BOTANICAL IMAGINATION

A volume in the series

The Environments of East Asia

Edited by Ann Sherif and Albert L. Park

Editorial Board: Anna L. Ahlers, David Fedman, Eleana J. Kim, and Micah Muscolino

This timely series brings an interdisciplinary lens to the study of the environments of East Asia, approaching questions of human-environment relations by bringing together scholars from social science, humanities, and STEM fields to challenge entrenched paradigms about East Asian societies' relationship with the environment. The series interrogates past and present societies, cultures, and environments with the aim of imagining and forging ways to a more sustainable and equitable future. Books in the series are freely available in open access through the generous support of the Henry Luce Foundation.

A list of titles in this series is available at cornellpress.cornell.edu.

BOTANICAL IMAGINATION

Rethinking Plants in Modern Japan

Jon L. Pitt
Foreword by Ann Sherif

CORNELL UNIVERSITY PRESS   ITHACA AND LONDON

Thanks to generous funding from the Luce Foundation, the ebook editions of this book are available as open access volumes through the Cornell Open initiative.

Copyright © 2025 by Jon L. Pitt

The text of this book is licensed under a Creative Commons Attribution-NonCommercial-NoDerivatives 4.0 International License: https://creativecommons.org/licenses/by-nc-nd/4.0/. To use this book, or parts of this book, in any way not covered by the license, please contact Cornell University Press, Sage House, 512 East State Street, Ithaca, New York 14850. Visit our website at cornellpress.cornell.edu.

First published 2025 by Cornell University Press

Library of Congress Cataloging-in-Publication Data

Names: Pitt, Jon L., author.
Title: Botanical imagination : rethinking plants in modern Japan / Jon L. Pitt.
Description: Ithaca: Cornell University Press, 2025. | Series: The environments of East Asia | Includes bibliographical references and index.
Identifiers: LCCN 2024032715 (print) | LCCN 2024032716 (ebook) | ISBN 9781501780967 (hardcover) | ISBN 9781501780950 (paperback) | ISBN 9781501780981 (epub) | ISBN 9781501780974 (pdf)
Subjects: LCSH: Japanese literature—20th century—History and criticism. | Japanese literature—21st century—History and criticism. | Plants in literature. | Motion pictures—Japan—History and criticism. | Plants in motion pictures. | Human ecology—Japan. | LCGFT: Literary criticism. | Film criticism.
Classification: LCC PL726.67.P5 P58 2025 (print) | LCC PL726.67.P5 (ebook) | DDC 895.609/364213—dc23/eng/20241030
LC record available at https://lccn.loc.gov/2024032715
LC ebook record available at https://lccn.loc.gov/2024032716

For PKS

Contents

Foreword by Ann Sherif	ix
Acknowledgments	xi
Note on Transliteration, Naming Convention, and English Translations	xiv
Introduction: Botanical Potential	1
1. Botanical Families: Osaki Midori, Moss, and Evolutionary Resemblance	29
2. Botanical Allegory: Metamorphosis and Colonial Memory in Abe Kōbō's "Dendrocacalia"	55
3. Botanical Media: Haniya Yutaka, Hashimoto Ken, Itō Seikō, and the Search for Dead Spirits	80
4. Botanical Regeneration: Fire and Disturbance Ecology in the Films of Yanagimachi Mitsuo and Kawase Naomi	115
5. Botanical Migration: Empathy and Naturalization in the Poetry and Prose of Hiromi Ito	149
Epilogue: Botanical Models	191
Notes	203
Bibliography	223
Index	231

Foreword

Ann Sherif

In close alignment with the sciences, environmental humanities seeks a place among disciplinary modes of inquiry that will "reveal deep and abiding connections between art and the environment," as those connections serve as sobering reminders of "our complicity in perpetuating" daunting climate and environmental issues, while also sparking realization of "our capacity to work toward solutions."[1]

In *Botanical Imagination*, Jon L. Pitt demonstrates the fertile workings of a botanical imagination in twentieth-to-twenty-first-century literature and cinema. Pitt employs the approaches of critical plant studies (CPS), a multidisciplinary field overlapping with botany in its focus on plant life, while drawing in multiple disciplinary approaches that have historically foregrounded the interests of human societies and individuals. Through its expansiveness, CPS develops modes of analysis encompassing artistic expression and the dynamic, mutual relationship between botanical life and humans. While environmental humanities may explicate long-standing codification of seasonal change and plant motifs evident in cultural Japan, CPS is grounded in values of reciprocity, humility, and learning systems thinking and ecology.

For Pitt, modern literature and film emerged as fertile ground for rethinking "the human through plant life." The twentieth-century writer Osaki Midori harnessed botanical imaginaries as a means of political and ethical critiques of "science in an era when technological progress was inseparable from empire building" and of gendered hierarchies. Knowledge of the science of flourishing and flowering of moss, plants, and trees fostered fresh creative outlooks in deeply troubled times. Pitt's exploration of the works of a diverse set of twentieth- and twenty-first-century artists who seek new ways to understand and represent the natural world—including prominent novelist and playwright Abe Kōbō, celebrated poet Itō Hiromi, and award-winning contemporary filmmaker Kawase Naomi, among others—demonstrates that a botanical flourishing in the arts has taken root across media, generations, and genres.

A key insight in *Botanical Imagination* relates to connections between canonical and dominant codification of seasonal change 四季, landscape 山水, and stylized and richly symbolic plant motifs 桜 in Japan's classical and popular cultures, on the one hand, and the writers and filmmakers who have fashioned a fresh understanding of plants through engagement with scientific discourses and emergent understandings of the connection between art and politics, on the other. Botanical representations play a major role in the culture of the four seasons, being imbued with talismanic and evoking enchantment. Natural motifs in classical poetry are immanent and sensual rather than transcendent. But does the enchantment simply vanish in the instant the reader stops believing, leaving us with nothing but a "natural . . . dead body lying dead beside the tracks of progress"?[2] This shift in the metaphorical landscape and concept of humans' relation to nature marks not so much a rejection of dominant ways of representing and imagining nature in the arts but rather a broadening of possibilities for knowing nature and imagining a right relation between humans and the natural world. Pitt clears a path for scholarly inquiry by employing analytical and methodological tools for understanding artistic production and aesthetic responses to linguistic and visual cultures and the natural world, entangled with changing historical conditions and ways of knowing worlds made fragile by humans. Environmental humanities scholarship centered on trees and plants, the dominant life-forms on earth, is motivated by resistance to despair, by hope that the arts will contribute to expanding our capacity to act as responsible stewards of this earth.

Acknowledgments

This book took many years to germinate and is the product of many hands. If not for the copious support and encouragement I received along the way, this book would never have come to fruition. I would like to thank my former professors in the East Asian Languages and Cultures and Film and Media Departments at the University of California, Berkeley, for planting the seeds in the early days of this project. Funding from the Japan Foundation was instrumental in allowing for research in Japan, including in the southernmost reaches of the archipelago, the Ogasawara Islands. I am thankful to the Japan Foundation for inviting me to participate in the inaugural cohort of the US-Japan Junior Scholars Networking Seminar, through which I had the great fortune of meeting Sakura Christmas, Alyssa Paredes, Daiichi Sugai, Wakana Suzuki, Satsuki Takahashi, and Karen Thornber.

I am indebted to Waseda University for providing me a place to read, think, and write during the year I spent conducting research for what ultimately became this book. A special thank you to Toba Koji for his guidance and generosity in serving as my faculty advisor at Waseda. Thank you, also, to the Center for Japanese Studies at UC Berkeley. This book would not have been possible without the labor of those who worked at the UC Berkeley C. V. Starr East Asian Library, the Waseda University Library, the National Diet Library of Japan, and the Langson Library at the University of California, Irvine.

I am grateful for my colleagues at UC Irvine. They welcomed me into the fold and offered tireless support. Thank you, Chungmoo Choi, David Fedman, Ted Fowler, Jim Fujii, Martin Huang, Kyung Hyun Kim, Susan Klein, André Keiji Kunigami, Margherita Long, James Nisbet, Bert Scruggs, Serk-Bae Suh, Bert Winther-Tamaki, Judy Wu, and Hu Ying. I have learned much from working with graduate students at UCI, and so I would like to thank Brandon Blackburn, Zane Casimir, Monica Cho, Hiroshi Clark, Megan Cole, Miguel Angel Quirarte Hernandez, Blossom Jeong, Soojin Jeong, Adam Miller, Sara Newsome, Nikita Prokhorov, Xiangu Qi, Yaqi Wang, Sophie Wheeler, Vanessa Wong, and Xiaoyang Yue.

For their unending generosity and friendship, I express my heartfelt thanks to Pedro Bassoe, Daryl Maude, and Linda Zhang, all of whom have read various parts of this book along the way and helped me sustain a life outside of the book through coffee, concerts, cake, and cinema. I have many other colleagues to thank for their friendship, advice, and encouragement since our shared time in Berkeley (and beyond), including Marjorie Burge, Xiangjun Feng, Julia Keblinska, Matt Mewhinney, Shelby Oxenford, Evelyn Shih, Wendy Wang, Chelsea Ward, Matt Wild, Melissa Van Wyk, and Lawrence Zi-Qiao Yang. A special thank you to Pat Noonan for his support and friendship dating back even further.

Over the past several years, I have been lucky to meet and receive valuable feedback from many scholars whose work I admire, including Jonathan Abel, Jeffrey Angles, Jakobina Arch, Reiko Abe Auestad, Vanessa Baker, Brian Bergstrom, Kate Brelje, Kathleen Burns, Andrew Campana, C. Anne Claus, Rebeca Copeland, Rachel DiNitto, Terese Gagnon, Weisong Gao, Kazue Harada, Brian Hurley, Joela Jacobs, Melody Jue, Megan Kaminski, Saeko Kimura, ann-elise lewallen, Jiajun Liang, Christine Marran, Anne McKnight, Natania Meeker, Lucas Mertehikian, Keitaro Morita, Chiara Pavone, Franz Prichard, Mina Qiao, Paul Roquet, Aike Rots, Eric Siercks, Douglas Slaymaker, Anthony Stott, Keijiro Suga, Wakako Suzuki, and Victoria Young.

I would like to thank the editorial board of the journal *Plant Perspectives*, the Plant Initiative, and the Literary and Cultural Plant Studies Network for helping create a vegetally minded community across the globe. The UCI Center for Environmental Humanities has been an important network that has helped shape ideas for this book. I would also like to express my gratitude to Dumbarton Oaks, as I learned much and met inspiring plant people as a virtual fellow in their Plant Humanities Lab in 2023. The UCI Humanities Center and the University of California Humanities Research Center have also been a great support over the past few years. This book was published with a support grant from the UCI Humanities Center.

This book has benefited from my participation in several conferences and workshops. Early ideas for chapter 4 were shared at a 2017 international workshop co-organized by UC Berkeley and the Research Institute for Humanity and Nature titled "Food, Agriculture and Human Impacts on the Environment: Japan, Asia, and Beyond." Parts of chapter 2 were presented at the virtual "Russia/Japan: Residues, Materialities, Environments" conference organized by Elena Fratto, Franz Prichard, and Ryo Morimoto in 2020. Parts of chapter 4 were presented at the University of Oslo "Animism and Ecocriticism Workshop," organized by Reiko Abe Auestad in 2022. Chapter 5 was developed in part through presentations at the 2022 Transpacific Workshop, held at UC Riverside and organized by Setsu Shigematsu, Anne McKnight, and John Kim, and at the Second International Environmental Humanities Conference on Critical Animal and Plant Studies, held (virtually) at Cappadocia University, also in 2022. The 2023 "Plant Animacies" workshop at Harvey Mudd College, organized by Kathleen Burns, helped clarify many overarching concepts in this book. I received valuable feedback at each of these gatherings.

Ann Sherif and Albert L. Park, the series editors with The Environments of East Asia series at Cornell University Press, have offered invaluable feedback along the way, making this a much better book than it was before their involvement. I could not have asked for better guides through this process. My sincere thanks to Alexis Shimon, who likewise saw potential in this project and helped it bloom. India Miraglia offered much-needed help in securing rights for the images included in the coming pages. The feedback I received from two anonymous reviewers helped push the book into a more critically precise direction, and I am grateful for their kind and insightful words.

I have thanked plants in previous publications, and this book will be no exception. Moss on the streets of Kyoto (a photo of which appears in chapter 1) taught me about multiplicity and the strength of laying low. The dendrocacalia tree taught me about perseverance and adaptation and about the joy and possible futility of the chase. The ice plant of Southern California has helped me grapple with notions of native, naturalized, and invasive. The cacti and wildflowers of the UCI Nature Preserve helped me process my grief during the COVID-19 pandemic. The many plants in my garden—passionfruit, papaya, sage, lavender, succulents, and chiles—have taught me about mutual aid and care work. I am indebted to these botanical teachers.

I am eternally grateful for my late father, Lawrence, my mother, Jacqui, as well as my stepfather, Jim. They have shown me nothing but love and support. Thank you also to my siblings, James and Cait. Over the years I spent working on this book, I was lucky enough to share my home with several more-than-human family members. Thank you Boba, Spruce, and Sugi for your own respective forms of support. Thank you also to Jem Fanvu for her knowledge of Pando and for getting me away from the desk and into the concert venues of Los Angeles.

This book is for Petronella Keryn Sovella, my partner in life and my biggest supporter. If this book is a plant, then we grew it together.

Note on Transliteration, Naming Convention, and English Translations

This book follows the modified Hepburn system of romanization in the transliteration of Japanese words. Macrons have been omitted in the case of common place names, such as Tokyo.

I follow Japanese convention by listing family names before personal names. The one exception to this is when I discuss the writer Hiromi Ito, who has expressed a desire to have her name written with personal name first and family name last and without a macron over the letter *o* in her last name when being discussed in English. I have honored her wishes.

All translations from Japanese into English are my own, except where otherwise stated explicitly.

Introduction
BOTANICAL POTENTIAL

This is a book about plants. More specifically, it is about plant life in Japan and how plants appear in a wide range of modern Japanese artistic media, including poetry, novels, and films. This may seem like a simple, obvious, even conservative topic, as plant life has been a recognizable element of conventional Japanese aesthetics for centuries. From cherry blossoms to bonsai trees to ikebana flower arranging, plants are conventionally associated with Japanese culture. Is there anything new or critical to say about plants in Japan? This book argues that there is and that looking more closely at plants can, at times, be a radical act. Several writers and filmmakers in Japan's modern period saw something new in plants that extended beyond classical Japanese aesthetics, and this botanical potential allowed them to rethink the question at the heart of humanities scholarship: What does it mean to be human? They reframed this question, asking: What would it mean for humans to be more like plants? They hoped that becoming more plantlike—a trope I call "becoming botanical"—could serve as an imaginative response to moments of crisis in Japan's modern history.

In the coming pages, I map out a botanical imagination that yearns to be plantlike.[1] It is this botanical imagination that gives rise to the trope of becoming botanical and to a botanical poetics (both discursive and visual) that erodes firm distinctions between human and plant.[2] Such plant poetics attempt to bring the logic of plant life into the very form of artistic creation. In other words, this book is interested in how plant life is featured in twentieth- and twenty-first-century Japanese literature and cinema not only at the level of content but also at the level of literary and cinematic form. Through close readings and textual analysis of literature and film, I look to identify the botanical qualities of literary and cinematic texts spanning nearly a century. This book is also interested in the role of plants within the sociocultural milieu from which a given botanical imagination sprouted. How and why were plants important to the artists under investigation here, and what informed their understanding of plant life in the first place? By focusing on plants at these three levels (content, form, context), I believe we are better able to appreciate just how significant a role plant life has played in the development of modern Japanese literature and cinema and in the larger sociocultural landscape from which artistic texts emerged.

Rethinking plant life in this way requires one to know a fair amount about plants, and there are many ways to know a plant. One can have an aesthetic understanding and know a plant's place in literary tradition, including its metaphorical meanings and poetic tropes. One can also have a scientific understanding and know its latinized name, its medicinal uses, and its place in evolutionary history. One can likewise have a spiritual understanding and know its connection to religious beliefs and rituals. The botanical poetics I examine in this book attempt to knit these varying epistemologies together and sculpt a botanical imagination that allows for new, more plantlike ways of inhabiting the world. The writers and filmmakers I discuss wondered what it would mean to not only understand a plant through one or more of these regimes of knowledge but also to understand *like a plant*. They have asked: Is it possible to know a plant on its own terms, to know a plant as a plant knows a plant? Is it possible to experience or imagine the world as a plant does? Could one create art from a plant's perspective, to write like a plant or create a film that embodies a plant's experience of the world in some way? Could attempting to do so be liberatory for humans, and if so, in what way?

Questions like these have been asked with urgency in the field of critical plant studies. Critical plant studies (henceforth abbreviated as CPS) takes the methodological tools of the humanities and applies them to the study of plant life to better understand the human relationship to plants and, indeed, to better understand plants themselves. In an era of increasing ecological precarity, with anthropogenic climate change and resource extraction (and the anthropocentric mindset that has fueled both) threatening the continued existence of our mutualistic relationship with plant life, CPS argues that it is imperative that humans attempt to better understand this form of life—a form much older and more plentiful than we humans are—for both their sake and our own. In the spirit of the environmental humanities, CPS urges us to learn to see plant life as foreground, not just background. This means decentering the human in the humanities and turning our attention to the grass beneath our feet, the moss clinging to our sidewalks, and the trees that tower over our heads. CPS says we need to think more about plants, and we need to think differently about plants. With the advent of CPS, plants are increasingly moving into the foreground of academic scholarship outside of the sciences and are helping to expand the parameters of the environmental humanities. While it may seem that plants make for particularly curious objects of study in the *human*ities, one can now find residencies in the *plant* humanities at Dumbarton Oaks and pursue the growing bibliography of CPS works cataloged on the website for the Literary and Cultural Plant Studies Network.[3]

As Jeffrey T. Nealon outlines in his 2016 book *Plant Theory: Biopower and Vegetable Life*, CPS has emerged in response to the more established paradigm of animal studies. Theorists in animal studies have worked hard to extend the humanities into the realm of the more-than-human animal, and for someone like Nealon, animal studies once appeared to offer much promise in thinking through Foucauldian notions of biopower: "If biopolitical studies began by pointing out that questions pertaining to human 'life' have become *the* political topics of the modern era (revolving around practices of identity, health, and sexuality), animal studies steps in to show how that notion of human-centered biopower is itself based on an originary exclusion and abjection of the other, animal life."[4] What Nealon ultimately came to realize, however, and what served as the impetus for his book was that "the plant, rather than the animal, functions as that form of life forgotten and abjected within a dominant regime of humanist biopower."[5] Plants, for Nealon and many others working in CPS, serve as the very limit of anthropocentric knowledge formation. It is not that plants exist further along a scale of abjection that finds humans on one end and more-than-human animals somewhere in the middle but rather that plants and their mode of life utterly upset this hierarchical schematic and that this disruption has serious implications for our conceptualization of biopower (and of the humanities more broadly). CPS argues that plants, when taken seriously, force us to rethink our basic assumptions about ethics, history, power, and even life itself.

For Nealon and other CPS thinkers, plants are *other* to the already other that is the more-than-human animal.[6] It is, to be sure, much easier to recognize the abjection of the animal than it is the abjection of the plant. This is because we humans can recognize shared modes of life in more-than-human animals, particularly in other mammals. We can look them in the eye; we can hear their cries of pain; we can witness them care for their young. More-than-human animals live in ways that resemble "living" to us, while plants, by and large, do not. Plants lack organs as we conventionally understand them. We are not privy to their modes of communication without the help of scientific apparatuses. They reproduce in ways that challenge our very notions of self and other, let alone gender and sexuality. Cut a piece of a succulent and stick it in the ground. Is what grows from the cutting the same plant as that which was cut? Or take aspens as another example. They grow in groves, but a grove is a singular organism made of many trees.

Should we say: "*It* grows in groves"? Where does one aspen end and another begin? These are questions Pando—a grove of over forty thousand aspen stems in Utah that has been categorized as a single organism—force(s) us to ask ourselves. Then there are those plants that thrive and reproduce precisely when animals (both human and more-than-human) eat of their body. Fruits are produced for this very purpose, to spread seeds in a form of reproduction markedly different from that of humans and more-than-human animals. Plants confound the way humans conceive of life, despite their overwhelming omnipresence in the world around us. Thus, while most human beings will admit that plants are alive, they will also contend that plants are just not as alive as humans or more-than-human animals.

CPS has emerged within academia as a means to take plants seriously, to wrestle with the theoretical challenges they propose, and to subsequently rethink the human in relation to the botanical realm. To a certain degree, the general public also seems to be in the midst of turning a more serious eye toward the world of plants. Peter Wohlleben's 2015 work of popular science *The Hidden Life of Trees: What They Feel, How They Communicate* and Richard Powers's 2018 arboreal novel *The Overstory* are examples of a growing field of public-facing publications (both fictional and nonfictional) that look to overturn trenchant preconceived notions about plant life—that they are silent, that they are immobile, that they are a lower form of life best left to the background of human action. Public opinion is incrementally coming around to rethinking the plant, in part with the help of popular documentary series that explore plant (and fungi) communication and intelligence.[7] The growing public awareness of the "wood-wide web"—the underground fungal network that connects trees and allows for the exchange of information among them—further points toward an uncanny acceptance that there is more going on in the botanical realm than meets the eye.[8]

Plant Awareness Disparities

With this growing interest in plant life comes an increasingly common claim invoked in CPS scholarship about so-called plant awareness disparity.[9] The argument goes that there is an inherent irony to the way humans conventionally think about plants, namely, that humans do not think about plants all that much, especially when we consider the fact that plants are the most abundant living organisms on the planet, accounting for 80 percent of the earth's total biomass.[10] It is not an exaggeration to say that humans could not survive without plants, although, as the Japanese agricultural historian and philosopher Fujihara Tatsushi reminds us, plants could indeed survive without us.[11] We humans are apparently not sufficiently aware of the fact that we are fully dependent on plants for our most basic survival. We breathe the oxygen they create and consume parts of their material bodies for our sustenance, but we are not properly cognizant of what this relationship means at a deeper level. CPS thinkers often claim that, for most of us, plants linger in the background, decorating our gardens and greening our parks (or helping to constitute the settings of our fictional narratives). They may be nice to look at, nice to smell and eat, and useful as raw materials and natural resources, but rarely are they the object of serious philosophical contemplation, either in humanities scholarship or in our daily lives. The argument goes that it is only within the past decade or so that academia and the general public have turned serious attention to the botanical world, that the recent interest in plants and plant communication (as I mentioned above) is new and unprecedented.

This is a useful claim to help justify the importance of CPS scholarship, to be sure. This book, however, pushes back against the idea of plant awareness disparity and argues instead that plants have been in the critical foreground of modern Japanese aesthetics (in both literature and cinema) and in philosophical discourse for decades. As the works I bring together in this book demonstrate, Japanese artists have taken plants seriously and thought deeply about the botanical realm long before the advent of CPS as a recognizable field of academic inquiry. Some seventy years before academics were reading the CPS theorist Robin Wall Kimmerer's influential work on moss, the Japanese modernist writer Osaki Midori was looking closely at moss and writing literary experiments that suggested humans and moss were much more alike than was conventionally believed. This is not to say that Osaki anticipated Kimmerer's specific theoretical insights about the plant. Osaki turned to moss against a backdrop of escalating war and colonial violence in 1930s Japan, and so moss meant something different to her than it does to Kimmerer. This difference is important.

Rather than make a blanket claim about plant awareness disparity among a generalized notion of the human, I want to suggest at the beginning of this book that there is an awareness disparity within CPS itself. This is an awareness disparity that, in attempting to take plants seriously, ends up abstracting them into decontextualized figures of metaphysics rather than recognizing them as historically situated subjects in their own right. Part of the rethinking of the plant at the heart of this book is a rethinking of the historicity of plant life, of why it matters when and where a given plant is situated. To speak of moss in general is to neglect the contingencies that inform both Kimmerer's and Osaki's botanical imaginations. By and large, the humanities no longer treat the human as a generalized/generalizable figure, recognizing instead that specificity and context matter greatly to historical configurations of the human. Now that the plant humanities have entered the fray, it is time to recognize that specificity and context matter with plants as well. The influential Russian botanist Kliment Timiryazev (whom I discuss in chapter 2) once asked: "Has a plant its history?"[12] This book intends to demonstrate that yes, a plant has its history, and this history is important.

History matters to the botanical imagination of the writers and filmmakers I discuss in the pages that follow. Like plants themselves, their botanical poetics did not grow out of a vacuum. I contend that by "following the plants" (to use the words of Gilles Deleuze and Félix Guattari) in works of modern Japanese literature and cinema, we can gain new insight into the moments of historical crisis that inspired artists to seek out knowledge of plant life and to imagine what it might mean to be more plantlike themselves. Following the plants in works of twentieth- and twenty-first-century Japanese literature and cinema reveals how writers and filmmakers were able to construct new forms of subjectivity, navigate historical turbulence, and attempt to resist certain forms of state violence. Bringing CPS into Japanese studies offers a way to think simultaneously about the place of plants in histories of imperialism and state control while also recognizing how plants became figures of resistance to such state power. This tension is at the heart of the book, a push-and-pull that finds plants participating in the very forms of violence that drove artists to turn to plants as a model of resistance in the first place. The trope of becoming botanical, as I theorize it here, is a potential that can be used to radical ends, but it can also be used to more conservative, reactionary, and even violent ends.

Ultimately, rethinking plants can, I believe, help us rethink Japanese literary and cinematic history. A closer look at Japanese literature and cinema can, in turn, help us rethink the parameters and stakes of CPS. Therefore, this book argues that writers and filmmakers in Japan have been engaged in rethinking the plant for nearly one hundred years, and it uses the insights of CPS to read works of Japanese literature and film where plants play important, if not always central, roles. It argues that these texts rethink what it means to be human by imagining what it would mean to be more plantlike. Inspired by plant life's ability to adapt in the face of adversity, the writers and filmmakers I bring together in this book attempted to weather moments of crisis by becoming anew, which is to say, by becoming botanical.

Toward *Shokubutsusei* in Japanese Studies

By claiming that there has been an awareness disparity in CPS when it comes to historicity, I do not mean to suggest that CPS scholarship has nothing to say about the plant histories discussed in this book. On the contrary, the inspiration for this book was reading Robin Wall Kimmerer's *Gathering Moss* (2003) alongside Osaki

Midori's moss-filled novella *Wandering in the Realm of the Seventh Sense* (1931). Kimmerer's poetic discussion of moss was informed by intersecting forms of knowledge, both conventionally scientific (Kimmerer is trained as a botanist) and Indigenous (she is a member of the Citizen Potawatomi Nation). What, I wondered, was informing Osaki's poetic discussion of moss in 1930s Japan? CPS invited me to follow the plants and find surprising connections among works of writers and filmmakers that were not immediately apparent, as well as surprising links between the Japanese state and artists who resisted the state in their work.

Thinkers like Kimmerer provided a theoretical foundation to rethink my approach to modern Japanese media and find a botanical potential lying in wait within Japanese studies. This is because CPS thinkers are continually diversifying our ways of understanding not only plants but also ourselves in relation to plants. In the process, CPS has worked to erode several supposed binary oppositions, principal among them nature and culture. When viewed as a whole, it becomes clear that the CPS project of moving plants to the foreground is not a means of moving other pressing issues into the background, be it ecological crisis, legacies of settler colonialism, systemic racism, sexism, and/or transphobia. Rather, plants offer us a way of rethinking these issues in new, less anthropocentric ways. As an interdisciplinary endeavor, CPS invites us to not only think about plants as either belonging to nature (what we might call their material face) or belonging to culture (what we might call their semiotic face) but also as active yet ambiguous beings that grow across the line separating the material and the semiotic. To truly know a plant is to know both of these faces and to see them as entwined. To this end, CPS likewise works to erode the firm distinctions between science and art. CPS acknowledges the pitfalls of dominant forms of science, including the potential for objectification and instrumentalization as well as science's complicity in histories of colonialism, racism, sexism, and resource extraction. But CPS is not antiscience. Far from it! Like the Japanese writers and filmmakers I examine in this book, CPS thinkers find great potential in the sciences, including (and perhaps especially) in nondominant forms of science. For the figures I discuss in the coming pages, it was an engagement with science (be it botany, evolution, or even spiritually inflected pseudoscience) that allowed them to know plants in new ways and bring these insights into their novels, poetry, and films. The botanical poetics I read into their works grows out of this engagement with science.

All the same, there has certainly been an awareness disparity in CPS regarding Japan (and many other non-Western cultural traditions, to be sure). Conversely, Japanese studies has heretofore been slow to engage with CPS scholarship. While Natania Meeker and Antonia Szabri claim in their coauthored work *Radical Botany* that we are in the midst of a "plant turn" in academia, no such turn has yet made serious inroads into the study of Japanese literature or cinema.[13] This is surprising for several reasons. First, as mentioned at the beginning of this introduction, plants have long held a significant place in Japanese culture not only in the realm of aesthetics but also in the realm of spirituality and religion. From Japan's earliest extant poetry and mythology all the way to contemporary anime and science fiction, plants abound in Japanese cultural production. Even the ubiquitous notion of "the transience of life" as embodied in the cherry blossom's scattering in the wind is arguably an attempt to rethink human existence through plant life. Such aesthetics have never been ideologically neutral, however, and several anthropologists and environmental historians of Japan have made clear the role that certain plants (including the cherry blossom) have played in Japan's imperial history.[14] Such entanglements between botany and empire extend into Japanese literature and cinema as well, but critical attention to plant life in the study of Japanese media has been surprisingly scant. This book looks to remedy that.

The second reason I find the lack of CPS in Japanese studies surprising is that CPS texts have been (and continue to be) translated into Japanese. Translations of books by Robin Wall Kimmerer, Stefano Mancuso, and Emanuele Coccia are all easily found in Japanese bookstores. It was not until around 2020, however, that Japanese scholars began to enter into dialogue with these CPS theorists. Most notable among those who have is Fujihara Tatsushi, whose 2022 book *Thoughts on Plants* (*Shokubutsukō*) collects essays written between 2019 and 2021 that discuss Japanese aesthetics and literary texts alongside insights from CPS thinkers like Coccia and Mancuso. As Fujihara explains in his introduction, it was his research on the relationship between agriculture and Japanese settler colonialism that first spurred him on to think and write critically about plant life and to theorize what he calls *shokubutsusei*—what we might translate as "botanicallity" or "plant-ness." Ultimately, however, I think the word is better left in the original Japanese, where *shokubutsu* means "plant" and *-sei* marks the nature or essence of something (and is usually rendered in English as the suffix "-ity" or "-ness"). My decision to leave Fujihara's term in its original Japanese is not because the term is untranslatable per se. It is, rather, meant to highlight the geographical and linguistic context in which Fujihara has developed his concept. Which is to say, Fujihara's *shokubutsusei* is an intervention into CPS that is expressly informed by his reading of and engagement with Japanese literature, history, and botanical scholarship, in addition to the more prevalent Western tradition that informs much of CPS theorization. To help widen the scope of CPS and draw attention to the specificity of Fujihara's scholarship, I have kept the term untranslated in the coming pages, as one might refer to a plant's scientific name rather than its common name. There is, I believe, an academic specificity to such an act.

In *Thoughts on Plants*, Fujihara puts CPS theorists like Coccia and Mancuso into conversation with Japanese authors like Miyazawa Kenji and Itō Seikō (who

I also take up, in chapter 3). He discusses cultural/material botanical figurations like *chinju no mori* (forests that surround Shinto shrines) and specific trees growing around his home of Kyoto. As he does so, he relativizes a received cultural tradition of botanical thinking that stretches back to Greek philosophy—a tradition that has by and large served as the basis of CPS. In its attention to Japan, Fujihara's work helps CPS open its eyes to historicity beyond the Western tradition, to different forms of knowing plant life in different historical contexts across time and place. Fujihara is not interested in a universal theory of "plant-ness" but rather in specific articulations of *shokubutsusei* that can be applied even beyond the botanical realm: "If we define the concept as such, we can use it to say things like, 'the *shokubutsusei* of this country has fallen into an alarming condition,' or 'this thinker is unique when it comes to the depth of their *shokubutsusei*.'"[15] The qualities of the *shokubutsusei* in Fujihara's hypothetical country are surely different than the qualities present in the hypothetical thinker mentioned in this quote. Just as there are different plants, there are different manifestations of *shokubutsusei*. The concept is powerful in its recognition of plant plurality and diversity.

Fujihara's *shokubutsusei* is an abstraction of plant life, but it is one intended to draw attention to particular and differing botanical characteristics throughout history. It is an abstraction in the plural. This is another reason for my keeping the term in its original language, as it can indeed be read as plural in Japanese. There are many articulations of *shokubutsusei* and not a singular "botanicallity" that cuts across all plants, let alone all humans or countries. The trope of becoming botanical—the primary focus of this book—is one such *shokubutsusei*, and as we shall see from chapter to chapter, there are many different articulations of becoming botanical. While the goal of this book is to make legible the parameters of these particular manifestations of *shokubutsusei*, Fujihara has implored all of us who work in the humanities to think more deeply about the *shokubutsusei* of our respective objects of study, be they literary, historical, or otherwise. *Shokubutsusei* is, in classic CPS form, an interdisciplinary concept that will hopefully inspire more CPS work in Japanese studies and beyond.

Widening the Scope of Japanese Environmental Studies

Thoughts on Plants is arguably the first text to emerge in Japan from within the current plant turn that CPS has helped steer, but it is by no means the first Japanese text to think critically about plant life. This is the third reason why it is surprising CPS has not yet made serious inroads into Japanese studies. Writers in Japan have been circling the questions raised by present-day CPS theorists for decades, but they have done so mostly outside of academia. This book brings together a somewhat unlikely group of thinkers and artists from Japan who were all deeply engaged in theorizing *shokubutsusei*. It is my contention that the texts I discuss in the coming pages belong within the corpus of CPS scholarship, even though they are not academic works in and of themselves. By putting CPS thinkers in conversation with Japanese writers and filmmakers, I want to demonstrate that works of Japanese literature and cinema have also engaged in "plant-thinking," a concept developed by Michael Marder in his book of the same name. According to Marder: "'Plant-thinking' is in the first place the promise and the name of an encounter, and therefore it may be read as an invitation to abandon the familiar terrain of human and humanist thought and to meet vegetal life, if not in the place where it is, then at least halfway."[16] Insofar as Marder's book (and most CPS scholarship) is devoted to traditions and knowledges of Europe and the Americas, this present study is an invitation to a different sort of encounter. It is an invitation for those interested in CPS to encounter plant-thinking in a different cultural/geopolitical context than they may be accustomed to (namely, Japan), while also serving as an invitation for those interested in Japan to encounter the theoretical world of CPS.

Put succinctly, this book is an attempt to bring CPS more fully into the realm of Japanese studies and to bring Japanese studies into the realm of CPS. It is also an attempt to widen the scope of environmental scholarship in Japanese studies more broadly. There is a need to widen the scope because a dominant paradigm has emerged within environmental approaches to the study of modern Japan and Japanese media: toxicity and environmental degradation.[17] In particular, the March 11, 2011, triple disaster of earthquake, tsunami, and meltdown at the Fukushima Daiichi Nuclear Power Plant in northeastern Japan (known in shorthand as "3.11") has had an enormous impact on environmental scholarship on and in Japan.[18] This makes good sense, of course, as these events are still unfolding and continue to impact lives both human and more-than-human. Important scholarship on literary and cinematic responses to environmental (often nuclear) crises of Japan's modern era has helped push the field of Japanese studies into a new, more ecologically minded direction.

The issue of environmental degradation has been raised in the study of premodern Japan as well, stretching back even earlier in the history of Japanese studies. Conrad Totman's classic environmental history of Japanese deforestation in the premodern period, *The Green Archipelago* (1989), looked to disabuse readers of what was (and continues to be) a trenchant stereotype, particularly in regard to classical Japanese aesthetics, namely that Japan has long had a harmonious relationship with nature. The ubiquity of natural imagery (including plants) in premodern Japanese poetry, prose, and visual culture has indeed contributed to an image of Japan as a nature-loving culture. Several critics since Totman have engaged in environmental scholarship with the goal of critiquing this notion of harmony. Yuki Masami, in her introduction to the 2018 collected volume *Ecocriticism in Japan*, explains that "quite a few scholars of different disciplines tend to see what appears to be a Japanese attitude of living in harmony with nature simply as culturally constructed and thereby often contradictory to Japan's social reality."[19] Yuki offers Haruo Shirane's *Japan and the Culture of the Four Seasons* (2012) as an example of this paradigm and singles out the book's concept of "second nature," which she glosses as "highly stylized nonhuman nature in literature and art."[20] Shirane uses his notion of second nature to argue (in a quote that Yuki includes in her introduction as well) that "the oft-mentioned Japanese 'harmony' with nature is not an inherent closeness to primary nature due to topography and climate, but a result of close ties to secondary nature, which was constructed from as early as the seventh century and based in major cities."[21]

Shirane's work suggests that Totman's history of premodern deforestation can sit comfortably alongside the notion that Japanese classical aesthetics expresses a "love of nature," for it is only the semiotic face of nature (i.e., second nature) that is to be found in premodern Japanese literature and visual art, not its material face (or "primary nature"). Indeed, Shirane opens his investigation into classical Japanese aesthetics' dependance on second nature by pointing out that many of the characters in the early eleventh-century classic *The Tale of Genji* are named after plants, but that *Genji*'s author, the aristocrat Murasaki Shikibu, would have primarily known these plants only through poetry, paintings, or in carefully "constructed" gardens.[22] Consequently, Shirane's second nature cannot locate the material face of *Genji*'s plants.[23] CPS could help. Although this current book does not focus on premodern works like *The Tale of Genji*, it hopefully paves the way for others to approach plant life more critically within the realm of classical Japanese literature and culture more broadly. There is botanical potential there, even if (or perhaps especially if) writers like Murasaki Shikibu knew plants only as "a substitute for a more primary nature that was often remote from or rarely seen by the aristocrats who lived in the center of (the capital city of) Heian," as Shirane claims.[24]

This potential extends to works that are less obviously concerned with plant life than the likes of *Genji* because what a CPS approach to the study of Japan allows, in either a modern or premodern context, is an expansion of what we deem an "environmental" text in the first place. One can look for the *shokubutsu-sei* of any given text and thereby engage in environmental scholarship on works that have not conventionally been thought of heretofore as eco-minded. The trope of becoming botanical—the central conceit of this book—is an environmental response to crises that do not necessarily appear environmental in nature. Only one of the texts examined in this book was written in response to the events of 3.11 (Itō Seikō's *Radio Imagination*, discussed in chapter 3). The rest look for the *shokubutsusei* of other moments in Japan's modern history, including crises brought on by war, colonial violence, postwar economic depression and rural depopulation, and emigration/immigration. What ties these seemingly discreet historical moments together are their entanglements with the botanical realm.

The books and films I bring together here show us how to think differently about plant life by pointing us in two directions. They show us what it could mean for humans to respond to moments of crisis in more plantlike ways, while also showing us that plants are implicated in said moments of crisis in the first place, even when they do not appear to be. The trope of becoming botanical is historically specific in its particular manifestations, but it is itself not historically contingent to any given time. Thus, this book covers nearly a century, from roughly 1930 to present day—a long stretch of time for a human, but not so long at all for a tree.

Men Are Grass

If plants have played such an important role in Japanese history and aesthetics (beginning with the earliest extant works of Japanese literature), then what, you might be wondering at this point, is ultimately so unique about the writers and filmmakers brought together here that they merit specific attention in this book? How are they not merely tapping into centuries of preestablished plant metaphors (like the cherry blossoms scattering in the wind) and/or engaging in a form of anthropomorphism that only serves to reinforce the kind of anthropocentrism that CPS actively attempts to dismantle? If one can discuss the *shokubutsusei* of any given text, then what is so special about the books and films discussed in the coming pages?

What makes the figures I bring together in this book unique is precisely that they do not perpetuate centuries-old botanical tropes but instead actively rethink the very relationship between plants and Japanese culture. Part of the rethinking at the heart of this book concerns both metaphor and anthropomorphism, two literary techniques that are frequently associated with the cultural understanding of plant life. The trope of becoming botanical is not metaphorical (at least in its conventional understanding), nor is it anthropomorphic. Instead, the trope rethinks metaphor along the lines of Gregory Bateson, author of the foundational *Steps to an Ecology of the Mind* (1972), when he argues that humans not only understand the living world primarily through metaphor but, in fact, a metaphorical logic structures the biological/material world itself. For Bateson, metaphor extends over the material/semiotic line, rendering the perceived binary untenable. He begins his argument on this account by offering the following well-known logical syllogism:

> Men die.
> Socrates is a man.
> Socrates will die.

He contrasts this with what he calls a "syllogism in grass":

> Grass dies.
> Men die.
> Men are grass.[25]

Bateson likens this second syllogism to metaphor and argues that, in the long history of evolution, "metaphor was not just pretty poetry, it was not either good or bad logic, but was in fact the logic upon which the biological world had been built."[26] For Bateson, how species have evolved and how we humans understand the relationships among differing species (as well as how we understand ourselves as humans) are determined by this metaphorical logic, through the give-and-take of similarity and difference. This is a radical rethinking of metaphor, one that moves from the page into the natural world all around us (and even within us). Bateson uses the traditional, semiotic logic of syllogisms and the material, biological fact of death to expose what appears to be an absurd conclusion: men [sic] are grass.[27] Bateson finds commonalities between humans and plants and consequently finds the *shokubutsusei* of the human. He posits that in this recognition of similarity is the potential for a new way of inhabiting the world, one in which our plantlike qualities are not mere anthropomorphism but rather the biological outcome of evolution. Taken seriously, Bateson's syllogism in grass presents us with a subjective experience that rethinks what it means to be human by asking: What if we truly understood ourselves, materially, as grass?

This question is raised throughout the present book and serves as a jumping-off point from which to theorize phytomorphism, or the attribution of plantlike characteristics to humans. Phytomorphism is this book's attempt to rethink anthropomorphism, turning the directionality of anthropomorphism the other way around. The writers and filmmakers I discuss were not interested in ascribing humanlike traits to plants. They sought the opposite. Phytomorphism allowed them, in writing and in film, to imagine just what it would feel like—affectually and sensorially—to experience the world as a plant might. Consequently, their figurations of phytomorphism take many forms, from Osaki Midori's scientific speculation that humans can reverse the course of evolution and inhabit plantlike states of mind (as discussed in chapter 1), to Abe Kōbō's more wild phenomenological speculations that find human characters moving at a very slow, plantlike speed as the rest of the world races by (as discussed in chapter 2). Phytomorphism allowed writers and filmmakers to imbue their fictional characters with a variety of botanical capacities, including extrasensory and out-of-body experiences (chapters 1 and 3), longer-than-human lifespans (chapter 4), and enhanced reproductive capabilities (what is referred to, in chapter 5, as an "aggressive fertility").

Throughout this book, I refer to these plantlike capacities as "botanical subjectivity"—a way of experiencing oneself as plantlike. Why would one want to experience the world in this way? For the figures I discuss in these pages, theorizing botanical subjectivity allowed for the construction of new ways to work through moments of crisis. Seeing oneself as grass was a subjective experience that held the potential to break wide open confining ideologies that (as explained in each respective chapter of this book) looked to solidify racial and gendered differences; that attempted to deny wartime atrocities; that tied nature-based spirituality to wartime aggression; that suggested futurity was only to be found in capitalist development; that attempted to control human migration as one might control an invasive plant species. Seeing oneself as grass seemed to promise new ways to adapt to worsening states of affairs. If grass can change with the seasons, why can't men, if they are grass?

In his book *Men Are Grass* (*Hito wa kusa de aru*, 2013), Hara Shōji describes the subjective experience suggested by Bateson's syllogism as a kind of "overlap" of human and plant life: "In (Bateson's) phrase 'men are grass,' humans do not stand outside of grass, separated from it and pointing at it. For both humans and grass, a self can only grasp itself as a projection within the other, and as a self that projects the other within itself. And so it can only grasp the other by means of searching for the self within that image that is projected. Humans and grass fluctuate and overlap."[28] By and large, the works I discuss in this book find a kind of liberatory potential in the fluctuation and overlapping of human and plant as Hara describes it. Phytomorphism names this fluctuation and allows the human to "grasp itself" in the search for a wholly new idea of the self within the botanical realm. In the process, phytomorphism explodes the very idea of individuated selfhood. Remember Pando, the aspen(s) I mentioned above? What would selfhood feel like for it/them? With this in mind, I stress throughout this book that a botanical subjectivity that sees itself as grass is necessarily a multiple subjectivity. Is grass singular or plural? Both? Is a human who sees themselves as grass a self or selves? Such ambiguity is at the heart of this book, where it becomes a radical gesture of rethinking the human.

Hara's reading of Bateson resonates with a set of fundamental questions that Elizabeth Grosz poses in the beginning of *Becoming Undone* (2011), her feminist reading of Darwinian evolution. Although she focuses on "the animal" in these questions, we can easily substitute "the plant" as the figure of the "nonhuman":

> What would a humanities, a knowledge of and for the human, look like if it placed the animal in its rightful place, not only before the human but also within and after the human? What is the trajectory of a newly considered humanities, one that seeks to know itself not in opposition to its others, the "others" of the human, but in continuity with them? What would a humanities look like that does not rely on an opposition between self and other, in which the other is always in some way associated with animality or the nonhuman? What kind of intellectual revolution would be required to make man, and the various forms of man, one among many living things, and one force among many, rather than the aim and destination of all knowledges, not only the traditional disciplines within the humanities, but also the newer forms of interdisciplinarity?[29]

Grosz's provocations serve as something of a starting point for this book, and thus I have quoted her at length. I take her call to interdisciplinarity seriously. CPS helps with this. The coming pages are my attempt to read the plant "within" the human or, to use Bateson's words, to read "men as grass." Bateson himself recognizes that such thinking appears absurd on the surface, but he argues that the natural world does not always align with strict logic: "Life, perhaps, doesn't always ask what is logically sound. I'd be very surprised if it did."[30] So, too, would be the writers and filmmakers brought together in this book.

Words Are Plants

For one of the writers I discuss in the coming pages, Hiromi Ito (the subject of chapter 5), not only is the line between the human and the plant quite blurry and overlapping; so, too, is the line between plants and language itself.[31] For Ito, words, too, are grass. She claims as much in a 2019 dialogue with her fellow author Machida Kō. Knowing Ito's love of all things plant, Machida suggests that the two most important things for Ito are "grass and words." Ito responds: "'Grass?' How rude. That's not precise enough. You have to know the various classifications, the Latin names for plants, their individual personalities. But I guess it is as you say. Those two are the most important things. Words and plants—for me they are the same thing."[32] Ito clarifies that "Words, like plants, and plants, like words, flourish all around us."[33] It may appear that Ito is rehearsing one of the oldest claims about Japanese literature here. In his preface to the classic imperial anthology of Japanese poetry, the early tenth-century *Kokinwakashū*, Ki no Tsurayuki famously writes: "The seeds of Japanese poetry lie in the human heart and grow into leaves of ten thousand words."[34] From the earliest musings on Japanese poetry, words and plants have overlapped. But Ito, in true CPS fashion, pushes us to think beyond the semiotic here and to "know the various classifications, the Latin names for plants, their individual personalities." Traditional poetics is not enough. To truly see "words as grass," one must strive to know plants in all the ways they might be known, including their scientific categorizations.

In her 2014 book *Tree Spirits Grass Spirits* (*Kodama kusadama*), Ito ruminates on one of the best-known poems of the Japanese premodern tradition, a late seventeenth-century haiku by Matsuo Bashō that reads: "Summer grass—all that remains of warriors' dreams."[35] Bashō's haiku appears to resonate with Bateson's claim that "men are grass," as it laments the passing of fallen warriors and memorializes them through the grass that grows on the battlefield in the wake of their defeat. Like the trope of the cherry blossom scattering in the wind, Bashō's grass poetically comments on the perceived transience of human existence. Bashō's haiku (and, indeed, haiku in general) has a *shokubutsusei* of its own, but it is not the specific *shokubutsusei* under investigation in this book. Bashō's grass, in its poetic rendering in the form of haiku, shows only its semiotic face. Taking Bateson's lead and moving beyond conventional metaphor, Ito—seemingly unsatisfied with notions akin to Shirane's concept of second nature—looks for the material face of Bashō's grass:

> For a long time, I had thought "summer grass" referred to large clumps of *seitaka-awadachisō* (*Solidago altissima*) or *ō-arechinogiku* (*Conyza sumatrensis*). I thought, "It's gotta be them, those symbols of life that grow out of and prosper on top of those that have already fallen into ruin and have faded away." But that wasn't the case. It would be one thing if they were plants that had come to Japan in the very distant past, but *seitaka-awadachisō* and *ō-arechinogiku* both arrived after the Meiji Restoration and couldn't have proliferated among the remains of warriors' dreams in the middle of the Edo period. It must have been an entirely different landscape all together.[36]

Rethinking plants in this way and yearning to know their particular capacities allow Ito's poetry to accomplish something we do not see in the history of Japanese classical poetry, namely, that words become plantlike at a *formal* level. If botanical subjectivity is a way of naming the overlap of humans and plants, then "botanical form" names the overlap of words and plants at the level of composition. Intimately familiar with the wild qualities of weeds and vines, Ito mimics their vegetal nature in her poetry through unruly prose and short, repetitive lines. Her poetry embodies their botanical form.

To read Ito's work is to experience something akin to looking out over a dense field of grass, of simultaneously focusing in on individual wildflowers and allowing the multiplicity of the field to wash over you. It is an affectual experience that arises in excess of the semiotic meaning of her words. Inspired by Ito's claim that words and plants are the same thing, I think in this book about how language and literary/filmic form can embody and mimic the materiality of plant life. I am interested in how the writers and filmmakers I take up have attempted to bring the logic of the botanical realm into the very structure of their art. Thus, I do not discuss haiku or other forms of premodern Japanese poetry. Instead, I locate a moss-like literary form in chapter 1—indistinct and repetitive at first glance but, like moss, carefully constructed and full of minute details on closer examination. I posit in chapter 2 that a story concerned with the objectivity bound up in the scientific naming of plants expresses this concern by employing objective language throughout the narrative. The expansive, haunting qualities of the forest are legible in the expansive, haunting volumes of Haniya Yutaka's philosophical prose that make up the epic novel at the heart of chapter 3. In chapter 4, I turn to cinema and discuss how the cyclical manner in which forests experience time is likewise inscribed into the cinematography and narrative development of two films, one directed by Yanagimachi Mitsuo, the other by Kawase Naomi. And chapter 5, devoted to Ito, examines the wild, weedy qualities of her poetry and prose. Plants thus enter the foreground not only in *what* all of these texts say but also in *how* they say it. In other words, the trope of becoming botanical not only imagines what it would be like to be more plantlike at the level of plot; it also strives to make whatever medium it finds itself in more plantlike as well. Modern poetry, prose, and film allow for sufficient formal flexibility such that the artists who work within them can rethink both themselves and their artistic media as plantlike. Men are grass; words are plants; and so, too, this book suggests, are novels, poetry, and films, through and through.

What It Is (and What It Is Not) to Become Botanical

As I am concerned with writers and filmmakers who question what it would be like to be more plantlike not only at the level of content but also at the level of form, I have not set out to write an exhaustive glossary of botanical thinkers and artists from Japan. While much has been written in Japan about plants, not all botanical writers—those writers that Fujihara would say are "unique when it comes to the depth of their *shokubutsusei*"—attempted to become botanical within the parameters I outline in this book. For this reason, I do not focus on some of the key figures in the history of Japanese botany, most notably Makino Tomitarō (1862–1957) and Minakata Kumagusu (1867–1941). Both wrote texts and conducted scientific experiments that are ripe for CPS theorization, but their particular *shokubutsusei* emerged from a different kind of botanical imagination than the one I map out here. Likewise, there are many modern and contemporary literary authors whose works prominently feature plant life but ultimately do not fit within the figuration of becoming botanical that I sketch in these pages. Renowned modern poet and children's author Miyazawa Kenji seems like an obvious choice for inclusion in this study (and, indeed, Fujihara discusses him at length in *Thoughts on Plants*). While Miyazawa Kenji's fictional world is populated with talking trees, his works never quite take on the formal qualities with which I am interested. Makino, Minakata, and Miyazawa all had fascinating things to say about plants, but there was nothing particularly plantlike about the way they said them.

Likewise, contemporary authors like Oyamada Hiroko and Hoshino Tomoyuki write compelling works rich in their respective *shokubutsusei*, but they lack the experimental step taken by the writers I do consider in this book, namely, what would it look like to not just write about plants but also to write like a plant. This formal consideration extends into the filmic texts I discuss as well, as the cinematography of these films experimentally embodies the botanical subjectivity I trace throughout the book in a manner other botanically inflected works of cinema do not. Thus, I do not discuss the films of Miyazaki Hayao and his Studio Ghibli, as wonderfully plant filled as they may be. Totoro may help the trees grow in the anime bearing his name, but there is nothing particularly arboreal about the way his film is structured.

Formal considerations are not the sole driving force behind the trope of becoming botanical, however. A plantlike form is an important part of the botanical poetics that this book looks to identify, but only insofar as form reinforces thematic content. The texts I examine in this book all point toward the inseparability of form and content—a concept that is itself quite botanical. Think, if you will, of a flower. Now think, if you will, like Hiromi Ito and imagine that plants and words are the same thing. As an example of expression (a quite literal expression of matter from the plant's body out into the surrounding atmosphere), where could one draw the line between a flower's form and its content? A conventional dismissal would claim that flowers harbor no content, only form. A bee would disagree. A bee can read the flower, interpret it, and decide whether or not to alight on its petals. This speculative realm of more-than-human hermeneutics is fertile ground for CPS and for pushing Japanese studies toward a *shokubut-susei* that both reads texts about plants and reads texts like plants. It is my hope that in reading this book, readers will, to some degree, start to become botanical themselves.

To entertain the idea that a human might learn to read texts like a plant, and that to do so would open the door to new ways of inhabiting and understanding the world, is not just to rethink what it means to be a plant; it is also to rethink what it means to be human. This is the central conceit of this book, that plant life offered modern Japanese writers and filmmakers a botanical imagination through which to craft a plantlike poetics that reworked human subjectivity in response to turbulent historical events ranging nearly one hundred years—events in which plants themselves served as historical actors. These botanical poetics allowed for a reconfiguration of subjectivity beyond the confines of the human body (as plants extend their being out into the atmosphere around them and the soil down below), beyond conventional sense perception (as plants sense the world in ways radically different than humans), and beyond human temporality (as plants move at a different temporality altogether and live on timescales incomprehensible to the human).

Of course, *subjectivity* is a notoriously thorny term. Throughout, I deploy the word in reference to how one experiences oneself as oneself. If we take plants and their multiplicity seriously—remember again the aspen(s)—then we can say a botanical subjectivity is one in which one comes to experience oneself as more than *one self*. As mentioned earlier, the idea of a multiple subjectivity is important to the works I examine in this book, for it is in reconfiguring human subjectivity to be multiple (as it would be for a plant) that the writers and filmmakers I discuss attempt to expand beyond the confines of crisis and to look for solidarities across bodies and timelines. They all saw becoming botanical as a means to adapt and construct models of futurity that may allow for growth beyond the immediate violence of the present, much like grass struggling up and through the hard concrete.

In naming this reconfiguration of subjectivity "becoming botanical," I am drawing from Deleuze and Guattari's *A Thousand Plateaus*, in which a "becoming" is an ongoing process where two or more entities enter into an alliance that creates something unprecedented, something that is "neither one nor two, nor the relation of the two; it is the inbetween."[37] Deleuze and Guattari's figuration of becoming is a challenge to ontological fixity. In her book *How I Became a Tree* (a pioneering CPS work that looks beyond the Western philosophical tradition), Sumana Roy characterizes *A Thousand Plateaus* as "a manifesto to claim another way of looking and living."[38] This assessment is apt, as Deleuze and Guattari's rhizomatic logic (and, indeed, form) rejects firm claims to "being" and the violence of strict definitions that may be leveraged against humans and more-than-humans alike. For Deleuze and Guattari (and Roy in turn), becoming names a striving, a gesture toward a new horizon of subjectivity, a different way of inhabiting the world that is flexible and oscillates between things. The figures at the heart of this book understood plant life as an embodiment of becoming, as an ever-changing and adapting form of life, and they imagined what it would mean to embody this botanical form of becoming themselves. These artists inhabit the in-between space of becoming—a space in between human and plant—in the belief that it holds possibilities for overcoming the crises unfolding dramatically, slowly, or even imperceptibly around them. Deleuze and Guattari ask (in a passage singled out by Roy): "What if one became animal or plant *through* literature, which certainly does not mean literally?"[39] The works examined in this book provide something of an answer to this question, as they inhabit a space in between literature (or cinema) and science. These works engage with evolutionary and ecological science as well as with pseudoscientific theories of plant communication popularized in Peter Tompkins and Christopher Bird's 1973 controversial best-seller *The Secret Life of Plants* (a text I discuss more fully below).[40]

In order to locate these texts in their respective zones of in-between-ness, I discuss how they are informed by science (and pseudoscience). I use scientific concepts as a means to read literary and filmic texts. My goal, in interdisciplinary CPS fashion, is to remind us that the realms of science and art are far from distinct, as I have already argued in this introduction.[41] Thus, in chapter 1, I illustrate how science inspired the botanical poetics of the poet, short story writer, and early film critic Osaki Midori (1896–1971). Osaki witnessed the impending storm of the Pacific War in the early years of Japan's Shōwa era (which began in 1926) and turned to the botanical realm to learn how to adapt to encroaching threats of Japan's militarization. Osaki found in the science of evolutionary thought a means to bring the human and plant closer together, forging a familial connection between humans and plants in deep evolutionary time. In an era when the ideology of social Darwinism was widely used to justify colonial expansion throughout Asia, Osaki's idiosyncratic take on evolutionary theory (written in texts that embody botanical form) pointed the way toward a potential future born of cooperation and not competition. For Osaki, becoming botanical was a utopian gesture made amid an unfolding national crisis that would eventually lead to a fully mobilized war, this despite the fact that she held her own familial connections to the practice of colonial agriculture on the Japanese-occupied Korean peninsula. Thus, while Osaki imagined a botanical becoming in the face of colonial violence, the Japanese empire was undergoing a botanical becoming of its own.

Osaki's work demonstrates that becoming botanical is not a panacea, and chapter 2 reinforces the idea that not all botanical becomings are utopian. Sometimes the concrete is too hard to break up and through, and sometimes the history of a given plant resists its abstraction into utopian imaginaries, even as it serves as inspiration for literary allegory. This is the ambiguous conclusion reached in Abe Kōbō's short story "Dendrocacalia," which was originally written in 1949 and then rewritten in 1952. This story is the focus of chapter 2, where I explain how, for the prolific author and critic Abe Kōbō (1924–1993), becoming botanical was the very site of crisis and not a means of overcoming it, despite the beliefs held by his Anarcho-Marxist contemporaries. "Dendrocacalia" is an allegorical tale in which a man transforms into a rare tree that only grows on the remote island of Hahajima in the Ogasawara (or Bonin) Islands, an archipelago with a long settler colonial history that became the site of some of the Pacific Theater's most deadly battles. In the narrative, the human-turned-tree is ultimately locked away in a government-controlled greenhouse, making explicit a fact that lies under the surface of Osaki Midori's work, that botanical science was instrumental to Japan's colonial project and any attempt to rethink human subjectivity as being more plantlike must reckon with this wartime legacy. At the same time, however, it is a work clearly informed and inspired by the insights of botanical science, one that uses plant biology to fascinating, experimental, and poetic ends. Abe's story may seek to keep our posthuman desires in check, warning readers that there are dark potentials held in becoming botanical, but it simultaneously points toward the critical potential for plant life to illuminate forgotten histories. In the in-between of these two chapters, we witness how the trope of becoming botanical can bloom in different ways, be they utopian, dystopian, or, indeed, somewhere in between.

Plasticity and the Malleability of Form

The transformation of the human protagonist into a tree in Abe's "Dendrocacalia" is the most literal figuration of becoming botanical that I discuss in this book. Yet in all cases of becoming botanical, there is a transformation that takes place, not necessarily at the physical level of a human body turning into a plant but rather at the level of subjectivity. As a process of ongoing change in the tradition of Deleuze and Guattari, I argue that becoming botanical is dependent on notions of "plasticity," a scientific concept that has been embraced and theorized in the humanities as well. Although we may want to associate the word *plasticity* with a hardness and stubbornness of form (like the ubiquitous plastic objects that surround us and threaten our oceans by not biodegrading), my use of the term is meant to indicate quite the opposite. Plasticity is the very malleability of form, the ability to transform and change, but not without some effort or resistance, of course. Philosopher Catherine Malabou, who has been a central figure in the concept's theorization, characterizes plasticity as "a sort of natural sculpting that forms our identity, an identity modeled by experience and that makes us subjects of a history."[42] Plasticity is what makes fundamental changes in identity and/or subjectivity possible in the first place. Plasticity makes legible the external pressures that occasion or force such changes (what Malabou here calls "history"). If human subjectivity is to transform into a more plantlike state, then it needs to be sufficiently malleable in the first place. If a transformation does take place, then the traces of the history that sculpted the new form must be legible in the form itself. A botanical hermeneutics, like the one I employ here in this book, seeks out the places where plasticity sheds light on historical subjectification.

All of the texts discussed in this book share the belief that whatever the human is, it is not fixed in time or place. Plasticity names the capacity (both positive and negative) for humans—and the very concept of the human—to transform. Plasticity turns being into becoming. Yet while it serves as the basis for my discussion of the term, Malabou's figuration of plasticity is firmly centered in the human realm, in large part due to its concern with the brain and neurobiology. Plasticity is, however, an operative term in the botanical realm as well. Phenotypic plasticity names, in Beronda Montgomery's words, the botanical potential for "change of form and function in response to dynamic environmental conditions."[43] The website for the VILLUM Research Center for Plant Plasticity at the University of Copenhagen explains that plasticity is especially important to plant life due to its sessile condition: "In contrast to animals, which are able to actively move away to avoid challenges such as a predators [sic] or a changing climate, plants have acquired the ability to biosynthesize an unprecedented array of structurally complex bioactive natural compounds with specialized roles in order to cope with environmental challenges."[44]

What happens when animals (in this case, humans) are also not "able to actively move away to avoid challenges"? This is the situation explored in the texts at the heart of this book (save for chapter 5, which is focused specifically on movement through plant migration). Unable to physically escape moments of crisis in Japan's modern history, the writers and filmmakers I assemble here attempted to take a note from the botanical realm and turn plastic, becoming "other to themselves," to paraphrase Malabou.[45] The plasticity of becoming botanical allows us to rethink the human not just as a subject of history (to return to Malabou's claim) but as an environmental subject as well, an "open, living system" that slowly but persistently adapts to (at times catastrophic) change.[46]

The crises I discuss in this book are indeed catastrophic, but they are often not spectacular, at least not within the texts' narratives. The writings of Osaki Midori respond to the violence of early Shōwa Japan, but they are not narratives of war and imperialism in and of themselves. Abe's "Dendrocacalia" comments on the colonization and military occupation of the Ogasawara Islands, but it does so allegorically. It is my contention that by moving plants to the foreground of these texts, we can glimpse the crises serving as, to quote Christopher Dole in *The Time of Catastrophe*, "both a backdrop to and condition for the intimate terrain of . . . everyday lives."[47] The mosses in Osaki's *Wandering in the Realm of the Seventh Sense* and the dendrocacalia tree in Abe's story tie these narratives into a larger historical ecosystem of war and colonialism. Plants become windows onto the historical moment of a given text. Move them to the foreground, and with them come historical and social contexts not otherwise obvious. Turning to plants and learning to understand their different temporalities allows us to see the slow unfolding of crisis and how a botanical plasticity allows for slow adaptation to slow violence (to borrow Rob Nixon's influential concept). If subjectivity is plastic, then we can see history's fingerprints in the mold as it becomes botanical.

The In-Between of Science and Spirituality

Throughout this book, I focus on texts where unspectacular crises structure the everyday lives of characters in damaging ways. I am interested in texts where crises largely hide in the background, as ubiquitous, unassuming, and easily ignored as the grass beneath our feet. Chapter 3, for example, begins by discussing a long-form, multivolume novel that grapples with the existential disillusionment of Japan's defeat in World War II. Said novel, written by Haniya Yutaka (1909–1997) and titled *Dead Spirits* (*Shirei*), does not focus on the war or any of Japan's postwar crises (US occupation and repatriation, for example) outright. The catastrophe of war and defeat is affectually palpable but not necessarily visible. While it is considered something of a masterpiece of postwar Japanese literature (Haniya began publishing it in installments soon after Japan's surrender, in 1946), few critics have considered it an environmental text. By foregrounding forests in our reading of the *Dead Spirits*, however, we can see the novel as an environmental response to the background of crisis that was the postwar moment. For in the novel, characters yearn for plasticity in the face of defeat, to become anew in the face of an unspeakable trauma. They transform and become anew among trees, becoming botanical by phytomorphically extending their subjectivity out into the surrounding forest.

Chapter 3 marks a shift in this book's discussion of plasticity and transformation. In the first two chapters, it is in the in-between of literature and science that the texts under investigation attempt to rethink the human as more plantlike. In chapters 3 and 4, spirituality enters the fray. CPS thinkers have been working to bridge the realms of science and spirituality through their focus on plant life.

Robin Wall Kimmerer's work does so within the context of Indigenous cosmologies of North America, for example. Something similar happens in the works I discuss in chapters 3 and 4, albeit in very different contexts from those of Kimmerer's work. In this section of the book, science and spirituality form an in-between that proves fertile ground for becoming botanical.

Anyone who has spent time in a forest (especially at night) has likely felt something akin to the mysterious/spiritual affect that Haniya writes into *Dead Spirits* and that filmmakers Yanagimachi Mitsuo (born 1945) and Kawase Naomi (born 1969) make present in their films (as I discuss in chapter 4). It may not be a religious experience for all, but something approaching the sublime seems to strike humans as they find themselves surrounded by a dark, dense green within the forest. Getting lost in the woods can be terrifying. For those in the middle of a crisis, losing oneself in the botanical realm can also be liberating. This is the conceit of the texts I discuss in chapters 3 and 4. In chapter 3, trees become a medium—by definition, an in-between—that facilitates exchange between the world of the living and the world of the dead (what I call "botanical media"). By becoming more plantlike and experiencing himself as part of the forest, the protagonist of *Dead Spirits* reclaims a metaphysically spiritual connection to trees that puts him in contact with the dead spirits of the novel's title. Trees have long held such associations with the dead in Japan, and *Dead Spirits* is Haniya's attempt to reconnect to this botanically spiritual realm in the aftermath of a war in which the state coopted religion to disastrous ends in the form of State Shinto.

Chapter 3 pairs *Dead Spirits* with a novel written under very different circumstances, a 2013 response to 3.11 titled *Radio Imagination*, written by Itō Seikō (born 1961). Like Haniya's work of the immediate postwar, Itō's novel turns to trees as a medium to connect to those who have died, in this case, in the wake of the earthquake and tsunami that occurred on March 11, 2011. Trees become a bridge connecting these two moments of crisis as well as figures of plasticity that allow these two writers to rethink the human, the plant, and spirituality itself. This trend toward a spiritual understanding of plants continues into chapter 4. Against the backdrop of economic depression occasioned by an increasingly globalized timber industry, the two films at the heart of chapter 4—Yanagimachi Mitsuo's *Fire Festival* (*Himatsuri*, 1985) and Kawase Naomi's *Vision* (2018)—straddle the line of science and spirituality in their focus on the decline of Japanese forestry. Both films read destruction by fire as a means of embracing plasticity. Employing both scientific notions of disturbance ecology and religious ritual, these two cinematic texts demonstrate that the transformations found in becoming botanical can be cyclical, and that, for plants, life and death can be cyclical as well. Set the forest on fire, and a new one will (eventually) grow back. At the intersection of science and spirituality, these films ask: What happens when humans, too, strive for this kind of botanical regeneration in the aftermath of fire? Is there a *shokubutsusei* that can lead to rebirth?

How Pseudoscience Haunts CPS

The in-between of science and spirituality has been fertile ground for becoming botanical in the literary and filmic works I discuss in chapters 3 and 4, but it also served as the site of one of the biggest scandals in the history of botanical science, the publication of Peter Tompkins and Christopher Bird's *The Secret Life of Plants*. A best-seller at the time of its release in the 1970s, *The Secret Life of Plants* tried hard to make humans think differently about plants. It did so, in the words of Michael Pollan, in the form of "a beguiling mashup of legitimate plant science, quack experiments, and mystical nature worship that captured the public imagination at a time when New Age thinking was seeping into the mainstream."[48] Stories of plant communication, including communication with the dead and with extraterrestrials, caused a sensation that ultimately resulted in significant backlash. As Pollan explains:

> [In] the view of many plant scientists "The Secret Life of Plants" has done lasting damage to their field. According to Daniel Chamovitz, an Israeli biologist who is the author of the recent book "What a Plant Knows," Tompkins and Bird "stymied important research on plant behavior as scientists became wary of any studies that hinted at parallels between animal senses and plant senses." Others contend that "The Secret Life of Plants" led to "self-censorship" among researchers seeking to explore the "possible homologies between neurobiology and phytobiology"; that is, the possibility that plants are much more intelligent and much more like us than most people think—capable of cognition, communication, information processing, computation, learning, and memory.[49]

The supposed junk science that is *The Secret Life of Plants* continues to haunt CPS scholarship. Its legacy is such that contemporary works engaging in rethinking the plant (and rethinking the human to be more plantlike) run the risk of dismissal as New Age pseudoscience. One of the reasons CPS has been slow to make inroads in both the sciences and the humanities is no doubt due to the tarnished legacy of Tompkins and Bird.

All the same, the history of *The Secret Life of Plants* is important to the trope of becoming botanical as I outline it in this book. This is because Japanese electrical engineer-turned-best-selling-parascientist Hashimoto Ken (1924–2007) is featured prominently in *The Secret Life of Plants* (and appears with his wife in the film adaptation of the book as well). I mentioned above that Japanese translations of CPS thinkers like Kimmerer and Mancuso can be found in Japanese bookstores. Often sitting next to them is the Japanese translation of *The Secret Life of Plants*. Hashimoto's belief that plants could speak with the help of polygraph machines and that plants could serve as a conduit between the world of the living and the world of the dead is a part of the reason the book has been discredited as pseudoscience. Yet Hashimoto's beliefs also feel at home alongside Haniya Yutaka's *Dead Spirits* and Itō Seikō's *Radio Imagination*. All three envisioned plants as media that could put humans in touch with dead spirits. I put the work of these three writers together in chapter 3 to once again show how literature and science (in this case, spiritually inflected parascience) are entangled. These three figures—Haniya, Hashimoto, and Itō—form an unlikely grouping that only makes sense in terms of a twice-haunted *shokubutsusei*, one that puts humans in touch with the dead and one that continues to haunt the legitimacy of CPS. Here is where the plant humanities can offer something of a resurgence (if not redemption) to figures like Hashimoto. From an environmental humanities perspective, the fact that the science of *The Secret Life of Plants* has been debunked does not mean it is any less interesting or worthy of study.

Quite the contrary! As a best-selling book that continues to be in print in both Japan and the United States despite its spurious claims, and as a work whose bogus propositions have seemingly influenced serious works of literature like Haniya's *Dead Spirits* and Itō's *Radio Imagination*, *The Secret Life of Plants* is an important cultural touchstone that we in the humanities who work in CPS can embrace and question the extent to which it inspired a generation (or generations) to look for plasticity in the botanical realm. For CPS thinkers like Stefano Mancuso and Monica Gagliano, i.e., those who actively engage in STEM research, the legacy of *The Secret Life of Plants* may present a burden to be overcome, but for us plant humanists, it is a text ripe with botanical potential. I believe that the particular *shokubutsusei* of the plant humanities allows us to give up the ghost, so to speak, and to seek the strange and revel in the paranormal possibilities plant life might offer on the page or on the screen, or even, I would argue, at the level of subjectivity.

Embracing the Untamable

It may seem surprising that rethinking the plant can lead one to a haunted, frightening realm, as it does in the works explored in chapters 3 and 4. If one does not get lost in the woods, plants do not appear all that threatening. Cacti might hurt if we touch them, but by and large, we humans feel as if we are in control of things when it comes to plants. Yet as Dawn Keetley has convincingly demonstrated, plants frequently appear in works of horror, from *Invasion of the Body Snatchers* (1956) to M. Night Shyamalan's *The Happening* (2008). As Keetley explains, "At its most basic, plant horror marks humans' dread of the 'wildness' of vegetal nature—its untameability, its pointless excess, its uncontrollable growth. Plants embody an inscrutable silence, an implacable strangeness, which human culture has, from the beginning, set out to tame."[50] In other words, the extreme plasticity of plant life—its ability to grow and change, ever so slowly but persistently—has, at times, made it a threatening figure when it has entered the foreground. What the writers and filmmakers brought together in this book have in common is a desire to embrace the "untameability" of plant life, to turn the horror of its "implacable strangeness" into a new, potentially liberatory form of subjectivity.

This is perhaps most true of the poet Hiromi Ito (born 1955), who earlier we saw claim that plants and words are "the same thing." Ito serves as the subject of chapter 5—a chapter that finds our investigation of becoming botanical in yet another state of in-betweenness. Much of Ito's oeuvre is set between Japan and the United States, as the writer lived in Southern California for many years and continued to travel to Japan at regular intervals to care for her aging parents. I identify the *shokubutsusei* of Ito's work as that of "botanical migration," using the scientific notion of secular migration—in which plants themselves migrate across land through successive generations—to draw out the ways in which Ito's work challenges biopolitical attempts to control the movement of human bodies. Ito's work teaches us that in becoming botanical, one can phytomorphically become untamable, unruly, and potentially nongovernable.[51] In the in-between movement of migration, Ito's poetry shows us that to be more plantlike is to be always in motion, as counterintuitive as that might seem. Anyone who has kept a garden and has tried to keep weeds out of a given area knows the tenacity of plants and their ability to sprout up where you least expect them. Trying to tame weeds is often a fool's errand. Ito's work asks: What if we humans were more like weeds?

Ultimately, this unruly spirit runs throughout all the works I discuss in this book, albeit to differing degrees. Although the story they collectively tell unfolds across nearly one hundred years, and although they turn to plants in response to different moments of crisis throughout those nearly one hundred years, many sought a form of resistance, be it subtle (as in the works of Osaki Midori) or brash (as in the works of Hiromi Ito). Becoming botanical often allowed the writers and filmmakers gathered here to rethink the human in defiance of hegemonic structures that looked to fix human subjectivity in ways that would prove beneficial to the state in one way or another. Ultimately, learning to embody the plasticity of one's own *shokubutsusei* and become more plantlike was (and remains) a radical act, even when (or perhaps especially when) state power also turned to the botanical realm as a form of control in the first place.

This is not to say that the majority of the figures discussed in this book were (or are) politically radical themselves. Some were, of course. Abe Kōbō and Haniya Yutaka both belonged to the Japanese Communist Party for a spell. But others are harder to claim as having produced works of resistance. Miura Shion (born 1976), whose 2018 plant-filled novel *A World Without Love* (*Ai naki sekai*) I discuss in the epilogue of this book, is a popular writer whose work seems far removed from contemporary politics. Yet, in its resistance to gender norms and genre conventions, Miura's novel is unruly in its own right. Of more serious concern is Kawase Naomi, who has received much criticism for the nationalistic overtones of her official documentary film covering the controversial 2020 Tokyo Olympics. The film I discuss in this book, *Vision*, nevertheless turns to the forest to advocate for change, community, and nongovernability, even if it does so in an ambiguous manner that may belie her nationalist tendencies all the same. Kawase's work reminds us, again, that becoming botanical is a potential that can be mobilized to different ends, at different points and times. Just like the plants themselves, there is great diversity in works of art that strive to be plantlike. It may take some time to see and better understand the radical *shokubutsusei* of some of these works. CPS can help.

This is because, at its core, CPS is itself a radical paradigm that can help us rethink many things: what it means to be human, what it means to be a plant, what it means to live, what it means to die, and, yes, what it means to resist. As a framework for building something new, plants hold much potential. This book maps how Japanese writers and filmmakers sought to actualize this potential. My hope is that this book likewise demonstrates the kind of botanical potential CPS and the plant humanities hold for rethinking Japanese studies. May it serve as a seed that struggles its way up through the hard ground that has kept the field fixed in place.

1

BOTANICAL FAMILIES
Osaki Midori, Moss, and
Evolutionary Resemblance

In June of 1930, the modernist writer and film critic Osaki Midori watched Max Fleischer's 1925 silent documentary *Evolution* at a movie theater in Tokyo.[1] The film recounts the history of the earth from its earliest days to the evolutionary descent of human beings. Osaki would write about *Evolution* in *Jottings on Film* (*Eiga mansō*), her column on cinema published in the periodical *Women's Arts* (*Nyonin geijutsu*) in August of the same year. She recounts having an out-of-body experience while watching the film, of it drawing her in and putting her in touch with the deepest of time before the mythological creator deities of Japan, Izanagi and Izanami:

> Within the space of about twenty minutes, my mind [*kokoro*] leaves the earth's surface, and is released into a time before the gods Izanagi and Izanami. . . . Within the space of about twenty minutes, I ponder a toy box-like philosophy. "I" become gas; "I" become a star; "I" become smoke; "I" become a slice of glacier; "I" become moss; "I" become a chameleon; "I" become a native. How skillful that a world without even the slightest whiff of culture can arouse a naïve empathy in viewers. There are not many films that fully absorb a viewer's mind, even for a second, into "moss," into "anger," into "laughter."[2]

In the darkened theater, Osaki visits various points on the evolutionary path toward humankind and imagines occupying other modes of being. Along the way, she loses a concrete sense of self. Her subjectivity becomes fluid, moving both through time and between states of matter. *Evolution* allows Osaki to rethink what it means to be human. Her mind is set adrift, and she repeatedly brackets the self-referential pronoun "I."

Of all the stops along the evolutionary path that Osaki visits while watching the film, she only mentions one example twice, moss. This is no coincidence. For Osaki, moss and evolutionary thinking go hand in hand. Moss appears throughout Osaki's oeuvre and has become something of a symbol for the writer herself. Amid the violent backdrop of Japan's early Shōwa period—a stretch of time beginning in 1926 that witnessed the intensification of Japanese colonialism and fascism—Osaki found in moss (and plants in general) a model for adaptation to rapidly changing (and, to be sure, worsening) times. Weary of a world increasingly at war, she became botanical and envisioned a world and a future in which firm divisions between humans and plants were replaced with familial bonds in deep evolutionary time. Osaki embraced the inclusiveness of evolutionary theory and rejected the exclusionary impulses of social Darwinism, with its survival of the fittest ideology, in an age when concepts of racial difference contributed to the rhetoric of Japan's colonial expansion.[3]

By the time Osaki watched Fleischer's film, the theory of evolution had been circulating through Japan for decades. The American academic Edward Morse's lectures on evolution at Tokyo Imperial University (where he taught for three years beginning in 1877) are often considered the point at which Charles Darwin's ideas were formally introduced to Japan. Morse influenced Japanese academics like Ishikawa Chiyomatsu, who would go on to be among the first to write about the theory in Japanese. However, what Morse introduced into Japan as evolutionary theory was in fact a form of social Darwinism that went on to impact political policy and theories of nation and empire building in the coming decades.[4] According to the historian of science Watanabe Masao, Morse's lectures were "a crude treatment of the subject (of evolution)" in which he "applie[d] examples from the animal and plant world indiscriminately to humans."[5] This abstraction of natural science and its application to the social realm was instrumental to the fledgling state of the Meiji period (1868–1912). By the early Shōwa period, it was the de facto interpretation of evolutionary thinking.

This chapter looks to highlight the in-between of literature and science (and evolution, in particular) through its focus on the writing of Osaki Midori, as evolutionary thought and plant life in Osaki's work bring together these supposedly opposing regimes of knowledge against the backdrop of Japanese imperialism. For as much as Osaki turned to a utopian vision of evolution to rethink the human as more plantlike and resist the exclusionary impulses of social Darwinism, her own life was thoroughly entangled in the crisis of colonial expansion—the very crisis she looked to overcome through her embrace of plants as kin in evolutionary time.

Plant science abounds in Osaki's oeuvre. Moss, in particular, becomes a meeting point of scientific and poetic speculation. As a primitive plant with no roots, moss was the perfect model for Osaki to craft a new (and yet extremely old) way of inhabiting a world turned upside down by crisis. Robin Wall Kimmerer writes in her poetic account of mosses that they "are the most primitive of plants and lack any such vascular tissue (to hold them upright)," but that it is precisely this "primitive" state that has ensured their flourishing.[6] Kimmerer sings the praises of mosses' simplicity and smallness, arguing that "being small doesn't mean being unsuccessful. Mosses are successful by any biological measure—they inhabit nearly every ecosystem on earth and number as many as 22,000 species. . . . Beautifully adapted for life in miniature, mosses take full advantage of being small."[7] Moss seems to have spoken to Osaki, suggesting that a way forward could be found in a movement backward in evolutionary time toward the small but resilient realm of plant life.

In Osaki's affinity for moss and plants in general, we see a desire to rethink the human and better understand the "I" that Osaki put within brackets in *Jottings on Film*. This desire is apparent in Osaki's best-known work, *Wandering in the Realm of the Seventh Sense* (*Dainana kankai hōkō*), which was published in 1931, just one year after she wrote about Fleischer's *Evolution*. It is also apparent in Osaki's poetry and the constellation of stories I call the "Machiko Cycle," which partially continue the story of *Wandering in the Realm of the Seventh Sense*.[8] The bracketing of the "I" in *Jottings on Film* is but one example of what we might call a fractured subjectivity in Osaki's writing. Such fracturing was not a mere literary conceit for Osaki, as it was for many writers who experimented with the aesthetics of literary modernism in Japan. Osaki struggled with mental health issues that became the subject of much of her work and ultimately ended her writing career. In 1932, only one year after the publication of *Wandering in the Realm of the Seventh Sense*, she left Tokyo and returned to her native rural Tottori Prefecture after suffering a nervous breakdown. By 1935, she had ceased writing altogether.

Like many of her modernist contemporaries, Osaki's work shows the influence of Freudian thinking and psychoanalysis on early Shōwa aesthetics. Osaki's personal experiences with psychoanalysis (which was still in its relative infancy in Japan in the 1930s) aroused an interest in unconventional subjective states as well as in science more generally. In his study of Japanese literary modernism, Seiji Lippit explains that it was precisely in this period that Freud's influence on literature and culture became significant.[9] Lippit offers two well-known modernist texts as examples—Yokomitsu Riichi's *Machine* (*Kikai*, 1930) and Kawabata Yasunari's *Crystal Fantasy* (*Suishō gensō*, 1931)—and explains how both "explore a realm of the psyche existing beyond conscious control but erupting from time to time into the space of consciousness and everyday life."[10] Osaki's work fits within this modernist paradigm in its attention to the reconfiguration of subjectivity in the violent decade of the 1930s.

Osaki was not the only modernist writer to be fascinated by plant life. Satō Haruo's 1929 short story "Record of Nonchalant" (*Nanshoran no kiroku*) presents a dystopian world in which the poor are turned into plants intended to decorate the homes of the rich, while Ryūtanji Yū began researching and writing extensively about cacti and succulents starting in the mid-1930s. What makes Osaki stand out among the better-known writers of her generation is her specific *shokubutsusei* (to return to Fujihara Tatsushi's term I discussed in the introduction to this book). Osaki ultimately sought a better model to understand the various ruptures of the early Shōwa era than was available in contemporaneous theories of psychology, of which she was intimately familiar through her own diagnosis of *shinkeibyō* (nervous disorder). In her poems and fiction, Osaki searched for a way of inhabiting a violent world that was not relegated to clinical psychosis. She ultimately found moss, and, inspired by the strength in smallness it provided, Osaki attempted to sculpt a more plantlike way of weathering the turbulence of the era.

The Uprooting of Colonial Modernity

The uncertainty of the times took its toll on Osaki, as it did on other contemporaneous writers of the 1930s. Some, like Yokomitsu Riichi in his novel *Shanghai* (published between 1928 and 1931), wrote explicitly about the violence unfolding in Japan's overseas colonies. Osaki did not. Yet the crises of the early Shōwa—and Japanese colonialism in particular—are legible in her work all the same if we foreground plants in our reading of her stories and poetry. This is because plant life played an important role in Japan's colonial project, and, as Osaki wrote of characters engaged in botanical science, she drew from her real-life familial connection to Japan's colonies. Osaki was intimately familiar with science's complicity in Japan's wartime agenda from her brother's work researching fertilizer use in Japanese-occupied Korea, but just as she attempted to rethink the human through plant life, so, too, did plants allow her to rethink science in an era when technological progress was inseparable from empire building. In her fiction, characters learn to read botanical science like poetry. They use psychology to theorize a moss-like subjectivity that pushes back against the patriarchy. They take the insights of evolutionary thought and posit a botanical family that made kin of humans and plants alike. In the in-between of science and literature, Osaki found a way to become more plantlike and turn the chaos and psychological unrest of her time into something creative that could grow and flourish.

Even still, Osaki's career as a writer was all too brief. Born in rural Tottori Prefecture in 1896, she spent only thirteen years in Tokyo as a writer, from 1919 to 1932. Although championed by her friend Hayashi Fumiko (who went on to become one of Japan's best-known postwar writers), it was only after several decades since Osaki had stopped writing that critics and the public took notice of her work. *Wandering in the Realm of the Seventh Sense* was republished in 1969 when it was collected in the sixth volume of *Collected Works—Discoveries of Modern Literature* (*Zenshū—Gendai bungaku no hakken*), titled *Dark Humor* (*Kuroi yūmoa*). This volume—edited by Ōka Shōhei and including works by Abe Kōbō (who is the subject of the next chapter) and Hanada Kiyoteru—reintroduced Osaki's work to a new generation. In 1973, Hanada, one of the most influential literary and media critics of his time, went on to publish an essay in which he called Osaki "his muse." Although she is by no means a household name, Osaki's reputation continues to grow even today, as does critical attention to her work.[11] Osaki's life has even been portrayed on film (as I discuss below), and a manga adaptation of *Wandering in the Realm of the Seventh Sense* was published in 2018.

Osaki's life as a writer in the early Shōwa period was, by all accounts, rough, both in terms of the political landscape of the times and in terms of her personal life. This particularly turbulent era saw both the massive destruction of the Great Kantō Earthquake of 1923 (which effectively leveled the city of Tokyo) and the transition from the relatively democratic Taishō era to the increasingly militaristic Shōwa era in 1926. Osaki's career coincided with an increase in Japan's colonial activities in Taiwan (which began the year before Osaki's birth in 1895) and the Korean peninsula (which began in 1910). The Mukden Incident of 1931—the year Osaki's *Wandering in the Realm of the Seventh Sense* was published—served as justification for Japan's invasion of Manchuria. The following year saw the May 15 Incident, in which a failed coup attempt resulted in the assassination of prime minister Inukai Tsuyoshi.

Political and colonial violence was unfolding all around Osaki, and, closer at hand, she struggled to make ends meet in Tokyo. Having to rely on her mother for financial support, Osaki watched as her contemporaries, like Hayashi Fumiko, gained greater notoriety than she did. In 1929, she lost her brother Tetsurō to illness, a family tragedy that some speculate contributed to Osaki's ever-worsening psychological condition.[12] Tetsurō had been a student of new Buddhist thought, and Kawasaki Kenko presumes that Osaki was likely introduced to many schools of academic thought (like evolution, psychology, and vitalism) via Tetsurō.[13] Osaki then lost her oldest brother, Atsurō, to tuberculosis in 1933. Atsurō had served in the navy until his untimely passing. There is a story of Osaki's contemporaries from *Women's Arts*, which included proletarian writer Toda Toyoko and Ōta Yōko (the latter of whom would go on to write of her experiences surviving the atomic bombing of Hiroshima), visiting Osaki's apartment and listening to her talk solely of her "grief."[14] The conventional portrait of Osaki is thus one of struggle and sadness.

Given Osaki's brief and by all accounts unhappy time spent as a transplant in Tokyo, it is easy to imagine she certainly felt out of place and uprooted in the colonial metropole. Many of her characters, including *Wandering in the Realm of the Seventh Sense*'s protagonist Machiko, come to the city from a rural elsewhere. It was plant life, and moss in particular, that allowed Machiko (and thus Osaki) to see the potential in this type of uprooting. Who needed roots anyway? Mosses flourish without roots.

With moss in mind, Osaki composed an idiosyncratic environmental literature that paid close attention to plants and their potential influence on human subjectivity from within the anxious, urban setting of Tokyo. In cramped attic rooms and hospital wards, her fractured characters (most of them women) dream of flourishing by forging new connections with the botanical realm in defiance of male relatives and male psychologists who pathologize and hospitalize them. Osaki's work attempts to resist such pathologizing and to instead greet the multiplicity of modern subjectivity as generative rather than debilitating.

Of Moss and Multiple Subjectivity

As is apparent in the title *Wandering in the Realm of the Seventh Sense*, Osaki was interested in capturing the extrasensory experience of nonnormative states of subjectivity in writing. She was fascinated with doppelgangers and moments of repetition and how these instances of multiplicity caused the human subject to experience the world in strange ways. This interest helped bring her to the question: How do plants experience the world? Like the other figures I discuss in this book, Osaki concluded that a plant's subjective experience is one of multiplicity. Theorists working in critical plant studies (CPS) argue that plants resist the easy categorization of "the individual" that is so fundamental to normative understandings of identity and subjectivity as well as mental health. Plants like mosses are themselves always already multiplicities. As Kimmerer writes: "Moss plants almost never occur singly, but in colonies packed as dense as an August cornfield."[15] Bryologist J. W. Bates likewise claims that "the colony rather than the individual is widely regarded as the functional unit for many bryophytes."[16] In general, to think of moss is to think of a multiplicity of moss, spread out over a rock or tree with fuzzy boundaries (see figure 1.1). Kimmerer recounts the difficulties of identifying mosses with her students: "Slowing down and coming

FIGURE 1.1. Moss as multiplicity. Photo by author.

close, we see patterns emerge and expand out of the tangled tapestry threads. The threads are simultaneously distinct from the whole, and part of the whole."[17] Such is their *shokubutsusei*, somewhere in between singular and multiple. This is the subjective state Osaki sought in becoming botanical. A unified subjectivity—a sense of oneself as *one self*—gets lost in the transformation that leads to a botanical subjectivity. Karen L. F. Houle refers to the act of becoming as "provisional co-creative zone(s) in which the 'parties' and their 'proper functions' are themselves effaced and augmented."[18] Augmented and effaced at the same time, things come together and lose themselves as themselves in the process of becoming. They form something new that is more than the sum of their parts. Osaki's work asks: Could inhabiting the world this way be liberating?

Drawing from her own life, Osaki created characters that struggled with *shinkeibyō* and looked for ways to free themselves of its burden in dangerous and depressing times. Sometimes her characters turn to film, sometimes to drugs, sometimes to poetry. Often, they turn to plants. In her 1932 short story "Miss Cricket" ("Kōrogijō"), for example, the anxieties of nervous disorder extend into the botanical realm:

> When he has to pass under the late spring paulownia blossoms, he constantly breathes out from his nostrils. This is probably to avoid, by means of a hasty breath in through the nose, letting the fragrance of a paulownia that is suffering from nervous disorder enter inside his body. After all, those with nervous disorders disavow others with nervous disorders. This is done to preemptively ward off sad feelings toward fellow travelers. Be as it may that there exists between himself and the paulownia blossoms the difference between humans and plants, on the grounds of their being similarly afflicted by nervous disorders, they are fellow travelers.[19]

For Osaki, humans and paulownia blossoms are "fellow travelers" as they move through the anxious uprooting of modernity. The play here between anthropomorphism and phytomorphism (the attribution of plantlike characteristics to humans) blurs the lines between human and plant, but ultimately, in this passage, we see a human character trying to disavow his connection to the botanical realm and maintain a singular subjectivity. This is because this passage is narrated from a doctor's perspective. It is a pathologizing of the becoming botanical that Osaki's work actually attempted to overturn.

Unusual psychological states shared between humans and plants become a site of possibility and transcendence in Osaki's other works. We see this in a poem dating from 1933 (one of the few works she created after leaving Tokyo):

> A human
> is truly a single, thinking reed
> a single
> slim
> reed that thinks of things
> a single plant, within a thin reed
> a spirit as wide as the cosmos.[20]

This poem, part of a longer series titled *Poems Dedicated to the Gods* (*Kamigami ni sasaguru shi*) is a play on seventeenth-century French philosopher Blaise Pascal's famous figuration of becoming botanical in *Pensées*: "Man is but a reed, the most feeble thing in nature; but he is a thinking reed."[21] Osaki's poem is also a tribute to nineteenth-century Scottish poet William Sharp, who appears several times throughout Osaki's work (including in "Miss Cricket"). Sharp secretly wrote under the female pseudonym Fiona Macleod, an instance of multiplicity that fascinated Osaki and attracted her to his (their) work. The idea of two poets inhabiting one body seemed to perfectly crystalize the potential Osaki saw in so-called abnormal psychology found in the fractured subjectivity of early Shōwa Japan. The poem continues:

> Fiona
> inside your chest
> deep within the gate to your soul
> she dwells, all alone.
> You are one side of a body.
> You are a doppelgänger.
> Oh,
> You,
> what a split poet.[22]

William Sharp/Fiona Macleod become a creative multiplicity of selves. While a seeming impossibility for a human, such multiplicity was the very stuff of the botanical realm. The *shokubutsusei* of Sharp/Macleod offered a model for Osaki to find something new in the anxieties (both societal and personal) that threatened to split her apart. Thus, while Pascal calls the reed "the most feeble thing in nature," Osaki does not. For all its feebleness, the reed is strong in its plasticity, that is, its ability to change, split, and accommodate two subjectivities at once. Osaki's botanical imagination grows from the same soil as this reed.

Just as Sharp is both himself and Fiona Macleod, so, too, is he both human and botanical. In the same poem, Osaki writes of Sharp: "fragrant olive smells of you" (*mokusei wa kimi no nioi*) only to reverse the attribution a few lines later as "you smell of fragrant olive" (*kimi wa mokusei no nioi*).[23] Sharp is the smell of fragrant olive, and fragrant olive is the smell of Sharp. The human and plant overlap and form an in-between. The human is but a reed, but in its singularity-as-a-multiplicity, it is unfathomably expansive. The human becomes botanical, forming something new and augmented, enveloped in fragrant olive. A splintered subjectivity finds liberatory form in Osaki's botanical poetics.

In poetry, Osaki likewise finds a way to rethink the science of evolution. In this poem dedicated to Sharp/Macleod, Osaki rethinks the human through the reed as both a reduction and an expansion. The material body of human-turned-plant is "slim" and "singular," but its immaterial spirit—its subjectivity—is "as wide as the cosmos."[24] This jump from the botanical to the cosmic reverses the trajectory found in Osaki's review of Max Fleischer's *Evolution*. While watching the story of evolution unfold in cinema, Osaki moved forward in evolutionary time and thus forward in biological complexity. The film, like the conventional understanding of evolutionary descent, travels from the cosmos toward the botanical realm: "'I' become gas; 'I' become a star; 'I' become smoke; 'I' become a slice of glacier; 'I' become moss." In Osaki's poem to Sharp/Macleod, on the contrary, the human becomes a plant that uproots (a reed, in the place of moss), *and then* ends up among the stars. What a transformation! Uprooting, Osaki discovered, can lead to such transcendence, should one seek the plasticity of plant life.

Repetition and the Plasticity of Form

Osaki similarly turns back evolutionary time in her unassuming masterpiece, *Wandering in the Realm of the Seventh Sense*. In the novella, a patient in a mental hospital eschews human subjectivity in favor of a "moss-like disposition." Osaki calls this phenomenon "species-reversal" (*shugaeri*), a term that echoes Deleuze and Guattari's figuration of "involution." For Deleuze and Guattari, involution is not merely the opposite or reverse of evolution. Rather, it is a creative movement that turns backward in the name of a kind of progress that "is in no way confused with regression."[25] *Wandering the Realm of the Seventh Sense* is full of attempted involutions, as its main character, Ono Machiko, intimately immerses herself in the miniature world of moss, that evolutionary ancestor of humans. She strives throughout to be more like moss.

It is difficult to summarize the plot of *Wandering in the Realm of the Seventh Sense*, not because so much happens in the narrative but rather because so little seems to happen. To fully appreciate it, one must look closely, as if one were inspecting a clump of moss. As Kimmerer has shown, moss is difficult to identify and requires a different kind of attention: "Learning to see mosses is more like listening than looking. A cursory glance will not do it. Straining to hear a faraway voice or catch a nuance in the quiet subtext of a conversation requires attentiveness, a filtering of all the noise, to catch the music."[26] This is the kind of attention that is required of *Wandering in the Realm of the Seventh Sense*, especially if we wish to identify the fingerprints of crisis that help shape the text. For what does happen in the novella happens slowly, nearly imperceptibly, and it happens several times, mostly within one location, the small, cramped house that Machiko shares with her brothers and cousin. Machiko is a teenage girl of indeterminate age with curly red hair. She uproots and leaves the countryside for Tokyo, where she comes to live with her two brothers, Ichisuke and Nisuke, along with their cousin Sangorō. It is a story about familial relationships, one that ultimately finds Machiko feeling closer to moss as an evolutionary ancestor than to any of her immediate male kin.

Each of the four main (human) characters considers themself a student, formally or otherwise. It is an odd household, with its haphazard mix of science and art. Sangorō prepares to retake the entrance exam for a music school. He practices on an old piano, annoying his housemates. Ichisuke studies a type of abnormal psychology referred to as "split psychology" (*bunretsu shinrigaku*)—a name that resembles the Japanese word for schizophrenia (*bunretsushō*) and also includes the same word for "split" that Osaki uses in referring to William Sharp as a "split poet." Ichisuke falls in love with a female patient who refuses to speak with him, and it is she who inhabits a moss-like subjectivity by means of species-reversal in defiance of his advances. Nisuke conducts research on plants, experimenting with the fertilization of radishes and mosses. The smell of his fertilizer wafts through the house throughout the story. Nisuke studies the "love lives" of moss, mixing different types of fertilizers to encourage their reproduction. Machiko, in turn, considers herself a student of poetry. She tries to capture, in verse, an elusive sensory experience that she calls "the seventh sense." Machiko is not taken seriously by her relatives, however. She is made to feel small, neglected, and used. As they hold forth in long conversations that last for pages at a time, Machiko cleans their rooms and cooks their meals. She is ignored for most of the novella. At one point, she becomes friends with a neighbor, but their relationship is short-lived. At the very end, she leaves the house to visit Ichisuke's clinic. This is the only action that takes place outside the confining walls of the run-down house she shares with her male relatives.

With its unusual and meandering plot, *Wandering in the Realm of the Seventh Sense* reads like a text trying to hold itself together in the face of neglect and near abuse. It is an experimental narrative, both in terms of content and form. Osaki initially envisioned the story as forming a closed loop, creating an ouroboros that ends where it begins.[27] Although she ultimately abandoned this idea, the circular logic of the text bears traces of its original plotting. There is a botanical quality to this cyclicality (a formal quality I explore in more detail in chapter 4). In touch with the cyclical rhythms of the atmosphere and the seasons in ways humans are generally not, plants embody a temporality of perpetual return that Osaki builds into the very structure of *Wandering in the Realm of the Seventh Sense*.

While the narrative form is temporally complex, Osaki's prose is deceptively simple. There is clarity at the level of the sentence that exposes the uprooted subjectivity floating underneath. Things seem almost too clear, as if Machiko needs to remind herself what she is narrating at all times. As the first-person narrator, Machiko repeatedly reminds readers who, what, and where things are, offering a kind of mapping that centers characters in space, to the point of stagnating narrative flow. The story develops in these repetitious clumps and clusters that look similar from a distance but reveal differences up close. In other words, the form of the story resembles the clumps of moss that come to serve as a key element to the plot. Moss is repetitive, like the narrative itself. Nisuke may encourage moss to fall in love and reproduce via spores, but moss can also reproduce asexually. Mosses can clone themselves, make duplicates via a process called "vegetal reproduction." Mosses are biologically repetitive.

Form and content thus overlap in *Wandering in the Realm of the Seventh Sense*, and this is a key element of the trope of becoming botanical. For example, as Machiko arrives at the house early in the story, she describes the mandarin oranges that grow outside and repeats the word *mandarin orange* (*mikan*) to a conspicuous degree:

> As Sangorō and I reached the house, the mandarin orange trees that formed a hedge surrounding the house were illuminated by the sun. The mandarin oranges were small in diameter and bumpy, their color no different from their leaves. This was when I first noticed. I was holding a string bag of mandarin oranges. It was a bag of leftover mandarin oranges that I had eaten while on the train, that I had unknowingly carried here. Anyway, the mandarin oranges from the hedge around this house were late bloomers. Later on, these mandarin oranges turned into poorly formed homegrown mandarin oranges: shockingly behind the season, full of bumps on their peels, full of seeds, and still small in diameter. They were sour mandarin oranges. However, beneath the light of the late autumn stars, these mandarin oranges looked beautiful.[28]

Machiko's narration is frequently repetitious in this manner. It is as if she must constantly take account of the material world around her or else risk getting lost. Yet the narrative repetition also makes legible the plasticity of Machiko's subjectivity (and the botanical form in which the text presents it). According to Catherine Malabou, "Repetition is plastic, it gives form to what it destroys. We have to think of a form created by destruction, the form of a new person, which is not the transcendental subject, but what undermines it, as the threat of its explosion."[29] In Machiko's repetitions, we can hear her coming apart. She splinters—or, as Malabou might say, she explodes—in order to become anew, to become multiple like moss.

The repetitions throughout the novella demonstrate how Machiko pays close attention to her environment and to plants in particular. She displays a form of intense noticing that CPS theorist Michael Marder aligns specifically with plant life. It is a form of noticing in which the distinction between subject and object dissolves:

> When I linger with plants, in thoughtful and physical proximity, I try to pay attention to their singular mode of attention. I notice, first, that plants do not attend to an *object* or *group of objects*. Their attention is inseparable from their life and growth. From a magnificent sequoia to a blade of

grass, a plant attends to the physical elements, precisely, because the elements are not objects and cannot be objectified. Only then, in such nonobjectification, are the elements and life itself respected in their proper being. Therefore, human attention convoked and directed toward life must strive, strange as this may sound, to be similarly nonobjectifying.[30]

Through her close attention to the physical world, Machiko strives to be "nonobjectifying" in this way. Thus she repeatedly tries to find a way into the seventh sense, that new, extrasensory mode of experience that would allow her to attend to her environment in the nonobjectifying way that Marder posits is possible for plant life. She believes poetry can accommodate this extrasensory subject position. The seventh sense eludes Machiko for much of the novella, however, and in her repetition, she ends up unwittingly highlighting objects like the mandarin oranges.

While Machiko's repetitive language does not allow for nonobjectification, it nevertheless accomplishes a kind of nonsubjectification. The pronoun "I" is used to an excessive degree throughout the novella, although Osaki never brackets it the way she does in her discussion of *Evolution* in *Jottings on Film*. Ironically, the repeated foregrounding of the first-person pronoun serves to destabilize any sense of a unified subjectivity precisely through its anxious attempts to solidify subjectivity. Machiko's brothers and cousin repeat subjects of conversations numerous times while talking to one another. Everyone repeats each other's names (often their full names) time and again, long after the narrative has made clear both who is being discussed and who they are in relation to each other. It feels self-conscious and somewhat paranoid, as if everyone is worried that they will become someone (or something) else unless they make explicit who they are in the first place. The formality of full names keeps everyone within the house (as well as the readers) at a distance. It exposes an artificiality and discomfort that comes across as anxiety. Early in the novella, cousin Sangorō mentions a book Ichisuke has asked him to purchase at the Maruzen bookstore called "'Doppel-something."[31] The anxiety over repetition, doubling, and identity abounds. To return to Malabou's claim about the relationship between repetition and plasticity, "it gives form to what it destroys." Names, subjects, objects—Osaki wants to "destroy" all of these in order to rethink the human and become anew. The narrative repeats names until they come to mean nothing. *Wandering in the Realm of the Seventh Sense* is not merely deconstructive in its stilted narration, however. Rather, in its repetitions and awkward exchanges, it constructs a moss-like form that accommodates a botanical subjectivity, a way of experiencing the world as moss might. Explode human subjectivity enough, and moss might just grow in the cracks.

Meeting Moss in Evolutionary Time

As she regularly cleans her brother Nisuke's room, Machiko marvels at the mosses that "spread out with the vastness of a forest" on his desk.[32] She discovers a different world in this mysterious and vast moss-covered landscape, one that eludes the confining clarity of the household in which she feels trapped and neglected. As she watches Nisuke work over this forest of moss, Machiko finally slips into the hazy, nonobjectifying (and nonsubjectifying) realm of the seventh sense. She enters into a new form of botanical subjectivity, where her senses become augmented and seem to take on a life of their own: "On the verge of falling asleep, I breathed heavily. I stayed awake for a short while by breathing air in through my nose, and then I breathed in again. While doing this, I inhabited a singular world of mist. There, my senses worked independently of each other, then merged into one, and then went astray again. My faculties continued incoherently on like this. Nisuke had just finished eagerly rubbing the top of the moss with a cotton swab, when his apron became hazy like mist, and transformed into clouds of various shapes."[33]

The new world that opens up to Machiko as she watches Nisuke work is indistinct and incoherent. It is a plastic world where things transform (like aprons into clouds). It is the seventh sense, a decidedly unclear subjectivity that Machiko describes as "a mental world shrouded in extensive fog."[34] Nozoe Nobuhisa's manga adaptation of *Wandering in the Realm of the Seventh Sense* highlights the bizarre qualities of this subjective state. It inserts a scene near the end of the story in which Machiko falls asleep and is led by a double of herself directly into the realm of the seventh sense. "This is the world you've wanted to know," says the doppelganger-Machiko against a moss-covered landscape populated by overlapping repetitions of portals and the faces of her male relatives growing out of moss spores.[35] It is a perfect visualization of becoming botanical, full of multiplicity and metamorphosis. Hamano Sachi's 1998 film adaptation of the story depicts Machiko's botanical subjectivity by superimposing her image over a closeup of moss (see figure 1.2). In this scene, Machiko physically embodies the small potentiality of moss; the exuberance she feels at having gained such knowledge is legible in the smile on her face.

What propels Machiko to such moments of epiphany is evolutionary thinking. Evolution is introduced into the narrative at the start of a long conversation between Ichisuke and Nisuke (which Machiko quietly, but closely, overhears). Ichisuke suggests (phytomorphically) that human emotions such as love are inherited from vegetal ancestors: "Seeing that humans fall in love, there is no reason mosses cannot fall in love. You could say that human love is an inheritance from moss. This perspective is certainly not wrong. The theory of evolution likely

FIGURE 1.2. Machiko among the moss in Hamano Sachi's 1998 film adaptation of *Wandering in the Realm of the Seventh Sense*.

imagines moss to be a very distant ancestor of humans."[36] Ichisuke then claims that he has witnessed humans inhabiting a moss-like subjectivity: "We can see a kind of evidence of this when humans are on the verge of waking from a nap and they suddenly find themselves returning to the mind of moss. It is a strange psychology, like clinging to a damp and humid bog, your body unable to move. This is evidence that the disposition of moss has been inherited by humans to this very day."[37] In this description, we see clear echoes of Machiko's own experience watching Nisuke work. As she drifted into a misty realm on the verge of sleep and her senses started working "independently of each other," Machiko embodied, in Ichisuke's words, "the disposition of moss." Machiko's becoming botanical, then, is an evolutionary inheritance, one that holds the potential for transcendence through involution.

In her feminist reading of Darwinian evolution, Elizabeth Grosz argues that Darwin's theory offers "the elements of an account of the place of futurity, the direction forward as the opening up, diversification, or bifurcation of the latencies of the present, which provide a kind of ballast for the induction of a future different but not detached from the past or present."[38] In other words, evolutionary thought provides a way to imagine the future as branching out and heading somewhere new from the present, like a plant does from its roots or rhizome. Flowers, stems, and leaves are different but not detached from their roots. Machiko takes note of this capability and attempts to embody it herself. As she becomes botanical, Machiko's mundane present branches off into a hazy future along a new evolutionary timeline in which the human is rethought as more plantlike.

For her brother Ichisuke, however, turning backward in evolutionary time in order to embody a moss-like disposition is a pathology that presents a serious problem. He complains to Nisuke of a patient recently admitted to his psychiatric clinic: "That patient is silent towards me, the split-consciousness she possesses is of a completely concealed nature. This is certainly inherited from the disposition of moss in ancient times."[39] Ichisuke explains that patients take on this moss-like subjectivity in response to the feeling of uprootedness, claiming: "Those humans that have inherited a moss-like disposition have a craving of wanting to put down roots in one place."[40] Ichisuke thus understands the connection between the uprooting of modernity and becoming botanical, but he diagnoses this becoming as a mental disorder.

There is a gendered element to Ichisuke's pathologizing of his female patient. Part of his conversation with Nisuke revolves around the fact that the patient in question is "not male" (*otoko de wa nai*). This somewhat curious phrasing is partially a critique of Ichisuke's history of harboring romantic feelings for female patients. If we consider the moss, however, we also find a subversion of sex/gender norms at play here. This is because mosses (and, indeed, plants in general) challenge conventional understandings of sexual differentiation (i.e., whether a moss can be identified as male or female). As Akiyama Hiroyuki explains in his 2004 book *The Story of Moss* (*Koke no hanashi*), mosses exhibit a complex biological development such that some possess male sex organs, some possess female sex organs, and some possess both simultaneously. In this, they resemble many other species of plant life. What makes mosses a uniquely complicated species in terms of sexual identification is their particular multiplicity. Akiyama explains: "In the case of mosses, they are connected below through their underground stems and their rhizomatic structure (which is a complexly entangled network, from which stems do emerge), and so it is difficult to recognize them as individual entities. According to their stages of development and the environment in which they are born and grow, they sometimes only display either male or female sex organs even though they biologically possess both, and so it can be difficult to judge whether they do in fact possess both sexes to begin with."[41]

Stella Sandford takes the question of sexual identification in plant life further than Akiyama. In her 2023 book *Vegetal Sex*, Sandford interrogates the historical development of botanists ascribing zoologically analogous notions of sex onto plant life. She points out that philosophers concerned with plants (such as Aristotle) did not entertain the idea of male and female plant life: "The idea of plant sex was not obvious for these thinkers because an answer to the question 'Do plants have "male" and "female"?' required an answer to another, more fundamental philosophical question: 'What are "male" and female"?'"[42]

Sandford argues that plants can lead us to this fundamental question in part because plants—and plants alone—exhibit a dibiontic life cycle, which she explains as "two different multicellular stages, also known as alternation of haploid and diploid generations (in one generation the organism has a singular set of chromosomes; in the other it has a double set.)"[43] What this means is that "although there are two generations in the 'individual' plant life cycle, there are at least three plants—one sporophyte and two gametophytes (one male, one female). The dibiontic life cycle thus further troubles the idea of the individual organism characteristic of the zoocentric model."[44] The *shokubutsusei* of the dibiontic life cycle thus simultaneously pushes against clear notions of both the male/female binary and suggests a radical reformulation of the plant as a multiplicity, insofar as Sandford claims that each plant is in fact "at least three plants." To what extent is Ichisuke's patient striving toward this type of sexual and subjective multiplicity by becoming botanical and adopting a moss-like disposition? Given Nisuke's primary research on moss reproduction, and further given the historical reality that plants' dibiontic life cycle was first identified in 1851 by William Hofmeister through the study of mosses and ferns, the question of sex and gender, and the subversion/rethinking thereof, is inseparable from the botanical imagination of *Wandering in the Realm of the Seventh Sense*.[45] It is also tied to the history of evolutionary thought, as Darwin himself expressed uncertainty about the distinction between male and female in plant life in his 1877 work *The Different Form of Flowers on Plants of the Same Species*.[46]

It is perhaps for this reason that for Nisuke, the student of plant biology, a moss-like disposition is quite natural. In his response to Ichisuke, Nisuke posits a certain amount of agency in the patient's psychological state, aligning it directly with the concept of involution. He claims that his brother's patient has performed a species-reversal and recounts a story he has heard of someone being born with a fox's tail: "They said it was a case of a human going against the course of evolution. . . . In addition to humans species-reversing back to foxes, it's also not a problem for human psychology to return to that of moss."[47] Of course, Nisuke does not know, or more likely does not care, that his own sister is attempting a species-reversal of her own.

While Nisuke's research on moss allows him to see a certain degree of agency in species-reversal, only Machiko can glimpse the full potential of becoming botanical. It is Machiko who names the botanical subjectivity arrived at through species-reversal "the seventh sense." While she fails repeatedly to capture the seventh sense in her poetry, it does momentarily offer her a means of escape, however brief, from the confines of her family and the home they share. In one particularly charged scene, Machiko brings her brothers boiled chestnuts that have arrived from their grandmother. Nisuke is hard at work on his moss research, studying the pollen that serves as a telltale sign that his moss has indeed fallen in love. After bits of a chestnut fall from Nisuke's mouth onto a notebook, Machiko notices the striking resemblance between the moss pollen and the chestnut powder. She once again starts to become botanical:

> Without thinking, I craned my neck and looked at the surface of the notebook. Then I knew. The moss pollen and the chestnut bits, they were the exact same color! And they had the same shape! And so I felt as if I had gained a vague but remarkable piece of knowledge—the poetic realm I was searching for, wasn't it this small world of powder? Moss flowers and the insides of chestnuts, now, scattered atop the notebook. Beside this are the tips of tweezers, the thin roots of moss, and the shadow of the perfume bottle under the electric light turned into a single beam of yellow light, stretching toward the cotton swab.[48]

The excitement of Machiko's narration here, with its uncharacteristic use of exclamation marks, is a moment of exuberance and possibility borne of the seventh sense. It is the pure possibility of becoming botanical within the small world of moss and powder, a world of smallness Kimmerer extols as she writes of mosses "[taking] possession of spaces from which other plants are excluded by their size. Their ways of being are a celebration of smallness. . . . In being small, limitation is their strength."[49] Machiko, who has been ignored and consistently made to feel small by her male relatives, seems to arrive at a momentary recognition of smallness as a form of strength in this way. The small world of moss and powder opens up to Machiko, and for a moment, she becomes anew. Unfortunately, the moment ends quickly. Her brother, who remains oblivious to the insight Machiko has gained, sweeps the possibility of becoming botanical away in an instant, as he "gathered the moss up in a hurry and brushed away the chestnut bits from the notebook."[50] It is only for a moment that Machiko finds a sense of escape in the mistiness of the moss forest before she is once again held back by one of her relatives. The transcendent world of evolutionary kin gives way to the confining world of patriarchal relationships.

Perhaps this was inevitable, for the near-utopian vision of evolutionary thought that Machiko finds in the seventh sense runs counter to the prevailing political adherence to social Darwinism in the early Shōwa era. Historians like Tessa Morris-Suzuki have demonstrated how evolutionary thought reinforced ideologies of racial purity and supremacy in Japan to justify imperial expansion, and how less overtly racist theories of cultural evolution likewise spurred on the creation of the Greater East Asia Co-Prosperity Sphere.[51] Osaki's idiosyncratic take on evolution was an attempt to rethink evolution as multidirectional. It thus denied the notion that evolution unfolded in an ever-progressing path. While not an outright condemnation of Japanese imperialism, there is nevertheless a form of botanical resistance to be found in the novella's turn back in evolutionary time. This is especially true when we consider the gendered dynamics under which Osaki's female characters attempt species-reversal. They become moss-like in defiance of a patriarchal scientific system that looks to pathologize them. There is thus much to celebrate in Machiko's momentary epiphany about the utopian possibilities held in an involutionary move to a moss-like subjectivity. The moss in question, however, is the subject of scientific experimentation, and it is precisely Nisuke's scientific work that places *Wandering in the Realm of the Seventh Sense* within Japan's colonial nexus. Moving moss even further into the foreground allows us to see how the small, seemingly sheltered home shared by Machiko and her brothers belonged to a world at war and how even the moss that brought Machiko into a moment of transcendence was fertilized by the spoils of colonial extraction.

Fertilizer in the Time of Colonial Modernity

By and large, critics have read *Wandering the Realm of the Seventh Sense*, and the place of science within it, in the context of *ero-guro-nansensu* (erotic-grotesque-nonsensical), a cultural aesthetic term used both contemporaneously in the early 1930s and retrospectively to characterize Japanese modernism as a decedent movement more concerned with sensual pleasure than with the increasingly unstable politics of the early Shōwa era.[52] This line of interpretation discounts Osaki's engagement with science and botanical life as either parody or nonsense. One can partly trace this tendency to read Osaki's work as humorous back to the republication of the novella in the 1969 volume *Dark Humor*. Seen as an example of "dark humor," the seemingly anthropomorphic quality of Osaki's moss—particularly the fact that Nisuke's moss falls in love—was understood as "grotesque."[53] Within the *ero-guro-nansensu* paradigm, *guro*, or *grotesque*, could refer to acts of sexual perversion.[54] On the surface, Osaki's sexually active mosses fit this designation.

However, as I have been suggesting throughout this chapter, the violence of Japan's colonial project serves as an important, yet often neglected, background for *Wandering in the Realm of the Seventh Sense*. Taking Osaki's moss seriously, instead of explaining it away as an example of *ero-guro-nansensu*, allows us to open a new window onto the historical moment from which the story emerged and helps us identify the ambient anxiety that hovers throughout the narrative. The novella's portrayal of plant research, as unscientific as it may appear, is tied directly to Japan's colonial project and, in turn, to Osaki's family history. Osaki had several family members living in Japanese-occupied territories, including Taiwan (her great-uncle) and Manchuria (her sister, Aya). Her third-oldest brother, Shirō, was an agricultural researcher at Tokyo Imperial University. He was deployed to colonial Korea and participated in the creation of governmental policies surrounding fertilizer use on the Korean peninsula. Osaki visited him numerous times in what was then the colonial capital of Keijō (modern-day Seoul).[55] In December of 1930, six months after Osaki watched *Evolution* and only three months before the publication of *Wandering in the Realm of the Seventh Sense*, Shirō published an article titled "Supply and Demand of Fertilizer and Its Management" (*Hiryō no jukyū to kono torishimari*) in *Chosen*, a magazine published by the colonial governor-general of Korea.[56] It seems clear that Shirō's research served as the model for Nisuke's research on moss. The novella takes on a new, dark aura once we read it with this in mind.

The uprooting experienced in Japan's colonies was of a different magnitude than the one experienced by those occupying the metropole. Agricultural reforms on the Korean peninsula initiated by the Japanese colonial government displaced farmers and denied them access to the fertilizers that were necessary for their livelihoods.[57] Such restrictions often resulted in violence. In the same year Shirō wrote of fertilizer management, local farmers battled with police in Gangwon Province over access to fertilizer and other necessities. Four people were killed and twenty-six were injured.[58] Fertilizer played a significant role in Japan's colonial project, as Fujihara Tatsushi recounts in his 2017 book *War and Agriculture* (*Sensō to nōgyō*). The development of chemical fertilizer was intimately tied to war, as the ammonia produced for fertilizer was likewise used in the production of gunpowder. Fujihara writes of how Chisso and Shōwa Denkō—two companies that developed chemical fertilizers—manufactured gunpowder in large quantities and how, for such purposes, Chisso (best known today for its polluting of the Minamata Bay and the subsequent methylmercury poisoning that afflicted residents in the postwar era) established a factory in what is now the North Korean city of Hungnam. The two companies constructed a hydroelectric plant that eroded mountains and lowered water levels in colonial Korea to produce large amounts of gunpowder and fertilizer.[59]

Around the same time that Osaki was writing *Wandering in the Realm of the Seventh Sense*, proletarian writers in Japanese-occupied Korea were creating literary responses to the establishment of the Chisso factory in Hungnam. These stories viscerally demonstrate the exploitation of local workers and the overall crisis of colonial extraction.[60] It is this crisis, diffuse as it may be for Machiko and her brothers, that wafts through the air of the house they share in Tokyo. For *Wandering in the Realm of the Seventh Sense* mentions the smell of ammonia as Nisuke boils his fertilizer. It speaks of a "yellow liquid" that Nisuke uses to fertilize his plants, making it clear that his research concerns chemical fertilizer in addition to the organic fertilizer he boils in ceramic pots. This subtle, amorphous atmosphere of crisis drifts through the narrative, and its violent undercurrent occasionally bubbles up to the surface in odd, gendered ways. At one point, Sangorō throws Machiko out a window. Later on, he cuts her hair against her will. As Sangorō ignores Machiko's tears and cuts her hair into a short bob, Machiko relates the violation she feels to that of being stripped naked: "My neck was suddenly cold, the unmistakable feeling of having my naked body fully exposed."[61] While obviously not commensurate with the real-world violence experienced in Japan's colonies, such moments in Osaki's fiction take on an uncanny hue of colonial domination and forced assimilation when read against her own familial connection to colonial Korea and subsequent awareness of botanical science's place in Japan's imperialism.

In her book on Osaki, Kawasaki Kenko tries to recuperate Shirō's work, writing that "What Shirō paid attention to as a colonial bureaucrat was a system of agricultural management that had become intensified to a high degree in terms of economics and rationality. This was not simply a matter of exploiting the colony for the sake of the home country."[62] Kawasaki argues that Shirō's approach was to teach farmers how to be self-sufficient in terms of fertilization and that he advocated for the formation of agricultural collectives. Yet at the same time, she recognizes that the national policies he helped create led to the downfall of organic fertilizers and the establishment of chemical fertilizer factories like the one in Hungnam.[63] It is difficult to separate Shirō, and thus the fictionalized version of him in *Wandering in the Realm of the Seventh Sense*, from the crisis experienced in colonial Korea. Osaki may not mention outright the implications of Nisuke's botanical research, but in her less-than-favorable portrayal of the character, she herself hardly seems interested in recuperating him. What she does seem interested in recuperating is plant life itself and the utopian potential it held despite its place in Japan's colonial network.

Love and Moss

Taking Osaki's moss seriously in *Wandering in the Realm of the Seventh Sense* not only exposes its entanglements within Japanese colonialism; it also allows us to see the extent to which Nisuke's research engages directly with scientific theories of evolution that circulated throughout Japan in the early twentieth century. Oka Asajirō, author of a best-selling treatise on evolution published in 1904 titled *Discourse on Evolution* (*Shinkaron kōwa*), included in his 1916 *Discourse on Biology* (*Seibutsugaku kōwa*) a chapter titled, simply, "Love" ("*Ren'ai*").[64] For Oka, talk of love was not anthropomorphic when applied to plant life. Rather, it was an operative concept within the scientific study of biology. He begins the chapter by claiming that "(there) are various methods for sperm and egg to meet, and for this reason breeding animals are equipped with a variety of organs.... However, the mere arrangement of equipment has no effect in and of itself. There must also be an extremely strong instinct that derives no satisfaction if this equipment is not put to use. In this is the root of what is called love in our world."[65] Oka uses the word *love* to name an instinctual drive that leads both animals and plants to reproduce: "As all animals and plants carry out sexual reproduction, there is necessarily a strong love between each egg and sperm cell."[66] In relegating the concept of love to an instinctual drive at the cellular level, Oka minimizes the differences among human, plant, and more-than-human animal, just as Osaki does in her writing. For both Osaki and Oka, love leveled the hierarchical playing field of evolution in yet another strike against the logic of social Darwinism. *Wandering in the Realm of the Seventh Sense* ends with Machiko falling in love with one of Ichisuke's colleagues. The suggestion is that Nisuke's experiments with making moss fall in love ultimately affect Machiko as well. Far from a story of anthropomorphism, one could say that Machiko's falling in love is, in fact, phytomorphic.

Oka Asajirō, like Osaki, was particularly fascinated by moss, and he, too, saw revolutionary potential in its multiplicity. As Gregory Sullivan recounts, Oka wrote an article in 1907 about *kokemushi*—aquatic invertebrates commonly referred to as "moss-animals" (the Japanese name literally translates to "moss-insects"). For Oka, moss-animals were an ideal life-form, a collective body constituted by a multiplicity of individuals. He advocated that it was in the best interest of the Japanese nation near the turn of the twentieth century to "recast human nature and eliminate our selfishness in order to become like moss-animals."[67] He even went as far as suggesting that if put on public display, statues of moss-animals would be more effective at teaching public morality than statues of religious or political figures.[68] Serious science, it seems, can be just as steeped in a bizarre logic as the *ero-guro-nansensu* aesthetics of literary modernism.

Although Osaki makes no explicit mention of Oka's work in her writing, his influential theories informed the scientific milieu in which she wrote. In its positing of love between mosses, *Wandering in the Realm of the Seventh Sense* was very much of its time. As the bryologist Arakawa Tomotsugu claims: "We can likely think that in (Osaki's time), the concept of 'love between mosses' was less out of place than it is in contemporary times and had permeated the society of the time."[69] The scientific language of plant love inspired Osaki to imagine what it could mean for humans and plants to share emotions. In this scientific speculation about the in-between of human and plant, she likewise found another form of becoming, one in the in-between of science and poetry.

Rethinking Science as Poetry

Throughout her oeuvre, Osaki envisions a common ground for science and literature that could facilitate the new becoming she sought in alliance with the botanical realm. In two stories from the Machiko Cycle, "Walking" (*Hokō*, 1931) and "A Night in Anton's Basement" (*Chikashitsu anton no hitoya*, 1932), a drama plays out between the poet Tsuchida Kyūsaku (who falls in love with Machiko) and his zoologist relative, Matsuki. Matsuki is disturbed by the scientific inaccuracies written into Kyūsaku's poems, such as Kyūsaku's claim that "crows are white." Matsuki knows objectively that crows are black. (To be sure, Matsuki would take issue with Bateson's claim that "men are grass," as discussed in this book's introduction.) Machiko comes to meet both men in "Walking" when her grandmother asks her to deliver food to Matsuki's house. Matsuki in turn asks her to deliver a jar of tadpoles to Kyūsaku's house. (It seems Machiko is ordered around even outside of Tokyo.) Matsuki raised the tadpoles in his laboratory with "the idea that when Kyūsaku goes to write a poem about tadpoles and sees the real thing, he will be unable to write poetry."[70] His prediction turns out to be accurate, and the story ends with Kyūsaku's frustration at the scientific interference with his poetic practice (a frustration shared with Machiko in *Wandering in the Realm of the Seventh Sense* when Nisuke brushes away the powder and gathers up his moss just as she is starting to becoming botanical).

While Matsuki thus appears to be an anti-art positivist, Kyūsaku learns to see the poetry hiding within Matsuki's scientific writings. "A Night in Anton's Basement" includes a list of fantastical-sounding scientific books authored by Matsuki: *The Condition of Appetite in Goats During the Period in which Paulownia Blossoms are in Full Bloom*; *The Vitality of the Chameleon*; *the Relationship Between Monkeys and Dreams*; *Mammoth, Human, Amoeba*; *An Analysis of Film-Emitting Animality*; *On Whether a Jar of Tadpoles on a Night in which Fragrant Olive Bloomed Out of Season Caused One's Heart to Change*.[71] This odd list of titles contains many recurring motifs in Osaki's work, including paulownia blossoms and fragrant olive trees. Kyūsaku takes the above-mentioned *On Whether a Jar of Tadpoles on a Night in which Fragrant Olive Bloomed Out of Season Caused One's Heart to Change* and reconfigures it, formally, as a poem:

> Out of Season
> A Night in which Fragrant Olive Bloomed
> A jar of tadpoles
> Did it cause one's heart to change?[72]

Kyūsaku remarks: "When I read this work's title, I mistook the Zoologist Matsuki for a lyric poet."[73] Machiko makes a similar remark in *Wandering in the Realm* of the Seventh Sense after secretly borrowing Nisuke's notes on his scientific research. She comments on the notes' poetic qualities: "I had read the notes for two of Nisuke's essays. One about his research on radishes called *On the Utilization of the Soil at the foot of Wasteland Mountain*, which fascinated me because it read as if it were Nisuke's lyric poetry, and *Changes in the Love Between Plants Based on the Temperature of Fertilizer* (his research on moss), which had secretly become my favorite thing to read."[74] Osaki includes sections of Nisuke's writing in *Wandering in the Realm of the Seventh Sense*, and it is written in the characteristic mix of Chinese characters and phonetic katakana syllabary that marks it as a scientific text of its time. In other words, Nisuke's scientific writing does not look anything like poetry. Machiko does not, like Kyūsaku, need to reformat the text to read it as poetry, however. For Machiko, there is a poetic affect to scientific writing that exceeds formal considerations.

Osaki was correct in believing that there was poetry to be found in the science of evolutionary thought, as, historically speaking, the two are bound together through the figure of Erasmus Darwin (1731–1802). Erasmus, grandfather to Charles, was a poet in addition to a physician and scientist.[75] In 1791, he published a collection of poetry titled *The Botanic Garden*. Consisting of two extended poems, the work is a combination of science and poetry, and it outlines the Linnaean system of taxonomy in rhyming couplets. One of the poems is titled *The Loves of the Plants*. It is a title that would have appealed to both Nisuke and Oka Asajirō. Its second stanza reads:

> From giant Oaks, that wave their branches dark,
> To the dwarf Moss, that clings upon their bark,
> What Beaux and Beauties crowd the gaudy groves,
> And woo and win their vegetable Loves.[76]

From the outset of evolutionary thought, it seems, mosses fell in love within a realm somewhere in between science and poetry.

Yet in *Wandering in the Realm of the Seventh Sense*, Machiko is ultimately unable to render the insights she gains about becoming botanical into poetic language of her own. After she reaches a new subjective state by closely observing the similarities between moss pollen and chestnut powder, she tries to write poetry of the seventh sense. She fails and instead composes a "love poem full of sadness." The poem laments not only her loss of a new botanical self but also the trauma of her hair being cut and her complicated relationship with her cousin Sangorō. Presented as a single line, the poem reads: "Although my grandmother sent me a scarlet kadsura flower, I can no longer put it in my hair. The kiss I received on my neck while my hair was being curled was, ah, lonely like the autumn wind."[77] Machiko's poem—the only one Osaki includes in *Wandering in the Realm of the*

Seventh Sense—laments the loss of her subjective agency at the hands of her male family members. Invoking the image of the kadsura flower, Machiko's words register the loss of a potential botanical becoming. Her modern haircut—the result of bodily violation—can no longer support the flower.

Just as Ichisuke's patient is rendered silent by her involution back to a moss-like psychology (a condition that causes Ichisuke much concern), so, too, does language fail Machiko as she tries to recount the new mode of subjectivity she glimpses among the moss. Yet like Ichisuke's patient, who finds agency in the silence of a moss-like disposition, Machiko's failure of language is actually no failure at all. Luce Irigaray finds in silence an ethical means to approach alterity, particularly that of plant life. She writes, in a work coauthored with Michael Marder: "Silence is crucial for a being-with, without domination or subjection. It is the first dwelling for coexisting in difference."[78] The moss-like psychology of *Wandering in the Realm of the Seventh Sense* is a being-with in this way. Better yet, it is a form of becoming-with that finds humans and plants occupying the same subject position. Machiko may express frustration at her inability to create poetry of the seventh sense, but for Osaki, silence itself was an ideal.[79] Machiko is ultimately more moss-like in her silence. Silence is a key part of the evolutionary process of species-reversal that brings Machiko to the botanical realm, where she can coexist with plant-kin in a nonobjectifying familial relationship. In silence, she becomes a member of a botanical family.

Botanical Rebirth

Osaki Midori yearned for change. She recognized the plasticity of subjectivity and strove for transformation in the face of an everyday eaten away by a slowly unfolding catastrophe. In the in-between of literature and science, she attempted to forge something new and to transcend the limits of both modern subjectivity and genre. As such, critics have treated *Wandering in the Realm of the Seventh Sense* as exceptional and out of step with its time.[80] Yet Osaki was very much of her time. In the early Shōwa period, she responded to the times by crafting a vernacular theory of evolution as a means of self-transformation. The act of writing occasioned a kind of rebirth for Osaki. In becoming botanical, her work has indeed transcended the Shōwa period. It would be rediscovered in the 1960s and go on to influence the next generation of writers as well as film and media scholars.

Osaki ultimately outlived the turbulence of the early Shōwa era. As previously mentioned, she retired from writing in 1935 and lived out the rest of her life in solitude. In a short 1973 essay on Osaki, the literary critic Hanada Kiyoteru characterizes her post-Tokyo life in a somber tone: "It is said the female author, who suffers from a nervous disorder, was, at her family's urging, forced to return to her native Tottori. After moving from hospital to hospital, last year she shut herself away in a room in her sister's home, spending her afternoons working diligently on small projects at home, and her nights absorbed in the novels of Shishi Bunroku and Kita Morio. This is not a romantic end to the life of a genius."[81]

Hanada writes from a place of deep respect for Osaki. One can feel his sadness as he imagines Osaki locked away, possibly against her will, with nothing but a few novels to read. However, it is possible to reframe Osaki's retirement from writing and her quiet final years as their own form of becoming botanical. To what extent is Hanada playing out the role of Ichisuke, pathologizing Osaki's silence as a fracture, as a deviation from what should befall a genius? The last lines of Osaki's 1929 short story "Osmanthus" (*Mokusei*) reads: "I am destitute moss that has begun to wither."[82] Did Osaki, in this short, sad sentence, predict her own eventual retreat from the world? Or did she become botanical in this moment, blazing a path toward something wholly new?

If we pay closer attention to the botanical realm, we can see even in this most dire of sentences the potential for something unprecedented in alliance with plant life. The bryologist Arakawa Tomotsugu writes of this line: "Usually, dried up moss has the image of something transient and broken. When moss dries out, it becomes frizzled. However, if given water, within moments it will suck it up and come back to life."[83] Robin Wall Kimmerer likewise claims that "most mosses are immune to death by drying. For them, desiccation is simply a temporary interruption in life."[84] This, too, is their *shokubutsusei*. Put simply, moss can help us rethink death as a "temporary interruption." Osaki passed away in 1971. Nearly thirty years later, the filmmaker Hamano Sachi would interweave Osaki's life story with the fictional narrative of Machiko in her film *Wandering in the Realm of the Seventh Sense: In Search of Osaki Midori* (*Dainana kankai hōkō—Osaki Midori o sagashite*). This cinematic portrait of Osaki unfolds like a botanical rebirth. While the narrative of *Wandering in the Realm of the Seventh Sense* progresses linearly in the film, the biographical portions move backward in time, presenting Osaki's death first and ending with a young Osaki surrounded by friends, overlooking the ocean from Tottori's vast sand dunes. As the onscreen Machiko lingers over the small world of moss on Ichisuke's desk, yearning to become botanical, the filmic "Osaki" springs back to life like a withered moss given water. As the screen goes dark and the film fades into silence as Osaki looks out over the water, one can imagine the reverse flow of time continuing on, until Osaki becomes a chameleon; becomes moss; becomes a slice of glacier; becomes smoke; becomes a star; becomes gas . . . and on and on.

2

BOTANICAL ALLEGORY

Metamorphosis and Colonial Memory in Abe Kōbō's "Dendrocacalia"

On April 6, 1949, the poet, novelist, and future playwright Abe Kōbō wrote a letter to fellow writer Haniya Yutaka. At the time, the two were members of a literary circle known as the Night Group (*Yoru no Kai*), which was founded the previous year by literary critic Hanada Kiyoteru (the same critic who lamented Osaki Midori's postretirement fate) and visual artist Okamoto Tarō, with the goal of developing an alternative art form to socialist realism by combining Marxist ideals with surrealist experimentation.[1] In this letter, Abe explains that his wife and frequent collaborator, the visual artist Abe Machiko, has recently fallen ill, and this has prevented more frequent correspondence. At the end of the short letter, Abe mentions a short story he was working on at the time: "I am currently writing a strange story called 'Dendrocacalia,' in which a human becomes a plant."[2]

Abe would publish "Dendrocacalia" (*Dendorokakariya*) four months later in the literary magazine *Expressions* (*Hyōgen*), and then revise and republish the "strange story" three years later, in 1952. "Dendrocacalia" is a story of plant metamorphosis, in which a man named "Common" becomes a dendrocacalia, a tree endemic to the remote Bonin or Ogasawara Islands, which lay about one thousand kilometers south of Tokyo. In the story, Abe uses plant metamorphosis as an allegorical model to explore colonial memory in the Japanese postwar era. With this allegorical configuration, the botanical becoming in "Dendrocacalia" differs from the one explored in the preceding chapter of this book, where moss provided a model for utopian desires to move beyond the contemporary moment. In the works of Osaki Midori, engagements with the botanical world opened up subjectivity beyond the confines of the human body and beyond human temporality, leading into the long durée of plant life and evolutionary deep time. This is not what happens in Abe's "Dendrocacalia."

To be sure, Abe Kōbō was immersed in an intellectual milieu in which plant life offered utopian visions of overcoming the postwar crisis. Anarcho-Marxist thinkers like Hanada Kiyoteru and Haniya Yutaka envisioned a new form of revolutionary subjectivity informed by their engagements with the botanical realm. In Haniya's epic novel *Dead Spirits*, which I discuss at length in the next chapter, the figuration of the forest plays a vital role in the construction of a subject position that bridges the rupture of Japan's defeat in war, while also bridging the rupture between life and death. Hanada likewise believed in the potential of plant life to help usher in political, artistic, and social change. In his 1949 essay titled *Animal—Plant—Mineral* (*Dōbutsu—shokubutsu—kōbutsu*), he posits a connection between a literary concern for the more-than-human (including plants) and the coming of revolution: "The popularity of erotic art predicts again and again the approach of revolution, just like the flight of the petrel that announces the coming of a storm. But that is not necessarily because decedent signs of the times appear within those works. It is because in the eyes of revolutionary writers, the human spirit and the body are carefully distinguished. The human body is perceived as animal, as vegetal, as mineral, and written about in an emotionless, ruthless manner without the slightest bit of sentimentality."[3]

For Hanada, rethinking the human body as more-than-human (as animal, vegetal, or mineral) was a sign of approaching revolution. It was plants in particular, however, that interested him in his 1973 essay *Do You Like Brahms?* (*Burāmusu wa osuki?*). Here, Hanada argues that a new attitude toward plant life can be found in Abe's "Dendrocacalia." In fact, Hanada draws a line between Abe's depiction of plant life and Osaki's treatment of moss in *Wandering in the Realm of the Seventh Sense*. For Hanada, these two works featured "plants of the twentieth century."[4] Considering the relationship between Abe's plants in "Dendrocacalia" and the dark history of the twentieth century leading up to the postwar moment (in which the story was written), Hanada's comment speaks not only to the revolutionary potential of twentieth-century plants but also to the violence witnessed by the same twentieth-century plants. The new attitude Hanada glimpsed in Abe's plants was thus both utopian and dystopian at the same time.

Abe links the dendrocacalia plant to colonial violence, and the botanical becoming he writes into the story that shares the plant's name turns dark. Gone are the new familial bonds forged through evolutionary thought in the works of Osaki. For Abe, the ontological ambiguity between human and plant ultimately leads to dehumanization, a negative post-humanism occasioned by the botanical world. "Dendrocacalia" suggests that there is, in fact, no means (botanical or otherwise) to transcend one's contemporary moment, despite what his fellow Night Group members may have believed. Through the enduring allegorical trope of plant metamorphosis, Abe turned to plants not to move beyond the lingering violence of the postwar but rather to bring such violence to light. The story positions becoming botanical as a means, to paraphrase Donna Haraway, of staying with the trouble of the Japanese postwar.[5]

Japanese rhetoric surrounding the relationship between colonial expansion and wartime violence has been (and largely continues to be) shrouded in disavowal.[6] "Dendrocacalia" exposes the living memories of Japanese colonialism that Abe feared were increasingly hidden in the postwar moment by turning to contemporaneous botanical science, which itself was in the process of exposing a previously hidden notion of life in plants. In the story, the work of Russian botanist Kliment Timiryazev plays a fundamental role in Abe's allegorical configuration of the disavowal of colonial memory. Timiryazev's *The Life of the Plant* (first published in Japan in 1934 and referenced directly in "Dendrocacalia") helped usher in a new understanding of plants that granted them a hidden world of inner experience (in other words, a *life*) that had previously been denied.[7] Abe uses this newly exposed understanding of plant life to likewise expose the dark history of Japan's colonization of the Bonin Islands.

Endemic Species, Endemic Histories

"Dendrocacalia" is the tale of an endemic species uprooted from the *gaichi* (a term meaning "exterior land" that was used to refer to colonized space) and pursued in the *naichi* (a term meaning "interior land" that was used to signify the Japanese mainland). The *gaichi* in question in the story is the Ogasawara archipelago, which is often referred to as the Bonin Islands in English. The full scientific name of the plant at the center of the story is *Dendrocacalia crepidifolia* (Nakai) Nakai (see figure 2.1). The name Nakai refers to the influential botanist Nakai Takenoshin, whom I discuss in more detail below. The use of a proper name at the end of a Latin species name indicates that the named individual (in this case, Nakai) was the first to publish a description of said species. Abe only uses the plant's Latin name in "Dendrocacalia" (and not the Japanese name, which is *wadannoki*). Abe held a degree in medicine from Tokyo Imperial University, and while he never practiced medicine, a familiarity with scientific terminology can be found throughout his oeuvre. "Dendrocacalia" is unique, however, for its use of botanical terminology.

Despite its speculative subject matter, "Dendrocacalia" (much like Osaki's *Wandering in the Realm of the Seventh Sense*) is quite clear at the level of the sen-

FIGURE 2.1. Dendrocacalia nameplate at the Koishikawa Botanical Gardens. Photo by author.

tence. Mutsuko Motoyama has argued that the style of "Dendrocacalia" is drastically more straightforward than any of Abe's previous work, claiming: "Words are no longer symbolic and do not suggest ideas other than their usual meanings."[8] This clarity of language speaks to both Abe's interest at the time in spreading literature to the masses (as evidenced by his involvement with Night Group and his work organizing among factory workers) and the influence of scientific literature on the narrative.[9] The short story's style performs the perceived objectivity of language inherent in scientific naming, while simultaneously narrating the violent consequences of such naming. At the same time, the use of the Latin name *dendrocacalia* speaks to the milieu in which the plant was taken up as a scientific object of study in Japan. In 1936, the Botanical Society of Japan published a series of articles that categorized the flora of the Bonin Islands. The articles were published entirely in Latin, save for a few passages in English. The dendrocacalia is featured in the fifth installment of this series.[10] If we take seriously Hiromi Ito's claim that "words and plants are the same thing" (as discussed in this book's introduction), then Abe's clarity of language and straightforward style become a formal choice related to his use of the scientific name *dendrocacalia*. The history of imperial botany and its use of latinized nomenclature is legible not only at the level of the sentence but also at the level of the word itself.

The dendrocacalia is a member of the Asteraceae family of flowering plants, which includes asters, daisies, sunflowers, and chrysanthemums. Within this large family, the dendrocacalia is unique. Endemic to the island of Hahajima, it grows only around Chibusayama, the mountain that stands as the highest point of the island and in the protected nature preserve called Sekimon. The unique ecosystems of the Bonin Islands have earned them the status of UNESCO World Heritage Site, and scholarly interest continues to grow as endemic species on the islands face increasing threats from nonnative species and climate change.[11] Just as the many endemic species of the Galapagos Islands helped Charles Darwin develop his theory of evolution, so, too, have the endemic flora of the Bonin Islands contributed to continuing scientific research. The islands have even earned the nickname "The Galapagos of East Asia."

Endemic species like the dendrocacalia are something of a puzzle. According to Itō Motomi, a researcher of plant evolution and biodiversity at Tokyo University, the origins of the dendrocacalia are mysterious: "From what kind of ancestors did (the dendrocacalia) evolve? In truth, we still cannot answer this question. We do not find a plant that closely resembles the dendrocacalia within the Asteraceae family."[12] For the Bonin Islands, the issue of unclear ancestry extends beyond the botanical realm and participates in the tension between internal and external (*naichi* and *gaichi*) that Abe stages throughout "Dendrocacalia." By the time Japan officially claimed the islands as colonial property in 1876, the Bonin Islands had already been a contested site for decades. Both Britain and Japan believed the islands to be rightfully theirs, and Commodore Matthew Perry famously made a visit to the islands a month before landing on the Japanese mainland.[13]

This contested history led to a diverse population of human inhabitants on the islands. Records of the first Bonin Islanders to enter the Japanese family registration system (*jinshin koseki*), which was established by the Meiji government in the 1870s, demonstrate this reality. Of the initial five islanders that registered, one was British, one was Spanish, and the remaining three were Pacific Islanders.[14] By 1882, the entire population of the islands was entered into the family registry, making the Bonin Islanders legal subjects of Japan.[15] Despite the status of the Bonin Islands as colonial *gaichi*, residents of the islands joined the same registry as *naichi* mainlanders. As the historian David Chapman explains, the islands were unique among Japan's colonies in this regard, as colonial territories such as Korea and Taiwan had their own "special colonial registers (*gaichi koseki*) that were administered by colonial offices and abolished after the end of the war."[16]

Thus, according to their family registries, the inhabitants of the Bonin Islands belonged not to the colonial space of the *gaichi* but rather to the *naichi* metropole, even if they had been born in Britain or Spain.

The ambiguity over the status of Bonin Islanders took on a potentially violent nature in 1944, as the Japanese government ordered the forced evacuation of the islands. As close to seven thousand residents "returned" to the *naichi* mainland that had not been their home, they faced a situation similar to the one Abe allegorically narrates in "Dendrocacalia." The Bonin Islanders were often greeted with suspicion and threats of violence in the *naichi*. As Chapman recounts, "with some members of this group having blond hair and blue or green eyes, the Bonin Islanders were often questioned about their origin and most times their interrogators were unaware of the existence of the Ogasawara Islands much less the small community of descendants of original foreign settlers."[17] When islanders were allowed back to their former home in 1946, they found it in ruins. US bombing raids had leveled much of the island of Chichijima, decimating buildings as well as plant life.[18] Eventually, the islands were returned to Japanese sovereignty in 1968 and remain official Japanese territory to this day.

Of the Interior and the Exterior

As discussed in the previous chapter, Japan's colonial project was deeply tied to the botanical realm through the extraction of natural resources and through scientific research that depended on imperial support and technologies. There is also a figurative connection between the rhetoric of colonialism and the world of plants that bears on Abe's allegory. As Christy Wampole has demonstrated, postcolonial identity politics often invoke botanical metaphors such as "uprooting, transplanting, and vegetal invasion."[19] (These are the very concepts in which Hiromi Ito's work revels and finds resistance, as I discuss in chapter 5.) A botanical metaphor is also present at the level of the Japanese language, as the Japanese word for colonization, *shokumin*, literally means "people planting," a translation of the Dutch *volkplanting*. "Dendrocacalia" makes clear this link between Japan's colonial history and plant life, as its protagonist becomes a dendrocacalia.

In the story, a man named Common (transliterated as *Komon* in Japanese) undergoes several transformations into the endemic plant. The name *Common* is unusual. It is possible that Abe's use of the name was a means of creating a character devoid of any real identifiable characteristics. He did this frequently throughout his career by giving characters initials for names, as he does in this story with another character referred to only as "K." However, given the story's concern with scientific naming and Linnaean classification, it seems likely that Abe means to layer the scientific convention of referring to the non-Linnaean name of an organism as its "common name." Understood this way, Common's metamorphosis into a dendrocacalia is more pronounced as he moves from a common name (literally) into the scientific name used as the title of the short story.

As the narrative opens, Common suddenly feels as if he is turning into a plant one day while walking and absentmindedly kicking a stone.[20] He feels the strong pull of gravity, and everything suddenly becomes dark. Within the darkness, however, he sees his own face "as if reflected in a train window."[21] The feeling is momentary and passes without incident. For the first half of the narrative, he is uncertain what is happening and struggles with the discomfort and near horror of bodily disintegration. He learns to turn his face back outward and resist metamorphosis. Common recognizes his becoming botanical as a kind of "illness."[22] Machiko's brother Ichisuke from Osaki's *Wandering in the Realm of the Seventh Sense* would agree with this diagnosis, as he repeatedly pathologized the "mosslike disposition" found in that novella as a form of mental illness.

A year goes by without Common experiencing another plant metamorphosis, until one day he receives a mysterious letter from someone identified only as "K." The letter asks Common to come to a café the following day. Common goes, believing the letter to be from a now-forgotten ex-girlfriend. Common undergoes another partial transformation while waiting for K at the café. During this metamorphosis, Common's senses become heightened, and he loses a clear sense of time. The anxiety of this experience causes him to leave the café, whereupon he finds himself among the city's bombed-out buildings (*yakeato*). Here, Common finally begins to accept his new existence as a plant. At this point, however, the director of a botanical garden (who serves as the story's antagonist) appears and remarks on the rarity of coming across the dendrocacalia plant in the *naichi*, that term meaning "interior land" and thus the metropole of the Japanese mainland, as opposed to the *gaichi*, meaning "exterior land," and thus the overseas territories of Japan's colonies. The classification of the plant as a dendrocacalia (a *gaichi* plant from the colonies) marks a turning point in the narrative and sets up Abe's allegorical play with notions of the interior and the exterior.

Abe uses the interior/exterior dichotomy in multiple registers throughout "Dendrocacalia."[23] Abe cites Kliment Timiryazev's claim from his classic work of botany *The Life of the Plant* (originally published in Russia in 1878) that humans and plants have no qualitative differences, only quantitative ones. This was a radical claim, as it proposed that plants, like humans, have an interior life. Timiryazev was a highly influential botanist in his native Russia. He was a contemporary of Charles Darwin and an adamant supporter of Darwin's theory of evolution.

Timiryazev wrote an account of visiting Darwin in England when Darwin was working with his son Francis on their study of the botanical world titled *The Power of Movement in Plants*. While Darwin's text influenced plant biology in Europe and the United States, it would not be translated into Japanese until 1987. Timiryazev's *The Life of the Plant*, however, was initially translated into Japanese in 1934 and went through three printings in the following thirteen years. Building from Timiryazev's claim that plants have an interior life, Abe works to destabilize the boundaries between the colonial binaries of an interior *naichi* and exterior *gaichi*. As Common becomes a tree uprooted from its native land, firm distinctions between *naichi* and *gaichi* begin to dissolve, just as the distinctions between human and plant dissolve through metamorphosis.

In order to explore the tension between the colonial markers of the internal *naichi* and the external *gaichi*, Abe focuses on the tension between the protagonist's interior subjectivity and the external world. He builds a bridge between the *naichi/gaichi* divide and the subjective interiority/exteriority divide through a close engagement with plant life. As Common turns into a dendrocacalia among the *yakeato* ruins of war, he feels as if "the whole of the exterior world was becoming himself."[24] This is an astute description of botanical subjectivity, akin to Emanuele Coccia's claim that "Plant life is life as complete exposure, in absolute continuity and total communion with the environment."[25] Yet where such botanical subjectivity proved generative for other writers and filmmakers, in "Dendrocacalia," it becomes a site of governance. For through the figure of this flowering plant endemic to colonial space, "Dendrocacalia" suggests that the external *gaichi* is not something that exists outside of postwar subjectivity (as disavowal suggests) but rather that colonial history is alive within the postwar subject. For this reason, the plant itself becomes, for the director of a botanical garden that serves as the narrative's antagonist, an object that must be captured and carefully controlled.

At the end of the story, the director of the botanical garden locks the dendrocacalia (and the colonial memory it embodies) away in a government-protected greenhouse, where its existence becomes static. The final image of "Dendrocacalia" is of the director laughing uncontrollably as he places a name card bearing the scientific name of the plant on the now fully metamorphosed Common. The 1952 version of the story features an illustration by Abe's wife Machiko that captures the horror of this moment—a sense of terror increased by the scientific coldness on display (see figure 2.2). Within Abe's allegorical configuration, the greenhouse is the site of disavowal and narrative control. It puts memories aside, where they can be manipulated and categorized by the state. It is a liminal space within the interior of the Japanese mainland where botanical specimens of the Japanese colonial exterior are forever marked as such.

FIGURE 2.2. Illustration by Abe Machiko of Common's metamorphosis into a dendrocacalia, included in the 1952 version of the story.

Utopian Idealism in Botanical-Anarchist Subjectivity

The introduction of overtly political themes into Abe's work caused critics, including his friend Haniya Yutaka, to position "Dendrocacalia" as a transitional text for Abe.[26] Some have argued that the story marked a change from Abe's existential and formally experimental early work like his debut novel *For the Signpost at the End of the Road* (*Owarishi michi no shirube ni*, 1948) to the more absurdist and Marxist themes found in his 1951 Akutagawa Prize–winning novella *The Wall—The Crime of S. Karma* (*Kabe—S. Karuma shi no hanzai*). The period in which "Dendrocacalia" was written was the most politically active period of Abe's career. In 1950, he would officially join the Japanese Communist Party (JCP) and would remain a member until 1962, when he was expelled for alleged disloyalty.[27]

Although "Dendrocacalia" is positioned as the beginning of Abe's embrace of Marxist thought, the seeds of his eventual discontent with Anarcho-Marxist ideology can be glimpsed in the story's phenomenological engagement with plant life. Given Abe's membership in the Night Group and the JCP around the time of his writing and rewriting "Dendrocacalia," it is likely that Abe was introduced to the plant research of Kliment Timiryazev within a politically charged context. Timiryazev was first introduced into Japan as a Marxist thinker, albeit one who looked to the natural sciences for inspiration. The first of Timiryazev's texts to appear in Japanese translation was published in 1931 in a collection titled *The Present Stage of Marxist Philosophy* (*Marukusushūgi tetsugaku no gendankai*). Included in this volume is a conversation between Timiryazev and Marxist philosopher Abram Moiseevich Deborin that took place in 1929. The two discuss natural science alongside the writings of Marx and Engels. In 1947, an article titled "Revolutionary and Scientist—A Short Biography of Timiryazev" ("*Kakumei to kagakusha—Timiriyazefu shōden*") was published by the JCP in its magazine *Science and Technology* (*Kagaku to gijutsu*). As the title suggests, the article offers a biographical sketch of Timiryazev's life, highlighting his major works and influence on contemporary Soviet scientists. It also recounts Timiryazev's interest in Marxism and his relationship with Vladimir Lenin.

Writers of natural science, including Ilya Mechnikov, Peter Kropotkin, Charles Darwin, and Jean-Henri Fabre, heavily influenced anarchist thought in Japan, offering Japanese anarchist and Marxist thinkers "scientific evidence from the biological world for a modern anarchist temporality and subjectivity."[28] The writing of the influential anarchist thinker Peter Kropotkin describes this subjectivity as plantlike. He envisioned a subjectivity that was more of "an agglomeration, a colony of millions of separate individuals than a personality one and indivisible."[29] For Kropotkin, becoming botanical fostered a multiple subjectivity in which "the individual is quite a world of federations, a whole universe in himself."[30]

Kropotkin helped Japanese Anarcho-Marxists forge links between a revolutionary subjectivity and plant life. Well-known writer and anarchist Arishima Takeo visited Kropotkin in Russia in 1906, where they discussed the ideas of Kropotkin's classic text *Mutual Aid: A Factor of Evolution*.[31] Kropotkin's concept of mutual aid posits that within the paradigm of evolution, the fittest species survive through cooperation rather than competition. Kropotkin directly opposes competition in *Mutual Aid* and argues that it is in fact unnatural to compete: "'Don't compete!—competition is always injurious to the species, and you have plenty of resources to avoid it!' That is the *tendency* of nature, not always realized in full, but always present."[32] For Anarcho-Marxist thinkers in Japan, Kropotkin's theory of mutual aid provided an alternative to the competitive impulses of social Darwinism.[33]

In 1927, a partial translation of *Mutual Aid* was published in Japan.[34] It included the first two chapters of the full text, and its title was reworked as *The Lives of Animals and Plants* (*Dōbutsu to shokubutsu no seikatsu*), a title similar to the Timiryazev text that Abe mentions in "Dendrocacalia." *Mutual Aid* is a utopian text, even if Kropotkin himself took issue with the term. In his *Modern Science and Anarchism* (1901), Kropotkin writes, "It would not be fair to describe (a society of equals) as a *Utopia*, because the word 'Utopia' in our current language conveys the idea of something that *cannot* be realized. . . . (It) cannot be applied to a conception of society which is based, as Anarchism is, on an analysis of *tendencies of an evolution that is already going on in society*."[35] Here we see how Kropotkin, like Osaki, drew from evolutionary thought in order to envision a society free of social Darwinism.

In "Dendrocacalia," however, Abe Kōbō ultimately critiques the utopian idealism of such an anarchist subjectivity informed by the botanical world. He does so by engaging directly with his own speculative phenomenological account of what a botanical-anarchist subjectivity would actually look and feel like, only to collapse the idealism of such subjectivity under the weight of colonial history. Abe's botanical imagination brought him to this speculation, a *shokubutsusei* ripe with criticality. Abe's *shokubutsusei* counters the claims that a utopian transcendence was possible in becoming botanical. This is because Abe follows Timiryazev by "giving plants their history."[36] The history of the dendrocacalia plant in postwar Japan was one of colonial violence.

Abe's own history and oeuvre at large are themselves inseparable from Japan's imperial project. Born in Tokyo in 1924 and raised in colonial Manchuria, Abe relocated to the Japanese mainland in 1946. During his prolific career as a writer, he wrote several stories set in the colonial space of the *gaichi*, including *For the Signpost at the End of the Road*, his 1952 short story "The Starving Skin" ("*Ueta hifu*"), and his 1957 novel *Beasts Head for Home* (*Kemonotachi wa kokyō o mezasu*). "Dendrocacalia," however, is unique in that it grapples with Japan's colonial project within the interior *naichi* of the Japanese mainland. Just as Abe's concern with coloniality makes scattered appearances throughout his career, so, too, does his interest in plant life. While his best-known work, 1962's *Woman of the Dunes* (*Suna no onna*), explores the relationship between the material world and human subjectivity in a sand-filled atmosphere devoid of plant life, several other works take up botanical life in order to question the status of the human subject. His 1957 short story "Lead Egg" ("*Namari no tamago*") portrays an imagined future in which humans have become more plantlike, with green skin and extremely long lifespans. His 1975 play *Green Stockings* (*Midori iro no sutokkingu*) features an experiment in which a human is turned into an herbivore and thus comes to subsist only on vegetation. Abe would even revisit plant metamorphosis late in his career with 1991's *Kangaroo Notebook* (*Kangarū nōto*), in which the protagonist begins to sprout radishes through his skin.

In a 1952 essay written about the advent of avant-garde ikebana (flower arranging), Abe paraphrases Jean-Paul Sartre's comments on Swiss sculptor Alberto

Giacometti (who was a contemporary of Abe's fellow Night Group member Okamoto Tarō): "Plants are free, but the human body is not free. To speak of the relationship between the model and artwork, plants are unpredictable (*gūzen*), and the human body is a foregone conclusion (*hitsuzen*)."[37] Abe found freedom in taking plants as a model to shed light on the disavowal of colonial violence in "Dendrocacalia." The fantastical qualities of plant metamorphosis likely helped the story navigate the US occupation censorship that was still a lingering reality for Japanese writers in 1949. In this regard, becoming botanical was a strategy of subversion.

Greening Week and Phytophenomenology

Throughout "Dendrocacalia," Abe engages in a speculative phenomenological account of becoming botanical that I refer to as phytophenomenology, with the Greek prefix *phyto* referring to plants (as it does in *phytomorphism*). In his experimentation with phytophenomenology, Abe demonstrates an acute understanding of plant life, likely drawn from his familiarity with the work of Timiryazev. Abe takes up the figuration of a utopian botanical-anarchist subjectivity espoused by thinkers like Kropotkin and carries it through to its logical (and literal) end point. "Dendrocacalia" explores what it would feel like to embody the kind of utopian subjectivity that Kropotkin called "a federation of digestive, sensual, nervous organs, all very intimately connected with one another, each feeling the consequence of the well-being or indisposition of each, but each living its own life."[38] Abe does this to critique the idealism bound up in such a figuration.

While the plant metamorphosis in "Dendrocacalia" is strange, to use the word Abe wrote in his letter to Haniya, the experiential account of Common's metamorphosis aligns with scientific theories of plant life all the same. For example, as Common inspects the interior of the café and the exterior world outside the window while resisting becoming botanical and waiting for K to arrive, the narrator remarks how Common's vision has become altered: "It was as if everything looked big, as if under a magnifying glass."[39] Common's heightened vision settles on and intensifies the facial features of nearby patrons at the café. The results are grotesque: "The faces of customers occupying the space around him stood out strangely: moles on the sides of their noses, warts under their ears, half-gold teeth, long nose hair."[40]

Theories of plant vision have circulated in scientific communities since at least 1905 when Austrian botanist Gottlieb Haberlandt proposed that the cells of a plant's epidermal layer act like convex lenses, giving plants a visual capacity. Francis Darwin (son of Charles) became a proponent of this theory and wrote of it extensively. In 1908, British botanist Harold Wager even published photographs produced using the epidermal cells of various plants.[41] Common's sensitivity to light and uncomfortable visual experience seem to capture some of the peculiarities of this proposed "plant vision." The list of heightened grotesque facial features registered by Common's plant vision suggests that a plantlike subjectivity would not be ideal but rather uncomfortable and disorienting.

As Common struggles with his newly altered vision, an unknown man enters the café. The man stares at Common, at which point Common's neck unhinges. His head falls forward, his eyes suddenly meeting his chest. Common realizes he is once again becoming a plant, and as he struggles to regain his composure, he notices a banner hanging on a sign outside promoting "Greening Week" (*ryokka shūkan*). This is a reference to a governmental program officially started in 1934 and resumed in 1947 (after having been suspended for several years between 1944 and 1946), in which Japanese citizens participated in rehabilitating the war-torn natural environment by planting trees (see figure 2.3). Greening Week was directly tied to the imperial house and featured an official ceremony conducted by the crown prince.[42] The slogan for the 1947 campaign was "Repair the ruined land of our country with peaceful green."[43] The type of rhetoric that linked peace and rehabilitation to plant life persisted as Greening Week continued into the postwar era. The stated objective of the 1950 campaign was "To extend Tree-Planting Greening Week to the whole country, in order to rehabilitate a peaceful Japan that is beautifully green and full of culture."[44]

Abe's critique of the idealism found in Greening Week is connected to his critique of the idealism found in Anarcho-Marxist thought. The rhetoric of Greening Week ironically echoes the language Kropotkin used to express his vision of a new anarchist subjectivity informed by the botanical world. Greening Week proposed an imperially approved cooperative notion of subjectivity. It encouraged individuals to think of themselves as part of a larger network composed of

FIGURE 2.3. A 1948 postage stamp promoting greening afforestation efforts. Source: Japan Post / Wikimedia Commons / Public Domain.

humans and more-than-humans alike. Greening Week's rhetoric resonates with Kropotkin's vision of "continued endeavours—as a struggle against adverse circumstances—for such a development of individuals, races, species, and societies, as would result in the greatest possible fullness, variety, and intensity of life."[45] The rehabilitation of the war-torn natural world was one such endeavor.

Upon seeing the banner for Greening Week, with its advocating for a botanical subjectivity, Common's body begins to dissolve. His internal organs "squeeze out to the exterior of his body."[46] The CPS theorist and self-proclaimed "plant neurobiologist" Stefano Mancuso explains how plant life functions through decentralization in this way: "Plants distribute over their entire body the function that animals concentrate in specific organs. Decentralization is the key. . . . [Plants] breathe with their whole body, see with their whole body, feel with their whole body."[47] As Common's organs "squeeze out," his perception likewise becomes decentralized in an unpleasant way. His hands become leaves. He loses a sense of time, and as he regains consciousness, he realizes it is already thirty minutes past the time K was supposed to have arrived.

This strange passage of time in "Dendrocacalia" is perhaps the clearest example of Abe's phytophenomenology. The story attempts to approximate the time of plants through a tactile awareness of spring. In the earlier, 1949 version of the story, spring is mentioned at the start of the direct address that begins the story: "Go ahead and kick a stone while walking down the street. What are you thinking about? Go ahead, say it. Where are you? I can tell you the season. It's spring. That spot where the stone rolled on the edge of the path—a dark, damp clump of soil. Green. Something . . . something is growing, right? Why, it's within you. Isn't there something like a plant growing within you?"[48] The mention of "a dark, damp clump of soil" offers a phytophenomenological account of how plants experience the seasonal time of spring, for, according to Mancuso, plants have an acute sense of touch: "In the plant world, the sense of touch is closely related to the sense of hearing and makes use of small sensory organs called mechanosensitive channels, found in small numbers everywhere on the plant but with greatest frequency on the epidermal cells, the cells that are in direct contact with the external environment."[49] Mancuso goes on to posit that plants in fact possess a unique sense unavailable to humans that helps find moisture and that this watery sense is one of fifteen senses that exist within the botanical realm that are unavailable to humans.[50] Perhaps Machiko's belief in a seventh sense (as discussed in chapter 1) was more scientific than poetic after all.

As Common waits for K at the café and experiences plant vision, he looks out the window and remarks on the lack of moisture. He presents the scene in surreal and near-horrific language: "The busy asphalt street near the station for the national railway line was already dry and white. Even the mixed shadows floated up dry and white. Bicycles lined up and raced by, breaking up the dried-up shadows into small pieces and setting them afloat."[51] As Machiko became botanical in *Wandering in the Realm of the Seventh Sense*, she watched as her brother's apron "became hazy like mist, and transformed into clouds of various shapes." Her utopian plantlike subjectivity found moisture, while Common's dystopian subjectivity cannot help but focus on the absence of moisture.

"Dendrocacalia" imagines what the passage of time for plants would feel like. As Common sits anxiously waiting for K to arrive, he resists the pull of plant metamorphosis, and he feels the flow of time change. As he progressively becomes botanical, human clock time becomes dry and elusive: "Gradually, as it fell in rhythm with the beating of his anxious heart, the ticking of the wall clock hanging overhead appeared to speed up. Time felt like sand falling through the spaces in-between his fingers."[52] Common feels as if time is moving more quickly because plant time is remarkably slower than human time. In tune with the seasons and the natural diurnal cycle of sunrise and sunset, plants experience a much slower form of temporality than humans are accustomed to. It is only through time-lapse cinematography that human perception is able to grasp the slow unfolding that is the movement of plants. Plant movement has been the object of time-lapse cinema from its earliest days. In 1896, German botanist Wilhelm Friedrich Philipp Pfeffer developed a method of time-lapse cinematography that first demonstrated how plants move.[53] In 1910, F. Percy Smith released his influential time-lapse film *The Birth of the Flower*, which makes a series of flowers opening their buds legible within human time. For this legibility to occur, plant time needed to be sped up to match human time. As the popularity of the 2022 BBC documentary series *The Green Planet* shows, there remains to this day a strong interest in speeding up plant time through time-lapse photography.

Common experiences what might be understood as the opposite of time-lapse cinematography. As he becomes botanical, human clock time gives way to plant time. Everything slows down within the embodied time Common experiences. Like a plant, any of Common's small movements (looking out the window, for example) likely take a long duration of human clock time. A moment of plant time (such as the opening up of a flower bud) could take several human hours. For Common, the world within the café rushes by at an entirely different temporality. In the time it takes for him to unfurl the leaves that had been his fingers, around half an hour passes, and he realizes he can no longer meet K, the mysterious stranger who invited him there in the first place.

Once again, Common's experience of botanical subjectivity is not utopian. It is not, in Kropotkin's words, a multiple subjectivity in which subjects are "all very intimately connected with one another, each feeling the consequence of the well-being or indisposition of each."[54] On the contrary, becoming botanical disconnects Common from others around him. His plant vision makes them appear grotesque. His plant time makes him miss the time of his appointment with K. Caught between two temporalities, Common anxiously runs out of the café.

Becoming Oneself, Otherwise

Leaving the café, Common enters the crowds on the street and hears the following announcement somewhere in the distance: "It is currently Greening Week. To all passersby: Let us love trees. Plants provide harmony for our hearts that are in ruins. Plants make our neighborhoods clean and beautiful."[55] Common then comes upon the *yakeato*, those literal ruins of the city leftover from the war, and the very material ruins Greening Week looks to move beyond. Among the remains of war, Common begins another transformation. The loss of distinction between interior and exterior is made explicit during this metamorphosis among the *yakeato* ruins (as briefly discussed above): "He had a sense that this time he was clearly becoming a plant. Or rather, he felt the whole of the exterior world was becoming himself, and a tube-like part that had been himself up until this point but was no longer himself was becoming a plant. Yet he felt no need to resist. Wasn't it just as the advertisement had said? 'Our hearts that are in ruins.'"[56]

Greening Week posits a utopian scenario in which the ravaged internal spirits of a nation are healed by repairing the ruined external world with "peaceful green." Common's sudden embrace of the Greening Week rhetoric temporarily portrays the botanical becoming in "Dendrocacalia" as similarly utopian, as it looks toward plantlike plasticity to forge a new subjectivity. Up until this point in the narrative, Common has resisted the pull of becoming botanical. The story has been highlighting the uncomfortable phenomenological experience of plant subjectivity, resisting the pull of the utopian rhetoric bound up in the botanical-anarchist subjectivity that was espoused by anarchist thinkers and Abe's contemporaries in the Night Group and the JCP. All of a sudden, however, Common lets go of such resistance.

In this moment, Common embraces plant metamorphosis as his subjectivity dissolves into the exterior world. It is here (and only here) that we find the potential for plasticity in "Dendrocacalia." As he feels himself "clearly becoming a plant" among the wreckage of past bomb raids, Common, too, admits to having a "heart in ruins." In the dissolution of a firm boundary between interior and exterior, Common feels the *yakeato* enter within him and glimpses how plant life can grow up through the remains of war: "It was as if the kind of rust that can only be seen in the *yakeato* had bled into him. A light pink color was blotted on the chimneys that remained and stood like pillars among the ruins, resembling a map. Even still, in the spaces between the crumbling, disordered slate and bricks, it seemed as if weeds were growing."[57]

Common understands that plant metamorphosis is his chance, to borrow a phrase from Michael Marder, to become himself, otherwise. Marder writes of plant life: "Plants are together with what they attend to, and their being is a being-together with air, moisture, soil, warmth, and sunlight. In their attention to the elements, they become themselves.... When I linger with plants, I find myself thus in a communion with everything they are and live with. I am together with myself differently as well; I become myself, otherwise."[58]

Through plant metamorphosis, Common becomes, if only for a moment, a different, radically other version of himself. For a moment he becomes a vegetal version that attempts to grow from and yet beyond the literal wreckage of the Japanese postwar. As Common surrenders to his botanical becoming, "Dendrocacalia" momentarily reads as a harbinger of the kind of revolutionary potential Hanada Kiyoteru saw in plants of the twentieth century. While not explicitly anarchist or Marxist in tone, the language Abe uses to describe Common's new subjectivity shares the utopian leanings of anarchist thinkers like Kropotkin. As Common feels "the whole of the exterior world . . . becoming himself," his sense of subjectivity is expanded far beyond regionally and temporally specific notions of national subjectivity.[59] For a brief moment (and only for a moment), Common becomes, as Kropotkin envisioned, "quite a world of federations, a universe in himself." He becomes like Osaki's reed mentioned in the previous chapter, that plant with a spirit "as wide as the cosmos."

The new form of subjectivity opened up in Common's botanical becoming is suddenly legible in the very narrative form of "Dendrocacalia." As Common embraces plant metamorphosis to move beyond a collective "heart in ruins," the otherwise straightforward and objective language of the short story gives way to a different kind of botanical poetics. Offset from the rest of the narrative, "Dendrocacalia" presents a portion of the ninth elegy from Rainer Maria Rilke's *Duino Elegies* (1923), a stanza that questions what it would be like to be a laurel tree. Abe was a great admirer of Rilke. For Abe, Rilke's work offered respite during the turbulence of the war: "The generation of us that had been born and raised in the war knew nothing but wartime philosophy. The word 'anti-war' never even reached our ears. However, for some reason, I could never adapt myself to war philosophy. Within the fear of rejecting the world or being rejected by the world, Rilke's world seemed like a wonderful den of hibernation. I indulged in Rilke's world, especially *The Book of Images* and *The Notebooks of Malte Laurids Brigge* . . . Rilke's world was a suspension of time."[60] Rilke continued to inspire Abe in the postwar era and is featured heavily in Abe's 1948 novel *For the Night with No Name* (*Na mo naki your no tame ni*). In "Dendrocacalia," Rilke's poetry becomes a part of Common's all-too-brief glimpse into a liberatory botanical subjectivity as well as a transformation at the formal level of the text. It is both a "suspension of time" and a suspension of the otherwise objective language of "Dendrocacalia."

As it slips into the realm of poetry, "Dendrocacalia" demonstrates a formal plasticity in the narrative that points toward the subjective plasticity Common experiences in this moment of metamorphosis. The original 1949 version of the story attributes the poem to Rilke, while the revised 1952 version does not. In both cases, however, a vague attribution follows the final line of ellipses: "Such poetry might have occurred to Common."[61] The insertion of this poetic take on becoming botanical (the very thing Machiko sought in *Wandering in the Realm of the Seventh Sense* but could never accomplish) seems to pass through Common. He becomes a medium—a plantlike trait that serves as the focus of the next chapter of this book. For a moment, Common seeks shelter from the violence of the postwar in the space of the botanical realm, as it provides a site of potential to reconfigure subjectivity. Common suddenly feels the comfort of becoming botanical: "I have decided to be reduced to a single plant, right here. Once determined, becoming a plant is a pleasant feeling. Why not become a plant?"[62] Common comes to understand the safe space that the botanical world provides. It is a space that, according to Marder, "provide[s] us with a very peculiar shelter where the traditional distinction between interiority and exteriority no longer applies."[63]

This utopian moment does not last for long, however. A voice rings out in surprise, identifying and interpolating Common for the first time as a dendrocacalia, using the scientific name for the plant. A man that we will come to recognize as the director of a botanical garden approaches the transformed Common and pulls out a "naval knife." The man remarks: "How rare to be able to collect a dendrocacalia in the Japanese *naichi*!"[64] With this act of scientific classification, the director of the botanical garden forecloses the possibility of Common's finding plasticity in the botanical world. The recognition of the dendrocacalia and its position within the Japanese colonial nexus shatters the utopian possibilities bound up in becoming botanical. The use of the plant's scientific name draws attention to the complicity of botanical science in Japan's colonial project. Likewise, the explicit use of the term *naichi* just as Common embraces the loss of distinction between his own interior subjectivity and the exterior world ("he felt the whole of the exterior world was becoming himself, and a tube-like part that had been himself up until this point but was no longer himself was becoming a plant") shatters the utopian idealism of transcendence.

Once this occurs, the peculiar shelter of a botanical subjectivity no longer provides any comfort. Instead, Common is confronted with the reality of violence as distinctions between interior and exterior dissolve. The interior subjective space that opens up in plant metamorphosis forces Common to reckon with the repressed wartime memories harbored within, just as he is forced to reckon with his own face staring back at him. Standing among the bombed-out remains of the city, with a military knife in hand, the botanical garden director prevents Common's attempts at moving beyond the historical realities of postwar Japan.

For the dendrocacalia plant is not, in the rhetoric of Greening Week, a "peaceful green." It is a reminder of Japan's external *gaichi*, a physical reality bearing witness to lands exterior to the Japanese mainland that had now, in the immediate postwar present of the narrative, either regained sovereignty (such as Korea) or found themselves in a state of political limbo at the hands of the US occupation (such as the Ryūkyū Islands or Okinawa and the Bonin Islands as well). The botanical garden director's recognition of the dendrocacalia in the *naichi* mainland marks a turning point. The remainder of the story finds Common trying to evade and ultimately kill the director (with the military knife, no less), while the director likewise attempts to convince Common to come live within the space of the botanical garden. He assures Common he will be safe in the garden, as it receives "government protection."[65] Through the figure of the dendrocacalia, and the artificial environment of the government-protected botanical garden, Abe presents an allegorical diagnosis of Japan's negotiation of wartime memory. Within this tale of plant metamorphosis is a critique of the "greening" or beautification of such memory. Abe's allegorical figuration finds governmental authority safely and securely tending to such living memories, keeping them manicured and carefully categorized. They are out of time, suspended in artificial animation, like plant specimens in a greenhouse.

At the end of the story, the dendrocacalia-that-once-was-Common is carefully arranged in a collection that bears nameplates and national flags. It has been categorized and assigned a place within the logic of the nation-state. Once Common's metamorphosis into the dendrocacalia is complete, there is no potential for further change. There is no further hope for plasticity. The dendrocacalia is preserved within what we might call "specimen time." The greenhouse denies the plant its place in a living history. For in the greenhouse, there is no space for, in the words of Timiryazev, a notion of "organic Nature as a vast whole which is ever changing and transforming itself."[66] There is only stasis, regulated by the infrastructure of botanical science.

The Limit Beyond Which a Subject Becomes an Object

Before Common is locked away in the greenhouse and after his encounter in the bombed-out ruins with the director of the botanical garden, he visits the library to research plant metamorphosis. There, he begins reading about Dante's *Divine Comedy* and Greek mythology, although he recognizes this as an "unscientific" way to begin searching for an explanation for something "actually occurring" in his body. Through his reading of Dante and Greek mythology, Common develops a folkloric/religious explanation for his plant metamorphosis. Within the *Divine Comedy*, the middle circle of the seventh level of Hell is populated by those guilty of the sin of suicide, whereupon they are turned into trees and become food for the mythical half-human/half-bird harpies. Common embraces this unscientific explanation and concludes: "Without knowing it, I guess I must have already committed suicide."[67]

Common decides he must kill the director of the botanical garden who has been pursuing him. When they meet again, Common accuses the director of being a harpy. The director then condemns mythology and offers a scientific explanation in its place: "Isn't Greek mythology a little unscientific, Mr. Dendrocacalia? It does more harm than good. Do you want to hear something more interesting? Have you read Timiryazev's *The Life of the Plant*? This is what it says: there is no qualitative difference between plants and animals. There is only a quantitative difference. In other words, plants and animals are scientifically the same."[68]

The Life of the Plant, originally published in Russia in 1878, participated in a revolutionary new approach to the study of plant life. By its very title, it grants a notion of "life" to the botanical realm. It views plants as subjects living their own lives, rather than mere objects of study. In his review of the Japanese translation of Timiryazev's text in 1934, Nakajima Seinosuke contrasts *The Life of the Plant* to the many popular books on plant science that can be found in "any used book store in Japan for around 30–40 *sen*."[69] Nakajima suggests that Timiryazev's text should serve as the basis for a new approach to the writing of popular science.[70] In his preface to the 1947 edition of *The Life of the Plant*, translator Ishii Tomoyuki echoes this review: "Popular books and general introductions devoted to the study of plants are extremely common both abroad and in Japan. However, I do not know whether another general introduction exists that is as unique and as excellent as Timiryazev's *The Life of the Plant*."[71] What Ishii finds particularly rare in *The Life of the Plant* is Timiryazev's scientific engagement with a mysterious energy within plants that Ishii aligns with vitalism.

The director of the botanical garden's claim that "there is no qualitative difference between plants and animals" can indeed be found in *The Life of the Plant*. Drawing from scientific research, Timiryazev investigates whether plants in fact exhibit characteristics that have previously been ascribed only to animals. These characteristics include movement, nutrition, respiration, stimulation, and finally, consciousness. Although he admits that the question of consciousness comes up against the limits of experimental inquiry and is thus scientifically unknowable, in each other case, he demonstrates that plants do in fact possess the same characteristics and internal processes as animals. Having reached this conclusion, he writes: "It follows that the difference between plants and animals is not qualitative, but only quantitative. The same processes take place in both kingdoms, but some of them predominate in the one and some in the other."[72] For Timiryazev, plants live *lives* in very much the same way as animals.

The Life of the Plant participated in a metamorphosis of scientific epistemology. It granted the botanical world a notion of life and exposed the previously hidden, internal forces of plants, granting them movement and potential consciousness. Having moved beyond the objective realm of the visible, Timiryazev asks: "Where is the limit beyond which an object becomes a subject?"[73] Common's botanical becoming in "Dendrocacalia" posits a similar question. Confronted with the hidden, internally repressed memories of colonial violence, the narrative questions how one becomes a subject of one's own history rather than an object within it. In *The Life of the Plant*, Timiryazev asks: "Has a plant its history?"[74] "Dendrocacalia" answers that it certainly does and that the question of who gets to narrate this history can be a matter of life or death.

The Imperial Lives of Plants

"Dendrocacalia" introduces the concept of plants having lives through the work of Timiryazev, but the notion of "the lives of plants" has its own history in modern Japan that extends beyond Timiryazev and sits directly within Japan's imperial project. Beginning in 1939, publisher Shinchōsha (who would go on to publish Abe Kōbō's collected works decades later) began selling a multivolume educational series titled *New Collection for Japanese Boys and Girls* (*Shin Nihon shōnen shōjo bunko*). The intended audience for this series was, as its title suggests, children. It included such nationalistic titles as *Stories of Patriotism* (*Aikoku monogatari*), *Stories to Purify One's Spirit* (*Kokoro o kiyoku suru hanashi*), and *Defending the Country* (*Kuni no mamori*). As these titles demonstrate, the aim of this series was to mold children into proper imperial subjects.

Yet the series also included less obviously propagandistic volumes on literature (including Chinese and Western literature, in addition to Japanese), as well as volumes on agriculture and natural science. The seventh volume, published in 1940, is titled *The Lives of Animals and Plants* (*Dōbutsu to shokubutsu no seikatsu*)—the same title used for the first translation of Kropotkin's *Mutual Aid* and essentially the same title as Timiryazev's *The Life of the Plant* (which in Japanese is *Shokubutsu no seikatsu*). In using the title of Timiryazev's text within an allegorical tale of Japanese colonialism, Abe (whether knowingly or unknowingly) entangles the utopian notions bound up in Timiryazev's and Kropotkin's texts to the propagandistic wartime text that shares the same name.

The Lives of Animals and Plants is divided into two sections, with the first half discussing more-than-human animals, and the second half taking up the botanical world. This latter half is attributed to Honda Masaji, a prominent prewar botanist who went on to assist the Shōwa emperor in botanical research after the war.[75] Botanical research was a key element to rehabilitating the image of the formerly militaristic emperor in the postwar, just as it was a key component to the colonial project. The same concept (the notion of life in plants) that inspired a transcendent vision of subjectivity among Anarcho-Marxists also helped justify the very wartime violence that thinkers in the Night Group looked to move beyond. The introduction to *The Lives of Animals and Plants* grants "lives" to both more-than-human animals and plants. In a playful tone pitched at the young reader, it attempts to arouse curiosity in the natural world: "Each of these innumerable animals and plants are carrying on with their lives as they please. The bees flying outside your window, the monkeys in the deep mountains—they each have their own lives. The wild grasses on the roadside, the giant trees on the mountain peaks that reach toward the heavens—they each have their own lives. Isn't it fun getting to know about the lives of these animals and plants?"[76]

For the writers of this propagandistic text, there is a logical progression that leads from the enjoyment of studying the lives of animals and plants to a nationalistic devotion to the Japanese Empire. *The Lives of Animals and Plants* functions within an ideology that naturalizes, through science and biophilia, Japanese nationalism. The introduction claims: "It has been said from long ago that there is not an evil person among those that love animals and plants. . . . A spirit that loves those animals and plants closely connected to human life develops into a spirit that loves its friends and the people around it. Furthermore, it develops into a spirit that loves its country."[77]

This posits that a love for the Japanese nation is as natural as a childlike love for animals and plants. Yet as much as this ideology attempts to tie nationalism to a scientific study of the material world, it nonetheless resorts to the language of the immaterial. The introduction relegates the love for animals, plants, friends, and ultimately the nation to the realm of the spirit or mind (*kokoro*). The separation of the material and the spirit in *The Lives of Animals and Plants* does not foreshadow the coming of revolution, as Hanada Kiyoteru believed. Instead, it uses the supposed objectivity of science to justify the subjective experience of a militarized nationalism. Such ideology speaks to a claim the director of the botanical garden makes in "Dendrocacalia": "A plant is purity itself—that word so full of pathos that has been expunged from everyday usage."[78] The implication of the director's comment here is that the concept of "purity" was expunged from everyday use in the postwar because of its ties to wartime rhetoric. The use of the language of "spirit" in *The Lives of Animals and Plants* belongs to the same rhetoric.

For Honda, an interest in the interior world of plant life helps condition the spiritual interior of the human subject: "Those who are capable of loving grasses and trees are always extremely happy and are able to possess beautiful spirits [*kokoro*]."[79] As the text's introduction lays out for the young reader, a beautiful spirit is one that will naturally love its country. In this, Honda's language resembles the rhetoric of *Airin shisō*, or Forest-Love Ideology, a pre- and wartime phenomenon that Tessa Morris-Suzuki calls "an intriguing mixture of ecological science and nationalist romanticism, which brought together elements from myth, literature, aesthetics and cutting-edge botanical knowledge."[80] The rhetoric of *Airin shisō* posited a natural link between the love of plant life and the love of the nation. The purported logic of this link between forest love and national love is exemplified in the opening lines of a short catalog that the Japanese Bureau of Forestry published for the 1910 Japanese-British Exhibition in London:

> Along the western shore of the Pacific, there lies a group of numerous islands stretched in a serpent like form covered with rich verdant growths over two thirds of the area of the land. These verdant growths are none other than the forests of the Empire of Japan. The wholesome effects produced upon the land and the people by these forests are both striking and remarkable. The Japanese by nature love their forests and derive enjoyment from the prosperous and luxuriant growths of the same. The burning patriotism and the refined aesthetic ideas of the Japanese are in a large measure the outcome of the influence exerted upon the minds of the people by these forests.[81]

As this text argues, proper love of and care for the botanical world equaled a form of progress that justified the expansion of the Japanese Empire. By 1910, the Bonin Islands had already been part of the "numerous islands" of the Empire of Japan for several decades.

The entanglements of plant research and Japan's colonial project are clearly legible in Honda's section of *The Lives of Animals and Plants*. Early on, he discusses how the colonial space of the *gaichi* served as a site for the study of botanical life. Honda recounts a researcher who "replanted several four-to-five-hundred-year-old lotus seeds that had been dug up from the peat soil of Manchukuo. After a few years, they all produced splendid spouts."[82] Honda's mention of the imperial puppet state of Manchukuo (Manshūkoku or Manchuria)—the *gaichi* space in which Abe Kōbō was raised—illustrates how colonial space was not only a source of resource extraction but also a site for botanical research. Honda's use of this colonial name *Manchukuo* among a discussion of plant life makes the history of Japanese imperialism forever inscribed within the pages of his *Life of the Plant.* Abe ends up doing the same (perhaps unwittingly) by inscribing Timiryazev's book of the same name within the pages of "Dendrocacalia."

On the (Scientific) Name

There is yet another piece of colonial history inscribed within "Dendrocacalia." It can be found in Abe's decision to use the Linnaean Latin name *dendrocacalia* for the *wadannoki*. As mentioned above, the full name for the *wadannoki* in binomial nomenclature is *Dendrocacalia crepidifolia* (Nakai) Nakai, with the last name referring to the botanist Nakai Takenoshin. Although Abe's text never attaches Nakai's name to the name *dendrocacalia* within the narrative, scientific literature on the dendrocacalia gives Nakai credit for having been the first researcher to publish a description of the plant. A 1936 article by Tsuyama Takashi, written in Latin and published in the *Journal of Plant Research* (*Shokubutsugaku zasshi*), claims that Nakai first published a description of the plant in 1928. Tsuyama includes Nakai's name in the official scientific nomenclature of the dendrocacalia.[83]

Nakai was a central figure of botanical research during Japan's colonial modernity. He was the foremost scholar of plant life in Japan's *gaichi*. Nakai published numerous studies of Korean flora, from which he hoped to craft a new method of classification for vegetal life beyond the Japanese Empire. As the historian Jung Lee explains, Nakai's work on developing a universal classification system for plant life is inseparable from the history of Japan's colonial project: "In conjunction with [colonial] expansion, the Japanese botanical establishment consciously chose an imperial path in modernizing Japanese botany. Nakai's systematics, based on Korean plants, was a product of an imperial strategy that secured a Japanese 'centre of calculation' through specimens collected from expanding Japanese colonial peripheries."[84]

The act of classification and naming once again bears traces of colonial legacy. The unique classification system Nakai developed grew out of his relationship to the specimens he studied in the metropole, not from plants living in their natural habitats. As Lee explains, Nakai only ever made short trips to the Korean peninsula and relied on specimens sent to the Japanese *naichi* from naturalists in the *gaichi*.[85] (He did, however, serve as the chief director of a botanical garden in Japanese-occupied Indonesia in 1942.)[86] For the most part, he studied and named colonial plants at Tokyo Imperial University, the same university where Abe studied medicine and Osaki's brother Shirō studied agricultural science. Tokyo Imperial University was Japan's only university to have founded a botany department between the years 1877 and 1918.[87]

In the revised, 1952 version of "Dendrocacalia," the antagonist of the narrative signs a letter to Common as "Director of the K Botanical Gardens." It has been speculated that the letter *K* refers to Tokyo Imperial University's Koishikawa Botanical Gardens. Inspired by European colonial precedent, the first director of the Koishikawa Gardens, Matsumura Jinzō, acquired specimens from colonial *gaichi* to exhibit within the gardens.[88] The allegorical image written into the fictional world of "Dendrocacalia" of the rare plant ending up in a greenhouse could well have been drawn from Abe's own encounter with a real dendrocacalia at Koishikawa.

As the director of the botanical garden in "Dendrocacalia" pins a name tag to a metamorphosed Common bearing the Latin name *Dendrocacalia crepidifolia*, he relegates Common's botanical becoming to the realm of colonial specimen, just as the historical figures who worked in the Koishikawa Botanical Gardens had done to the actual plants collected from colonial space during Japan's colonial modernity. Although the director of the botanical garden in the fictional world of the story claims that finding a *gaichi* plant in the *naichi* is a rarity, within the real world of botanical research, it was not so rare at all. This is especially true of plants like the dendrocacalia that bear the colonial marker that is the name *Nakai*. As botanical research continues to use the name *Nakai* as part of the *wadannoki*'s scientific name, the life of the dendrocacalia remains tied to its place within Japanese colonial history. As such, it continues to be a plant of the twentieth century, even well into the twenty-first century.

3

BOTANICAL MEDIA

Haniya Yutaka, Hashimoto Ken, Itō Seikō, and the Search for Dead Spirits

Tokyo's Inokashira Park is well known today for its cherry trees. Every year, the park is swarmed with visitors who come to view the blossoms of the five hundred or so trees that grow throughout the park. Particularly beloved are the trees that line the pond in the park's center. Crowds gather and marvel at the blossoms reflected in the water's surface. They eat, drink, play music, and celebrate the new growth of spring. It is a lively scene, one that recurs year in and year out. Yet, to paraphrase the Russian botanist Kliment Timiryazev, whom I discussed at length in chapter 2, these trees, too, have their history, one that ties them to Japan's wartime empire and the rebuilding of the nation in the postwar period.

Inokashira Park was not always associated with cherry blossoms. For novelist and literary critic Haniya Yutaka, Inokashira Park, as he encountered it in the early Shōwa era, was a dark, mysterious, forested space: "I moved to the Tokyo neighborhood of Kichijōji in 1934. At that time, Inokashira Park was a dense forest of cedar trees. . . . In order to walk on the solid path through the park, one had to enter into the cedar forest. As you walked, it was cedar trees the whole time. . . . You would suddenly start trembling. . . . You'd get the feeling something was passing behind you."[1]

Visitors to Inokashira Park today would likely not recognize Haniya's haunting (and perhaps haunted) vision of the park. This is because the cedar (or *sugi* in Japanese) trees that once lined Inokashira's pond are no longer there. The cherry trees that line the pond today were largely planted after Japan's defeat, making them part of the greening efforts discussed in the previous chapter.

FIGURE 3.1. Felling trees in Inokashira Park in 1937. Courtesy of Midori Toshokan Tokyo Green Archives.

Fifteen thousand trees, the majority cedars, were removed from Inokashira Park during the war (see figure 3.1).[2] There is a grim, well-known tale about these trees that begins on November 24, 1944, when the US military began an aerial bombing campaign over Tokyo. Their first target was the Nakajima Aircraft Company's Musashino Plant, located near Inokashira Park. The Nakajima Plant produced engines and other components for Japanese military aircraft and was ultimately bombed nine times, resulting in the deaths of over two hundred plant workers.[3] The plentiful cedar trees of Inokashira Park that Haniya recalls in the quote above were allegedly cut down in the wake of these deaths. The story goes that they were used to construct caskets for those who perished in the Nakajima Plant bombings.[4] Most of the cherry trees that now line the pond were planted to replace these once-abundant cedars.

The memory of these felled cedars is inscribed into the novel that Haniya began publishing in the year following Japan's surrender, the multivolume epic *Dead Spirits* (*Shirei*, written between 1946 and 1995). *Dead Spirits* explores a wide range of existential and metaphysical questions in response to the crisis that was the immediate Japanese postwar period. *Dead Spirits* is not, however, a work of spectacular crisis. Nowhere in the novel do we see mention of the US occupation (which lasted on the Japanese mainland from 1945 to 1952) or the day-to-day struggles of Japanese citizens trying to survive in the bombed-out wreckage of the nation. Instead, the crisis to which Haniya directly responds in *Dead Spirits* is an existential one, certainly informed by the difficulties of Japan's postwar reality but not limited to them. *Dead Spirits* has been called "Japan's first metaphysical novel," and as we shall see, it was the violence of wartime Japan that brought Haniya to metaphysics in the first place.[5]

It was likewise metaphysics that brought Haniya to the realm of plant life. Throughout *Dead Spirits*, the figuration of the forest plays a vital role in the construction of a new subjectivity that bridges the rupture of Japan's defeat and helps process the trauma of death. The forest in question bears a striking resemblance to the Inokashira Park that Haniya remembered from the early Shōwa period. The forest is a dark space, haunted by a presence never seen but felt in other sensory (perhaps extrasensory) ways. In volume one of the novel, protagonist Miwa Yoshi takes a late-night walk with his friend Kurokawa Kenkichi through a heavily forested park that resembles Inokashira from Haniya's description above: "The wind seemed to pick up, as the tips of the leaves on the trees of the park (which was home to many broadleaf trees) started rustling fiercely. It wasn't the cold wind of winter, it was an unnerving reverberation, an irritating sound that seemed piercing. They could hear behind them the intermittent quiet sounds of a spring bubbling. They passed through the long, dark tree-lined path of the park."[6] The "unnerving reverberation" that sounds throughout the forest persists, and Miwa and Kurokawa, like Haniya himself, cannot shake the feeling that "something was passing behind" them. As readers, we feel this ghostly presence twice over when we consider the history of Inokashira's forests. The titular "dead spirits" of the novel belong to the humans lost in war and the trees of the lost forest, purportedly cut down to help lay the dead to rest.

In chapter 2, I discussed how Abe Kōbō's short story "Dendrocacalia" turned to the botanical realm to implore readers to reckon with Japan's wartime history and to not use the trope of becoming botanical to move beyond the lingering violence of war too quickly. Abe was critical of the type of greening efforts that we find in Inokashira Park (with its replanting of cherry trees) and of botanical science more broadly for its complicity in Japan's colonial project. To a certain degree, Haniya (who was Abe's contemporary in the Night Group) heeds this warning in *Dead Spirits*. Although written over the course of five decades, Haniya's novel never leaves the dark forests of Inokashira Park and never moves beyond the moment of existential crisis that was the immediate postwar moment. This is because it is in this haunted, forested space that Haniya rethinks the human in the face of defeat and rethinks what it means to become botanical in the process.

He does so by paying close attention to trees and by theorizing them as a form of media that can help channel the dead spirits of the novel's title.

This chapter focuses on a fantastical *shokubutsusei* of the forest. It examines, beginning with the work of Haniya Yutaka, how trees connect the living with the dead. The forests of *Dead Spirits* are home to what I call "botanical media," in which trees mediate between the novel's protagonist Miwa Yoshi and the ghostly remains of war that haunt the narrative. This ghostly affect manifests as *kehai*, a word repeated throughout *Dead Spirits* that connotes a vague sense of "presence" or "trace." The botanical medium of the forest puts protagonist Miwa Yoshi in touch with this presence occasioned by loss. It offers a nonverbal means to work through the violence of the Japanese postwar, a violence that is, to return to the language of Christopher Dole and colleagues: "both a backdrop to and condition for the intimate terrain of . . . everyday lives."

By focusing on trees as botanical media, this chapter links the crisis of the immediate Japanese postwar period to a more recent crisis in modern Japanese history: the March 11, 2011, triple disaster of earthquake, tsunami, and meltdown at the Fukushima Daiichi Nuclear Power Plant (hereafter referred to as "3.11"). Just as Haniya saw the forest as a medium to connect to the haunting spirits of the Japanese postwar era, so, too, does novelist and rapper Itō Seikō, in his 2013 novel *Radio Imagination* (*Sōzō rajio*), turn to the spiritual affect of trees to connect the living to the dead in the wake of 3.11. *Radio Imagination* is a fantastical reflection on loss that presents a paranormal scenario in which survivors of 3.11 can make contact with the victims through the medium of a spirit radio. The spirit radio is hosted by a deceased DJ who broadcasts via botanical media from the top of a giant cedar, a tree not unlike the ones removed from Inokashira Park.

In its attention to the otherworldly realm of death, this chapter moves away from the scientific understanding of plants that informed the botanical becomings of chapters 1 and 2. Both Haniya and Itō sought a different kind of in-between in their figurations of botanical media, one influenced more by spirituality and paranormal affect than evolution or botanical science. However, this chapter also demonstrates how, in addition to inspiring a new kind of botanical imagination, the spiritual affect of plants also inspired a new kind of science, albeit one that is dismissed as pseudoscience today. An important episode in the historical trajectory that this chapter maps—beginning with the cutting down of cedar trees from Inokashira Park and ending with Itō Seikō imagining a cedar tree serving as a radio tower able to communicate with the dead of 3.11—is the rise to prominence of the electrical engineer and popular parascience writer Hashimoto Ken. Hashimoto's writings on plant communication, which would ultimately earn him a place in the infamous work of botanical pseudoscience *The Secret Life of Plants*, allow us to draw Haniya and Itō into a heretofore neglected lineage of botanical writers who looked to rethink the human by rethinking the line between life and death. It was a line they redrew in the botanical realm.

Dead Spirits and Fractured Subjectivities

Haniya Yutaka grew up amid a backdrop of violence, through the turbulent history of pre- and interwar Japan. Like Abe Kōbō, he grew up in a colonial space. Haniya was born and spent the first part of his life in Japanese-occupied Taiwan. There he claims to have experienced something akin to the fracturing of subjectivity I discussed in chapter 1. Haniya recounts: "You could say that the structure of my thinking is fractured (*bunretsukei*). This fractured form of thinking began with my childhood in Taiwan. Generally speaking, I remember feeling uncomfortable in my existence there."[7] The fracturing Haniya speaks of was a direct product of violence: "People's fathers, my parents' friends, they would physically attack the Taiwanese people. And they were Japanese, just like me. In other words, I was friends with these attackers. So, in remembering the discomfort in all of that, I now realize it was the beginning of a certain fracturing."[8] Haniya has written that witnessing such violence made him "hate the Japanese" and that having to reconcile the fact that he himself was Japanese caused him to develop a distrust in self-identity.[9] Haniya thus experienced the crisis of colonial violence close at hand, although from a relatively safe remove, to be sure. Nevertheless, the physical violence that led to Haniya's fractured form of thinking left a lasting impression that would go on to inform his antiauthoritarian politics and his radical literary career, stretching all the way to his role as a leading voice in the ANPO (an abbreviation of the Japanese word for security treaty, *Anzen Hoshō Jōyaku*) protests of the 1960s that looked to halt the renewal of the US-Japan Security Treaty.

Haniya moved to Tokyo in 1923 and eventually enrolled in the Nihon Daigaku preparatory school where he was exposed to the Marxist and anarchist thought that would later influence his critical writing. In 1930, he was expelled for poor attendance and began working for an office associated with the *Zenō Zenkoku Kaigi*, the communist faction of the prewar agrarian movement.[10] The following year, he joined the Japanese Communist Party and was arrested for his political beliefs in 1932.[11] After the failed coup attempt in 1932 known as the May 15 Incident, treatment of political prisoners in Japan worsened, and Haniya spent over a year and a half in incarceration.[12] In prison, he would suffer from recurring, debilitating bouts of tuberculosis. Haniya would ultimately perform *tenkō*, the process by which leftists were forced to renounce their ideological beliefs and pledge allegiance to the imperial throne. According to Haniya, the *tenkō* statement he submitted read: "Within our solar system, the earth will be the first to collapse. The imperial system will collapse before this, but it will last for quite a while."[13] With this metaphysically tongue-in-cheek statement, Haniya was released from prison. In 1945, he helped found the influential literary magazine *Modern Literature* (*Kindai Bungaku*). It was in this magazine that he began publishing *Dead Spirits* in serial installments.

Technically an unfinished novel, *Dead Spirits* is a work of staggering length. It spanned nine volumes by the time of Haniya's death in 1997. The first four volumes were published beginning in the immediate postwar moment of 1946, with Haniya continuing to write new chapters periodically for the rest of his life.[14] Haniya characterizes the work as his attempt to "take flight from the constraints of the modern age" and says that the novel calls for nothing less than "a revolution of existence."[15] It was during his imprisonment that Haniya decided to rethink existence from the ground up: "My wanting to write a novel that could somehow break free of modern notions of time and space, as well as from one's own body—that started while I was in prison. Which is to say, I came to think that a revolution just at the level of society was not good enough. There needed to be a revolution at the level of existence itself."[16] In this statement, we see Haniya's disaffection with the Communist Party. Indeed, *Dead Spirits* has been read as "an unflinching critique of the Japanese Communist Party and Stalin's Russia."[17]

In Haniya's desire for a "revolution at the level of existence," we also see a desire to rethink the human more metaphysically, to reconfigure subjectivity beyond the confines of the human body. Haniya writes that one of the things he sought to resolve by writing *Dead Spirits* was the violence at the base of life that he believed could be glimpsed in the food chain, namely, that life feeds on other forms of life. This was an insight he claims to have first learned as an adolescent, as he witnessed the violence against Taiwanese colonial subjects. Haniya explains that plant life provides a framework to move beyond what he saw as the exploitation that underscores life itself: "Plants are able to photosynthesize with just sunlight and water. They don't eat other beings. They're fine with just light and water."[18] From the confines of a prison cell, Haniya turned to the nonviolence of plant life and envisioned a way to become anew that would eventually bring him into the expansive realm of the forest. *Dead Spirits* became his environmental response to the existential crises of his youth and his contemporary moment.

Like Osaki Midori's *Wandering in the Realm of the Seventh Sense*, not much happens in *Dead Spirits*, despite its length. Also like Osaki's novella, it displays a botanical poetics and embodies a botanical form. Where Osaki's work formally resembled moss in its repetitions and circular structure, *Dead Spirits* is vast like a forest. It stretches on and on. It is easy to get lost within. As Haniya wrote new chapters throughout his life, sometimes taking many years in between, it follows a temporal unfolding (both in terms of narrative and in Haniya's timeline in writing the work) that mimics what I call "forest time"—a concept I develop in chapter 4 of this book. If, as Hiromi Ito claims, words and plants are the same thing (a statement I discuss in this book's introduction), then *Dead Spirits*' words have grown into formidable trees, daunting in number and complexity. One could wander in the forest of *Dead Spirits* for years and still not see everything there is to see within. This chapter presents just a small glimpse into its depths.

The novel unfolds largely through extended philosophical conversations, along with limited narration, in order to tease out the histories of a complicated web of characters: protagonist Miwa Yoshi and his formerly imprisoned activist brother, Takashi; Miwa Yoshi's fiancée and her mother; Yoshi's student friend Kurokawa; the vociferous and argumentative Kubi Takeo; the aphasia-ridden former prisoner Yaba Tetsugo; a pair of hospitalized mentally ill sisters named "God" and "Nighty-Night;" the philosophical doctor Kishi, who is in charge of the mental hospital where many of the characters find themselves. The narrative ultimately reveals that Miwa Yoshi, Miwa Takashi, Kubi, and Yaba are, in fact, biological brothers.

The overall tone of *Dead Spirits* is contemplative and mournful. The novel distills the trauma Haniya himself experienced in the interwar period and transmutes it into a haunting affect. There is dreamlike quality to the work, legible in the poetic gloss that opens the novel:

> Wandering in the space between ill will and the abyss
> Like the cosmos
> Those dead spirits that whisper[19]

These ambiguous yet suggestive lines set the stage for the ghostly affect that will inhabit the text from within its dark forests. A polyvalent sense of loss runs throughout *Dead Spirits*. At times, the loss is concrete and personal, such as the loss of family and friends. At times, it is abstract, such as the loss of certainty in a belief in absolute truth. Japan's loss in war hangs over the novel like a specter. It is not discussed outright, but it haunts the characters of the novel as they try to understand what it means to have survived into the postwar. Aphasia—the loss of language to silence—is a recurring motif. Where silence was a significant part of the botanical becoming written into Osaki's *Wandering in the Realm of the Seventh Sense* (insofar as it allowed characters to inhabit a "moss-like disposition"), silence in *Dead Spirits* speaks to the complicated status of language in the postwar landscape of Japanese literature. This is because *Dead Spirits* was published amid discussions of the wartime culpability of Japanese writers. The editors of *Modern Literature* published a journal titled *Literary Signpost* (*Bungaku jihyō*), the most popular feature of which, according to James Dorsey, "was a regular column called 'Literary Prosecution' (*bungaku kensatsu*), in which the editors and a host of others took literary figures to task for reactionary wartime writings."[20] In postwar Japan, language could be dangerous, and what one said in the past rang into the present with a newfound, threatening clarity. Haniya understood this all too well from his years in prison and his subsequent forced *tenkō*, the ideological conversion mentioned above. It was Haniya's commitment to leftist politics even after his renunciation of the Communist Party that kept him from being labeled complicit in the war effort.

Dead Spirits' narrative begins in a world where the war has ended but the damage lingers on. In the opening scene, Miwa Yoshi visits his friend Yaba Tetsugo in the mental hospital. Yaba has developed aphasia after an incident with the warden of the prison in which he was being held. The narrative never makes clear the origins of Yaba's aphasia. Miwa Yoshi is told several different stories concerning Yaba's treatment in jail, but ultimately there are no definitive words that explain the trauma Yaba underwent as a political prisoner. Yoshi's brother Takashi (who is also on parole from prison) is a resident of this hospital as well and is bedridden with "an unfortunate mental illness" (*fukō na seishinbyō*). Although not confined to the hospital, Miwa Yoshi himself also exhibits signs of a fractured subjectivity, as language fails him time and again. Throughout *Dead Spirits*, Yoshi experiences excruciating emotional anguish as he attempts and fails (most often within the woods) to speak the words "I am myself" ("*Ore wa ore da*"). In this existentially unstable state, he looks throughout the narrative to reconfigure his subjectivity in a space beyond words, much like Machiko in Osaki's *Wandering in the Realm of the Seventh Sense*. Where Machiko turned to the small, indistinct realm of moss to become botanical, Miwa Yoshi turns to the expanse of the forest, a botanical space that Michael Marder suggests is ideal for the kind of existential rethinking Haniya sought: "Paradoxically, in order to recover ourselves we must lose ourselves better by learning to grow *outward*, to be an excrescence that, while remaining rooted, knows how to grow *with* nonhuman others—the elements, plants, and animals. The best place for this apprenticeship is the forest."[21]

Assemblage, Attunement, and *Kehai*

As Miwa Yoshi takes long walks in tree-filled areas of Tokyo, his subjectivity begins to extend out into the forest around him. He becomes, in Marder's words, "an excrescence" that "grows outwards." The more he spends time among trees, the more Miwa loses a sense of himself and develops a botanical subjectivity in its place. As I have been theorizing in this book, a botanical subjectivity is multiple, a way of experiencing oneself as more than one self. As he becomes more plantlike and lets go of the confines of his body, Miwa Yoshi enters into an assemblage with the forest, a form of becoming in which individual entities are rendered part of something larger than themselves. Assemblages give rise to something new that is more than the sum of its parts. Jane Bennett writes that assemblages "are not governed by any central head. . . . The effects generated by an assemblage are, rather, emergent properties, emergent in that their ability to make something happen . . . is distinct from the sum of the vital force of each materiality considered alone."[22] Entering into an assemblage with the forest allows for the metaphysically new becoming that Haniya sought while in prison. It allows for a way to escape notions of self-identity that plagued Haniya since his childhood in colonial Taiwan.

As Miwa walks in the forest with his friend Kurokawa, he becomes a part of the forest assemblage, merging with the atmosphere around him: "The damp atmosphere coiled around the skin of the trees. It was the fragrant scent of night. Within the dark stand of trees, the sound of their feet as they stepped reverberated as if chips of the trees were gently being torn off. The howling wind continued to shake the treetops. The atmosphere cooled."[23] Miwa and Kurokawa, like the trees, are surrounded by a damp atmosphere in which something seems to always be bubbling up to the surface, born of movement and sound. Sound is important in *Dead Spirits*. Human characters may suffer from aphasia, but the forest consistently emits a droning hum. Miwa hears and senses static or a rumble in the forest that others cannot. As Miwa enters into the forest assemblage, he attunes himself to the atmosphere in a manner similar to the way a listener tunes in to a radio broadcast.

Since his childhood, Miwa has felt this sonorous presence in the forest. It is both haunting and threatening, and it renders him speechless:

> In his childhood, at such times as when Miwa would play alone at the edge of the forest, he would suddenly become frightened. He had a feeling as if, from somewhere in the still silence of the forest, an indistinct rumble was occurring. Or rather, it welled up suddenly from the lonely environment unhindered. It was a presence that seemed to be hunting him down. A presence that seemed impossible to escape, no matter how hard he tried to run away, crying. . . . And so, no matter how much he was comforted, he was unable to explain a thing about that presence that pressed down around him.[24]

Miwa is attuned to the existence of something ghostly pursuing him through the medium of trees. As a child, this presence terrified Miwa, but as an adult, he comes to see it as a site of potential. In the aftermath of war, this presence becomes a space of the in-between. It is a presence not quite alive but not quite dead, not quite human but not quite plant. *Dead Spirits* names this potential *kehai*.

Haniya uses the word *kehai* throughout the novel to reference Miwa's sense that someone, or something, is standing behind him, hidden just out of reach, both there and not there—a faint rumble, like radio static. Toward the end of his walk with Kurokawa, Miwa begins to feel the *kehai* presence of someone standing among the trees (just as Haniya himself had felt walking through Inokashira Park): "He began to have the feeling that in the dark stand of trees—the center of which was difficult to see—there was someone standing. The space around him that moved in tandem with him felt like a grey wall that he was propping up while it also propped him up, or like an expanding, endless mist. It was a portent that he had secretly named 'cosmic presence' [*uchūteki na keihai*]."[25] *Dead Spirits* posits that the human can make contact with this "cosmic presence" should one rethink oneself as part of the forest and attune oneself to the ineffable sounds of botanical media. For someone like Haniya—imprisoned, often ill, forced to renounce his political ideals—tapping into this larger cosmic *kehai* provided a way forward in the face of great uncertainty. It pointed toward the revolution at the level of existence he deemed necessary in the postwar moment.

The word *kehai* appears after the novel's first mention of a forest, which occurs in a temporal flashback. Miwa Yoshi and his friend Yaba Tetsugo are walking back from high school to their dormitory when "approaching the edge of a park where trees with yellowed leaves grew thickly," they encounter a young girl pulling a dog's ear, causing it to cry in a way that "reminds one of the extreme suffering of a battered human being."[26] Yaba steps in to end the dog's suffering, pulling the young girl's ears in turn. In response to Yaba's response, a bystander cries out, "She's mentally ill" and calls Yaba a "bastard," to which Yaba replies, "I am Yaba Tetsugo."[27] Although in the narrative present of the novel Yaba is suffering from aphasia, in this flashback, he is able to declare his subjective identity in a manner that will elude Miwa Yoshi throughout the story (as Miwa is time and again unable to say "I am myself"). As Yaba states his name, all action in the forested park comes to a halt, except for a mysterious presence that emerges: "In an instant, a silent presence [*kehai*] came over."[28] With the violence of the scene (however we choose to interpret it) now over, the wordless atmosphere of *kehai* emerges as a cosmic presence. The dead spirits of the work's title whisper within this forested presence in the aftermath of suffering.

The notion of *kehai* is botanical. In his theoretical text *Trees, "ke," and "ki"* (*Ki to ke to ki*, 1993), the architect and critic Takizawa Kenji argues that there is a direct connection between the mysterious force of *kehai* and trees. He postulates that the words share a linguistic origin, as the word for *tree* in Japanese is a homonym for the first character of the compound word *kehai*, namely the vital force of *ki/ke* (the word *tree* is also read as both *ki* and *ke* under differing circumstances). Takizawa writes that trees "naturally signify the earth below, but they also possess the capability to extract the life energy [*ki*] from this dark world of dead spirits [*shirei*] that we know as the earth, and bring it up to the bright world known as the heavens.... We can imagine there was once a connection between the terms 'vital energy' ('*ki*') and 'tree' ('*ki*')."[29] Takizawa's use of the phrase *dead spirits* here is uncanny. While it is doubtful that he meant to reference Haniya's novel, his description of *kehai* can easily be applied to *Dead Spirits*. Takizawa describes a phenomenological account of *kehai* that strongly echoes Miwa Yoshi's childhood experience of being "hunted down" by a feeling of *kehai* in the forest: "The omen of terror born from the darkness is the drifting of '*ke*' in the vicinity.... In the small environment enclosed within forests, the terror was likely comprehensible as something pressing down upon the body, a feeling like a god's curse or the spirit of someone dead was just behind you."[30]

Trees have a long history in Japan as spiritual objects occupying the middle position of the medium between humans and the supernatural realm. In Shinto belief and practice, trees become sacred as *yorishiro*, which are material objects said to house *kami*, the spirits of Shinto cosmology/ideology. Sacred trees are known as *shinboku* and are marked with ropes called *shimenawa* that encircle their trunks (see figure 3.2). The spiritual essence of trees can also be found in the concept of *hashira*, the sacred pillars used in shrine architecture. In each case, trees are a medium that mediate between the human world and the spiritual realm. Although much contemporary research on Japanese religion (including Japanese Buddhism and Shintoism) has questioned and critiqued the origins of such beliefs as *somoku jōbutsu* (the ability of plants to gain Buddhist enlightenment) and *shinboku*, there is nevertheless a long history of spiritual ideology and practice in Japan that has deemed the botanical world (and trees in particular) sacred.[31]

Dead Spirits is undeniably a spiritual novel, although it is certainly not a religious one. It does not invoke religious imagery such as *shinboku*, nor does it speak in Shinto terms of *kami* residing in the trees. Instead, *Dead Spirits* is Haniya's attempt in the postwar moment to reclaim the natural world as a site of spiritual connection outside the fascistic confines of State Shinto ideology that helped justify Japan's wartime colonial expansion. In chapter 2, I discussed how, through the ideology of *Airin shisō*, forests (and the love thereof) were used to justify Japanese patriotism in the wartime period. That Haniya would return to the forests in the postwar period demonstrates his desire to not only rethink the human from within the forest but to also rethink the forest as a site of transformation and potential resistance.

FIGURE 3.2. Sacred tree at Tōshō-gū Shrine in Nikkō. Photo by author.

The trees of *Dead Spirits* are not figures of Shinto animism, although they borrow some of Shinto's spiritual affect. Rather, they are media that occasion a "sense of vital interconnectivity," to borrow a phrase from the environmental media theorist John Durham Peters.[32] The forest is a medium in *Dead Spirits* in the sense that it is, in Peters's words, an "enabling (environment) that provide(s) habitats for diverse forms of life."[33] Forests become an enabling environment for Miwa Yoshi to become botanical as he strives toward a new form of subjectivity that expands beyond the confines of his body into the haunted atmosphere that surrounds him, where diverse forms of life commingle with dead spirits. The forest is also a medium in the manner described by the environmental philosopher and media theorist Takemura Shinichi, who uses the language of multiplicity to account for the forest as an assemblage: "Not 'a forest' as a gathering of mere trees, but a forest as a singular moving body [*undōttai*], in which the 'singular' is simultaneously 'many.' A forest in which things that come to exist and things that are made to exist dissolve into one in time and in space."³⁴ For Takemura, like Peters, a medium is an enabling environment: "Trees exist . . . as a singular matrix in which various forms of life spontaneously come to be."³⁵ Talk about botanical potential!

Miwa Yoshi experiences the forest as a matrix in this way. For Miwa, the forest is a medium in which things come into being and pass away suddenly:

> At night, Miwa Yoshi would open his window and gaze out on the dimly lit park. The elm trees drew dark shadows, and he could see their leaves fluttering noisily in the wind. There was no one to be seen within the park. Suddenly, he would have the feeling that he could hear the sound of hoarse coughing behind him. It seemed like a cough uttered unconsciously by an indistinct body that was about the same height as himself. While controlling his impulse to abruptly turn around, he stood still and listened closely. He could hear what sounded like the reverberation of wings rubbing together, from insects he couldn't see that were hidden in the cracks of the pillars, along with the creaking of the floorboard joints. When he slowly turned around to look, of course . . . there was a lonely void in which not a single shape could be found.³⁶

Staring out into the darkness of the matrix of the forest medium, Miwa Yoshi experiences the presence of something just behind him. He is attuned to a presence that is both there and not there, and he lingers on through a reverberating *kehai* that resembles the empty presence of radio static:

> A reverberation that spread forth like a shadow did not disappear into the void. Covering his ears, he weaved his way through the faint buzzing that quietly murmured like a small stream, and before long a certain groaning could be heard. . . . It was a presence of a certain condition in which every moment was meshed together—every moment in which his sense of self piled upon another sense of self, where he wanted to cry out a certain phrase but was unable to. It was a frightening groan that brought with it an unpleasant expression, one that formed the strange scowl of gnawing down on oneself while trying to say the words "I am..."³⁷

Within the matrix of botanical media, Miwa experiences, to paraphrase Takemura, the singular as many. Moments are meshed together, differing selves are piled atop one another. Within the buzzing of the forest, Miwa Yoshi becomes botanical, inhabiting a multiple subjectivity. He cannot finish the sentence "I am myself" because he is no longer himself. He has become a part of the forest and, phytomorphically, has lost the human capacity to declare an individuated identity.

Understood through the language of media, forests become a clear site of plasticity, that capacity for transformation that I have been arguing is central to the trope of becoming botanical. In Takemura's image of a "moving body" that is both singular and many, we can see the very process of perpetual change and transformation that plasticity names. From the confines of his prison cell, Haniya yearned for a plasticity sufficient enough to accommodate a revolution at the level of existence itself. To be sure, the plasticity Haniya found in the forest was a destructive plasticity, a radical form of transformation that Catherine Malabou describes in language easily applied to the traumatized characters of *Dead Spirits*: "Something shows itself when there is damage, a cut, something to which normal, creative plasticity gives neither access nor body: the deserting of subjectivity, the distancing of the individual who becomes a stranger to herself, who no longer recognizes anyone, who no longer recognizes herself, who no longer remembers her self."[38]

Entering into the forest assemblage requires the "deserting of subjectivity." Miwa's inability to say "I am myself" is the encapsulation of what Malabou calls "the distancing of the individual." Malabou writes further of the subject undergoing the radical changes of destructive plasticity: "We return nowhere. Between life and death we become other to ourselves."[39] In the aftermath of Japan's loss in war, with friends and relatives hospitalized and unable to speak, Miwa Yoshi responds to the existential dread of having nowhere to return by yearning to become something new, something "other to himself." He seeks this otherness in the forest, where, drawn into an assemblage with tree media, he finds himself becoming botanical somewhere, in Malabou's words, "between life and death."

On *Kyotai*

Botanical media facilitate an exchange between Miwa Yoshi and the world of the dead, but they offer no concrete language from which to name this new botanical subjectivity. Trees may emit a low, haunting hum throughout the novel, but they do not speak in an anthropomorphic way. Trees are, to invoke Marshall McLuhan's famous formulation, a medium, not a message. The closest Miwa can come to naming his new subjectivity is the term *kyotai*, or "empty body"—an empty signifier that names its own falsehood. The "*kyo*" of *kyotai* has many meanings, including a hollow or a void. In spite of clear connections to Buddhist cosmology, the word is Haniya's neologism, and it serves as both a metaphysical rejection of Japan's wartime political ideology and the seeds for a botanical resistance to an anthropocentric mindset that we can read as environmental. The human body was central to the ideology of Imperial Japan, both in the material form of its subjects and in the abstract form of the National Body, or *kokutai*. While postwar writers like Tamura Taijirō rediscovered the sensuality of the body after Japan's defeat, Haniya registered the falsehood of the individuated body, pointing instead to the interconnectedness of human beings and nature. Fujii Takashi's work on what he calls a "Post-Anthropocentric" tendency in Haniya's writing goes as far as to claim that we can read *Dead Spirits* as a novel of the Anthropocene and that Haniya's posthumanism ends up showcasing the extent to which humans have had a disproportionate impact on the health of the planet writ large.[40]

Whether or not we find an *environmentalist* message within *Dead Spirits*, it is clear that the reconfiguration of subjectivity bound up in the concept of *kyotai* is *environmental*. It is also metaphysical—a spiritually inflected environmental framework through which to rethink the human. Miwa coins the term *kyotai* in response to his repeated inability to speak the words "I am myself" within the botanical realm of *kehai*, most often during his long walks through the woods. In volume two, he sets out late at night to wander alone, and the narrative is characteristically metaphysical as it offers the following aside to frame Miwa's walk: "In the wandering of the intoxicated self within vast space, a cosmic consciousness eventually arises."[41] Miwa Yoshi's walks, for all of their mundanity, are cosmic. They put him in touch with a vastness much larger than the confines of his skin: "He was within a kind of mysterious rustling of the night, one he would find difficult to explain. It was not simply loneliness. There was a singular space, so to speak, along with him, one which moved in tandem with him."[42]

Emanuele Coccia has argued that plants are intrinsically cosmic beings, as the process of photosynthesis puts plants in intimate touch with the cosmos. Solar energy is converted by their leaves into "living matter." "Photosynthesis," Coccia writes, "is, in this sense, a cosmic process of fluidification of the universe, one of the movements through which the fluid of the world constitutes itself."[43] As they perform this process of helping constitute the world (and, more directly, the atmosphere), plants become media. To explain this, Coccia quotes Kliment Timiryazev, the Russian botanist I discuss at length in chapter 2. Timiryazev writes: "The plant plays a role of a mediator between the Sun and the animal world. The plant, or rather its most typical organ, the chloroplast, is the connection that brings together the activity of all the organic world—everything we call life—to the center of energy of our solar system: such is the cosmic function of the plant."[44] In *Dead Spirits*, Haniya extends the mediative properties of plants (in the form of trees) to not only bring together "everything we call life" but also to bring together life and death.

Drawn up into a cosmic consciousness opened up by tree media, Miwa Yoshi feels the boundaries of his subjectivity dissolve. He becomes part of something much larger than himself, which makes him feel as though his own individuated sense of self is shrinking: "While the radius that moved in tandem with him (that radius that was in fact himself) gradually narrowed, the end point of this contraction seemed like a dot that was too small for the eye to see. It was like the pointed end of a funnel that seemed to have been pricked by a needle. . . . And with that small dot that was like the end of a needle, he transformed into an infinitesimal particle."[45] As Miwa feels himself simultaneously expanding (to the natural world around him) and contracting (to an infinitesimal sense of self), he feels the need to declare himself an individuated subject: "There was only one thing that Miwa Yoshi—who had become that singular existence of the infinitesimal—wanted to shout from the bottom of his heart. . . . It was, namely, the singular phrase: 'I am myself.'"[46] Once again, Miwa is unable to speak this singular phrase. Something prevents him from completing the self-declaration: "It was undoubtedly foolish, generally speaking, but once he began to mutter the words 'I am,' he was unable to continue muttering the final word 'myself.'"[47] Miwa Yoshi's subjectivity lingers half-spoken in the forest, fractured at the level of the sentence. *Kyotai* names this cosmic fracturing and releases Miwa from the confines of his body. It allows him to identify as more than himself, as "other to himself," to return to Malabou's phrase.

The novel introduces the term *kyotai* via a conversation between Miwa and Dr. Kishi at the mental institution. The two discuss Miwa Yoshi's lack of interest in living. After Kishi warns Miwa that such feelings are akin to suicide, Miwa corrects him by explaining that what he is in fact seeking is not death but rather the state of *kyotai*. Kishi thinks again of death: "Hmm, well. . . . You want to become a ghost. . . . Why, somehow, we've certainly entered into a strange conversation befitting a mental institution."[48] Dr. Kishi asks Miwa Yoshi if he believes in God. When Yoshi replies in the negative, Kishi asks, "And yet . . . you wish for *kyotai*. . . . Isn't that itself a form of divinity? Of course, your subject here is very complicated, and I recognize it is a form of contradiction."[49] Miwa Yoshi interrupts: "Right, it is contradiction itself."[50]

For Miwa Yoshi, contradiction is generative. His desire for *kyotai* is not a desire for death but rather for a kind of rebirth among botanical media that puts him in contact with the dead. *Kyotai* thus embraces the seeming contradiction of yearning for rebirth within the realm of dead spirits. *Kyotai* is Miwa Yoshi's cosmological means of forging a new subjectivity within the forest, where he faces the contradiction of becoming botanical both *despite* and yet *specifically because* he cannot say "I am myself." It is the contradiction of reimagining oneself as something other than oneself. It is the result of reimagining the human as plantlike, as a multiple being, and, in Coccia's words, as "the only breach in the self-referentiality of the living."[51] It is the seeming contradiction of rethinking the human through plant life.

Hashimoto Ken and *The Secret Life of Plants*

In *Dead Spirits*, Haniya imagines how trees as botanical media can open up a channel of wordless communication between the living and the dead, but in a 1992 conversation with Tachibana Takashi, Haniya also questioned whether humans could engage in some form of direct communication with plants themselves. He recounts a story he heard concerning plants' response to vibrations, suggesting that plants communicate via sound and that they could possibly understand language:

> They say there is a difference between flowers that have been told to "Bloom into beautiful flowers!" and flowers that have not been told to do so. They say that the ones that have been spoken to will bloom beautifully. The first people to realize this said that the reason wildflowers grow and bloom so well near airports is due to the vibrations of the airplanes. . . . That if you play flowers Mozart and Beethoven, that they prefer Mozart. That trees also respond to vibrations. They say the writer Endō Shūsaku says things to his plants like that: "Bloom into beautiful flowers!" This is just a guess, but perhaps in reality, trees do respond to vibrations.[52]

Haniya goes on to claim that because humans are essentially "anthropocentric" (*ningen chūshin shugi*), they have not yet conducted ample research on whether or not sound elicits such responses from plants. Tachibana tells Haniya that, actually, there *are* experiments being conducted in greenhouses in which Mozart's music is played for plants. He reports that he has heard plants prefer soft music.[53] Then, as if suddenly realizing the esoteric and bizarre turn their conversation has taken, Tachibana mentions the mystical world of Haniya's *Dead Spirits*: "All of these things—*kehai*, spirits, the existence of objectively real objects from the other side that are invisible to the eye, the concept of *kyotai* which comes up again and again in *Dead Spirits*, the existence of things that have not yet come to be—these all belong to another dimension, don't they?"[54]

With this question, Tachibana acknowledges the relationship between the ideas Haniya explores in *Dead Spirits* and theories of the paranormal. Their conversation naturally flows from Haniya's experience of *kehai* in Inokashira Park to the parascience of experimenting with plant communication. Tachibana's claim that the botanical figures of *kehai* and *kyotai* "belong to another dimension" demonstrates how the forests of *Dead Spirits* are botanical media. According to Tachibana, they sit in the middle of two different dimensions. Tachibana and Haniya's discussion of parascience entangles *Dead Spirits* within the same pseudoscientific milieu as one of Japan's most prominent writers of the paranormal, Hashimoto Ken. In recollecting stories of experiments on plants involving classical music, it is likely that Tachibana and Haniya were discussing the best-selling (and highly controversial) study of plant parascience that introduced Hashimoto Ken to the world stage: Peter Tompkins and Christopher Bird's *The Secret Life of Plants* (1973).[55] *The Secret Life of Plants* was translated into Japanese in 1987, only five years before Haniya and Tachibana's conversation. Chapter ten of *The Secret Life of Plants*, titled "The Harmonic Life of Plants," discusses at length the history of sound experimentation on plants and mentions how "airport-level noise" has been used to "awaken seeds."[56] It further discusses a series of experiments in which cucurbit gourds were exposed to either rock music or classical music, and it details how they responded differently to each. Although Haniya and Tachibana never mention *The Secret Life of Plants* by name, their discussion of airport noise and plants' preference of classical music could easily have been drawn from this chapter of the text.

Hashimoto Ken appears in the third chapter of *The Secret Life of Plants*, titled "Plants That Open Doors." The chapter discusses experiments that use electricity to communicate with the botanical realm. It focuses on researchers who took inspiration from the controversial work of Cleve Backster, a central figure in plant pseudoscience who worked for the US Central Intelligence Agency and used his experience with polygraph machines (or "lie-detectors") to test the limits of what he called "primary perception." Primary perception, according to the title of Backster's book of the same name, refers to the belief in "biocommunication with plants, living foods, and human cells."[57] Backster claimed that communication with plants was indeed possible through the medium of the polygraph machine.

In one sense, Hashimoto Ken and Haniya Yutaka were opposites of one another. Haniya wrote of trees as botanical media that served as a conduit to the ineffable spiritual presence of *kehai*. He did so through the challenging medium of a multivolume novel that was full of philosophical musings and literary allusions.[58] Hashimoto, on the other hand, wrote of botanical media as a direct means of speaking with plants and dead spirits, and he did so through accessible books of popular science and television appearances. Hashimoto became something of a media sensation, as he and his wife appeared frequently on Japanese television to demonstrate their ability to speak with plants. Footage of the Hashimotos and their talking cacti (in which they attempt to teach a cactus to speak the Japanese syllabary) can be seen in Walon Green's 1979 documentary film *The Secret Life of Plants*, which is based on Tompkins and Bird's book (and features a soundtrack by Stevie Wonder). Despite their differences, however, both Haniya and Hashimoto were interested in the liminal status of the botanical realm as a site of possibility.

Like Haniya, Hashimoto's turn to plant life was a response to the trauma of Japan's wartime period, albeit from the other side of the political spectrum. According to the autobiographical account posted on the website of the Japanese Parascience Association (*Nihon Chokagakukai*), Hashimoto was drawn to science as an expression of his fervent nationalism for the Japanese military empire: "It was said that in war, victory or defeat was decided by the quality and quantity of scientific weapons. However, the leaders of Japan at that time said things like 'We will definitely win because the Japanese people have an unsurpassed spiritual strength' and 'Japan is the land of the gods, and so a divine wind will blow.' I disagreed with their thinking and committed myself to expend all my energy so that Japan would win the war. I had always wanted to become an inventor if possible, so I thought I would invent a new weapon for Japan."[59]

Hashimoto's nationalist desire to invent weapons of war brought him to Tokyo Imperial University in 1945 to study science—the same institution at which Osaki Midori's brother Shirō and Abe Kōbō had studied. However, Hashimoto's dreams of aiding the war effort quickly evaporated: "A divine wind did not blow, and in the end, Japan was defeated. Japan was unable to develop a new weapon, but the United States developed the atomic bomb. I thus lost my life's purpose."[60] Hashimoto's lamentation that "a divine wind did not blow" demonstrates the extent to which Shinto ideology was infused into the rhetoric of war. The notion of a "divine wind," or kamikaze, was mobilized to famously horrific ends. In seeking to reestablish a metaphysical relationship with the natural world in the postwar moment, Haniya was resisting the kind of State Shinto ideology that Hashimoto claims to have viewed as "his life's purpose."

Hashimoto's willingness to discuss his complicity in Japan's imperial project sets him apart from the other figures I discuss in this book. Hashimoto himself makes it clear that his interest in science was driven by his militaristic nationalism. Instead of turning to the botanical realm to grow beyond the violence of war, Hashimoto found in plant life a new direction for his belief in the divine once the divinity of the imperial system was thrown into question. In the aftermath of Japan's surrender to the United States, Hashimoto's belief in the existence of a divine force did not diminish but rather found a home in New Age parascience. Just as we find botanical science entangled in Japan's wartime empire (as discussed in chapters 1 and 2 of this book), so, too, do we find an imperial legacy within botanical pseudoscience.

Hashimoto writes of his confusion with and ultimate conviction in the scientific relationship to nativist (i.e., Shinto) modes of spirituality: "Do gods still exist even though a divine wind did not blow and Japan lost the war? I, who loved science and wanted to become a scientist, kept on believing in the existence of gods."[61] After being introduced to Taniguchi Masaharu's spiritually inflected scientific text *Truth of Life* (*Seimei no jissō*, 1937), Hashimoto found a new purpose and devoted himself to the scientific study of the spiritual/paranormal realm during an age when new religions flourished in the postwar loosening of restrictions on religious practice. He would go on to found the Japanese Parascience Association and develop the "alphacoil," a machine that Hashimoto claimed could solve all kinds of health and psychological issues.[62] His appearance in *The Secret Life of Plants* would cement his status as a leading figure of parascientific plant research—up until the fervent backlash against the book, that is.

That Haniya Yutaka would ultimately be drawn to the dubious findings of *The Secret Life of Plants* merits a look at Hashimoto's own engagements with the botanical realm. To a certain degree, Hashimoto looked to rethink the human through plant life, but I am not suggesting that his work offered the same promise of botanical resistance as did the other figures I discuss in this book. Rather, Hashimoto demonstrates the ambiguous position of becoming botanical, namely that it can be used both as a means of resistance and for serving state power depending on its mobilization. To be sure, Hashimoto's vision of teaching plants to speak was an anthropomorphic dream, far from the phyotomorphic tendencies of becoming botanical. Nevertheless, he belongs to a history of modern Japanese writers who saw, in plant life, a way to communicate with the dead.

In 1966, Hashimoto published an account of parascientific research titled *Mysteries of the Fourth Dimensional World* (*Yojigensekai no shinpi*). The work became a bestseller and was in its eighteenth printing by the time Tompkins and Bird wrote *The Secret Life of Plants*.[63] *Mysteries of the Fourth Dimensional World* is a hodgepodge of supernatural claims that draw equally from scientific evidence and spiritual speculation. Chapter titles include such wide-ranging topics as "Animals Have Precognition," "A Telepathic Phenomenon Anyone Can Experiment With," and "Does the Spirit World Exist?" For Hashimoto, the paranormal realm was a place of dead spirits, and like Haniya before him and Itō Seikō after him, Hashimoto imagined making contact with these spirits. In the fourth section of *Mysteries of the Fourth Dimensional World*, titled "Challenging Modern Biology," Hashimoto offers an account of haunted media, to borrow Jeffrey Sconce's term. In a subchapter titled "Is a Spirit Radio Possible?," Hashimoto explains how, late in his life, Thomas Edison conducted research on "spirit radios" that were able to communicate with the dead. Although Edison was ultimately unable to make contact with the spirit realm via radio, Hashimoto suggests that recent technological developments could make the completion of a spirit radio actually possible. The issue, argues Hashimoto, is overcoming the signal-to-noise ratio and determining where exactly the message emerges from the medium. It would take his discovery of Cleve Backster's work on plants and polygraphs for Hashimoto to theorize that plants could be the medium through which this spirit radio could be actualized.

Talking Cacti and Spirit Radios

After learning of Backster's "discovery" of plant communication, Hashimoto began his own experiments with botanical subjects and eventually became a proponent of plant intelligence. With the help of his wife, Hashimoto began attaching polygraph machines to cacti to teach the plants how to speak and sing. Hashimoto would go on to author numerous books about communicating with plants, including *How to Talk with Plants* (*Shokubutsu to ohanashisuru hō*, 1995) and *Plants Have Minds* (*Shokubutsu ni wa kokoro ga aru*, 1997). Although these texts share *Dead Spirit*'s interest in the otherworldly status of the botanic realm, they posit the opposite scenario of the wordless subjectivity of *kyotai* that Miwa Yoshi finds within the forest. In *Dead Spirits*, Haniya turned to the liminal presence of *kehai* to rethink human subjectivity as more botanical. Hashimoto, however, attempted to rethink botanical subjectivity as more human and claimed that direct communication via language is possible between humans and plants. Hashimoto assured readers, "You too can talk with plants!"[64] His books abound with anthropomorphic drawings of plants that turn the multiple subjectivity of the botanical realm into an individuated, humanlike mode of being (see figure 3.3).

Hashimoto claimed that plants could understand human language and respond through the polygraph machine: "I have claimed that 'plants too have minds,' and have attached polygraphs to cacti. When I called out to these cacti, 'Cactus-san, Cactus-san, if you do have a mind, please move the needle of the polygraph machine,' the needle of the polygraph made large movements."[65] *The Secret Life of Plants* portrays Hashimoto's experiments in a playful light: "Transformed and amplified by Dr. Hashimoto's electronic equipment, the sound produced by the plant was like the high-pitched hum of very-high-voltage wires heard from a distance, except that it was more like a song, the rhythm and tone being varied and pleasant, at times even warm and almost jolly."[66] The sounds produced by the cacti are a far cry from the sounds of the forests in *Dead Spirits*, which give Miwa Yoshi a "feeling as if, from somewhere in the still silence of the forest, an indistinct rumble was occurring. . . . It was a presence that seemed to be hunting him down."[67] Hashimoto's parascience turns the liminal, haunting rumbles of *kehai* into an accessible language that is "warm and almost jolly." This is indeed the feeling we get watching Hashimoto's wife teach a cactus to speak Japanese in the film version of *The Secret Life of Plants*. It is uncanny but also quite humorous to hear the cacti respond "ah" (i.e., the first sound of the Japanese syllabary) at Mrs. Hashimoto's prodding.

There is nevertheless an uncanny echo of the Hashimotos' experiments with polygraphs in Haniya's *Dead Spirits*. The fifth volume of the novel, which Haniya

FIGURE 3.3. Illustrations intended to show how plants grow well when exposed to classical music but not when exposed to "hard rock." From Hashimoto Ken's *How to Talk with Plants*, page 77.

published in 1975 after a twenty-six-year hiatus, introduces a concept that Miwa Yoshi's friend/secret brother Kubi calls the "Telephone Box of the Dead." Kubi proposes that if the body of someone dying were attached to electric probes, a machine would be able to receive transmissions from the body at a cellular level and move a needle to indicate a response from the dying consciousness. In effect, Haniya is describing a polygraph machine and imagining that it could serve as a medium to speak directly with the dead or at least those on the cusp of dying. It is possible Haniya borrowed this idea from Abe Kōbō's science fiction novel *Inter Ice Age 4* (*Dai-yon kanpyōki*, published between 1958 and 1959), in which a dead body is attached by electrodes to a computer equipped with artificial intelligence. It is unlikely, however, that Haniya was familiar with Hashimoto's work at this point of writing *Dead Spirits*, as it would take a few more years for *The Secret Life of Plants* to appear in Japanese. Nevertheless, their shared interest in the polygraph as a medium for extrasensory communication is striking, if not outright mysterious.

To be sure, Hashimoto never proposed attaching electrodes to human bodies, either alive or dead. Still, he was passionately interested in finding a way to communicate with those who had passed on to the other side. In a 1971 article published in the journal *Mental Science* (*Seishin Kagaku*) titled "Singing Cacti" ("*Utau saboten*"), Hashimoto explains that his ultimate goal with plant research is to invent a spirit radio, not unlike the one that would come to serve as the premise of Itō Seikō's *Radio Imagination* some forty years later. Where Itō's spirit radio functions as a medium that brings together the living and dead in the aftermath of the national/natural catastrophe that was/is 3.11, Hashimoto imagines his spirit radio as a more personal medium that can connect one to their deceased grandparents.[68] Hashimoto believed plants could serve as the missing piece to this spirit radio. Throughout his career, he fervently claimed that plants have minds, and yet in his figuration of the spirit radio, he refers to plants as machinelike, effectively denying them the kind of subjectivity he posits elsewhere: "What kind of apparatus exists to change spirit waves [*reiha*] into electricity, so that we can receive them? I am conducting various experiments, but I have not been able to find a spirit wave transducer.... Minerals have proven complicated, but it seems living beings could work. Not higher living beings like humans, but rather simple beings. Plants more so than animals, or bacteria—beings that are closer to machines."[69]

As he proposes that plants could be the perfect medium to receive spirit waves, Hashimoto upholds an evolutionary hierarchy that places humans above other living beings (a hierarchy Osaki Midori rejected in her work). Even though plants can speak, sing, and make contact with the dead, they are, according to Hashimoto's logic here, nonetheless at the bottom of the evolutionary ladder. Drawn into an assemblage with humans, dead spirits, and electric apparatuses, plants seemingly trade their "secret lives" for the role of machines. They become specimens, objects of experimentation, much like the dendrocacalia at the end of Abe Kōbō's story that I discussed in chapter 2. Hashimoto's cacti are ironically stripped of the very voice his experiments originally sought to find. Instead, they become only a channel for the voice of dead spirits. They become pure medium, devoid of any *kehai* or presence of their own.

Curiously, a cactus also appears in Haniya's *Dead Spirits*. In the fourth chapter, we are introduced to Ogi Tsuneko, a young woman who lives next door to a Korean man named Yi Poyan. Yi tends to a solitary cactus in his room. Ogi recounts that Yi believes that "cacti are the strongest plants in the world."[70] For Haniya, the cactus is meant to stand in for Yi's "self-reliance": "Cacti live in the desert and support themselves with only the smallest amount of moisture. This is meant to resemble Yi's spirit."[71] Far from the expansive role he gives trees in the novel, the cactus functions at the barest stage of symbolism. For Haniya, cacti were neither medium nor message, but merely metaphor.

Shinboku and the Fear of Plasticity

Trees occupy an even more complicated place in Hashimoto's work than cacti. This is because trees, more so than any of the plants he discusses, were tied to Shinto belief. If Hashimoto truly did lose his life's purpose once the "divine wind" did not blow during WWII, and if he truly did wish to continue "believing in the existence of gods" all the same, then it was the tree that allowed him to combine his faith in a Shinto cosmology with the pseudoscience of the paranormal. In *How to Talk with Plants*, he includes a chapter titled "Do You Believe in 'Tree Spirits?'" ("*Anata wa 'ki no tama' o shinjimasuka?*") that discusses the tradition of *Ushi no koku mairi*, or the "Ox-hour Shrine Visit," in which a "deeply jealous woman" visits a Shinto shrine around two o'clock in the morning and nails a straw doll meant to represent their rival in love into a *shinboku*.[72] Hashimoto explains that the purpose of this ritual was to enact a curse on the woman's rival, ultimately resulting in their death.[73] This tradition, Hashimoto argues, should not be dismissed as mere superstition. Hashimoto wants readers to take the *shinboku* seriously.

Religion and spirituality overlap in Hashimoto's writing in strange ways. The tension between science and religion is the main topic of his 1988 book *Science? Or Religion? (Kagaku ka? Shūkyō ka?)*. In this book, he once again recounts his disillusionment with Japan's loss in war, writing that while the postwar era of peace was something to be happy about, "we Japanese also lost a certain something, something important: piety (patriotism)."[74] Hashimoto's clear conflation of religious piety with nationalism is striking. The specter of imperial divinity (and Hashimoto's grief over its loss at the end of WWII) hangs over the rest of this book, which goes on to sing the praises of the alphacoil and its potential to heal the sick. In his earlier book *Mysteries of the Fourth Dimensional World*, Hashimoto claims that what parascience looks to uncover is precisely the presence of gods: "Long ago, a scholar once claimed: 'If God did not exist, it would be necessary to invent him.' This is true. There are gods. Deep in your subconscious, in a world of higher dimensions that far surpasses the third and fourth dimensions.... There we find unlimited law and knowledge, and in addition, we find a human-like personality and unlimited love. I believe we are inclined to give this the name 'god.' Parapsychology is in the process of discovering gods."[75] This is typical of Hashimoto's take on religion. He presents a New Age in-between that enfolds things like ESP and communication with the dead into an amorphous spirituality that avoids direct connection to established religion, except in the cases where Hashimoto laments the loss of a nationalistic belief in Shinto and emperor worship that enabled the Japanese during wartime to "survive each day while feeling able to endure extreme hardship in order to attain their objective."[76]

By and large, Hashimoto does not discuss plant life when he ruminates on "gods" and the possibility for parascience to become a new form of spirituality. Yet Hashimoto's discussion of *shinboku* is an exception, and it is one that complicates his parascientific view of "gods." This is because *shinboku* are tied to Shinto ideology, a system of belief that propelled his interest in science in the first place. Hashimoto has a difficult time reconciling a Shinto view of *shinboku* with his belief in plant communication. In what comes to resemble Haniya's figuration of *kehai* in *Dead Spirits*, and of Miwa Yoshi's feeling of a "presence that pressed down around him" in the forest, Hashimoto describes a menacing, spiritual atmosphere that surrounds *shinboku*: "*Shinboku* are without exception very old trees. Most likely, from long ago, humans have felt the presence of tree spirits in very old trees. For example, even when people today stand in front of giant trees that are a thousand years old, they likely feel that particular atmosphere that floats through the air around them. They feel a sense of intimidation that is somewhat spiritual."[77] Hashimoto argues that the "Ox-hour Shrine Visit" ritual involved a form of telepathic communication between humans and *shinboku*: "Human scorn is directed into the trunk of the *shinboku* as the nail is driven in. In a manner of speaking, an intense telepathy is cast (toward the *shinboku*)."[78] What is curious here is that elsewhere, Hashimoto excludes "regular" trees from the capacity of telepathic communication. Despite his firm belief in telepathy and plant consciousness (an idea he explores in detail in a chapter from *How to Talk with Plants*, titled "Plants' Words Might Be Telepathic"), the idea of tree telepathy becomes somewhat suspect: "Up to now, I have seen many instances of plants having miraculous abilities, but I imagine that even for a tree, (telepathic communication) is an abnormal situation. This type of abnormal situation—a paranormal phenomenon unthinkable to the average human—was likely quite rare."[79]

Within a body of work that purports to explain a step-by-step method to communicate with plants, Hashimoto loses certainty when it comes to trees. His sudden hesitation to claim that humans can communicate with trees speaks to the history of the *shinboku* (to once again paraphrase Timiryazev) and its place in nativist notions of spirituality. *Shinboku* were special. They possessed a Sacred *shokubutsusei* that was not to be confused with other trees. Thus, by and large, Hashimoto focused on other, less ideologically implicated forms of plant life. He did not attach trees to polygraph machines. He did not attempt to teach trees the Japanese language, as he did with cacti. This is because bound up in the figure of the thousand-year-old *shinboku* was an "intimidating" force that was also spiritual. If Hashimoto wished to keep believing in the gods, then he would need to leave trees alone in his research.

In the crisis of defeat in war he thought was divinely inspired, Hashimoto held on to the *shinboku* as divine, denying it a place in his new paranormal worldview. In an attempt to explain the haunting aura of the *shinboku*, Hashimoto ultimately turns to the psychoanalytic language of projection: "In psychology, there is a rule that states, 'what you fear manifests itself.' Just like a movie where the things burnt into the film appear on the screen, the world of the unconscious eventually gets projected onto the three-dimensional world of ours."[80] What Hashimoto truly seemed to fear by continuing to project a nativist spirituality onto the *shinboku* was precisely the kind of plasticity that Haniya found in regular trees, like those he remembered in Inokashira Park. Hashimoto may have believed in the plasticity of human subjectivity (insofar as parascience depends on this), but unlike Haniya, Hashimoto did not posit that trees could occasion a rethinking of the human.

In his work of arboreal philosophy *Cosmic Tree* (2004), Takemura Shinichi argues that trees do indeed have their own history, but that it is history that cannot be limited to a singular human construct like spirituality: "When we say, in one breath, a *thousand-year-old tree*, it does not connote a tree that has continued to live without change for a thousand years as a singular self. The expression should be read as signifying a multiple 'narrative' in which various histories are interwoven, and as an incessantly reorganizing self."[81] A tree, in other words, is a multiplicity, and as a multiplicity, it comes up against the limits of ideological interpolation by systems of belief like Shintoism. For Hashimoto, the tree, as an "incessantly reorganizing self," was too plastic. In works like Haniya's *Dead Spirits*, the tree could be rethought as something new, as something spiritual but not tied to nativist tradition. For all of the potential Hashimoto saw in plant life, and in his pseudoscientific approach to understanding plant life, he ultimately feared the transformative plasticity bound up in this kind of botanical becoming. He may have believed that he could teach plants to be more like humans, but he never questioned what it would mean for humans to be more like plants.

Hashimoto Ken's books sold well in the era of *The Secret Life of Plants*, but today, they are long out of print. They are obscurities to be found in used bookstores, not on shelves next to translations of CPS texts—although, as I recounted in the introduction to this book, the Japanese translation of *The Secret Life of Plants* remains in print. The infamous legacy of *The Secret Life of Plants* has undoubtedly impacted Hashimoto's own legacy. Nevertheless, his experiments have gone on to have a ghostly afterlife of their own. In 2017, filmmakers Elise

Florenty and Marcel Türkowsky released *Conversation with a Cactus*, a nonnarrative experimental film that reflects on and reenacts Hashimoto's research on plants. The artists' statement in the official press release for the film reads:

> *Conversation with a Cactus* is an exploration of self and other, myth and history, truth and false, seen through a cosmology of signs and stories that reveal the different ways in which the Hashimoto experiment was received. The film retraces the utopia the experiment generated, and the way it was perverted by the japanese [sic] media. With a defiance of the division between documentary and fiction, the experiment becomes itself object of the film's incapacity to demystify the Hashimoto legend. Eventually something else is more important than the question of whether Hashimoto's findings are valid, whether plants are therefore able to sense, speak or think: the concept of a possible other speech, a post human perspective on the world that the figure of the witness-bearing plant embodies.[82]

In its concern with a "post human perspective on the world," Florenty and Türkowsky's *Conversation with a Cactus* rethinks Hashimoto's work and finds a way to transform it into something far more in line with contemporary CPS thought. It turns Hashimoto's pseudoscience into a kind of visual poetry with its own botanical poetics. In the medium of cinema, Hashimoto's legacy finally becomes botanical.

Itō Seikō and Botanical Life

We can find traces of Hashimoto's legacy in other places as well. In his 1983 examination of cacti titled *Cacti Illusions* (*Shaboten gensō*), the novelist and cacti enthusiast Ryūtanji Yū writes of witnessing experiments on television in which polygraph machines were attached to cacti to facilitate communication. Although he does not state outright that it was the Hashimotos in front of the camera, we can likely assume it was. The television demonstrations inspired Ryūtanji to conduct his own experiments with cacti and polygraphs. Ryūtanji argues that cacti make for the ideal specimens because they are mere "blisters" that fill up with gas like balloons, unlike trees and grasses that are fibrous. This, Ryūtanji argues, makes them more conducive to electricity.[83]

More recent, however, is Itō Seikō's 2013 novel *Radio Imagination*—one of the best-known literary responses to 3.11. *Radio Imagination* presents a scenario that could have been taken directly from the pages of one of Hashimoto's largely forgotten texts. The story of a deceased DJ broadcasting out to the living and dead in the aftermath of 3.11, *Radio Imagination* presents trees as botanical media. Over sixty years after Haniya began writing *Dead Spirits*, Itō Seikō likewise embraced the mysterious realm of the forest as a means of working through trauma. *Radio Imagination* searches for plasticity in the botanical realm in response to the haunting losses occasioned by 3.11 and finds hope rather than fear within the cosmic presence of trees.

Itō Seikō has had a diverse career. He started performing as a rapper in the late 1980s, and he published his first novel, *No-Life King* (*Nō raifu kingu*), in 1988. Since the 1980s, Itō has continued writing both fiction and nonfiction while also creating music and contributing to Japanese television, radio, and cinema. Upon its release, *Radio Imagination* was his first novel in over fifteen years. Perhaps more than anything, Itō is well known for his writings about plants. In 1999, he published *Botanical Life* (*Botanikaru raifu—shokubutsu seikatsu*), a collection of online journal entries that spanned several years and discussed the plants Itō cared for on the veranda of his Tokyo apartment. The nonfictional work was subsequently made into a television drama, cementing Itō's reputation as a plant fanatic.

In *Botanical Life*, Itō Seikō writes directly of *kehai* in relation to plants. Like Haniya before him, he finds an aural quality to this presence: "The wind has become warm since around the end of April. A presence [*kehai*] that I find difficult to describe permeates the space among the plants which I cannot determine are either alive or dead. It is a subtle presence, but it is also blatant. . . . The plants emit this *kehai* throughout the veranda like a chirping cricket hidden from sight."[84] Much like Miwa Yoshi in *Dead Spirits*, the subtle presence of *kehai* renders Itō speechless in *Botanical Life*: "I nearly lose all words in front of these green beings [*midoritachi*] that possess a short but tremendous life force [*ikioi*]."[85] In language that resembles both the figurations of disturbance ecology in the films of Yanagimachi Mitsuo and Kawase Naomi, which I discuss in chapter 4, and the overwhelming destructive and reproductive power of plants found in the work of fellow "botanical writer" Hiromi Ito, which I discuss in chapter 5, Itō Seikō envisions the green life force of plants—a force he phytomorphically believes exists within humans as well—as simultaneously deadly and regenerative:

> Plants are a singular life form that emerge from planetary systems. They adopt a curious green substance from the exterior world, and silently wait for something. Like the previously mentioned *kehai*, I don't know what this "something" is. It is a "something" that is threatening, yet also desirable. I have the feeling that perhaps that "something" is the destruction of all life on earth. From that day forward, the cosmic substance called "green" that exists within each of us will cover the earth. At times I am shocked that I, too, am wishing for this day along with the plants.[86]

Itō's daily encounters with plants on his veranda give way to this complex, cosmic philosophical take on the relationship between plant and human life, and the relationship between life and death themselves. Itō views plants as both singular and multiple, infused with a "green" essence or life force that exists within human subjectivity, ready to emerge and cover the globe in "the destruction of all life on earth." Written in 1997 (two years after the final volume of *Dead Spirits* was published and also the year of Haniya's death), this passage from *Botanical Life* anticipates the coming of creative destruction. Read in the hindsight of the Tōhoku triple disaster, it eerily presages the stakes of *Radio Imagination*.

Radio Imagination reads like the curious offspring of Haniya's *Dead Spirits* and the writings of Hashimoto Ken. Like *Dead Spirits*, characters in *Radio Imagination* become botanical within assemblages with the forest. They look to move beyond the trauma of loss by becoming botanical. And like a page out of Hashimoto's parascience, the botanical assemblages of *Radio Imagination* become media in the form of a spirit radio that can communicate with the dead. The majority of the novel is told via direct address in the manner of a radio broadcast, through the voice of a deceased DJ named Ark. Miraculously, DJ Ark's broadcast reaches out to both the living and the dead in the aftermath of 3.11. He broadcasts from atop a giant cedar tree (which, again, is *sugi* in Japanese). From the top of this tree, the deceased DJ Ark gives a voice to those who have recently lost their own. He engages in on-air conversations with both living and dead "callers," several of whom recount their traumatic experiences. It is a work of many voices, a kind of collaborative narrative that is held together by the conceit of the radio program.

The novel arouses the spiritual affect of trees by drawing an explicit connection between the cedar tree and purported ancient spiritual beliefs. In an exchange with an elderly listener, DJ Ark is reminded of the spiritual significance of the cedar and the deep connection between dead spirits and the natural world. This spiritual connection is not of the kind Hashimoto wrote of in his discussion of *shinboku*. Instead, we find a more diffuse, more plastic form of spirituality that runs throughout *Radio Imagination*. The listener's story to DJ Ark is full of ellipses and contradictions, far from formalized: "I have heard that from time immemorial spirits [*tamashi*] have floated up to the top of trees. Spirits crawl the earth. . . . Since the arrival of Buddhism . . . we Japanese feel . . . the spirits of those who have passed have not only gone off to the far away Pure Land. They have surely merged [*dōka shite*] with trees and boulders. . . . They are closely watching over the living. . . . The other side is right there."[87] Within the spiritual logic of *Radio Imagination*, DJ Ark's dead spirit finds its natural place atop the cedar where it merges with the tree, as spirits have done "since time immemorial." But this spiritual merging, for all its connection to the past and nativist ideology, gives way to something new. The cedar tree forms an assemblage with the dead spirit of DJ Ark and becomes a spiritual medium that Itō incorporates into the medium of radio. The sacred tree transforms into a radio tower. If *The Secret Life of Plants* made it possible to imagine plants listening to music, *Radio Imagination* makes it possible for the botanical realm to broadcast music to listeners, both living and dead.

Moving Forward with the Dead

The botanical radio broadcast is DJ Ark's attempt to help the traumatized subjects of Japan's largest modern natural disaster cope with loss. Nearly twenty thousand people lost their lives on March 11, 2011, as a magnitude 9.1 earthquake off the northeast coast of Japan's main island Honshū set in motion a tsunami that reached over an estimated 130 feet in size. These two natural disasters resulted in a third, human-made disaster—the catastrophic meltdown at the Fukushima Daiichi Nuclear Power Plant. Like Haniya in the immediate postwar, Itō looked for a way to adapt to a radically changed world in the face of these crises. Also like Haniya, he saw in the botanical realm a framework for change in the face of unspeakable trauma. *Radio Imagination* is the story of how botanical media leads to plasticity and a rethinking of the human in the wake of 3.11. Put differently, *Radio Imagination* is the story of a post-3.11 botanical imagination.

DJ Ark explains that he named his son Sōsuke (the first character of which means "grass") "with the hope that, as he grew, he would be vibrant and able to bend in the wind, however it may blow." This is the plasticity the novel seeks, as *Radio Imagination* is populated with characters struggling to bend in the metaphorical wind of a post-3.11 Japan.[88] The resilient, ever-changing tree and the supple blade of grass bending in the wind present a new form of subjectivity that responds to the pervasive fear of both present and future catastrophe, a reasonable fear given the still-unfolding nuclear event and the ever-present possibility of future earthquakes and tsunamis. Plasticity allows for the construction of what Catherine Malabou calls "the post-traumatized subject" who, she claims, "disconnects the structure of the always already. The post-traumatized subject is the *nevermore* of the always already."[89] The post-traumatized subject is, in other words, like the "incessantly reorganizing self" that Takemura Shinichi finds in trees. Plant life helps Itō and the characters he writes into *Radio Imagination* learn how to grow anew as post-traumatized subjects.

Much like Abe Kōbō in "Dendrocacalia," however, Itō is cautious of moving too quickly past the trauma of crisis. Itō decides to "stay with the trouble" (to once again borrow Donna Haraway's phrase) by lingering with the dead spirits of 3.11. The novel's fourth and penultimate chapter is narrated from the perspective of S (a Fukushima volunteer who serves as the focus of the novel's second chapter as well) and consists entirely of a conversation between S and a woman with whom he has been engaged in a romantic relationship. Over the course of their conversation, it becomes clear that the woman has died in the disasters of 3.11. S discusses the important role the spirits of the dead play in constructing a future-oriented national subjectivity: "All we can do is remake this country together with the dead. Who are we that we continue to put a lid on the situation as if nothing happened? What will happen to this country?"[90] Despite its invocation of national identity, it is here that we find Itō's call to resistance. As a novel that looks to bring light to an unfolding crisis increasingly covered up by the state and news media, *Radio Imagination* resists like a tree and grows up and out of the "lid" put on the situation. As it does so, it finds common roots with past crises.

S looks back over Japanese history, finding in the past not a repetition of the "always already" but rather the potential for remaking: "At the time of the Tokyo air raids . . . and at the time when the atomic bomb was dropped on Hiroshima, and the time it was dropped on Nagasaki, and all the times of all the other many disasters, did we not move forward hand in hand with the dead? Yet, at some point, this country stopped being able to hold hands with the dead. Why is this? . . . I think it's because we stopped listening to their voices."[91] The assemblage of DJ Ark and the cedar tree restores the ability for the living to hear these voices. It opens a channel to the ghostly realm that Haniya likewise opened in the wake of war, including the "Tokyo air raids" of which Itō writes. Itō thus suggests that the only way to adapt and become anew is to look to the past for precedent and to look for a way to connect to the dead as a means of moving forward.

The giant cedar tree broadcasting out to the living and the dead seems to accomplish this need to both embrace the past and yet move on. Taking the *shokubutsusei* of trees seriously, we can see how trees like the one at the center of *Radio Imagination* are, to return to Takemura's claim, "a multiple 'narrative' in which various histories are interwoven" and "an incessantly reorganizing self." This image of the tree as a collection of histories that come together and support the growth of something new operates on several levels in Itō's work. It is in this image that we find the formal qualities that make *Radio Imagination* a work of becoming botanical. As a collection of voices speaking to one another—some alive, some dead, overlapping, and all contributing to the medium of the radio show—the novel itself comes to resemble a tree in its multiplicity and overlapping temporalities. At the same time, this is also the subjective state that the novel proposes as a means to rethink the human. *Radio Imagination* suggests that we

FIGURE 3.4. Radiation survey in Iitate. © Christian Åslund / Greenpeace.

should all become like the cedar itself, a medium that connects to the dead and to the past. It is in opening oneself up in this way that one allows a future to emerge.

Yet there is a bitter irony in Itō's arboreal futurity. This is because large swathes of forest (including many cedars) have been irradiated in the wake of 3.11 (see figure 3.4). Their future is murky at best, having not received the "decontamination" efforts towns and cities have. Radioactivity continues to circulate through forest ecosystems, impacting more-than-humans and humans alike.[92] The Japanese Forestry Agency has been hesitant to cut down these irradiated trees, fearing exposure to forest workers. At the same time, according to Satoru Miura, "radioactive contamination of forests has affected people economically and altered rural lifestyles, as forests comprise 71% of Fukushima Prefecture and many people make a living from harvesting forest products. Large-scale radioactive contamination of forests is the main problem interfering with revitalization and reconstruction following the Fukushima nuclear accident."[93] What kind of future can emerge from such a forest? If the prewar cedars of Inokashira Park became part of the "dead spirits" that haunt Haniya's writing, the cedars of the irradiated forests of Fukushima become something else in Itō's *Radio Imagination*. They become figures of the undead. They become botanical media that stand between humans and ionizing radiation that threatens to foreclose any possibility of an easy adaptation to crisis.

Botanical Subjectivity as Media, All the Way Down

The ninth and final volume of Haniya's *Dead Spirits* (published in 1995) presents an even murkier, less certain vision of the future than *Radio Imagination*. The principal characters all gather at a birthday celebration for Mrs. Tsuda, the mother of Miwa Yoshi's fiancé Yasuko. They sit around a large table and discuss many of the philosophical concerns the text has raised in its previous eight volumes over the span of nearly half a century. Miwa Yoshi and Yasuko discuss Miwa's philosophical difficulty in recognizing himself as an individuated subject. Miwa tells Yasuko, "The impression I am given is that throughout the history of existence, thinking that 'I, am, myself' is a singular trap meant to keep one existing."[94] In the final moments of the narrative, Miwa Yoshi is finally able to declare that "I am myself," albeit in a fractured form separated by commas. He concludes that the belief in the unified subjectivity that the phrase "I am myself" names is merely a "trap" set to keep one living, a subjective trap set in the name of futurity.

Yasuko counters by mentioning a previous conversation the two shared with their friend Kurokawa in chapter 8: "[Kurokawa] said: 'There is a "self" that is "the first of its kind in the universe." ... A creation that is entirely new and completely terrifying.'"[95] In this exchange, Yasuko offers Miwa Yoshi the promise of plasticity, of a future as a subject "[disconnected from] the structure of the always already," to return to Malabou's language. Yasuko offers the promise of a subjectivity that is "the first of its kind in the universe." Staring ahead into the darkness, Miwa loses his ability to speak and replies that he can "say no more." As the novel once again returns to silence, the figuration of botanical media emerges: "Afterwards, the reverberation of those short, blunt words were drowned out by a murmuring which unexpectedly arose above the long, narrow table. It was, so to speak, a deep, deep, deep murmuring that was difficult to hear, a murmuring that leaked out in a never-ending welcome from large, old floorboards of firm, woody substance in secret small rooms. It was like the reverberation of a secret and profound arboreal symphony [*mokushitsu kōkyōkyoku*] that plays on and on from distant and dim ancient forests."[96]

Language fails Miwa Yoshi once again, and the deep, cosmic reverberation of *kehai* returns. Like the cedar tree of *Radio Imagination*, the ancient forest medium of *Dead Spirits* broadcasts an unending musical score. Yet unlike the final song broadcast in Itō's novel—Bob Marley's "Redemption Song"—the "arboreal symphony" that hangs in the air of the final chapter of *Dead Spirits* does not offer a clear promise of a future. It does not offer any redemption. Instead, it remains in an infinite loop of indeterminacy, "forever welcoming" but "difficult to hear."

Not all forests were as "distant" and "difficult to hear" for Haniya, however. In a short 1986 essay/fragment that was likely intended for *Dead Spirits* titled "Echo" ("*Kodama*"), the forest begins to reverberate deep *within* human subjectivity, phyotomorphically: "Something dwells deep in the dark forest within my heart. When I cry out, 'I am myself,' all that comes back is the cruel, never-ending reverberation of 'You are still not yourself.'"[97] Haniya calls this reverberation a "mysterious echo that eternally negates, from deep in the dark forest within my heart."[98] With a dark forest deep inside his heart, Haniya (and/or perhaps Miwa Yoshi) is denied an individuated subjectivity, and he becomes a botanical medium *himself*, through which a never-ending echo (a word that literally translates from the Japanese *kodama* as "tree spirit") reverberates on and on, forever reminding him that he is other to himself.

As Haniya writes of his own subjectivity becoming a medium, he highlights how one medium can become an environment for yet another medium to emerge, as John Durham Peters has argued.[99] We see in this essay how the medium of writing is the enabling environment that provides a habitat for botanical media to emerge. For as much as Haniya and Itō were concerned with making contact with the dead, their works give life to language in the form of novels. Both Haniya and Itō ultimately suggest that writers themselves are, first and foremost, mediums. In the second chapter of *Radio Imagination*, during the long van ride from Fukushima to Tokyo that takes up the entirety of the chapter, a group of Fukushima volunteers discuss the role of spiritual mediums in communicating with the dead. They recount an experience of witnessing spiritual mediums at a memorial ceremony held at the Hiroshima Peace Park. S, who is a writer by trade and suffers from hearing problems, laments that he is unable to hear the mysterious spirit radio broadcast about which the others talk. He discusses the status of writing with his fellow volunteer Kimura, who tells the group: "I don't understand much about writers, but I think that they are those that hear voices in their hearts and give expression to them as words. It's not that they talk to them directly like spiritual mediums, but they turn the voices into words later on."[100] Kimura does not see writers as spiritual mediums that can speak directly to dead spirits, but he nonetheless views them as channels through which the words of the dead can emerge.

This is true of Haniya and Itō themselves. As they sought to become botanical and embraced trees as media, these two writers, separated by decades of turbulent history, became a type of media through which the *kehai* presence of dead spirits found a voice. Like Miwa Yoshi in *Dead Spirits*, they were no longer bound to a singular subjectivity that would declare "I am myself." Instead, they could embrace the space in between the "I am . . ." and the "myself," leaving it open as a channel for something new, for transformation. In the space of that medium, they brought forth, in words, the haunting reverberation that emerges in the space between trees, as *Dead Spirits* describes it: "The faint reverberation of trees rubbing up against each other from deep within a dark forest somewhere far, far away."[101] Perhaps if, as readers, we attune ourselves in the right way, we can hear something new in this botanical symphony, something interwoven with the past but sprouting new branches all the same.

4

BOTANICAL REGENERATION
Fire and Disturbance Ecology in the Films of
Yanagimachi Mitsuo and Kawase Naomi

In 2005, the Japanese Forestry Agency initiated the Kizukai Movement, a so-called People's Movement (*minzoku undo*) dedicated to the promotion of domestic wood use. In 2013, the agency commissioned an animated television commercial in which cute stop-motion bears made of wood deliver the following message: "Let's build the future out of wood."[1] Compared to the murky spiritual visions of the future that Haniya Yutaka and Itō Seikō glimpsed in the forest in the aftermath of crisis (as discussed in chapter 3), the Kizukai Movement proposes a clearer, brighter vision of Japan's future. It is a future in which the Japanese consumer is encouraged to buy products made of domestic lumber. While the word *kizukai* in the name *Kizukai Movement* means "using wood," it is also a homophone for a word that can be translated as "concern" or even "anxiety." According to the rhetoric of the Kizukai Movement, increased consumption of domestic timber resources can help alleviate national anxieties by revitalizing failing rural economies and restoring ecological balance to Japan's forests.

This seemingly contradictory idea—cutting down trees to help save the forest—is explained in further detail in a promotional advertisement for the movement (featuring the bears from the television commercial) published in the *Yomiuri Shinbun* newspaper:

> When you cut trees, the forest becomes healthy. Doesn't it seem unexpected to say so? Actually, in Japan, the resources of the forest continue to increase year by year. Meanwhile, there are forests which have fallen into ruin without periodic thinning. Therefore, shouldn't we make more

use of the domestic timber that has been thinned? From trees, houses. . . . From trees, buildings. . . . From trees, cities. . . . Now, as the potential of wood is rapidly widening from advances in technology, Japan's forests and ways of living are becoming more prosperous. With these hands, we can build a future in which we live together with nature.[2]

The idea is that, for the sake of Japan's future, there must be a return to the domestic forest, but not in the way Haniya or Itō envisioned, whereby humans learned to rethink themselves as a part of the greater forest ecosystem. The return to the forest envisioned by the Kizukai Movement is a return to domestic *forestry*, i.e., to the utilization of plant life as a resource. This return is needed, the movement argues, because the postwar greening efforts discussed in chapters 2 and 3 of this book have resulted, by the early 2000s, in mature forests that no longer adequately sequester carbon dioxide. Now is the time, they say, to turn these mature forests into consumer goods, thereby sequestering carbon and creating space for new trees to be planted. The Japanese Forestry Agency argues this point in a 2014 report: "In Japan, forests that were planted after World War II have begun to reach maturity and are ready for harvest. For circular utilization of such forest resources, the role of wood products industry is indispensable."[3] Below this claim is a colorful drawing of a forest represented as a circle, with the words "Well-balanced forest use" inside. Drawn as a part of this "well-balanced use" are a number of consumer products, including buildings, paper, and even drink containers.

Consumption of wood products is shown as part of a natural process, linking a personal, affectual relationship with wood to the overall health of not only the forests but also the nation itself and finally the planet at large. The Kizukai Movement website boldly declares: "Stop global warming with the use of domestic wood products." The logic of this neoliberal claim (as well as the impetus for the creation of the Kizukai Movement) emerges from the goals of the Kyoto Protocol:

> In the First Commitment Period of the Kyoto Protocol [the five-year period from 2008 to 2012], Japan committed to a reduction of CO_2 emissions by 6% from 1990 levels. 3.8% of this was to be achieved through the increased absorption rate of CO_2 by domestic Japanese forests. However, in Japan, forests inaccessible for maintenance have grown, and as they continue to fall into ruin, the success of the Kyoto Protocol carbon dioxide reduction objective has become doubtful. Because of this, the Forestry Agency, beginning in 2005, commenced with the "Kizukai Movement" initiative as a people's movement. Through proactive use of domestic wood, the movement encourages the revitalization of mountain villages, and the creation of healthy forests that amply absorb CO_2.[4]

The argument is that to "create" new forests that can better absorb CO_2 emissions, Japan must use more domestic wood and cut down trees to reverse the effects of climate change. In the process, Japan's rural villages will be "revitalized."

That nearly 70 percent of Japan's landmass is today covered in forests may seem surprising in this era of mass deforestation and ecological scarcity. As Conrad Totman writes, quite bluntly, in his classic 1989 account of premodern Japanese forestry *The Green Archipelago*: "Japan today should be an impoverished, slum-ridden, peasant society subsisting on a barren, eroded moonscape characterized by bald mountains and debris-strewn lowlands. Instead, it is a highly industrialized society living in a luxuriant green realm."[5] Environmentalists have used Japan's long history of forest management to argue for a tradition of conservation efforts, often seen as an expression of Japan's so-called unique love of nature. The reality, of course, is far more complicated. To be sure, part of the story of Japan's enduring forests can be traced to premodern governmental restrictions and efforts at reforestation beginning in the early modern Tokugawa period (1603–1867), but far from growing out of a recognition of the intrinsic value of forests for their own sake (an ideology linked to *Airin shisō*, as discussed in chapter 2), Totman argues that conservation and reforestation efforts grew in response to exploitative deforestation stemming from the construction of monumental architecture intended to broadcast the power of the imperial throne.

The other half of the story, namely Japan's post–World War II "economic miracle," has even less claim to notions of sustainability. As Peter Dauvergne writes in his 1997 account of Japan's exploitative forestry practices in Southeast Asia: "All countries cast ecological shadows. But Japan's is perhaps the world's largest. This is in part because of limited Japanese natural resources and rapid economic growth since World War II . . . Japan's sixteen general trading companies have triggered widespread environmental degradation in resource-rich countries."[6] Much of this degradation has come from the importation of tropical timber from Southeast Asia, to the extent that, in 1997, Dauvergne claims: "Japan has been the world's largest tropical timber importer since the 1960s."[7] When trees became scarce in one Southeast Asian country, Japan turned to another, contributing to mass deforestation in the region at large. All the while, Japan's own forests—many of which are timber plantations in the first place—sat relatively untouched. Hence the need for "revitalization."

This chapter follows chapter 3 and stays in the forest, but it turns to a new medium: cinema. I examine in this chapter cinematic representations of the crises surrounding Japan's "forgotten" forests. Following the collapse of the Japanese Empire and the subsequent loss of colonial resources, Japan began afforestation efforts at home while simultaneously exploiting timber resources throughout

Southeast Asia. All the while, local forestry industries in Japan's rural regions suffered from economic decline and depopulation. As John Knight has demonstrated, the forestry laborer workforce decreased by over four-fifths in the decades between the 1960s and the 1990s.[8] The films I discuss in this chapter grapple with the consequences of Japan's postwar economic imperialism from within rural forestry villages left behind by the postwar economic miracle. Like other texts discussed in this book, they do not revel in spectacular crisis; rather, they are concerned with the violence of Japan's economic imperialism in Southeast Asia only insofar as said violence can be understood as "both a backdrop to and condition for the intimate terrain of . . . everyday lives," to return once again to the words of Christopher Dole et al. in their introduction to *The Time of Catastrophe*.[9] Both films discussed in this chapter focus on the local forestry economy and the effects of its collapse on the figure of the *somabito*, a traditional name for the foresters who have lived and worked in rural Japan stretching back as far as the late fourteenth century.[10]

These films—Yanagimachi Mitsuo's *Fire Festival* (*Himatsuri*, 1985) and Kawase Naomi's *Vision* (2018)—depict the decline of rural forestry communities and feature *somabito* who strive for ecological, economic, and spiritual regeneration in the face of economic crisis. In other words, they share the Kizukai Movement's concern with notions of futurity and yearn for a similar notion of revitalization. But far from proposing a capitalist solution steeped in neoliberal responsibility placed on the consumer, these two films offer a far more radical (and, indeed, far more ecological) solution: burn it all down. Only by clearing away what has come before, these films suggest, can something truly new take hold. This chapter presents the most radical (and perhaps even dangerous) rethinking of plant life and the human presented in this book—a rethinking that, taken to its logical end point, can be used to justify violence. However, both films present their respective moments of violence as ritualistic. Violence becomes part of a spiritual relationship to the forest, a necessary rite that sets things right. The films I discuss in this chapter take the logic of plant life, specifically its ability to regrow and thrive in the aftermath of destruction, and link it up to local spiritual practice in the name of futurity.

The *somabito* of these films come to recognize the generative possibilities inherent in fire's destructive capabilities and realize that their own future depends on the long-term health of the forest ecosystem. They embrace the logic of disturbance ecology, a *shokubutsusei* of the forest in which fire opens space for new growth. In the act of embracing this mode of destructive-yet-regenerative ecological thinking, the *somabito* characters come to see themselves as part of the forest, not unlike the characters of the novels discussed in chapter 3. But what makes the films discussed in this chapter different from the novels discussed in chapter 3 is the extent to which human characters rethink themselves as a part of the forest. They put plants first and prioritize the best interests of the forest, even when such rethinking results in their own death, as well as the deaths of their immediate family members. By becoming botanical through the logic of disturbance ecology, the *somabito* of these films embody a botanical imagination and embrace death as a way forward. However, if we pay close attention to plants and allow their *shokubutsusei* to serve as a framework through which to read the violence and embrace of death on display, we see that both *Fire Festival* and *Vision* not only rethink the human as more plantlike; they also rethink death itself as both ritual and botanical.

Disturbance Ecology

Fire Festival and *Vision* demonstrate how disturbance and destruction help sculpt and maintain both the material ecology of the forest and a botanical subjectivity that sees itself as a part of the forest. The multispecies anthropologist Anna Tsing describes the importance of disturbances in facilitating the resurgence of ecosystems: "Disturbances, human and otherwise, knock out multispecies assemblages—yet livable ecologies come back. After a forest fire, seedlings sprout in the ashes, and, with time, another forest may grow up in the burn. The regrowing forest is an example of what I am calling *resurgence*. The cross-species relations that make forests possible are renewed in the regrowing forest. Resurgence is the work of many organisms, negotiating across differences, to forge assemblages of multispecies livability in the midst of disturbance. Humans cannot continue their livelihoods without it."[11]

We can see in Tsing's figuration of disturbance ecology something similar to Catherine Malabou's notion of destructive plasticity, as I have been invoking it in this book. As the forest ecosystem is destroyed by fire and subsequently reconfigured, so, too, is subjectivity as it becomes botanical. The transformative properties of fire kindle a rethinking of the human. As Catherine Malabou explains, violent transformation can be generative: "Destruction too is formative. A smashed-up face is still a face, a stump a limb, a traumatized psyche remains a psyche. Destruction has its own sculpting tools."[12] Just as the *somabito* sculpts the forest with his axe or chainsaw, the films of Yanagimachi and Kawase use the image of destruction by fire to carve out a notion of the future for the fading horizon of the *somabito* and the multispecies assemblage that is the forest.

Although the science of disturbance ecology is the model through which I argue that the films discussed in this chapter become botanical, once again, a spiritual understanding of plant life is paramount to the transformation at each film's core. Both *Fire Festival* and *Vision* stage the plasticity of disturbance ecology via a spiritual relationship to the forest that is inscribed into the respective settings of each film. They each make legible a spiritual presence that permeates the forest, not unlike the presence of *kehai* that floats throughout the texts discussed in the previous chapter. Whereas Haniya's figuration of *kehai* was decidedly nonreligious, the spirituality found in both *Fire Festival* and *Vision* is closely tied to local manifestations of Shinto and Buddhist practice. Where Haniya resisted a State Shinto that abstracted such practices to imperial ends, the religious affect of the films discussed in this chapter are closely tied to the land and the very ecological connections between humans and plant life that the films look to renew.

This spiritual presence is visible in both films in part through cinematography that creates what I call a *cinematic-botanical subjectivity*. As the camera floats between the trees of the forest and the human foresters, the films of Yanagimachi and Kawase portray forests as multispecies assemblages that give equal weight to the subjectivity of both, creating a visual botanical poetics. Here is where these films take on a plantlike form, a trait I have been arguing is necessary for the trope of becoming botanical. The subjectivity fashioned by each film's cinematography is multiple and at a scale and tempo more aligned with the botanical realm than the human realm. Read against the long religious history of the film's settings (the Kii Peninsula in *Fire Festival* and the Yoshino region of Nara Prefecture in *Vision*), the free-floating subject position sculpted by each film's cinematography likewise takes on an all-seeing perspective inhabited by the *kami*, or local gods, that move among the trees. This botanical-spiritual presence participates in the enacting of disturbance ecology, leading to a revitalization of economically depressed rural communities far outside the capitalist framework proposed by the Kizukai Movement. Therein lies their botanical resistance.

Fire Festival and *Vision* understand that disturbance renews the "cross-species relations that make forests possible" (to return to Anna Tsing's claim), but they arrive at this conclusion in dramatically different ways. *Fire Festival* reaches the conclusion that destruction is necessary for resurgence through its fiercely masculine protagonist Tatsuo, a character so egoistic and vulgar that critics at the time of its release were largely unable to recognize the ecological logic he embodies and subsequently dismissed him as a "pigheaded reactionary" and the film overall as "not ecological."[13] *Vision*, on the other hand, reaches the logic of disturbance ecology through the outright elimination of the human ego at the level of the species. Unlike *Fire Festival*, it does not cling to the notion of a unique, individuated character who ultimately must sacrifice himself for the greater good of the forest ecosystem. Rather, *Vision* takes the ecological logic of disturbance ecology and imagines that the destruction of fire can usher in a future in which *all* of humanity undergoes an evolutionary change that results in the dissolution of the human ego. It suggests that anyone can become botanical by adopting the subjectivity of the *somabito* and embracing the generative potentiality of destructive plasticity.

Another significant difference between the two films concerns the politics of their writers. This chapter places side-by-side two figures whose politics appear at sharp odds with one another: the prominent postwar novelist and critic Nakagami Kenji and director Kawase Naomi. Nakagami, who wrote the screenplay for Yanagimachi's *Fire Festival*, was a fervent critic of the Japanese state, a stance informed by his Burakumin (or outcaste) status in Japan.[14] Kawase Naomi, on the other hand, has recently demonstrated nationalist sympathies, as glimpsed in her official two-part documentary film covering the highly controversial 2020 Tokyo Olympics.[15] While their respective relationships to the state sit on opposite sides of the political spectrum, both Nakagami and Kawase think deeply about plant life in their work, and both arrive at the logic of disturbance ecology as a means of regeneration. That these two share an affinity for the forest and its regenerative *shokubutsusei* demonstrates the ambivalence inherent in becoming botanical. As we have seen in previous chapters, becoming botanical, for all of its radical possibilities, also holds the potential to be activated in more conservative contexts. Once again, this chapter demonstrates that context matters. After all, not all fire leads to regeneration.

The Otherworldly Atmosphere of *Fire Festival*

Yanagimachi's *Fire Festival* opens with an image of fire. Flames burn against a black backdrop as the film's opening credits run, for nearly three minutes, accompanied by a ghostly score written by the renowned composer Takemitsu Tōru. In these opening moments, droning tones of low-end brass instruments are punctuated by swells of shrill flutes that give way to a quiet undercurrent of marimba. The flames these sounds accompany are almost certainly from the torches used in the ritual Fire Festival of the film's title. The Fire Festival (which is held annually in the city of Shingū on the heavily forested Kii Peninsula in Wakayama Prefecture) is a ritual of purification performed to welcome the coming of spring. Within the cosmology of the festival (which is properly called the Lantern Festival, or *Otōmatsuri*), fire leads to new growth. By the film's end, protagonist Tatsuo will embody the logic of this festival and leave a fiery legacy behind. He will kill himself and his family for the greater good of the forest.

It is a shocking tale but one well in line with Yanagimachi's provocative cinematic oeuvre. Yanagimachi began his career with the 1976 film *God Speed You! Black Emperor* (*Goddo spiido yū! BLACK EMPEROR*), a 16mm documentary that follows a *bōsōzoku* motorcycle gang. His second (and first feature) film was a 1979 adaptation of Nakagami Kenji's tense and violent novella *A 19-Year-Old's Map* (*Jūkyūsai no chizu*). In 1982, he released *Farewell to the Beloved Land* (*Saraba itoshiki daichi*), a harrowing tale of a violent drug addict set against the pastoral beauty of Yanagimachi's native Ibaraki Prefecture. *Fire Festival* was Yanagimachi's fourth feature-length film. Nakagami Kenji produced the screenplay, marking his first foray into screenwriting. He subsequently wrote a novelization of the story as well.

Fire Festival is set in the small village of Nigishima, on the Kii Peninsula in the Kumano region of Mie Prefecture (also known by its historical name Kishū). Nigishima is home to lush, mountainous forests that have supported Tatsuo (played by Kitaōji Kinya) and his family since time immemorial. The Kii Peninsula was also Nakagami Kenji's birthplace and a frequent setting for his work. Nakagami had previously explored the region's complex intersections of history and mythology (and, yes, plant life) in his 1977 book *Ki Province: The Tale of the Land of Trees and the Land of Roots* (*Kishū: Ki no kuni, ne no kuni monogatari*). The forested landscape of the Kumano region, it has been said, is a place in which "the mythologies of the past *inhabit* the present."[16] Kumano is home to many important religious sites and is the birthplace of Shūgendō, a form of Buddhist asceticism that is intimately tied to the mountains and waters of the region. This spiritual history infuses the landscape of film and plays a central role in its eventual embrace of disturbance ecology. Characters in *Fire Festival* frequently discuss the Yama no Kami, the "mountain goddess" who resides in the forest and with whom Tatsuo is shown to have a singular relationship. The presence of the Yama no Kami is signaled both visually and aurally: branches waving in the wind seem to signal the *kami* manifesting itself through botanical media (as discussed in chapter 3), as does Takemitsu's haunting score.

The spiritual landscape of Kumano holds religious and political significance that is inseparable from images of death, fire, and rebirth and stretches back to Japan's earliest extant mythological histories. According to the *Nihon shoki*, an official mytho-history dating to 720 AD, the Hana no Iwa Shrine in Kumano marks the spot where Izanami (a deity who, along with her male counterpart Izanagi, gave birth to both the islands of Japan and the myriad gods, as briefly mentioned in chapter 1) was entombed after dying while giving birth to the deity of fire.[17] The Kii Peninsula is likewise home to the mythological site in which Japan's first emperor ascended the land. This latter belief plays directly into the film's narrative, as the villagers of Nigishima attempt to use the myth to rebrand their town as a potential site for tourism once the local economy falls on hard times.

The rich confluence of history and spirituality has made Kumano a popular pilgrimage destination for centuries. D. Max Moerman explains how this rich tapestry of religious and political history has resulted in Kumano's otherworldly aura. Kumano, he argues, is seen as a place that has "contained a multiplicity of other worlds: the homelands of an ancestral past and the celestial paradises of Buddhist rebirth."[18] Yanagimachi himself has spoken of *Fire Festival*'s setting as just such a place of otherworldliness: "I went time and again into the mountains of Kishū to hunt for locations . . . I went all over the place. And while I wouldn't go so far as to say these were unique experiences, I encountered enough phenomena along the way that I can imagine that kind of world: one in which the present world and the other world [*takai*] coexist."[19]

Yanagimachi's description of Kumano resembles works discussed in chapter 3 of this book, as they presented the forest as a meeting place for the living and the dead. Indeed, the forests (and forestry) of Kumano are tied to the spiritual history of the region, as the Hongū Shrine (one of the three major shrines of Kumano) enshrines the deity Ketsumiko no Ōkami, a god connected to the forested mountains and the forestry industry of the area more broadly.[20] The Kii Peninsula is famous for its old-growth cedar (*sugi*) and cypress (*hinoki*) forests, although ecologists and historians remind us that these forests are far from primeval. According to entomologist Gotō Shin, the cedar forests of Kumano are both a natural legacy of the region and a product of Japan's postwar "greening" efforts to rehabilitate the war-torn landscape.[21] Conrad Totman claims that human management and planning of the region's forests can be traced back much earlier, to the eighteenth century.[22] In either case, it is clear that humans have long lived and worked in these forests, and their understanding of the plant life that populates the forests is both scientific and spiritual. As an exploration of the failing forestry industry in Nigishima, *Fire Festival* lingers in the forest, giving long stretches of screen time to the tree-filled landscape, one that has historically existed in the flux of human management (see figure 4.1). As *somabito* sculpted the forests of Kumano for generations (managing the cycles of death and renewal in the forest ecosystem), they likewise sculpted a subjectivity through destructive plasticity and became botanical. This is Tatsuo's goal in *Fire Festival*—to usher in a new cycle.

Forests of Conflict

Fire Festival portrays the Kumano region as an ecosystem in dire need of change and regeneration. Like many rural communities in postwar Japan, Nigishima suffers from depopulation and economic depression. By the time of the film's release, rural depopulation (*kasoka*) had been acknowledged as a crisis for over a decade. In 1970, the first national law aimed at countering depopulation took

FIGURE 4.1. The forested landscape of Nigishima in *Fire Festival*.

effect. The goals of this countermeasure were fourfold: "to prevent excessive decreases in population," "to strengthen the infrastructure of local communities," "to improve the welfare of local residents," and "to correct regional disparities."[23] When the law was revised and reenacted ten years later in 1980 (five years before the release of *Fire Festival*), these objectives were partially rewritten to better address the economic effects of depopulation. The first objective of the 1980 version of the law reads: "promotion of depopulated areas." Gone is the language of strengthening infrastructure. In its place is a call to "increase employment."[24]

Fire Festival features several flashbacks that demonstrate the optimism the village experienced in the early years of Japan's postwar economic regrowth. The film highlights the completion of the Kisei Honsen Railway Line in 1959, an important piece of infrastructure that connected Mie Prefecture and Wakayama Prefecture along the Kii Peninsula. The enthusiasm and hope for the future witnessed in these flashbacks contrast sharply with the village's narrative present roughly twenty years later. The railway has not solved the region's economic woes. Both the lumber and fishing economies have become unsustainable in this remote area. As *Fire Festival* opens, the village has decided to rebrand itself as a tourist destination, a decision very much in line with the depopulation countermeasures discussed above. The focus of this revitalization is a proposed aquatic park that would commemorate the ascent of Japan's legendary first ruler, Emperor Jimmu, and effectively end the traditional livelihoods of the village. There is an irony at play here. The villagers believe the only way to survive as their local economies collapse under the weight of the state's increased dependence on imported natural resources is to construct a monument celebrating the divine authority of the imperial household.

Not all of the villagers consent to this plan, however. Nigishima's forest people (the *somabito*) and its ocean people (those involved in fishing) are at odds over the village's prospects for the future. The fishing community embraces the idea of the aquatic park, while Tatsuo adamantly opposes the development and changes it will bring to the forest ecosystem and the profession of the *somabito*. He believes these changes will not lead to regeneration. The tension between the village's vision of the future and Tatsuo's embodiment of an older, now largely incomprehensible (to his fellow villagers) way of inhabiting the world is at the heart of *Fire Festival*'s tale of becoming botanical. For the creators of the film, Tatsuo is as much a representative of the mythological era that resides within the otherworldly space of Kumano as the mythological Emperor Jimmu. Nakagami Kenji saw Tatsuo as directly linked to Japan's earliest mythology. In a conversation with the feminist critic Ueno Chizuko, Nakagami likens Tatsuo (at Ueno's suggestion) to the figure of Susanoo, brother of the Sun Goddess Amaterasu within traditional Japanese mythology. Susanoo is a wild and excessive figure, much like Tatsuo. Nakagami sees *Fire Festival* as "the tale of the final Susanoo—the one that leads into destruction."[25] Yanagimachi echoes Nakagami's eco-mythologizing, claiming that, with *Fire Festival*, he wanted to explore a world in which the separation of humans and the natural world had not yet occurred: "I wanted to go back to the Jōmon Period [a pre-agriculture, prehistoric time, c. 7000 BC–300 BC] . . . and incorporate that period of mythology into contemporary life in a very concrete way. Back then human beings and animals were not separated but were harmonic and fused."[26] Tatsuo's subjectivity is fused in the way Yanagimachi describes. He is not separate from the forest and its spiritual presence. Rather, he is an integral part of it.

Where in the previous chapters of this book writers turned to new theories of evolution and botanical science (and paranormal pseudoscience) to forge a new relationship with the botanical world, in *Fire Festival*, Yanagimachi and Nakagami attempt to return to prehistoric understandings of plant life (however idealized they may be) in order to rethink the human. According to film critic Ogi Masahiro, Yanagimachi's mythical imagining of Jōmon-era harmony between humans and more-than-humans belongs to a world not fully domesticated. He invokes botanical language to make this point:

> When a certain botanist told me that "the English word 'domestication' cannot be rendered into Japanese," I was shocked. Of course, one can find a matching idiom in an English-to-Japanese dictionary, such as *kainarashi* (tamed) or *junchi* (acclimatization). But, the botanist said, the

substance of the concept (of domestication) cannot be found in Japan. This claim was something of a hyperbole. But I had occasion to think about it, and I had a thought that stood out—Encyclopedia Britannica concisely summarizes the concept of domestication as "a process of genetic reorganization in which wild animals and plants are cultivated to live within a household for human benefit."[27]

The thought that stood out to Ogi after reading this definition was that the Japanese are a "misfit" people that never fully made the historical transformation from a hunter/gatherer existence to that of an agriculture-based existence. He claims this helps explain the contradiction of a people that "openly destroy nature and yet worship natural objects."[28] For Ogi, Tatsuo represents a plant or animal that is only partially domesticated: "While I watched Yanagimachi Mitsuo's *Fire Festival*, I entered an odd state of exaltation. I thought, 'This is it.' This was my hypothetical Japanese misfit, that fundamental contradiction between 'gatherer' and 'cultivator.'"[29] Tatsuo's practice of forestry contributes to this misfit subjectivity. As a *somabito*, he does not fit in the changing world of Nigishima or that of postwar Japan writ large. He is an anachronism facing the crisis of being left behind by a rapidly changing national economy that benefits from the exploitation of timber resources abroad. In their adherence to the traditional profession of forest management (and their adherence to its sometimes-brutal ecological logic that results in the death of more-than-humans), the *somabito* are misfits. Inamoto Tadashi has referred to *somabito* as "woodcutter(s) of a former age."[30] *Fire Festival*, in turn, asks how the *somabito* might be able to usher in a new age.

Those in favor of building the aquatic park think tourism will revitalize the village. This was a common response to the economic woes of rural Japan around the time Yanagimachi filmed *Fire Festival*, as John Knight explains in relation to Hongū, near Nigishima: "By the late 1970s and early 1980s, forestry was in decline, and the strategy of *kigyo yuchi* (the beckoning of industry to rural areas) was widely seen to have failed as the scale of industrial relocation was not sufficient to offset trends in rural depopulation. The rural exodus continued. . . . National subsidies such as support for rice prices, infrastructural investment, and general revenue support for rural municipalities looked endangered. . . . Some new source of employment was seen as vital. Tourism expanded greatly throughout the 1980s but it did not meet local developmental aspirations."[31]

While efforts to build a tourist economy in the area did not pan out, in *Fire Festival*, members of the local Nigishima community (along with developers from the city) pressure Tatsuo to sell his family home, as his land sits within the proposed site for development. Tatsuo's family is the last holdout. The local land broker explains to Tatsuo's wife and mother that if they refuse to sell, the plans for the aquatic park must be abandoned. Tatsuo's mother is begrudgingly open to the idea of selling the land and is tasked with convincing Tatsuo to change his mind. In the film's final scenes, Tatsuo visits the neighboring town of Shingū to participate in the annual Fire Festival. It is here that the film arrives at its botanical solution for change. Believing that he is doing what is best for the continued survival of the forest, Tatsuo returns home and kills his entire family (including his mother, wife, and two children) before turning the gun on himself. Nakagami took inspiration for this murder-suicide from an actual event that occurred in the Kumano region in 1980.[32] Although the specifics differ from those depicted in the film, Nakagami clearly saw in the horrific incident a model through which to explore the crisis of *kasoka*, or rural depopulation. Nakagami rendered this horrific incident environmental, for through his murder-suicide, Tatsuo brings the ritual fire of the Fire Festival home and introduces a disturbance akin to a forest fire into the ecosystem of Nigishima in order to, in Anna Tsing's words, renew the "cross-species relations that make forests possible." In the process, he controversially takes on the role of a martyr, sacrificing himself for the greater good of the forest. Tatsuo reaches the outermost boundaries of becoming botanical, and his violent actions open up the potential for a future made possible by his own fiery death.

Cinematic-Botanical Subjectivity

As he acts on behalf of the forest, Tatsuo embodies a shocking form of botanical subjectivity. Through his death, Tatsuo appears to put his human needs aside and do what is best for the future of the forest. Yet there is a curious tension at play in *Fire Festival*, as Tatsuo is the only member of the *somabito* forestry community shown to have this ecological knowledge. While the film goes to great lengths to show how Tatsuo sees himself as part of the forest, it ends up highlighting the uniqueness of Tatsuo's character. Ultimately, *Fire Festival* carves out an egoistic botanical subjectivity available only to Tatsuo and not to the other *somabito* characters in the film. It is a far cry from the utopian, multiple botanical subjectivity of Osaki Midori (as discussed in chapter 1) and also a far cry from the botanical subjectivity of Miwa Yoshi discussed in chapter 3. In becoming botanical, Miwa Yoshi was unable to declare "I am myself." Tatsuo's sense of "I" is overbearing in *Fire Festival*. This is why his enactment of disturbance ecology takes the form of suicide. He believes, egotistically, that he must become a martyr and that his death can become the very disturbance that leads to the regeneration of the greater ecosystem.

The botanical subjectivity that leads Tatsuo to believe that he alone can renew the forest is legible in the opening moments of the film. As the opening credits fade out, a high-angle wide shot of a cedar grove (in which a group of foresters are diminished and barely visible) appears and changes to a shot of a cedar falling directly toward the camera, its angle moving downward with the movement of the falling tree. This is followed by a low-angle shot showing the group of foresters at work. From here, the camera returns to a wide expanse of trees, with several distant mountains visible in the background. Tatsuo emerges and partially fills the foreground, along with his younger friend and coworker Ryōta. A cedar begins to fall directly toward the two men (and the camera). Tatsuo calmly warns Ryōta to move out of the way and then casually walks out of frame. As the two return to the frame and begin trimming the newly fallen tree of its branches, the camera pans up, looking back out over the forested mountains in the distance. The camera moves from the high treetops into the world of the foresters and further down to the perspective of Tatsuo, only to return to where it started among the tall trees, bringing together different scales of the forest, both human and more-than-human, but clearly marking Tatsuo as centrally important.

Famed cinematographer Tamura Masaki's camerawork suggests a flowing subjectivity that moves through the assemblage of trees and Tatsuo himself. It is a cinematic-botanical subjectivity. Indeed, Yanagimachi has claimed that several scenes of the film are meant to demonstrate the perspective of the trees themselves.[33] Tamura's cinematography highlights the relationship between the *somabito* and the trees to which they tend and portrays the work of the *somabito* as a natural and necessary cross-species relationship that maintains the ecological health of the forest. Yet it is Tatsuo and his unique botanical subjectivity that serves as the crux through which *Fire Festival* develops its ecological vision of forest health. He is repeatedly shown as having intimate knowledge of the forest that eludes everyone else. He alone knows when trees will fall and when rain will stop. He alone knows what will please and what will anger the Yama no Kami that presides over the forest. He repeatedly calls the spiritual presence "his girlfriend" and exposes his naked body to please her.

Even with this overwhelmingly strong sense of self, Tatsuo experiences himself as a part of the forest. He, in turn, thinks as a part of the forest. In one scene, Tamura's camera pans from a medium angle over a darkened forest grove, where we see Tatsuo and his crew standing on ladders hacking away at branches through the gaps between trees. The axe blades hitting wood is the only sound we hear. The camera pulls up toward the forest canopy, and light streams in between the branches. Ryōta calls out for Tatsuo, shattering the relative silence. Suddenly it is revealed (in an apparent temporal jump) that the two men stand on opposite sides of a gorge, their lewd conversation echoing back and forth over the gorge's expanse.

The scene is stunningly verdant. The men speak with an exuberance that carries over the mountain, as if they are overcome by the life teeming around them. Ryōta informs Tatsuo that he has caught something in his hunting trap. As the men run over to see Ryōta's handiwork, they discover he has used a sacred tree to make the snare. As the men begin to panic, Tatsuo tells them not to worry. He reminds them that the Yama no Kami is his girlfriend. He then squeezes the blood out of the dead bird that has been caught in the snare and smears it up his arm. *Fire Festival* suggests that a sense of order has been restored by Tatsuo's ritualistic embrace of death. The cedar tree directly behind Tatsuo suddenly begins to rustle, as if in agreement with Tatsuo's actions. The tree and Tatsuo come together in this moment, and a botanical subjectivity flows between them to alert viewers to the fact that they are partners in maintaining the proper balance of the forest. Throughout the film, Tatsuo is shown to have this kind of unique insight into an ecological system that includes humans, more-than-human animals, and plants, as well as the spiritual beings that inhabit the mountains and sea. This forest thinking affords him an intimate ecological knowledge of what the forest needs to renew itself.

Tatsuo has an epiphany in the forest near the end of the film. The scene in question opens with the silence of the forest, the only sound to be heard emerging from Tatsuo's axe as it strikes a giant cedar and echoes across the forested expanse. After a few trees fall, the film cuts away to a scenic shot of the forest reflected in water. The ghostly soundtrack of Takemitsu Tōru's score becomes audible. The high-pitched swells of flute come and go against a low rumble, just as they did in the opening moments of the film. We then see the group of *somabito* looking up, commenting on the coming rain. The otherworldliness of the music overlaps with the dark atmosphere visible in the rain clouds that come to fill the screen. A thick mist descends on the mountains. The *somabito* decide to descend the mountain in anticipation of the approaching weather. Ryōta continues to work, and the sound of his chainsaw becomes hidden in Takemitsu's increasingly ominous soundtrack. Suddenly the atmosphere becomes palpable and the mysterious spiritual aura that has clung to the forest throughout the film materializes as a heavy rain that floods the land. The rain's near-deafening sound erupts over Takemitsu's score and covers over all other noises. The heavy rain drenches fallen trees and the *somabito* alike. Everything within the forest matrix comes together through this atmospheric intrusion.

Once again, Tatsuo is singled out as having a unique insight into the significance of this event and its implications for the ecology of the forest. Tatsuo and Ryōta climb down the mountain together, but Tatsuo stops at the base of a massive tree. Ryōta pleads with Tatsuo to keep going, but Tatsuo brushes him off, stating that the rain will soon stop. He leans back on the tree and confidently declares: "I know the mountain" (*Yama no koto wa ore ga shittoru*).[34] Tatsuo (in his egoistic role as protector) holds Ryōta in an embrace for a brief spell to keep him warm, until Ryōta decides to leave Tatsuo and head down the mountain alone. Throughout the film, the *somabito* share a homosocial bond that brims with both violent and sexual energy. They talk openly about sex and engage in physical contact through wrestling and the like. The bond between Tatsuo and Ryōta is particularly close. It is clear throughout that Ryōta idolizes Tatsuo, admiring his sexual prowess. Ryōta enters into a sexual relationship with Tatsuo's childhood sweetheart/current sexual partner Kimiko and, in one scene, adopts Tatsuo's characteristic way of walking while visiting Kimiko. The tenderness Tatsuo shows Ryōta in the scene in the rain, however (as he embraces him in silence and holds Ryōta's face against his chest) seems too much for Ryōta to bear. It is as if, in the lack of wildness or violent affect, Ryōta is no longer able to share affection with Tatsuo. Or perhaps it is the fear of the coming storm that sends him running. In either case, it is clear that Ryōta does not understand the mountain or the Yama no Kami in the same way Tatsuo does and that this understanding bears on the homosocial and potentially sexual energy that flows between them.

Once Ryōta leaves, Tatsuo faces the massive tree, spreads his arms wide, and embraces it with his whole body (see figure 4.2). Takemitsu's score reemerges, signaling the presence of the Yama no Kami. A close-up of Tatsuo's hands shows him slapping and groping the tree in a manner equally violent and sexual. Yanagimachi has characterized this scene as Tatsuo having sex with the Yama no Kami.[35] The camera pulls back into a wide angle that diminishes Tatsuo at the bottom of the massive cedar. As he continues to pound his body against the tree, the rain suddenly stops.

Tatsuo then has an ecological epiphany that links the spiritual renewal of the Fire Festival to the material renewal of the forest ecosystem through disturbance ecology. A forceful wind blows from the foreground of the frame into the background where Tatsuo stands embracing the tree. Tatsuo walks through the trees blowing about violently in the wind and watches as one tree breaks and falls into the front of the frame. The camera now moves behind Tatsuo, who stares at the fallen tree for a moment before declaring: "I understand" (*Wakatta*). Something important has passed between the forest and Tatsuo, and his egoistic botanical subjectivity is encapsulated in this statement. He understands what the forest needs him to do, but no one else (including the viewer) has access to this knowledge until the final moments of the film.

In this scene, Tatsuo alone understands the wishes of the Yama no Kami and the greater forest assemblage. He subsequently thinks like the forest. He becomes botanical and finally understands what the forest wants him to do in response

FIGURE 4.2. Tatsuo's "sex scene" with the Yama no Kami in *Fire Festival*.

to the threat of development. He now knows something about the relationship between destruction and resurgence, between death and futurity. At the forest's behest, Tatsuo taps into the spiritual legacy of the land and attends the Fire Festival, where he partakes in the ceremonial ritual of renewal by fire. He then returns home and commits murder-suicide as the Yama no Kami watches over him approvingly.[36] In the final moments of his own life, Tatsuo becomes botanical through death within the logic of disturbance ecology. Like a forest fire burning wildly only to open space for new growth, Tatsuo uses the regenerative properties of destruction to create space for a potential future for the forests of Nigishima. The revitalization Tatsuo sets in motion is a far cry from the "future made out of wood" that the Forestry Agency would envision just a few decades later.

Fire and Futurity in the Forest

The Fire Festival plays a brief yet important role in the vision of the future that Yanagimachi presents. Images of the Fire Festival do not appear until the final fifteen minutes of the film and only constitute approximately five minutes of the film's running time. Yet the festival provides Tatsuo with an answer for how to renew a forest ecosystem that is no longer viable. The Fire Festival introduces the potential for plasticity. Through the destruction of fire, the forest assemblage can change, regrow, and become anew in Tatsuo's absence. The festival is an ancient ritual held in Shingū, Wakayama Prefecture every year on the sixth day of February.³⁷ As the film demonstrates, the ritual is exclusively for male participants. A large group of men all wearing white share a sacred flame, passing the fire between wooden torches. The men ascend the 538 stone stairs of Kamikura Shrine and eventually enter a sacred building on top of the mountain. Shut inside, the men must endure the painful smoke and fire until the doors are opened, at which point they descend the stairs. The Fire Festival welcomes the New Year and carries with it the significance of a "fire renewal" (*hi no kōshin*).³⁸

Tatsuo concludes that it is only in his absence that something new can grow, that he is like an old, dying tree blocking the sun from the forest floor. Tatsuo enacts the destructive power of ritual when he kills his mother, wife, children, and himself. As his killing spree is briefly interrupted by the return of his children, the three wooden torches he carried in the Fire Festival (one for Tatsuo and two for his young sons) can be seen hanging in the entryway to the house. The film lingers briefly on these torches as if to suggest they have reignited through Tatsuo's destruction. *Fire Festival* thus links, quite problematically, the symbolic regenerative properties of fire to Tatsuo's murder-suicide.

From a botanical perspective, however, fire can be an important element of a healthy ecosystem, leading to physical regrowth and reconstitution within a material ecology of the forest. As Sara E. Jensen and Guy R. McPherson remind us: "Fire has been a part of nearly all the world's ecosystems for millennia. It plays a crucial and irreplaceable role in the ecosystems that support all life. . . . Fire is both inevitable and ubiquitous."³⁹ Ecologically speaking, fire can be beneficial. As Nathaniel Brodie et al. explain: "Repeated disturbances, such as periodic wildfire, are critical influences on ecosystem development, patterns of forest age-classes across the landscape, and species evolution."⁴⁰ Certain plants, called pyrophytes, have evolved to tolerate and even thrive as they come into contact with fire. Certain trees, for example, have evolved to develop thick bark that prevents fire from damaging the living tissues within. In addition, there are trees that produce serotinous cones, which only open and spread their seeds when they reach a high enough temperature through fire.

Fire can indeed lead to regeneration and to a notion of futurity predicated on the destruction of the present. This connection is reinforced and performed in the Fire Festival, as it leaves the old year behind and welcomes the new. As Tatsuo comes to think like the forest, he gains an ecological understanding of this relationship between destruction and regeneration. In Tatsuo's forest-thinking, he and his family must burn in order for the forest, and thus the village of Nigishima, to live. Of course, this line of interpretation is dangerous and risks justifying extreme domestic violence. This is particularly true given the fact that Nakagami based his screenplay on a real-life incident of familial murder-suicide, as discussed above. For all of its thought-provoking figurations of botanical subjectivity, *Fire Festival* ultimately reaches a highly dangerous conclusion and exposes the dark potentials that also lay within the realm of becoming botanical.

Botanical becomings, as I have been discussing them throughout this book, take place in the loss of an individuated self as it forms an alliance with the botanical world in the service of sculpting something new. But instead of envisioning plant life as an alternative to a backdrop of violence, *Fire Festival* envisions becoming botanical as a necessarily violent act in and of itself. Nakagami Kenji reinforces the botanical nature of Tatsuo's murder-suicide in his conversation with Ueno Chizuko, where he claims that Tatsuo's death resembles that of bamboo: "After bamboo plants go to seed, they completely dry up. They are completely destroyed. It is that kind of image. That's what was in my mind at the time (I wrote it)."[41] Like bamboo, Tatsuo withers and dies in order for the seeds of potentiality to emerge. Unaccounted for in Nakagami's image of the bamboo going to seed, however, is that act of Tatsuo killing his own children (and wife and mother). The slippage here between the human and the botanical renders Nakagami's botanical becoming dystopian even as it strives toward a new opening of futurity.

Even if we take Nakagami's image of the bamboo going to seed at face value, the final moments of *Fire Festival* do not make clear what exactly will grow from these seeds of potentiality. It ultimately does not present a clear-cut vision of the future. In the aftermath of Tatsuo's murder-suicide, the film cuts to a few scenes demonstrating how quotidian life continues in Nigishima. The village's merchants close up shop and head home. *Fire Festival* ends with a shot of Tatsuo's hunting dogs sitting calmly and looking over a cliff at the harbor below. The sun is setting, casting a pinkish light over the water. Takemitsu's ethereal score, with its high-pitched flutes, drowns out any diegetic noise. Suddenly, the film cuts to a close-up of the water. A black substance is seen bubbling up to the water's surface from below. Dead fish float to the surface, filling the frame. Sunlight reflects brightly against the oil collecting at the water's surface until the screen turns a uniform shade of red that evokes the color of both fire and blood. A group of village fishermen stand on a dock looking out at the water. The red of fire/blood reflects back onto them, tinting their devastated faces.

Throughout the film, it has been rumored that Tatsuo has been responsible for dumping oil in the ocean to protest the building of the proposed marine park. The villagers now look perplexed. With Tatsuo dead, how did the oil get there? The suggestion is that Tatsuo has not "died" in the manner that humans conventionally die. Rather, by becoming botanical, he has survived in the forest in the way a plant might. He is no longer corporal, but he is still a part of the forest, albeit in a new way. Simply put, his death is a part of the life of the forest, a necessary condition for the maintenance of a cyclical ecosystem. If Tatsuo were shown the images produced by the Kizukai Movement, he would likely argue that it is not just the trees we need cut down to usher in the next forest cycle but also the anthropocentric worldview that renders trees nothing more than resources in the first place. Rather than "building a future out of wood," Tatsuo would advise that we build a future *as wood*.

Fire Festival ends with one last wide-angle panoramic view of Nigishima. A red sun hangs low between two mountains above the water. In the center of the water is the area where the oil has surfaced, which reflects the sun in a way that makes it look as if the water is on fire. The screen slowly fades to black but does so in a manner that leaves the bright red oil spill in the center of the frame illuminated as the final image of the film. In the end, it remains unclear if Tatsuo's fiery act has prevented the development of the aquatic park and the ecological damage it is sure to bring. In short, *Fire Festival* does not present us with an image of the future but rather lingers on the state of possibility that Tatsuo's death opens up. The final image, in which the very site of the proposed development appears to burn, suggests that perhaps it, too, has been set aflame by Tatsuo's becoming botanical in death. Anna Tsing claims that in the aftermath of disturbances such as fire that "livable ecologies come back." *Fire Festival* does not reward viewers with an image of the livable ecology of Nigishima coming back. It does, however, attempt to plant the seeds for this possibility, however devastating the immediate present (and likely traumatic aftermath) of the film's ending may appear to be.

The *Somabito* in the Films of Kawase Naomi

The economic precarity of Japanese *somabito* villages did not improve in the years following *Fire Festival*'s release. With the collapse of Japan's "Bubble Economy" at the end of the 1980s, rural depopulation and economic downturn continued to afflict rural villages. Legal countermeasures intended to combat rural depopulation were repeatedly revised. The 2000 version of the law introduced new language into its objectives once again. Where the 1980 version (as discussed above) called for the "promotion of depopulated areas," the 2000 version called for "the promotion of self-reliance in depopulated areas." This neoliberal turn is bolstered by yet another new objective: "to form regions [*kokudo*] with distinctive beauty."[42] Such revisions hold a certain irony when we consider areas like the ones portrayed in Yanagimachi's and Kawase's films. These regions struggle to be self-reliant because of the collapse of the timber industry, and the beauty of these regions is tied to the forests to which they cannot adequately tend—forests that are largely a product of postwar greening efforts that also looked "to form regions with distinctive beauty." In any case, the governmental countermeasures have not proven effective, and in 2022, more than half of all municipalities in Japan were designated "depopulated areas" for the first time since the classification began with the 1970 law.[43]

For Kawase, the plight of the *somabito* amid the ever-worsening depopulation crisis was felt close at hand in her native Nara Prefecture:

> For more than ten years I have felt that "something is strange with the mountains" and that if we don't do something about it, something bad will happen. The forestry profession is in decline, the people connected to it are aging, and the young people that could take over are leaving. It's a dangerous job—the roads are not maintained, and two acquaintances of mine died in accidents involving the felling of trees. If you get hurt, it can take two hours to get to the nearest hospital because the work is so deep in the mountains. The state of the forest is the state of humanity. I want to pass along to future generations a beautiful forest, and the idea that we continue living along with it.[44]

Kawase's filmography demonstrates a strong investment in the relationship between the human and botanical world, in particular within the forests of Nara. Many of her films prominently feature plant life and explore the impact of plants (and trees in particular) on human subjectivity. Her 2018 film *Vision* feels like an answer to the question left hanging at the end of Yanagimachi's *Fire Festival*: Just what kind of future is opened up in the destruction of fire? While *Fire Festival* finds the potential for futurity in its final fiery moments (an image screenwriter Nakagami Kenji likened to bamboo going to seed and then drying up), it does not offer a clear vision of what would grow in the aftermath of Tatsuo's death. Its ending leaves the future open, dangling in possibility. *Vision* closes this loop by mimicking the unfolding of cyclical time as experienced by the forest and tying the future back to the past.

Kawase has explored the ecological connections between the *somabito* and the forest beginning with her debut feature-length film *Suzaku* (*Moe no Suzaku*, 1997). *Suzaku* shares many similarities with *Fire Festival*, including the verdant cinematography of Tamura Masaki. Set within the forested landscape of Nishiyoshino in Nara Prefecture, *Suzaku* narrates the economic decline of the local logging community. The village and forests of Nishiyoshino lie some seventy kilometers west of Nigishima (the setting of *Fire Festival*), and, like Nigishima, the Yoshino region is a crossroads of several overlapping histories. It holds long-founded significance as a mythological and spiritual site while also being home to a long history of forest management. In a narrative echo of *Fire Festival*, the father of the Tahara family (the family which serves as the narrative focus of *Suzaku*) concludes that he must die in order for something new to grow. As he can no longer support his family, the Tahara patriarch kills himself, creating a disturbance in the village ecosystem meant to open space for renewal.

In the same year she released *Suzaku*, Kawase returned to her documentarian roots and released *The Weald* (*Somaudo monogatari*, 1997), a film that follows the hard lives of the *somabito* (or, in this case, *somaudo*, a variant of the word *somabito* that is used in the Japanese title of the film) of Nishiyoshino, the same setting as *Suzaku*. The film plays like a supplement to *Suzaku*, depicting the actual *somabito* that served as the inspiration for the fictional narrative of Kawase's first feature film. On her official website, Kawase explains that she attempted with the documentary to envision a future for the economically disenfranchised forestry community: "Replacing the 'facts' of the life they have spun with my own 'truth,' I spin a tale in cinema, so that this may become a film that continues from the past to the present, the present to the future."[45] She discusses the *somabito* phytomorphically, as if they were themselves trees imbued with a resilience that could weather the storm of economic depression: "I was given a lot of hints on how to enrich life from the *soma* people who live in Hirao, Nishiyoshino-mura, Nara Prefecture. The accumulation of their lived days has taken root in the earth and returned to nature. Just as massive trees withstand the wind and the rain, the cold and the heat, these people endure the twists and turns of life by simply existing, developing deep wrinkles."[46] Kawase would return to this image of the *somabito* as a resilient tree some twenty years later in *Vision*.

In *Vision*, Kawase finds the future for the *somabito* that she sought in both *Suzaku* and *The Weald*. *Vision* is a botanical becoming in the form of an eco-fable that finds life and futurity in the aftermath of fire. The film articulates the principles of disturbance ecology, as I have been discussing them in this chapter, wherein ecological disturbances such as fire are necessary for the continued health of an ecosystem. Like *Fire Festival* before it, *Vision* arrives at this conclusion through a deep investment in the ritual/spiritual traditions of its setting. Unlike *Fire Festival*, however, it does so without the presence of a singular, egoistic character at its narrative center. Rather, it explicitly imagines, through destruction and renewal, that the human ego itself can be overcome. It imagines that the entirety of humanity can become botanical.

Forest Time

Like *Fire Festival*, *Vision* is set in a region of deep political, religious, and mythological significance. The film takes place in Kawase's native Nara Prefecture, in the mountainous and highly forested region of Yoshino, the same setting as her earlier films *Suzaku* and *The Weald*. Yoshino is located at the southern end of the ancient province of Yamato, home to the imperial capital of Heijōkyō (present-day Nara) from AD 710 to 794. In several respects, Yamato Province is a point of origin for the modern Japanese state. It is here that Buddhism became tied to the imperial court. Central to the legitimization of the court was the embrace of Buddhism as a quasi-state religion, which led to the construction of monumental Buddhist temple complexes, including Tōdaiji—a marvel of sacred wooden architecture and one of the causes, according to Conrad Totman, of Japan's early deforestation.[47] These forests, in their contemporary form, are the focus of *Vision*.

Photographer Dodo Arata serves as the film's cinematographer, his second collaboration with Kawase. Dodo's cinematography moves between the scales of the forest, from the minuscule life found on the forest floor to the *somabito* climbing and felling trees, and even farther up to the expansive forest canopy. The forest canopy is full of rich colors: deep greens that give way to more autumnal hues of red and yellow as the narrative progresses through the seasons. Bright light streams through the tops of the trees for several moments, and fog moves throughout the spaces between giant trees, illuminating the spiritual aura characteristic of Yoshino that clings to humans and more-than-humans alike. Katherine Connell has referred to the film's cinematography as "vegetal camerawork" (see figures 4.3–4.5).[48] Indeed, as the camera moves through the forest in this manner, it highlights the interconnectedness of the cross-species relationships that make up the forest assemblage (to return to Anna Tsing's language) and presents a botanical subjectivity that is shared throughout the forest among humans, plants, and spiritual entities. This subjectivity finds further expression within a cyclical and ritual unfolding of time.

It is clear in *Vision* that the village of Yoshino is suffering from the economic decline that also afflicted Nigishima in *Fire Festival* some thirty years before. In the opening scenes, we see Tomo (a *somabito* who lives a secluded life in the forest) use a chainsaw to fell a large cypress. A few scenes later, we see a group of elderly villagers (likely *somabito*) sitting in the forest lamenting how much the forest and the community have changed and how many people have left the village behind. Even as it highlights these hardships, *Vision* offers hope for the *somabito* profession in a way that *Fire Festival* did not. In its cyclical vision of time, the film sees an unbroken link among the *somabito* of the past, present, and future.

Late in the film, Tomo begins to teach the ways of the *somabito* to Rin, a young character with a complex backstory who represents the future of the forest ecosystem within cyclical time. (I explain Rin's role in the film in detail below.) Tomo takes Rin to the marketplace where the large cypresses that have been felled in the forest are sold. As the two lean in and appreciate the impressive size of a particular tree, Tomo tells Rin they have to work in the forest for the sake of future generations: "It's not just us, right? The previous generation, the generation before

FIGURE 4.3. Cinematographer Dodo Arata's "vegetal camerawork" in *Vision*.

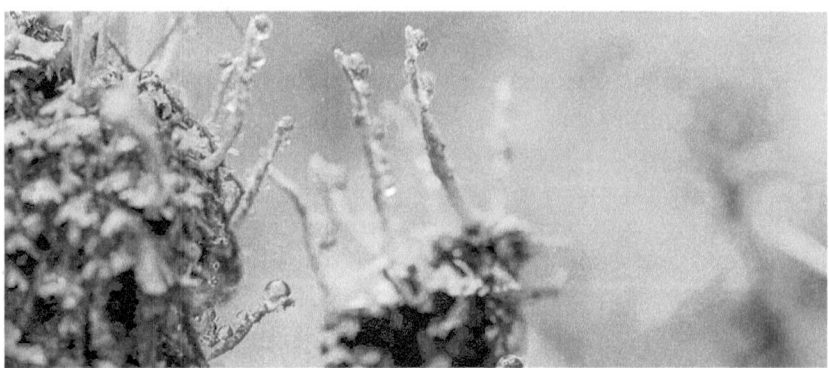

FIGURE 4.4. Cinematic-botanical subjectivity on a small scale in *Vision*.

FIGURE 4.5. The expanded scale of cinematic-botanical subjectivity in *Vision*.

that, and even further back, those people before us grew and raised these trees. That's why they are here now. We have to work hard and link up with them." Tomo's vision of time in this dialogue links generations of *somabito* (past, present, and future) together within the assemblage of the forest. He recognizes that the lifespan of the forest is far greater than that of human beings and that the work of past *somabito* informs the work of the current *somabito*. Their felling of the forest in the past (a period of destruction) cleared space for the trees of the present (a period of regeneration). Extrapolating forward, he explains to Rin that their work in the present will likewise influence the *somabito* of the future.

This cyclical time is *Vision*'s approximation of what I call "forest time." Forest time attempts to capture the complex manner in which the assemblage of the forest experiences time, i.e., its temporal *shokubutsusei*. In *Vision*, forest time is entangled with the ritual flow of time inscribed into the spiritual landscape of Yoshino. Disturbance ecology, with its alternating periods of destruction and regeneration, draws the *somabito* into forest time. Because a forest is not a singular entity but rather a web made up of "cross-species relations," as Anna Tsing claims, forest time does not follow the straightforward, linear timeline of the human (i.e., birth, life, death). The short durée of the human lifespan is only part of the much longer durée of the forest. Forest time is a cycle of many births, many deaths, and many rebirths. Individual humans and trees may die, but the forest remains to see the birth of new humans and new trees that come to reconstitute the forest anew.

Vision attempts to embody this temporal botanical imagination and make the long durée of forest time legible in its roughly two hours of running time. The film stars Juliette Binoche, who Kawase met in France at the 2017 Cannes Film Festival. Binoche plays Jeanne, a travel writer who ventures to the remote forests of Yoshino in search of a mythical herb named "vision." (Like the title of the film, only the English word is used.) Jeanne meets Tomo (played by Nagase Masatoshi), who tells her that his job is "saving the forest," and Aki (played by Natsuki Mari), a blind woman deeply connected to the forest. It becomes clear that Aki is a mythological figure. She occupies a narrative space similar to *Fire Festival*'s Yama no Kami, a spiritual entity belonging to the forest. It is suggested throughout the film that Aki is actually a tree (or group of trees) in human form. In certain moments, she is shown performing dancelike movements in the forest that mimic the swaying of trees in the wind. In such moments, she communes with the forest in such a way that she appears to be one of the surrounding trees.

At the start of the film, Aki is shown to have a special knowledge of the ritual unfolding of forest time. She tells Tomo that she is one thousand years old, born "when the stars were born." Aki states early on that the time has come to ritually renew the forest, claiming (in an echo of Kawase's own claim quoted earlier in this chapter) that "there is something strange [*okashii*] with the forest lately." Aki's role throughout the film is to teach the other characters the ecological necessity of burning down the forest in order to restart the cycle of forest time. Unlike Tatsuo in *Fire Festival*, Aki is not a "misfit," to return to Ogi Masahiro's assessment. In calling Tatsuo a misfit, Ogi claims Tatsuo is out of place in his contemporary moment. As time in *Vision* operates cyclically, the past is not out of place in the present but rather comes back around to structure the future, just as dead trees (or "snags") can become a site of regrowth for plants. In the same scene in which she claims to be one thousand years old, she tells Tomo that she hopes to meet him again when she "turns seventeen years old." The comment bewilders Tomo (and the viewer) due to Aki's advanced age. Her comment speaks, however, to the botanical subjectivity on display in *Vision* through its development of forest time. Within *Vision*'s complex timeline, the past is never just the past. The past can become the future, and one-thousand-year-old humans can turn seventeen again. Thus, like Osaki Midori, who saw something botanical in cyclical narratives and repetition, Kawase attempts to make the very narrative structure of *Vision* more plantlike.

Ritual Renewal through Fire

As the spiritual center of the forest and the only character to understand the strange flow of forest time, Aki sets the film's narrative in motion. She enacts a plan to introduce disturbance into the ecosystem to keep the cyclical flow of change in flux. In order to address the "something strange" in the forest, Aki needs Jeanne and Tomo to fulfill ritualistic roles within her plan, which ultimately ends in the forest catching fire. Jeanne arrives in Yoshino with only a faint idea of her purpose. It is as if something beyond her control has called her to the forest. She says her goal is to find the herb "vision," but her knowledge of the plant is tenuous at best. She is unclear where she has heard of it, but Jeanne believes in the tales of vision's magical powers, which purport that the herb has the ability to "end human pain." Arriving in Yoshino, she meets Tomo at a local shrine. Although their meeting appears accidental, it was in fact fated to happen, as Aki told Tomo to go pray at the shrine on that particular day and time. In secretly arranging this meeting, Aki has set up the conditions to ensure that the cyclical regeneration of the forest will eventually occur.

The regeneration that Aki sets in motion is ritualistic and seems to be connected to the shrine where Jeanne and Tomo meet. At the shrine, Jeanne notices a painting on one of the walls. It depicts a forest with several trees on fire and what looks like a white cloud or gust of wind passing through the forest. Tomo tells Jeanne that the painting has been there since long ago. As they talk, the film cuts from the painting to the forest around Tomo and Jeanne, making it clear that the forest in the image and the setting of the film are one and the same. In the film's fiery climax, it is revealed that this image depicts a reoccurring event. As the film cuts away in its final moments from the charred forest back to the ancient painting of fire it presented at the film's beginning, it shows us the future by returning to the past. The loop closes, ready to start again. We learn in the end that the "vision" Jeanne has been seeking is not a medicinal herb but rather this very ritualistic fire. "Vision" is not itself a plant but rather the conditions for plants (and humans who rethink themselves as plants) to grow anew, once again.

The characters of *Vision* must fulfill ritualistic roles to make these conditions for regrowth possible. In doing so, they get swept up in the cycle of forest time. They become something akin to archetypes or mythological figures that are devoid of individual egos. This egoless state is an ideal that *Vision* sees as a possible future for all of humanity through the plasticity of becoming botanical. To be sure, the extreme plasticity of *Vision*'s characters makes it difficult for viewers to understand their motivations and histories within the narrative. Their stories keep changing, to a degree that borders on infuriating. As they get written into forest time, the logistics of their personal histories get complicated and confusing. For example, when Aki meets Jeanne ostensibly for the first time, Aki remarks: "It was you, wasn't it?" No explanation is given for this comment. It will only make sense once the film later establishes a new, cyclical history for both characters. Although Jeanne arrives in the village of Yoshino a stranger, she quickly becomes a part of the forest assemblage, and her past is rewritten (or, in more ecological language, "renewed"). Jeanne becomes (in the past) the mother of Rin, the young character Tomo teaches to be a *somabito*, as discussed above.

Rin is introduced to viewers in a bewildering manner. He mysteriously appears in the forest after Aki has died midway through the film. *Vision* suggests that Rin is thus a new iteration of Aki, who is herself a manifestation of the trees in the forest. Remember the aspens from this book's introduction? Rin and Aki seem connected in a similar way. They are both offshoots of the same forest organism. But "Aki" is also a ritual role that Rin comes to play. Because Rin appears in the forest following Aki's death, it seems as if Aki's comment that she will see Tomo again when she "turns seventeen" may be referring to this moment. Although Rin seems too old to be seventeen, he does, in one scene, pick up a cicada shell and make a vague comment about how "there were many gathered long ago." In an earlier scene, Jeanne speaks of the seventeen-year cycle of certain cicadas with Tomo. Therefore, as viewers, we have been primed to consider that the strange figures of Aki and Rin may emerge and die off in cycles, just like cicadas—or, perhaps, like aspen. Yet within the narrative web that Aki sets in motion, Rin becomes Jeanne's son, fathered by a *somabito* character who was accidentally shot by a hunter in the forest before Rin's birth (a scene viewers will come to recognize as the opening scene of the film). As Jeanne falls into the forest time of *Vision*'s complex narrative, she, too, becomes an archetypical/ritualistic/botanical figure. She becomes botanical as a reproductive element of the forest assemblage. In becoming the mother of Rin, she simultaneously becomes the mother of Aki and thus a mother figure to the forest itself, contributing to its regeneration/rebirth within forest time.

The Liveliness of Destruction

The complex web of cyclical time that drastically changes Jeanne's personal history (turning her into the mother of Rin) unfolds slowly in *Vision*, as one might expect of forest time. As Jeanne comes to stay with Tomo and continues her research on the plants of the forest, she spends time outdoors and begins to have visions of her own. For the majority of the film, it is unclear if these visions are memories or premonitions. We will come to understand by the film's end that they are the "backstory" of Jeanne and her relationship with Rin's father. They tell, in fragmentary form, the new history that Jeanne adopts within forest time. As Jeanne starts to see these visions, we viewers see her subjectivity regenerating itself.

Jeanne's knowledge of "vision" comes to her in a similar manner. She speaks with Tomo about "prime number cicadas" that only emerge from the ground every seven, thirteen, and seventeen years. Jeanne links the cycle of prime number cicadas to the periodic cycle of the herb "vision," which she now states confidently as 997 years. She says that if her calculations are correct, it has been 997 years since it last appeared. Given Jeanne's lack of knowledge concerning "vision" up to this point, her newfound certainty is surprising. How has she gained this knowledge? How long has she been living with Tomo in Yoshino? *Vision* is not concerned with these questions or with making a clear narrative arc. Like many other developments to come, Jeanne's understanding of the cycle of 997 years comes out of nowhere, as if the forest is revealing itself to her as it sees fit. Jeanne ultimately decides to return to France but promises Tomo that she will come back to Yoshino soon. She is convinced "vision" will "release its spores" in either the fall or winter.

Jeanne then returns to Yoshino in the fall. The leaves of the trees in the forest have turned bright red, approximating the image of fire before they die off in winter. From this approximation of fire, the film turns to an actual image of fire (albeit one made with CGI). We see Rin walk in the forest and up to a giant tree that has been showcased throughout the film.[49] Rin begins swaying, mimicking the movements of the trees around him, just as Aki had previously done. In an illustration of the nonlinear nature of forest time, Rin sees both Aki and the man who was his father (the man who became Jeanne's ex-lover in her rewritten history), both of whom are ostensibly dead. They begin swaying along with Rin, and the forest bursts into flames. As the disturbance of fire is introduced into the ecosystem, forest time appears to reset. The past (as embodied in Aki and Rin's father) participates in the fiery event of "vision" and gives birth to the future (as embodied in Rin). Tomo sees the smoke from the forest fire and rushes into the woods. On the way, he hears the barking of his beloved dog who had tragically died a few scenes earlier. Aki's disembodied voice emerges from the forest, telling Tomo that he "is not alone." Tomo then finds Jeanne standing at the edge of the fire. He screams for Rin and tells Jeanne they need water. Jeanne, however, has already become botanical and understands the regenerative event taking place. She responds to Tomo, "We don't need water. 'Vision' is about to be born."

As "vision" is born, the past, present, and future come together. The ritual by fire is complete, and destruction has given way to liveliness. The film cuts from Aki to Jeanne's ex-lover (who is grasping a blanket), to Rin, who has now taken his father's place, holding the same blanket. The camera focuses on glowing embers and the charred remains of trees. Jeanne, Tomo, and Rin look over the scorched wreckage. The sound of birds and the flowing of water can be heard. Tomo remarks, "The mountain is lively, isn't it?" (see figure 4.6). These are the final words spoken in the film. They mark not only the renewal of the ecosystem through disturbance ecology but also a renewal of subjectivity. As the forest burns and starts anew, so, too, does Tomo's understanding of his place in the world. He now understands that he is "not alone," that he is multiple, that he is botanical.

FIGURE 4.6. The "liveliness" of the burnt forest in *Vision*.

Tomo sees a renewed sense of life teeming in the forest in the aftermath of destruction. He begins to think like the forest and understands the logic of disturbance ecology, that futurity comes from destruction and death. In the final moments of the film, all three characters (Jeanne, Tomo, and Rin) have arrived at this ecological epiphany and have participated in its ritualistic enactment. Where in *Fire Festival* it was Tatsuo's death that took center stage in the disturbance of fire, it is new life that emerges from within the remains of *Vision*'s fire ritual. Producer Yamamoto Reiji likens the vision event to the ritual Yamayaki festival in Nara, where the mountainside of Wakakusayama is set ablaze annually in the month of January.[50] He explains the event of "vision" as "a scene in which the forest regenerates through wildfire."[51] Echoing Nakagami Kenji's claim that Tatsuo's suicide in *Fire Festival* was like a bamboo going to seed, Kawase explains the ecological disturbance of "vision" as that which is necessary for the potential of futurity to emerge: "'Vision' is the 'seed of potentiality' that exists within us, that helps us accept things and then overcome them. . . . 'Vision' is necessary to move into a new world [*tsugi no sekai*]."[52]

For all of its teeming life, however, the "new world" that Kawase envisions nevertheless opens up through the death of certain organisms within the forest assemblage (including Aki and Rin's father). As Brodie et al. claim in regard to disturbance ecology: "There are winners and losers in every disturbance event; the death of established organisms creates new niches and living space for others."[53] This was Tatsuo's plan in *Fire Festival*, as he killed himself and his family to create new space for the future to take hold. As discussed above, however, *Fire Festival* does not show the results of his action. In *Vision*'s final moments, we actually see the future (as do Jeanne and Tomo) in the "lively" sound of birds and water flowing within the charred forest. We also see it in the figure of Rin, who is poised to become the new spiritual center of the forest (a position previously occupied by Aki), as well as the next generation of *somabito*, having been taught the profession by Tomo. We see a future growing from the remains of the past.

Evolution and the Destruction of the Human Ego

What makes *Vision*'s figuration of becoming botanical so extreme is that it imagines that fire can sculpt *all of humanity* anew, effecting an evolutionary change in the human species at large. Jeanne tells Rin near the end of the film that there "are people who say that human beings are still raw." The fire of the "vision" event is meant to address this rawness, this imperfection that leads to "pain," as Jeanne stresses throughout the film. Like Osaki Midori's work examined in chapter 1 of this book, *Vision* turns to evolutionary theory and posits that through the regeneration of the forest, humans can evolve into something new, something more botanical. *Vision* imagines an evolved form of humanity that no longer possesses an individuated human ego separated from the natural world. It imagines an evolved form of subjectivity that experiences itself as ecologically enmeshed within something larger. In other words, it imagines an evolutionary change that affords all of humanity the kind of botanical subjectivity inhabited by the *somabito* characters in *Vision* (and *Fire Festival* before it). The new becoming it imagines is, in a cyclical fashion, quite old. It is a return to the way *somabito* have inhabited the region of Yoshino for centuries. Given Kawase's politics, it is hard not to recognize a certain decontextualized idealization of the past here and a subsequent desire for regression. As Kawase has claimed: "The state of the forest is the state of humanity."[54] *Vision* presents us with an ambiguous view of evolution through circular time, a change at the scale of the human species that bends toward a seemingly romanticized notion of Japanese tradition (as bound up in the figure of the *somabito*).

What is unambiguous, however, is that Kawase sees disturbance as a necessary precondition for change, whatever the outcome of that change may be. Elizabeth Grosz argues that disturbance events are precisely what drive evolutionary change: "Natural selection, while it operates as an ordered and ordering network of processes, is in fact made up of nothing but thousands, millions of accidents, momentary events, that lead to the death of some, not because they were less well adapted but because they were, say, in the wrong place at the wrong time."[55] The "vision" event (the fire that renews the forest) is similar to one of "these millions of small events" as it forces the forest ecosystem to change and adapt accordingly. A sense of plasticity is necessary to survive and thrive in the aftermath of fire. *Vision* strives to grant humans this evolutionary plasticity. Yet the "vision" event presented in the film is not an accident. It is a recurring ritual. The characters of *Vision* (both human and more-than-human) are not "in the wrong place at the wrong time." Within the cyclical logic of forest time, they are in the exact right place, at the exact right time to usher in the future. Aki has made sure of this by secretly setting up the initial meeting of Tomo and Jeanne and by dying to make space for Rin to emerge. Like Osaki Midori's *Wandering in the Realm of the Seventh Sense*, Kawase's *Vision* posits a degree of agency over evolution. By becoming more plantlike, the characters of these works (separated by nearly one hundred years) find a way to navigate evolutionary time and redirect its flow.

Jeanne introduces evolutionary language in a monologue addressed to Rin (who, in this scene, she does not yet know is/will become her son): "In the ancient part of the human brain there is an aggressive instinct that is passed down genetically. And it seems that it will never change. We evolve so slowly." The camera

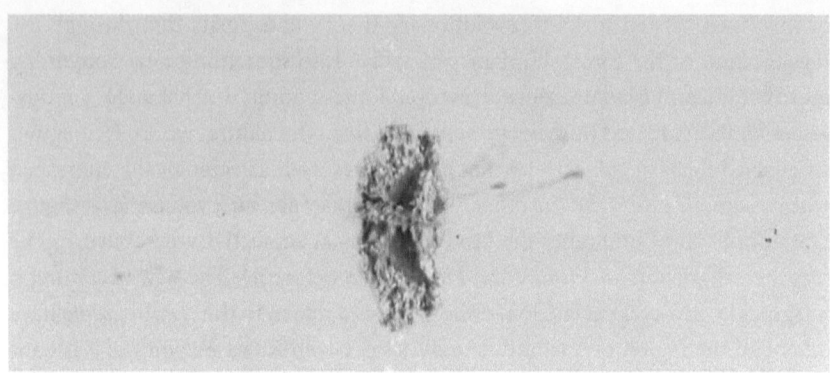

FIGURE 4.7. Abstract futurity in *Vision*.

moves from Jeanne and Rin to a rippling shot of water flowing and then presents an abstract image: a pale blue screen that is revealed to be the surface of water only when an unidentifiable substance (perhaps a clump of gold leaf/gold paint or some sort of metal) drips into it (see figure 4.7). The shift in imagery is striking. The majority of the film has been spent in the forested realm, and yet suddenly, we are transported somewhere different, somewhere beyond the realm of botanical subjectivity. There is something strange about the image of water. It is either in reverse or upside down, but the lack of perspective makes it difficult to tell. This ambiguity is pivotal, as it poses a question that gets to the heart of Jeanne's words: Is the figure in the image coming together, forming something new? Or is it breaking apart? Ultimately, it does not matter, as within the logic of disturbance ecology, coming together and breaking apart are not contradictory images. A forest fire does both. It creates new life by breaking apart certain "multi-species relations" and bringing together others. Like the fiery event of "vision" at the end of the film, this image of gold dripping into water is an image of futurity as well as an image of ongoing change that makes visible Jeanne's longing for human evolution. It is likewise a perfect encapsulation of the difficulty in pinning down Kawase's political stance in the film. Neither fully progressive nor fully retrogressive, the substance changes depending on how the viewer looks at it.

We then cut to a different image of futurity, one more literal: the interior of a hospital, where a newborn child is being handed to a parent. A new generation appears to be in the process of being born. We quickly return to water. This time, the shot is submerged below the surface, and we see air bubbles moving up to the surface. This series of images (the only ones of their kind in the film) bring us out of the local ecosystem of the forest and into a wider, more abstract visual space. This change in imagery highlights Jeanne's move into philosophical abstraction as she continues to discuss the aggressive nature of the human ego. She continues:

"We still carry that aggression inside. War and atrocity are acts of murder that only humans commit. No other living species commits such acts. Perhaps 'vision' is like us humans—with the power to create and the power to destroy. Maybe with its self-destruction it sends us some kind of message, at an instinctual level." In its embrace of evolutionary thought and disturbance ecology, *Vision* suggests that the transformation required for humanity to see the liveliness of disturbances such as forest fires requires the destruction of the ego through becoming botanical. It requires self-destruction, not the self-reliance called for by governmental countermeasures against rural depopulation. With Jeanne's monologue and Dodo's cinematography throughout, *Vision* presents an ecological picture of the future that privileges ecosystem assemblages over individuated selves. Many selves (human and more-than-human) die by the end of *Vision*, but the forest matrix lives on, as do the ritual roles necessary to maintain the forest ecosystem.

Kawase aligns the destruction of the ego with the embrace of alterity, an opening up to the other that mirrors the process of becoming botanical: "In the experience of (accepting the other), there is also the experience of losing what one holds dear. There is the destruction of the ego [*jibun o oshikoroshite*]."[56] For Kawase, this shift in subjectivity allows one to better see the future and enter into cyclical time:

> Even if one is not able to accomplish what one needs to do for those people living in the same generation contemporaneously, one can sculpt out a form that will enable the next generation to do so. Humans, at most, live 100 years. What can one accomplish in 100 years? If one links oneself up with what people of the next generation will want, then one can begin to think within a span of 200 years. . . . In the past, we didn't grow fruit trees on the land so that we ourselves could eat, we grew them for our grandchildren.[57]

The future that Kawase envisions is clearly utopian, idealistic, and heteronormative, if not outright naive. Yet Kawase's utopian evolution emerges from devastation, from within the wreckage of fire. On the one hand, there is a disregard for those who perish in the flames. At the same time, the seeming contradiction of *Vision*'s ending, in which Tomo remarks on the liveliness of the forest as he looks over its charred remains, speaks to the potential for humanity to evolve in a more ecological manner. This, *Vision* suggests, is the ultimate form of regeneration for the *somabito*. It is a regeneration not merely at the level of economic recovery but a species-wide embrace of the logic that the *somabito* embodies, one both violent and ecological.

In *Vision*, destruction sculpts the forest anew, forming fertile ground for a future to take hold. It is a future born, in Kawase's words, from the "seed of potentiality." Although *Vision* shows viewers images of this future in its final moments, it remains unclear whether or not the fire of "vision" could ever truly affect the kind of widespread evolutionary change that would lead to a species-wide botanical becoming. If, however, Kawase is correct in asserting that humans can only accomplish so much in their short lifespans, and thus must rethink themselves within the long durée of forest time, then perhaps this uncertainty and all of the various ambiguities at the heart of *Vision* are ultimately not a problem. A future sculpted through destructive plasticity may enable the next generation (or the one after that) to better envision their own path toward regeneration, no matter what ideology set the forest aflame in the first place. All that future generations would have to do to become botanical would be to burn it all down one more time and start anew, yet again.

5

BOTANICAL MIGRATION
Empathy and Naturalization in
the Poetry and Prose of Hiromi Ito

On June 27, 2019, Tokyo's Waseda University hosted an event featuring poet Hiromi Ito (1955–).[1] Ito read from *Wild Grass on the Riverbank* (*Kawara arekusa*), her 2004 book-length narrative poem that tells the story of a mother and her children uprooting and moving between two zones, "the riverbank" (*kawara*) and "the wasteland" (*arechi*). *Wild Grass on the Riverbank* is a tale of migration between these two settings, both of which are based on geographical locations that Ito herself has called home. The riverbank resembles the subtropical landscape of Kumamoto Prefecture in southern Japan, and the wasteland resembles the desert landscape of Southern California. Like much of Ito's literary work since the late 1990s, the poem grapples with her experience living and traveling between these two spaces.

Where chapters 3 and 4 of this book stayed rooted in the spiritual realm of the forest, this chapter takes flight and examines a surprising *shokubutsusei* of plant life, namely, its ability to migrate. While the conventional understanding of plants points to their sessility as a clear marker of difference from humans and more-than-human animals, we nonetheless commonly invoke the language of movement when referring to certain plant species as "invasive." Hiromi Ito's work rethinks the human by rethinking plants as beings constantly in motion. For Ito, paying close attention to plants becomes a way to make sense of one's own migratory existence and also a way to resist state control of other migratory bodies. Central to Ito's rethinking of humans and plants is their shared intergenerational existence. In chapter 4, Kawase Naomi advocated for humans to think botanically by "linking up" with future generations. Ito's work extends this thinking across national borders. Writing nearly a century after Osaki Midori (the subject of chapter 1), Ito demonstrates that the trope of becoming botanical has a plasticity of its own. While it no longer responds to the direct violence of Japan's empire, it has transformed into a botanical imagination that responds to the violence of the twenty-first century more broadly. Becoming botanical serves, in Ito's writing, as a critique of conservative anti-immigration policies in both Japan and the United States.

This is true of *Wild Grass on the Riverbank*, a work so full of botanical poetics that Ito claims plants are the real protagonists of the narrative.[2] Plant life is so pervasive in the poem that Ito has described experiencing a moment during its writing in which she could no longer tell if she herself was a human or a plant.[3] Formally, the poem unfolds like a plant, utilizing an urgent, messy mix of short, repetitive statements and longer narrative passages that mimic a vegetal nature (a *shokubutsusei*) that Dawn Keetley has described (in relation to the genre of plant horror) as having "pointless excess" and "uncontrollable growth."[4] The repetitive quality of the language echoes Machiko's narration in *Wandering in the Realm of the Seventh Sense*, but Ito's language is far messier and more urgent than Osaki's understated, moss-like disposition. There is an energetic liveliness to Ito's poetry that resembles the growth and movement of the vines that slither throughout the poem's narrative.[5] (Lest we forget, Ito has claimed that plants and words are the same thing, as I discussed in this book's introduction.) As the poem progresses, phrases repeat and images proliferate in a way that threatens to overtake the narrative flow, as if the plants poetically depicted in Ito's writing are themselves overgrowing the boundaries of the story:

> And the vines crawled from window frame to window frame
> Just outside, the sky was blue, the sea sparkled, the wind blew
>   across the
> wasteland
> In the wasteland
> The sage dried
> Where it stood
> The sage dried
> Where it stood
> We forgot what was happening inside and walked around
> Little brother scratched his skin raw
> The sage dried
> Where it stood[6]

Plants are active characters in *Wild Grass on the Riverbank*, moving throughout the narrative as they propagate and repeat an endless cycle of birth, death, and rebirth (not unlike the forests in Kawase's *Vision*). They take on human form, and humans likewise exhibit plantlike characteristics. They fight, resist, and struggle to survive, especially as they move to new soil.

Like the trees discussed in chapters 3 and 4 of this book, plants grow in *Wild Grass on the Riverbank* at the intersection of science and spirituality. There are long sections of the poem that repeat plant names (along with poetic variations of their names) in an incantation-like manner. Ito has been referred to as a "shamaness of poetry," and sections like the following contribute a sense of otherworldliness to the botanical realm:

> *Erigeron canadensis, Conyza sumantrensis,*
> *Sorghum halepense,* Great wasteland *japonica, Asteraceae,* Wasteland princess, no,
> *Humulus, Cayratia, Boehmeria nivea,* Wasteland, no, Barbarian, Great, Princess
> *Sorghum,*
> Wasteland *cyperus microiria,* Wasteland *rumex japonicus,* Wasteland *erigeron.*[7]

In chapter 2, I discussed Abe Kōbō's use of scientific nomenclature as an allegorical move linking plants to Japan's colonial project. In Ito's botanical poetics, science and spirituality are fused to the extent that Latin names themselves become sacred. In a scene from her poetic prose collection *Tree Spirits Grass Spirits* (*Kodama kusadama*, 2014), Ito hangs houseplants from the branches of a pepper tree in her yard and connects their scientific names to the chanting of Buddhist sutras: "Standing and chanting the many magic spells belonging to the branches of the still-young pepper tree, concluding with the sacred mantra from the Heart Sutra: *Asplenium, Nematanthus, Aeschynanthus,* Gate Gate Paragate."[8] At the very end of *Wild Grass on the Riverbank* (after the conclusion of the poem's narrative), Ito includes a section titled "Guide to the Plants in this Book," which reads like a field guide giving scientific information about the poem's botanical protagonists. Like Osaki Midori, Ito finds a creative space in the in-between of science and poetry, but she adds spirituality into the mix.

In this capacious in-between of poetry, science, and spirituality, Ito moves plants to the foreground to highlight the precarity of migratory bodies, both human and plant. Before she began reading at Waseda University, Ito discussed a tragic image that had been circulating throughout the international media the day before. It was a photograph that Ito said resembled the story she poetically tells in *Wild Grass on the Riverbank*. The image depicts a Salvadoran father and his young daughter face down along a riverbank. Both father (twenty-six-year-old Óscar Alberto Martínez Ramírez) and daughter (Valeria, just shy of two years old) have drowned. With Valeria on his back, Ramírez had attempted to cross the watery border of the Rio Grande to seek asylum in the United States. It is a photograph that seemed to perfectly crystallize, in the words of British newspaper the *Guardian*, the "grim reality of the migration crisis unfolding on America's southern border" in the year 2019.[9] How could this image also speak to *Wild Grass on the Riverbank*, a narrative poem written in Japanese fifteen years before, in which the main characters are not, according to Ito herself, the immigrant mother and children of the story but rather the plants that populate the riverbank and wasteland?

The answer to this question can be found in becoming botanical. In both her poetry and her prose, Hiromi Ito explores the potentialities and the tragedies of familial migration through a close (at times almost obsessive) engagement with plant life. Ito's works track the movements of both humans and plants as they cross national borders, focusing on the echoes that reverberate between the status of plants as native, naturalized, and/or invasive and her experience as a Japanese woman living between the United States and Japan in an era when immigration has become increasingly politicized and restricted. Many of Ito's works, including *Wild Grass on the Riverbank*, as well as collections of prose that draw directly from her life as an immigrant, explore how humans and plants have long been in a state of migration. In particular, the history of Japanese plants migrating to the US has impacted the way human migrants have been conceptualized and controlled. This is a history Jeannie N. Shinozuka traces in her book *Biotic Borders* (2022), where she reminds us that "the mass migration of Japanese plant and insect immigrants by the late nineteenth century coincided with the formation of new racial categories and landscapes, the hardening of biotic borders, and dramatic changes in agricultural practices, ushering in a new era of biotic exchanges that altered not only the lives of Japanese people in America, but American society at large."[10] Ito's work reflects on this history and looks for ways to navigate said racial categories and landscapes. It does so by rethinking plants.

Rootlessness and Being Controlled "Like a Plant"

Contrary to the common image of the plant as that which is *rooted* in place, Ito's works suggest that migratory humans and plants share a condition of *rootlessness*. Christy Wampole has argued that "Rootedness is a primary organizing trope that accommodates the need to feel connected to something outside the self . . . this subterranean, botanical form seems the ideal metaphor to communicate that desire."[11] In Ito's work, however, the connection to "something outside of the self" is found precisely in the movement of uprooted bodies. Her wild poetry and cultivated prose show how humans become botanical as they uproot and leave their native soil and eventually adapt to new environments. This is plasticity at work. Ito's writing presents a record of the subjective experience of this adaptation or acclimatization, an ongoing process she aligns with naturalization. The word *naturalization* applies to both humans and plants. Humans become naturalized as they are granted legal citizenship, while plants become naturalized once they are considered an established part of an ecosystem that is not their native home.[12]

In Ito's poetry and prose, a botanical subjectivity emerges through the process of naturalization. It emerges, for example, in the young girl Natsukusa, who serves as *Wild Grass on the Riverbank*'s narrator, as she comes to understand her experience existing between the riverbank and the wasteland—which is an existence between Japan and the United States—in botanical terms. She thinks to herself in an internal dialogue marked off by parentheses: "(I want to become a plant that grows vines)/ (I want to become a plant that grows spikes full of seed)/ . . . (I want to be naturalized)."[13] This is a hope that runs throughout Ito's work. It is a hope to become botanical through the rootless act of migration.

For Ito, becoming botanical is a form of resistance to the biopolitical control of human migration. As Shinozuka argues, "Much of the current rhetoric in the media continues to tap into the native-invasive binary and discussions of human migration across US borders. But few scholars discern how politicians presently draw upon language that has historically been deployed against plant and insect immigrants, in addition to other unwanted foreigners."[14] Catriona Sandilands is an exception to Shinozuka's claim, as she argues that state policy on migration operates through a dehumanizing, botanical logic of its own: "People and animals are increasingly organized and controlled *like and even as plants* in a neoliberal biopolitical universe."[15] For Sandilands, the human body is increasingly controlled like a plant, and "what is at the forefront of current political debate is where and when and how we are to live as reproducing, productive bodies who serve the polis by way of being, simply, alive. Growing. Populating. Spreading. Invading. Vegetating."[16] Ito's work confronts this vegetally inflected form of biopolitical control by resisting the "being, simply, alive" that Sandilands describes and forging instead a "becoming, complexly, alive" in alliance with the botanical realm.[17] In other words, Ito's poetry and prose resist the biopolitical control of migratory bodies—a form of control that Sandilands claims treats humans "*as plants*"—by taking the botanical logic being imposed on humans and finding an emancipatory quality within it. Ito's writing declares: "If you treat me like a plant, then I will respond, fiercely, like a plant."

Wild Grass on the Riverbank revels in the vegetal qualities of "growing, populating, spreading, and invading" and finds, through these qualities, an experience of migration shared between humans and plant life. The recognition of this shared experience gives rise to what I call "botanical empathy," which is a deep identification with other migratory bodies that bridges a gap of alterity believed to exist between humans and plants, and among humans of different nationalities. Botanical empathy is an emergent property of becoming botanical. It comes close to the radical sense of collectivity that Karen L. F. Houle finds in the botanical realm as she argues that "plant-becoming opens up thinking about relations as transient alliances rather than strategies. It credits the accomplishment of identity and intimacy as a *radically collective achievement*, crossing faculties, bodies, phyla."[18] Through botanical empathy, Ito's writing forges an international and multispecies collective of migrants, both human and plant, that stretches across generations and attempts to resist state control of when, where, and how one can live and create new life.

Secular Migration

Hiromi Ito began her career as a poet in the late 1970s, publishing her first poetry collection in 1978, titled *Sky of Plants* (*Sōmoku no sora*). Her early poetry tackles taboo and often-gendered subject matter. One of her best-known poems, "Killing Kanoko" (*Kanoko koroshi*, 1985), is a graphic meditation on abortion and postpartum depression.[19] Ito's frank discussions of sexuality and violence, along with her "shamaness-like" performance style, have made her a prominent figure in contemporary Japanese literature and earned her a reputation as "the igniting force behind the subsequent flourishing of 'women's poetry.'"[20] In addition to numerous poetry collections (including collaborations with photographer Nobuyoshi Araki), Ito also began writing literary nonfiction early in her career, including her 1985 essay collection/instruction manual on pregnancy and breastfeeding titled *Good Breasts, Bad Breasts* (*Yoi oppai warui oppai*). Poetry and literary nonfiction have remained the twin pillars of Ito's prolific career ever since.

In the early 1990s, Ito began living between the United States and Japan, staying in Southern California for three months at a time (as determined by her tourist visa) and then returning to Kumamoto, the southern prefecture in Japan that her aged parents called home. In 1997, Ito acquired a Permanent Resident Visa (or "Green Card") and settled in the San Diego suburb of Encinitas with partner Harold Cohen (the British-born artist who developed AARON, a computer program that uses artificial intelligence to generate artistic images) and her three children (two of whom she relocated from Japan and one fathered by Cohen).[21]

After Cohen's death in 2016, Ito returned to Japan and has been living between Kumamoto and Tokyo ever since.

It was in the United States that Ito began to write seriously and critically about the botanical realm. She has described how tending to houseplants and garden plants helped create, in her Southern California home, a familiar atmosphere reminiscent of Japan.[22] Over time, Ito's love of and care for plants developed into a form of political critique. Confronted with her own precarious existence as an immigrant in the United States in the wake of the September 11, 2011, terrorist attacks (a precarity that only increased with time, culminating with the anti-immigrant platform espoused by the Trump presidential campaign in 2016) and with the reality of immigration and asylum seekers entering Southern California along the US-Mexico border, Ito looked to plants to make sense of migration and its control by the state.[23]

In Ito's work, plants are not apolitical, aestheticized objects. Nor are they immobile bystanders bearing witness to the long unfolding of human migration throughout history. Rather, they are active participants in that history. Plants move, travel, and migrate. They engage in what the early American ecologist Herbert Mason has called "secular migration," a type of migration that he describes as "often persistently directional through long time, and always (involving) the lineal succession of individuals."[24] Secular migration is a form of movement and acclimatization that takes generations to achieve. Using the secular migration of naturalized plants as a model, Ito casts her own history (and that of her family) as part of a much larger movement of human bodies across time, space, and generations. It is a movement that includes asylum seekers like Ramírez and his daughter, whose photograph Ito aligned with *Wild Grass on the Riverbank*. To be sure, Ito's experience in Southern California is not commensurate with the tragedy that befell Ramírez and other asylum seekers along the southern border of the US. However, what Ito's particular botanical becoming makes possible is a compassionate recognition that uses a plantlike logic to find similarity in the act of migration while also maintaining the alterity and particularity of individual experiences. Becoming botanical allows Ito to theorize a shared struggle against biopolitical control of migration that is not equally distributed, a fact that holds true for both humans and plant life.

Migration is not an individual traversal of distance in Ito's work. Like plants that participate in secular migration, Ito casts migration as a familial/reproductive project that spans time in addition to distance. This form of migration echoes the vegetative qualities that Sandilands proposes are those most controlled in contemporary biopolitics: growing, populating, spreading, invading.[25] This is made clear when *Wild Grass on the Riverbank* states imperatively: "Be carried from your native land to foreign soil, where you will grow wild and propagate."[26]

By the end of the poem, Natsukusa will leave her mother in the riverbank (i.e., Kumamoto) and return to the wasteland (i.e., Southern California), where she will realize her desire to "become a plant that grows spikes full of seed" and naturalize through the process of endless, botanical reproduction:

> In the middle of the wasteland, I spread out my arms and
>   legs wide and
> crouched down
> And that's how I grew a stem
> A bud was born from the tip of the stem
> It swelled
> And swelled
> And opened
> And took in everything
> The stem continued to grow
> Giving birth to one bud after another[27]

Natsukusa's "giving birth to one bud after another" is an image of secular migration, which Mason describes as "the linear reproductive succession of individuals through time."[28] It is a reminder that migration is not merely the movement of bodies from point A to point B but is also a process that unfolds in a long durée through the creation of new life in new soil. *Wild Grass on the Riverbank* (as well as many of Ito's other works) portrays migration as an ongoing process in this way, forever unfolding, unstable, and in flux within the deep time of plant life.

In the Migratory Middle of Nation and Family

In the preceding chapters of this book, I have argued that becoming botanical served as a point of departure and a route by which writers and filmmakers in Japan attempted to rethink the human and the plant, to reconfigure subjectivity, and to head somewhere new in response to crisis. In other words, I have argued that becoming botanical led to a migration away from the human realm and into the realm of vegetal life. In Hiromi Ito's writing, however, it is the literal act of migration itself that leads to becoming botanical. Ito's tales of human and botanical migration suggest that while immigration is, in Mason's figuration of secular migration, a "linear succession of individuals through time," it is not experienced as a unidirectional process. It is, rather, an unending negotiation of one's place between two or more geographical points, as well as points in time. It is a process that unfolds in the in-between zone of becoming. The movement is the point. And the movement is, counterintuitively, plantlike.

Much of Ito's work since the 1990s has focused on her experience of shuttling back and forth between the United States and Japan. There is a kinetic energy to these texts as they recount the endless comings and goings of Ito herself and the semifictionalized characters modeled on members of her immediate family. *Wild Grass on the Riverbank* opens with the frenetic movement of migration from a child's perspective (the young narrator Natsukusa):

> Mother led us along
> And we got on board
> We got on, got off, then on again
> We boarded cars and busses
> Then we boarded planes
> Then we boarded more busses and trains and cars[29]

This unsettled movement reoccurs throughout the poem following the frequent relocation of the family at its narrative center. This sense of kinetic movement runs throughout Ito's oeuvre. Both *The Thorn-Puller* (*Togenuki: shinsugamo jizō engi*, 2007) and *A Father's Life* (*Chichi no ikiru*, 2016) recount the turbulent period Itō spent traveling between Southern California and Kumamoto while caring for her dying father. More recent works like *Twilight Child* (*Tasogareteyuku kosan*, 2018) and *Travels* (*Michiyukiya*, 2020) find form in their back-and-forth movement between various locations in the United States, Japan, and Europe. Taken collectively, these works narrate an unending series of migrations that form the creative core of Ito's writing.

Understood as an unfolding, ongoing process of movement and subsequent acclimatization across time, migration in Ito's work becomes, to borrow another term from Deleuze and Guattari, an enactment of the "middle"—a zone of heightened possibility that brings previously separate points together, where they can create something new: "The middle is by no means an average; on the contrary, it is where things pick up speed. *Between* things does not designate a localizable relation going from one thing to the other and back again, but a perpendicular direction, a transversal movement that sweeps one *and* the other away, a stream without beginning or end that undermines its banks and picks up speed in the middle."[30]

The figurative image of a "stream without beginning or end" that "undermines it banks" captures the creative flow of migration in texts like *Wild Grass on the Riverbank*. As Ito's writing shuttles between Japan and the United States (and other countries as well), it produces a sense of a "middle" that destabilizes national identities. Ito's characters (including the semifictionalized versions of herself and her family members that she writes into her prose pieces) do not identify as wholly Japanese or American. Instead, they move through the middle of these identities by becoming botanical. This is the case in *Tree Spirits Grass*

Spirits. Here, Ito includes a chapter that unfolds in the middle of interstate travel and destabilizes national borders by recounting a road trip with her youngest daughter, called Tomé in this case, from Southern California up north to Washington State: "Around this time, I had been thinking about naturalized plants. In Japan, the season for summer grasses had just begun. Along the riverbanks of Kumamoto, the young stems of *seitaka-awadachisō* (or Canadian goldenrod) are surely beginning to grow all at once. *Seitaka-awadachisō* and *matsuyoigusa* (or Chilean evening primrose) are both originally from North America, and I decided that I wanted to see someplace where they grew, at their own pace, in native soil."[31]

The movement of Ito and her daughter up the West Coast of the United States is set alongside the (much longer, much older) movement of naturalized plants: Canadian goldenrod and Chilean evening primrose (see figures 5.1 and 5.2).

FIGURE 5.1. *Seitaka-awadachisō* (Canadian goldenrod). Source: Helge Klaus Rieder / Wikimedia Commons / Public Domain.

FIGURE 5.2. *Matsuyoigusa* (Chilean evening primrose). Source: Patrick Alexander / Public Domain.

Itō knows these plants from her native soil of Japan, where they have been naturalized, but she wants to see them in their native soil of North America, which is also "native" soil to her daughter.

These overlapping histories of migration cross in the middle and give Ito a chance to reflect on her own place in the middle of a family lineage that stretches across national borders. The chapter ends with Ito and Tomé driving home via Highway 101 and passing by forests of redwood trees. In a later chapter of *Tree Spirits Grass Spirits*, Ito writes of how the giant redwoods of California used to be categorized within the same family as the *sugi* (or Japanese cedar) before the advent of the APG (Angiosperm Phylogeny Group) system of categorization separated the two: "The *sugi* which have grown native in Japan since time immemorial, those *sugi* that started out as tiny grasses—it made me happy that those *sugi* were close relatives to these giant trees. . . . And now that the Taxodiaceae family has been incorporated into the Cupressaceae family and the sequoias and the *sugi* have been separated, I have become absolutely and completely devastated."[32]

The reclassification of sequoias in the 1990s removed them from an extended family that once stretched across national borders and included the Japanese *sugi* (that tree that served as the focus of chapters 3 and 4 of this book). Ito's point here is that such classifications are arbitrary, prone to change, at the whim of those in power. Like migration itself, the classification of migratory plants is in a kind of flux that can separate families. As she and Tomé stop along the road to view the same sequoias while returning home to Southern California, Ito comes to recognize that even without a direct familial relationship between the Japanese *sugi* and the sequoia (Ito uses the word *shinseki*, or "relative," in the above quote), she and Tomé are nevertheless related to these trees through a shared determination as migrants to survive in California for many generations into the future:

> The plants growing around the large trees (which were small by comparison) were full of leaves and blooming flowers. Each one embraced the sunlight and blew in the wind, glistening. The large trees accompanied innumerable small trees. In other words, in this case, the several-hundred-year-old trees were all female. I too was female. Tomé, who I had taken along with me, was a young woman—she too was female. The young sprouts which were the trees' offspring were shorter than we were. The fresh green of these young trees, which seemed as if they were holding out their tiny hands, told me, with a determined expression that resembled the clenching of tiny teeth, that they planned to live for several hundreds of years to come.[33]

As Ito stands in the middle of the road, in the middle of a road trip with her daughter, she finds solidarity with the giant redwoods. She sees an overlap in their migratory histories and understands that secular migration places her in the middle of this history, with a past and "several hundreds of years to come." It is a sentiment echoed poetically in *Wild Grass on the Riverbank*:

> And as the sprouts of new trees grow over thousands of years
> They will become a forest
> As the trees grow, they will pass through
> Thousands of years of adolescence and
> Thousands of years of menopause
> And each year they will drop fruit and seedpods with hundreds
>   of seeds
> They will drop them one after another onto the ground
> And new sprouts will grow[34]

In both scenes, we see, in Sandilands' words, "an attentive and lively practice in which the possibilities for ecological kinship are able to germinate, proliferate, and even effloresce."[35] As a space without firm boundaries, the zone of the middle (Deleuze and Guattari's "stream that undermines its banks") encourages such ecological kinship by eroding the ontological distance between humans and plants. The blurring of national boundaries becomes a blurring of familial boundaries as well, as Ito extends a notion of kinship to plant life (a gesture Osaki did as well, in chapter 1).

In another chapter of *Tree Spirits Grass Spirits*, titled "Living Trees and Dying Trees" ("*Ikiteiru ki to shindeiku ki*"), Ito further encapsulates the notion of the middle as she lies beneath a famous camphor tree, the Jakushinsan no kusu in Kumamoto. The piece begins by recounting the shock and heartbreak Ito and her family suffered as a beloved pepper tree is cut down in their neighborhood in Southern California. She recalls how each family member had a personal relationship to this tree and suggests that the removal of the tree severs a tie that once helped to bind her family together. The chapter then takes flight and recalls a trip Ito made from California back to Kumamoto with her daughter Kanoko and Kanoko's American husband. Shortly after they arrive in Japan, Ito's aged father passes away. Consumed by grief and overwhelmed by the necessary errands pertaining to her father's death, Ito decides to accompany Kanoko (who is pregnant) and her husband to see the nearby giant camphor tree. As they arrive, Ito begins to think about family lineage and death, placing herself in the middle of a flow of time (from her father, to herself, to her daughter, to her daughter's unborn child) that she finds replicated in the leaves of the tree:

> The tree was in a well-maintained park, but there was no one around. Flowers bloomed in clusters along the path leading from the parking lot: violets, veronica plants, henbits, tiny and common vetches. Kanoko and her husband held hands and walked around the giant camphor. I laid down on the bench that had been placed under the tree.
>
> I looked up, looked at the tree, looked at my hands, looked at the sky. It was a lightly cloudy sky. It was a giant, giant tree covered in wrinkles. They were tired, sad hands covered in wrinkles. As I was gazing at them, I realized I'd made a big mistake. I'd just been thinking that the red color on camphor trees this time of year was from new growth. But that wasn't so. It was the old leaves that had turned red, and they were mixed in with the green of the new buds. The red leaves rustled in the wind, and rained down to cover the surface below, just like a cherry tree as it loses its blossoms.[36]

Ito invokes the classic image of the cherry tree losing its blossoms (although a step removed through the camphor tree) to reflect on the passing of her father and her own aging glimpsed in her "tired, sad hands covered in wrinkles." Yet unlike the cliché trope of cherry blossoms scattering and signaling the transience of life, the camphor tree simultaneously presents "the green of new buds" as its older leaves fall. Through this unceasing cycle of birth and death embodied in the Jakushinsan camphor (which is believed to be eight hundred years old), life (and Ito's place in the middle of it) becomes, to return to Deleuze and Guattari's words, "a stream without beginning or end." Life becomes a perpetual botanical becoming that moves across generations. The tree is the embodiment of "becoming, complexly, alive," to return to my reworking of Sandilands' figuration.

The piece does not end here, under the camphor tree, but keeps moving and returns to Southern California. Ito mentions yet another tree, one she notices as she brings her youngest daughter Tomé to and from school. At first, Ito is unsure if the tree is a wax tree or a bead tree. As Tomé brings her a branch of the tree one day, Ito concludes that it is, in fact, a bead tree: "Of the Meliaceae family, the genus *melia*, native to Asia, native to Kumamoto."[37] This encounter with a bead tree, which has, through secular migration, arrived and taken hold in Southern California from Asia, provides Ito a chance to reflect on her own place in the middle of secular migration—a middle between Japan and the United States, and a middle between her parents and her children:

> I remembered that long ago, when I had first moved to Kumamoto, people had told me that those trees along the highway were wax trees.
>
> Be that as it may, the trees growing along the highway are not wax trees, they're bead trees. It was three years ago that I realized this, in the April that my mother died, in that busy time I spent traveling between California and Kumamoto during April and May. During that time, the bead trees started blooming here and there, and then they bloomed in full.
>
> Wax trees and bead trees actually look exactly alike, but their flowers are different. The flowers of the wax tree don't draw attention. The flowers of the bead tree are gorgeously vibrant and bloom in May. And so now, these flowers that Tomé picked in our neighborhood in Southern California—these were undoubtedly from a bead tree.[38]

The bead tree entangles Kumamoto (and with it, the death of Ito's mother and father) and Southern California (where her young daughter picks its flowers). Ito and her writing flow through the middle of this entanglement, in "another way of traveling and moving" that Deleuze and Guattari describe as "proceeding from the middle, coming and going rather than starting and finishing."[39] This way of moving is a form of becoming, one that is shared by both humans and plants, by both the bead trees that grow between Kumamoto and Southern California and by Ito and her children, who likewise grow between Kumamoto and Southern California.

Alterity and Fertility in the Botanical Realm

Ito rethinks the human by challenging any claim to identity or subjectivity tied to place. While local spirituality and history were instrumental to the botanical becomings discussed in chapter 4, Ito offers something different in her work: a multiple subjectivity rooted in the rootlessness of unending movement, much like Deleuze and Guattari's "stream without beginning or end that undermines its banks." There is, in this figuration, an uncanny visual echo of the watery border where Ramírez and his daughter tragically succumbed to the cruel logic of national separation, as discussed above. Yet the figurative unending stream is also where Ito's writing draws together migrants of all types (human and plant alike) and forges a sense of solidarity that resists biopolitical control by stretching across borders both national and special (as in "species") through the act of becoming.

Deleuze and Guattari famously liken the unending process of becoming to a rhizome, that plant-borne structure that I called, in chapter 1, messy and uneven, leading somewhere new and venturing into uncharted territory. They claim the rhizome "has no beginning or end; it is always in the middle, between things, interbeing, *intermezzo*."[40] The humans and plants that populate works like *Wild Grass on the Riverbank* and *Tree Spirits Grass Spirits* are rhizomatic in this way. They exist between Japan and the US in an unending process of adaptation. It is through an embrace and a championing of the migrant as an "interbeing" that Ito's work constructs its notion of botanical empathy. After all, the migrant, in Ito's literary universe, is plantlike, and plants, in the words of Michael Marder, "simply cannot be conceived as individual organisms, but instead as subjects with deeply pluralistic identities, ranging from their own decentralized intelligence ... to their interdependent survival. On the face of it, plants' radical otherness has to do, in part, with this fluidity of the distinction between self and other."[41] What is empathy but a "fluidity of the distinction between self and other?"

Writing from within the middle, Ito breaks down the barriers between humans of differing points of origin as well as between humans and plants. She creates characters that identify somewhere between human and botanical. In her 2005 prose collection *Aunt Green-Thumb* (*Midori no obasan*), Ito imagines that she herself may even be part plant: "It's possible that in the process of growing up, I was, without my knowing it, violated by crawling and creeping vines, stalks, and leaves. I was meant to be human, but there's the possibility that I have the blood of plants mixed in somewhere."[42] Within Ito's literary universe, the line between the human and botanical realms is a permeable border, as permeable as the national borders that both humans and plants traverse. As such, the human characters of her poems and prose phytomorphically exhibit plantlike characteristics.

This is particularly true of *Wild Grass on the Riverbank*, in which seemingly human characters are able to regenerate cut-off appendages.[43] They are able, like plants, to wither and die, only to be reborn in spring (a *shokubutsusei* I discuss more at the end of this chapter). The naturalized plants of the riverbank (i.e., Kumamoto), become kin to protagonist Natsukusa and end up becoming a manifestation of herself. About halfway through the poem, a new "sister" appears named Alexa (which is written in Japanese as *Arekusa*, a homophone for "Wild Grass"). The poem suggests that Alexa is in fact a kind of avatar of the naturalized "wild grasses" that surround Natsukusa and her family. Eventually, Natsukusa realizes that Alexa is not a sister but rather a part of her own psyche that has been projected out into the botanical realm:

> Alexa was me
> The wild grass was me
> I was Alexa
> I was the wild grass
> We were exactly alike, just like *Erigeron canadensis* and
>   *Conyza sumatrensis*[44]

The two plants listed in the last line, called *himemukashiyomogi* and *ō-arechinogiku* in Japanese and commonly called *fleabane* and *horseweed* in English, are difficult to differentiate by sight. Natsukusa sees herself (and her other "self," Alexa/*Arekusa*/Wild Grass) in and *as* these naturalized plants. They become anthropomorphized first as part of Natsukusa's family and then as a manifestation of her botanical subjectivity. The poem engages in this anthropomorphism in order to then engage in phytomorphism. The zone of the middle opens up in the movement between these two "-isms."

Ito has written of the difficulty she experienced in reaching this point of indeterminacy between humans and plants. In *Tree Spirits Grass Spirits*, she describes the challenges she faced writing about naturalized plants in *Wild Grass on the Riverbank* while doing justice to their more-than-human characteristics: "Every summer during the period in which I wrote this poem, I would look out toward the riverbank and watch the *Sorghum halepense*, the *Conyza sumatrensis*, and the *Solidago altissima* rise and fall as they blew in the wind. I thought a lot about them. How could I put them into words? Would I be able to represent their movements, their life force, exactly as I saw them?"[45] Ito recounts that it took years to properly capture the way these naturalized plants moved in the wind, ultimately arriving at this section from *Wild Grass on the Riverbank*:

> *Sorghum halepense* fell over and got back up
> *Solidago altissima* was still young, its stalk and leaves were green

> It was pushed over by the wind, as if to say, you, get over there,
> then it pushed the next stalk
> The next stalk too, pushed the next stalk as if to say, you,
> get over there
> The next stalk after the next stalk also pushed the next stalk as if to
> say, you, get over there, you, get over there
> You, get over there, *Solidago altissima* was pushed over, you,
> get over there, was pushed, you, get over there
> You, get over there
> The kudzu vines squirmed, grew up
> Onto the embankment, stuck out their tips, waited, then grew tired[46]

Unlike *Wandering in the Realm of the Seventh Sense*'s Machiko, who struggled to write nonobjectifying poetry about the moss she observed (as discussed in chapter 1), Ito finds a way to capture the very essence of plant life in verse. She explains that once she found the right language to describe these plants, "(an) emotion ... like malice came out on the surface of it. I don't know why it turned out this way, when I was intentionally trying to push emotion aside."[47] The subjective power of plant life rises to the surface of Ito's poetry against her own intentions, as if the plants used Ito as a medium to find a voice and will of their own—a phenomenon discussed in chapter 3 of this book.

Even as she writes of human characters becoming botanical and forging international and multispecies alliances, Ito acknowledges the limits of truly knowing and/or embodying the botanical world. This is particularly true of her prose writings, which tend to be more overtly autobiographical in nature and thus tied more closely to a human point of view. Ito writes time and again of her identification with naturalized plants in *Tree Spirits Grass Spirits* while inevitably upholding the radical alterity of plant life. The book's opening chapter, "The Plants in My Front Yard" ("*Zentei no shokubutsutachi*"), speaks of Ito's inability to fully embody the botanical life force for which she yearns. It begins, much like *Wild Grass on the Riverbank*, in media res: "Returning to Southern California from Japan early in the New Year, I found the sky blue and the air dry and hot at both the Los Angeles airport and the small airport closest to where I live. At the airport in Kumamoto, a light snow had been falling."[48] Ito goes on to describe the various trees and flowers that populate her yard in Southern California. She writes of the oxalis:

> When its long flowering season comes to an end, oxalis withers all at once, and each one uproots from the soil. But at that point they have already left behind many small radish-like bulbs within the earth. It's a fertility more amazing than that of mice or rabbits.

> Each bulb sleeps a whole year and then opens its eyes in spring. They grow and spread out their leaves and clump together luxuriantly, blooming dignified yellow flowers. I couldn't help but feel that with their way of life as "naturalized plants," and with that very name, that they were somehow of my own flesh and blood. I had prayed for the kind of aggressive fertility they had, but I only gave birth to three children. I didn't have enough strength. It was disappointing.[49]

Ito simultaneously calls naturalized plants "of (her) own flesh and blood" and recognizes that they possess an "aggressive fertility" that exceeds the capabilities of a human like herself. She admits to "praying" for this botanical capacity and being disappointed by not actualizing the botanical becoming required to make it possible. Yet there is a way in which Ito *was able* to enact such a botanical becoming. As Natsukusa endlessly propagates at the end of *Wild Grass on the Riverbank*, Ito is able to accomplish, through poetry, what the oxalis accomplishes in her backyard. Ito writes of Natsukusa "giving birth to one bud after another." Ito may not have attained the "aggressive fertility" of plant life that she found necessary for secular migration in real life (and in the autobiographical prose that recounts this failure), but she is able to carve a space in the middle for Natsukusa to do so. It is here, in the middle of a botanical imagination, that *Wild Grass on the Riverbank* finds radical empathy for kindred, migratory spirits, be they tree, grass, or human.

Invasive Role Models and Fellow Countrymen

The indeterminacy between migratory humans and plants found in Ito's work extends into the legal realm of forced removal, where the lines between weeding undesirable plants and deporting undocumented immigrants blur. There is a reoccurring association in Ito's writing between the removal of naturalized (invasive) species of plants and the precarity Ito herself has experienced as an immigrant in the United States. A section near the end of *Wild Grass on the Riverbank* links the removal of the invasive ice plant to the removal of "invasive" immigrants:

> Just now, I was pulling out some ice plants,
> They're growing rampant,
> That plant originally didn't grow here naturally, someone brought
>   it from
> somewhere else, it's really robust, very strong, it's crowding out
>   and killing
> all the plants that grow here naturally, our only hope for reclaiming an

environment for the plants that grow here naturally is to get our hands dirty and tear them out at the roots, we need to eradicate them,
    but I can't
get them all[50]

This scene is repeated in *Tree Spirits Grass Spirits*, where Ito writes of the non-native species growing in a small park near her house in Southern California. She describes the removal of the ice plant as akin not only to deportation but also to genocide:

> Even in that park next door to our house, non-native plants find their way in. Since the park is designed to protect native species, the non-native plants are, of course, forcibly exterminated. One that's seen as particularly hostile is ice plant, which was planted as ground cover, and holds water in its leaves and grows easily, spreading out all over, covering everything up, destroying everything in its path. Sometimes the organization that manages the park conducts a large-scale assault on the ice plant, and the corpses that have been uprooted are piled up in heaps. I know they're plants, but there is no other word I can use besides "corpses." It's a terrible sight, and I have to cover my eyes.[51]

Ito is horrified by the sight of the dead ice plant (see figure 5.3). She empathizes with this invasive species and refers to their uprooted bodies as "corpses," a word used in reference to plants throughout *Wild Grass on the Riverbank* as well.

FIGURE 5.3. Ice Plant Pulling Contest, Monterey, California. Source: Photo by Steven L. Shepard, Presidio of Monterey Public Affairs.

The native-invasive dichotomy has become a topic of discussion within critical plant studies and has served as the central concern for such studies as Shinozuka's *Biotic Borders* and Banu Subramanian's *Ghost Stories for Darwin* (2014). What does it mean to empathize with an invasive species, especially in an age of ecological precarity? Subramanian's take on the issue resonates with Ito's empathy for the invasive ice plant:

> There are striking similarities in the qualities ascribed to foreign plants, animals, and people, and these debates track each other. The xenophobic rhetoric is unmistakable. The point of my analysis is not to suggest that we are not losing native species, or that we should allow the free flow of plants and animals in the name of modernity or globalization. Instead, it is to suggest that we are living in a cultural moment where the anxieties of globalization are feeding nationalisms through xenophobia. The battle against exotic and alien plants is a symptom of a campaign that misplaces and displaces anxieties about economic, social, political, and cultural changes onto outsiders and foreigners.[52]

Subramanian's diagnosis of a cultural moment in which anxiety over "economic, social, political, and cultural changes" feed into xenophobic ideology that gets displaced onto the botanical realm is precisely the background of crisis against which Ito writes. Like the other texts discussed in this book, Ito's books often do not make spectacles of crisis. Rather, xenophobia and the crises of anti-immigration policy serve as an undercurrent that runs throughout much of the writing Ito produced while living in California. Far from being a "displacement" of this xenophobia onto plant life, Ito's empathy for the ice plant is an empathy for the unruly migrant unwilling to submit to control. As Subramanian makes clear: "As long as exotic/alien plants know their rightful place as workers, laborers, and providers, and controlled commodities, their positions manipulated and controlled by the natives, their presence is tolerated."[53] Ito feels more akin to those plants that don't know their "rightful place."

Another question arises: By expressing a deep empathy for the plight of the ice plant, is Ito not reinforcing, to a certain extent, an anthropocentric worldview? Michael Marder has warned that such anthropocentrism can come specifically from an empathetic approach to plant life: "When humans empathize with plants, they, thus, ultimately empathize with themselves, turning the object of empathy into a blank screen, onto which essentially human emotions are projected. A presumably sensitive ethical approach veers on the side of instrumentalization, in that it uses the plant as a means for personal catharsis and an outlet for the content of bad conscience."[54] To be sure, Ito's empathy for plants does become an empathy for humans (who share their migratory movement). But her botanical empathy does not serve as an "outlet for the content of bad conscience," as Marder cautions. Instead, it serves as a radical destabilizing of an anthropocentric worldview, one that has instrumentalized and discounted the value of not only plant life but migratory human lives as well.

Ito expresses a deep concern for the plight of the migratory ice plant and concludes the chapter by extending this empathy toward fellow human migrants: "Even though I've learned that naturalized plants have exterminated the native plants, I've come on over to the side of the invasive, and resigned myself, thinking, 'Hmm, well, the native plants were weak, and so it goes.' If anything, naturalized plants are the ones that are fierce and indefatigable, and, to an extent, it seems that they served as my role models."[55]

Ito boldly declares invasive species her "role models." As role models, invasive naturalized plants teach Ito of the persistence necessary for secular migration, or the unruliness necessary for resistance. They likewise teach her about phenotypic plasticity, which Marder characterizes elsewhere as a "ceaseless striving toward the other and becoming-other in growth and reproduction."[56] Invasive plants also teach her to empathize with those humans deemed "invasive," a term that carries significant weight in the border community of Southern California that Ito called home at the time of writing.

Ito's claim that invasive species are her role models is striking because it not only redeems the unwanted plants that populate Southern California; it also casts Ito alongside these unwanted migratory bodies. Ito's botanical empathy reaches what Marder calls "the extreme," in which "to empathize with plants is to recognize in ourselves certain features of vegetal life, rather than to project the metaphysical image of human existence onto other life-worlds."[57] In other words, Ito's empathy is phytomorphic. The feature of vegetal life that Ito recognizes in herself is the "fierce and indefatigable" resolution to naturalize, to transform and become anew in new soil.

While I read Ito's embrace of the invasive as a form of resistance to biopolitical control of human bodies in immigration, I nevertheless acknowledge a potentially dangerous quality to her language here as it veers toward the social Darwinist logic that Osaki Midori rejected in her work (as discussed in chapter 1). Ito's claim that the flourishing of the ice plant is justified because the "native plants were weak" takes on a colonialist hue, especially in the settler-colonial space of California. It is somewhat difficult to square such logic and language with Ito's stated interest in Native American culture. She claims one of the main reasons she came to California was to study Native American poetry and storytelling. At the heart of Ito's writing on migration is a question that Marder articulates well in botanical terms: "How could one draw together the world of human beings and that of plants, while resisting the temptation to sacrifice the specificity of either perspective?"⁵⁸ We can modify this question to address humans of different nationalities as well: How could one draw together the varied experiences of humans migrating to the United States, while resisting the temptation to sacrifice the specificity of each individual set of circumstances? Ito's writing attempts to answer these questions through becoming botanical. For it is within the botanical realm that Ito's work maintains a sense of poetic wonder at the radical otherness of the plant world, which she then extends to those human refugees less fortunate than herself. A similar sense of poetic wonder is in turn extended to the Indigenous peoples of the United States. Ito's long-form narrative poem *Coyote Song* (*Koyōte songu*, written between 2005 and 2007) includes narrative elements from the folklore of various Native American tribes, including the Nez Perce, the Ponca, the Winnebago, and the Alsea. It is a poetic tribute to a "United States" that far predates the arrival of the ice plant and all that it stands for metaphorically.

There is, to be sure, a potential for oversimplification in Ito's botanical empathy. Reducing a diverse population of humans (and/or plants) with differing circumstances and struggles to the general category of "immigrant" can just as easily swing toward the kind of xenophobic rhetoric Ito's empathy looks to overcome. Yet we can also see in Ito's self-identification with marginalized immigrant communities a kind of reclamation of power. It is as if Ito recognizes the power held by the word *immigrant* (a power used to xenophobic ends by the US immigration enforcement agencies for much of Ito's tenure living in Southern California) and redirects its totalizing simplicity to destabilize any claims to a "native" belonging to place. If it sounds overly simple, that is because it *is* overly simple to Ito: *all bodies migrate*, even those deemed "native." In *Tree Spirits Grass Spirits*, Ito writes of *kyūrigusa*, or "cucumber grass," as a vegetal example of the arbitrariness of such designations as "native" and "naturalized": "They say cucumber grass is a naturalized plant. Even so, they say it's an ancient naturalized plant, one that came around the same time as the ancestor of barley. How in the world could we call this a 'naturalized plant?' Is it right to do so? If it were humans we were talking about, wouldn't they already be considered fellow countrymen? As a humble immigrant myself, this is a question I can't let go of."⁵⁹

Focusing on the deep history of plant migration, Ito asks: Where does the distinction lay between "native" and "naturalized" or between "immigrants" and "fellow countrymen?" Based on her experiences as an immigrant in the United States, Ito is aware that such distinctions lay in the hands of those in power. Throughout *Wild Grass on the Riverbank*, there is a tension between the freedom of movement found in the botanical realm and the biopolitical control exerted on migratory human bodies by governmental agencies. The fear of arrest and deportation looms over the poem. Within its opening pages, Natsukusa describes her experience with immigration authorities at the airport in the wasteland of Southern California, as the poem gives way to an extended section of run-on prose:

> It took one day and one night to reach immigration, the route was lined with many, many immigrants who had run out of energy, collapsed along the way and shriveled up, no matter how wealthy the country, they never make the path to immigration any shorter, their wealth won't help us, there is just sadness, curt answers and pain, those places are nowhere in particular, and to make matters worse, there is no guarantee we'll even make it through, little brother didn't notice but I did, our passports were bad passports, I had noticed alright, at immigration in every country, the men made unfriendly faces and stared at their computers, that's because our passports are bad passports.[60]

Here, at the start of *Wild Grass on the Riverbank*, innumerable desperate human bodies become botanical and "shriveled up" (*hikarabiteimashita*) as they wait endlessly for a chance to enter the United States. They embody, in their dried-up husks, Sandilands' claim that humans are "controlled *like and even as plants*" in the contemporary biopolitical control of human migration. Ito recognizes this and decides to turn it on its head. If migratory humans are controlled "like plants," then they can, to again paraphrase Sandilands, grow, populate, spread, invade "like plants."

By the end of *Wild Grass on the Riverbank*, Natsukusa will come to see herself as one of these desperate bodies rendered plantlike, but she finds freedom in the fact that such self-recognition in the botanical realm can lead to new possibilities. In the last section of the poem, Natsukusa returns to the wasteland without her mother. Her experience at the airport immigration office is markedly different than her first time through. While there remains a legal challenge to Natsukusa's entry (she still has a "bad passport"), she learns how to move through the middle:

> The man who worked there stared at his computer
> How long, he asked
> How long have you been away from this country?
> I told him
> The man who worked there looked at his computer and gave
>   me a stamp
> There is a dirty spot on your passport
> The man who worked there told me,
> You can't get rid of the dirty spot,
> In order to solve this problem,
> You have no choice but to transform
> So that you look like those who grow here naturally,

> Even though you didn't grow here naturally to begin with
> (Be carried from your native land to foreign soil, where you
>   will grow wild
> and propagate)
> *Paspalum urvillei*
> *Verbena brasiliensis*
> *Conyza sumatrensis*[61]

This is Natsukusa's true moment of epiphany. It is here that she learns she must become botanical and naturalize in order to avoid legal trouble. The poem hinges between human naturalization, in which Natsukusa is told she must become a legal citizen to "solve the problem" of her passport, and plant naturalization, as it lists three of the naturalized plants featured throughout the poem. Through secular migration, these three plants naturalized to the riverbank of Kumamoto. It is now Natsukusa's turn to do the same in the wasteland.

This epiphany is not singular. It blooms in Natsukusa's botanical subjectivity, opening out to a multispecies collective that incorporates all migratory bodies she encounters in the wasteland. She leaves the airport with her younger brother and sister and finds herself in the middle of just such a collective that includes both humans and plants:

> We left the airport building, and we waited for the bus a long time while keeping ourselves out of the rain, we got on board the bus and shook back and forth for a long time, the windows of the bus were miserably dirty, the people (got) on board and got off a few at a time, all of the people had left the places where they had been born naturally and had come here, the things growing here were alive, living, life, live oaks, sage thickets and cacti and agave . . .
>
> And that's how we reached the wasteland
>   Familiar landscapes, trees, and plants
>   There were things that had grown there naturally
>   There were things that had come from elsewhere and spread[62]

The wasteland becomes the sum total of "things that had grown there naturally," like "live oaks, sage thickets and cacti and agave," and "things that had come from elsewhere and spread," like those humans who had "left the places where they had been born naturally." The native, naturalized, and invasive all become "fellow countrymen" in the middle.

As she arrives in her old neighborhood, Natsukusa once again encounters human immigrants who have "dried up." She realizes they are no different than herself:

> There were bodies of immigrants who had run out of energy along the
> way and dried up
> There were whole families who had nowhere at all to go
> And had just laid down there and were sleeping soundly
> Mother had once told us, the *immigrants* are dead
> Mother used the unfamiliar word *immigrants*
> She said, we're *immigrants* too . . .
> They were told,
> This isn't where you're supposed to be,
> Go home,
> Shut your mouth,
> Just line up over there
> But even so, they came to this country
> They left behind their languages
> And we were just like them[63]

Within the botanical realm, Ito and her characters are "just like" those naturalized plants that left their native homes and "just like" those human immigrants told to "Go home." Natsukusa realizes she is "just like" those immigrants who "are dead," immigrants who have died tragic deaths but can somehow come back to life through becoming botanical (a *shokubutsusei* that I will discuss in the concluding paragraph of this chapter).

Natsukusa is able to see herself in these "dried up" husks of migratory bodies because she has spent the majority of the poem learning about naturalized plants. Before leaving the riverbank, she shares a conversation with an immigrant man who teaches her the names of several unfamiliar plants. Their conversation hinges on the fact that one of the plants, *Paspali urvillei* (*tachi-suzume-no-hie* in Japanese), is not featured in the "plant book" Natsukusa uses to identify the plants of the riverbank. The man explains that it is "newly naturalized" and thus not included in the book. He teaches Natsukusa about the prevalence of migratory plants, showing her that plants from elsewhere have adapted to the riverbank and become an integral part of their ecological fabric. At the same time, he speaks of the difficulty of acclimatization to a new environment, a difficulty shared by humans and plants alike:

> But this one is different,
> *Paspalum urvillei* is from South America,
> It reached here about the time I was born,
> We grew up together, the whole time, here on the riverbank.
> But neither of us has ever gotten used to the place,
> Not *Paspalum urvillei*, not me,

> We're not used to the climate or the landscape here, we don't understand the
> language or what people are saying, neither *Paspalum urvillei* nor me have
> much to do with people, we don't talk, we don't get accustomed to things . . .[64]

Natsukusa (who, as discussed above, has a botanical alter ego in the form of Alexa/*Arekusa*) thus learns to process her own experience of migration (first to the wasteland, then to the riverbank, and then back again) through the migratory experience of naturalized plants. But she also learns of the difficulty of acclimatization. As the man tells her, not all migrants "get accustomed to things."

This is true of Ito herself (or at least it is true of the semifictionalized version of herself at the heart of her work). Before she could find the literary (and critical) potential in uprooting, she would first need to find a way to acclimatize to her new surroundings in Southern California, just like the many naturalized plants there. In order to grow, populate, spread, and invade (to use Sandilands' figuration once again), she would need to turn plastic and transform. Just as it took Ito several years to capture the movement of naturalized plants in words (as she claims was the case in *Tree Spirits Grass Spirits*), so, too, would it take her several years to identify with migratory plants in a radical way and to find the botanical poetics from which to posit a notion of empathy that moves between migratory humans and plants.

The Struggle for Acclimatization and Plasticity

Ito began writing about migration after she arrived in Southern California in the late 1990s. Her early works written in California, including *House Plant* (*Hausu puranto*, 1998) and *La Niña* (*Ra nīnya*, 1999), do not make a clear link between the secular migration of plants and human migration in the way her later works do. Yet they are both works of a botanical imagination. *House Plant* and *La Niña* are attempts to find a language that can describe the process of acclimatization that is required to reach the status of naturalization.[65] Although they do not fully develop a notion of botanical empathy, they display a plantlike plasticity as they record the process of adaptation to a new environment. *House Plant* stages the difficulties Ito and her family faced settling in Southern California in the form of a semiautobiographical novella.[66] Some of these difficulties are linguistic. The novella portrays the first-person narrator (who is based on Ito but remains nameless throughout) struggling to learn English. She worries about losing her ability to properly communicate in Japanese as well.[67] From its opening lines, the narrator of *House Plant* pays close, plantlike attention to the climate of Southern California: "When I come out of the building the sky is very blue. The sunlight very dry, everything very Californian. I feel as though the sky is teasing me, the blue sky, the sunlight. It doesn't matter what I'm doing, doesn't matter what state I'm in; the sky never changes in the slightest. The sky is sky, very blue and clear."[68]

The narrator struggles to describe this non-Japanese climate with Japanese words: "I've been trying to find a suitable word to describe the blue sky, but I haven't found one. In Japanese we say *an-autumn-clear-sky* or *a-Japanese-cloudless-sky, a-spring-like-autumn-day*, but they all mean autumn weather in Japan, a clear, cloudless blue sky. But much calmer."[69] How, Ito asks, can one acclimatize to a new environment without the right words to describe even the climate itself?

Ito's follow-up to *House Plant*, titled *La Niña*, poses this question as well. The title is a play on words, as *la niña* (or "little girl" in Spanish) refers both to the daughter character in the text (a fictionalized version of one of Ito's daughters) and the weather pattern of the same name that influenced the climate of Southern California around the time Ito wrote the story. The novella's narrator (again based on Ito but nameless in the story) struggles to comprehend the increased rainfall that is characteristic of la niña weather. She likewise struggles to understand the gendered aspect of the name *la niña* and envisions it as a kind of migration of its own: "La niña—that small thing (feminine noun), that female child, those little girls, those daughters, no, I don't think it's plural, even if it is a feminine noun. But the image I have is of multiple girls making their way across the waves, headed this way."[70] In *La Niña*, Ito (or, rather, the narrator based on her) has not yet found the creative space of the middle. She experiences discomfort with the climate of her new home that exacerbates the personal struggles each family member experiences trying to adapt to their new lives in California. The narrator's daughter develops an eating disorder, while the narrator herself wrestles with painful memories of her ex-husband, whom she has left behind in Japan. Ito repeats a refrain throughout the narrative that speaks to the uprooted feeling of existing between Japan and the United States: "Two spirits, one body" (*Kokoro wa futatsu, mi wa hitotsu*). This phrase could easily be deployed to describe a botanical subjectivity, which I have been arguing throughout this book is a multiple subjectivity. Ito's use of the phrase in *La Niña* is far from botanical, however. It does not point toward a creative embodiment of plantlike qualities that Ito writes into her later work. Here, in *La Niña*, "two spirits" in "one body" is a hindrance to acclimatization. It prevents the narrator from being present or moving forward. It is not liberatory.

Both *House Plant* and *La Niña* are early steps toward becoming botanical, but they do not move beyond the metaphorical figuration of uprooting. Both focus on their narrator's isolation in her new home. In *House Plant*, the loneliness of uprooting becomes palpable after the narrator's one American friend, Claris, moves away. The narrator feels that she was able to communicate with Claris, claiming that when "talking with Claris, I never felt that any of my words were getting lost."[71] Once Claris moves away, however, the narrator remarks that her "life was silent for a while."[72] In this silence is a loneliness that permeates the text, producing what appears to be a strong desire for "rootedness," defined by Christy Wampole as "a conservative desire for comfort. Comfort here means the existential consolation of strength-giving sameness."[73] As the narrator of *House Plant* feels different and out of place in her surroundings, she looks for examples of "strength-giving sameness," but she cannot find any.

In these early California novellas, Ito has yet to find the sameness in difference that she writes into the botanical empathy of later texts. Overall, *House Plant* sees difference as a hindrance to acclimatization. Yet there is a moment in which the narrator finds something approaching a sense of community among fellow migrants. She attends a dinner party with her husband (named Aaron, likely after the computer program developed by Ito's partner Harold Cohen) and her friend Claris (who was still living there at the time). The remaining guests are, like the narrator, not US citizens. Among them is a woman the narrator refers to as "Dietlin(d)," the final letter of her name bracketed to highlight the fact that the narrator is unable, as a native Japanese speaker, to properly pronounce or hear the compound consonant of *nd*. Although the narrator dreads attending the party ("They cause me so much distress"), she finds a sense of camaraderie with the foreign guests: "Tom, Tomasz, and Agosz are always in and out of the country. When they're here, they're here; when they're not, they're not. When they are here, we see them, and when they aren't, then that's all there is to it. Whenever they return, we see them again. Dietlin(d) is the same way, and me too."[74]

The group shares stories of dealing with the US Immigration and Naturalization Service (INS), which was the agency in charge of immigration matters until it was dissolved in 2003.[75] They offer each other tips on how to avoid the legal troubles associated with overstaying one's tourist visa. The narrator ends up recounting how she ran into trouble after overstaying her own visa. When she attempted to return to the United States, she had difficulty passing through immigration at the airport. Told she would experience these issues every time she attempted to return to the United States, the narrator decides to apply for a Permanent Resident Visa. Her application is rejected:

> It said rejected, but it told me I could come to the consulate for an interview if I wished. I went; at the consulate, there was a little, little window. I had to talk to the window, stooping down, bending my whole body. I had to stoop, bending my whole body, to talk to the window. Voices

were transmitted back and forth through a microphone. The consul and the interpreter said I hadn't proved that I didn't want to immigrate. Of course, I said, I don't have any desire to leave my country for good, but they wouldn't believe me. You have to prove it, they said. So I said I have my own house here; I have my family here. I explained in many ways, but they didn't have their listening ears on. Before I had finished talking, the interpreter had already opened her mouth and said, that's not proof, you have to prove it much more convincingly. . . . And before I could catch my breath the interpreter yelled triumphantly, you haven't proved it! *Pom, pom, pom*, she stamped, stamped, stamped on the last pages of the passports, APPLICATION REJECTED, APPLICATION REJECTED, APPLICATION REJECTED. I say this three times because she first stamped my passport, then the kids'. There was nothing I could do; I was speechless; the window slammed shut in front of my nose.[76]

It is this traumatic experience (based on an experience from Ito's own life that she has written about several times in several different texts) that leads her to marry Aaron, who has an easier time naturalizing. In this dinner party scene, we see the first inklings of what Ito will eventually formulate into a botanical empathy. *House Plant* collects a group of people who have migration in common, but the dinner party does not necessarily bring them closer together. The narrator gets into an argument with the other non-US citizens at the party, trying to convince them that overstaying one's visa will lead to the kind of legal difficulties she has experienced. Although she tries to express empathy for their shared precarious situation, her words fall on deaf ears.

The dinner party scene in *House Plant* is an image of shared migrancy, but Ito does not seem to have the botanical language yet to draw the narrator and the other guests together into a radical collective that could resist state control. A similar thing occurs at the end of *La Niña*. The novella ends at the Los Angeles International Airport, as the narrator has decided to bring her children back to Japan for a period of time. Although they arrive at the airport late at night, the narrator finds other parents traveling as well: "We sat in the corner of a coffee shop. Even though it was the middle of the night, the LA airport was bustling. There were many other ethnic [*esunikku*] parents with children besides us. The parents were feeding their children. It was always around this time that planes going to Asia, South America, and the Near and Middle East took off."[77] Here again, Ito writes herself (through the nameless first-person narrator) into a scene surrounded by other migrating humans. She does not, however, make an explicit link between their deterritorialization (to borrow a term from Deleuze and Guattari) and the migratory nature of plants, a link I have been arguing allows

Ito's later work to form more radical alliances between humans and plants alike. Without migratory plants serving as a medium through which Ito can process her own migratory experience, the other "ethnic" families remain "other."

While the botanical realm does not help the narrators of *House Plant* and *La Niña* understand their place (or the place of the other dinner party guests or the migratory families at the airport) within secular migration, plants do figure prominently in both novellas. Newly transplanted to Southern California, the narrators are unfamiliar with much of the plant life in the region. Much like her uncomfortable relationship with the English language and the climate, *House Plant*'s narrator displays a tense relationship with the flora of Southern California. Eucalyptus trees, in particular, become an ominous presence:

> Every time I go shopping I see it. The road goes downhill. And as it continues winding along, I look out over the lower landscape ahead. It looks a bit hazy, so I know maybe there are eucalyptus trees. But when I drive into that landscape, there aren't just a few trees here and there; I am overwhelmed. The whole world is full of eucalyptus trees. I can't see the sky at all. The road is engulfed, left and right; the huge eucalyptus trees cover everything; even in the daytime it's gloomy here. Going downhill, winding or dead-end—it's like that everywhere.[78]

The sheer number of eucalyptus trees overwhelm the narrator, blocking out the sun, rendering the world "gloomy." In an ironic twist, it is plant life that keeps the narrator from realizing her own plantlike plasticity. Throughout *House Plant*, eucalyptus trees stand as a hindrance to acclimatization. In the narrator's eyes, they stand out in the otherwise verdant landscape. As she describes her neighborhood, we get the sense that the eucalyptus trees do not belong. The narrator's own anxiety over being uprooted becomes embodied in the trees: "This is a nice residential area—suburban, open, lots of Mexicans, though few Asians. Not much crime. At least this is a safe community to live in—that kind of place. The whole area is well irrigated, and most of the houses are surrounded in green. Shopping malls also are surrounded in green. Fruiting lemon trees, avocado trees, blooming bougainvillea. But we can spot a eucalyptus tree here and there, standing, growing, swaying, inhumanely, barrenly."[79]

The eucalyptus tree brings something like discomfort to the narrator. Yet there is a curious inversion taking place here. In the previous quotation, the eucalyptus trees are presented as thriving to the point of overwhelming the narrator, yet in the later quotation, they are spotty and unwelcome. They sway "inhumanely, barrenly." The narrator views these trees as an impediment to her own thriving, as they prevent her from growing anything new in her garden: "The ground is barren. Nothing grows. Even so, I've never given up; I planted many things and nothing grew. Someone told me that it was because of the eucalyptus trees. That's why, I thought."[80]

Ito's later works see the thriving of unwelcome species like the eucalyptus as a virtue (as with ice plants, which become a role model). As she praises the invasive qualities of naturalized plants, Ito expresses a conviction to do whatever it takes to acclimatize in *Tree Spirits Grass Spirits*. There, she sees herself as plastic, as a "fierce and indefatigable" naturalized plant that may even force out "weak" native plants.[81] This fierceness is all but absent in *House Plant*. Plant life does not offer any promise of plasticity that might help the narrator adapt to her new surroundings. The botanical subjectivity opened up in *House Plant* is confusing and confining: "The character of the eucalyptus trees around my house and the confusion under them can be seen from far off. The messiness of the lives of the people who live there—you can tell everything. I don't want to be discovered so easily—I don't, but there's no way of hiding. I'm overwhelmed by that endless blurred impression that is where I live."[82] By the time Ito began publishing *Wild Grass on the Riverbank* in 2004, her impression of her surroundings in Southern California had sharpened. The hazy, uneasy feeling of being out of place, as witnessed throughout *House Plant*, is replaced by a near-obsessive attention to the naturalized plants that have taken root and flourished in Southern California. *House Plant* may acknowledge the eucalyptus as a migratory species; it does so with an uncertainty that characterizes the novella and distinguishes it from Ito's later work: "I don't know whether it was before the Gold Rush or afterward that they were building the railroads and they brought the eucalyptus tree from Australia and planted them to use for railroad ties. . . . I heard this story somewhere. I'm not sure whether it's true or not. It was either Aaron or Claris who told me, but both of them came to California from somewhere else."[83]

The elements to construct a notion of botanical empathy are present here: migratory humans (the narrator, her husband Aaron, and even the American-born Claris) and migratory plants (the eucalyptus that has overstayed its welcome once it was no longer deemed of use to humans), all occupying the same space that has become their home. The novella suggests a commonality between these various humans and plants, but it does not draw these migratory beings into a multispecies collective, the way *Wild Grass on the Riverbank* does as Natsukusa returns to the wasteland and remarks:

> Familiar landscapes, trees, and plants
> There were things that had grown there naturally
> There were things that had come from elsewhere and spread[84]

La Niña comes closer to reaching a botanical revelation leading to acclimatization. While the eucalyptus trees in *House Plant* alienate the narrator and prevent her from adapting to Southern California, the acacia tree (another non-native plant deemed invasive in California) teaches the narrator of *La Niña* about diversity and perseverance. As she brings her husband (who, just like in *House Plant*, is a fictionalized version of Ito's then-partner Harold Cohen) to physical therapy after he undergoes surgery, the narrator of *La Niña* notices acacia trees surrounding the building. We see a moment of intense focus and clarity as the narrator describes how the acacia trees are all different, despite being of the same species:

> I drive around incessantly, secretly continuing to observe the acacia, and I've gotten quite acquainted with them. I've noticed that even though they are all "acacias," they are not all the same. There are some that flourish as if crawling along the ground, and there are some that become tall trees. There are those that stand up straight as a pole, no matter what their flowers look like, and there are those that have long tongue-like parts that hang down, and then there are those that seem like clouds. But each one is yellow, and there is no doubt that they are all acacias.[85]

This is a scene of acclimatization. The narrator becomes more familiar with her surroundings and gains a kind of knowledge about how to survive in foreign soil. Although not spelled out explicitly, this scene perfectly illustrates the tension Ito works through in her formulation of botanical empathy. The migratory human sees herself in a naturalized plant species (the acacia), and likewise comes to understand something about the migratory experience, namely, that there is great diversity among those that share the common act of becoming through migration.

Acacias appear again near the end of the novella. This time, the narrator observes how the individual trees fade away as they become a part of a collective of plants that together dye the landscape bright colors as they flourish:

> After the color of the acacias had faded and disappeared from the vicinity, mustard grass bloomed all over the canyon. The canyon was dyed yellow. Everything was, from the canyon to the hills. A fair amount of the empty lots as well, and the embankment too.... While we sped down the freeway, I thought to myself, "A full field of mustard grass, a full field of mustard grass, a full field of mustard grass," forever and ever....
>
> Then wild poppies, as orange began to be mixed in with the yellow. Dwarf marigolds, too, were yellow and orange, and the nasturtium that creeped about, it too was yellow and orange, and then wildflowers of all kinds of colors (I didn't know their names) bloomed here and there. The acacias went back to just being trees, with leaves that were just leaves. They were just green, hidden quietly in the spaces between the other trees.[86]

Once again, the narrator pays close attention to the landscape of Southern California as she tries to make sense of her own place within it. She displays a botanical subjectivity without fully understanding the implications of her experience. The scene is a subtle comment on naturalized plants. While marigolds are native to California, both mustard grass and nasturtium are considered invasive species. They are, in other words, migratory plants that have learned how to acclimatize and flourish. They are also beautiful. As they spread across the land, their bright colors eclipse the beauty of the acacia trees. Invasive species, the narrator learns, have their merits, even if these merits are merely aesthetic.

A full field of nonnative species that come together to create a beautiful landscape—again, it is not spelled out here in *La Niña*, but Ito is certainly circling around the kind of connections between botanical migrancy and human migrancy that will become the focus of *Wild Grass on the Riverbank* and *Tree Spirits Grass Spirits*. The narrator of *La Niña* is witnessing the results of a successful (perhaps too successful) acclimatization. She is not yet able to become fully botanical, however, for she has not learned the potential for creativity of the middle, repeating instead the novella's refrain: "two spirits, one body." It would take Ito a few more years to fully acclimatize and see herself and her migratory experience in a field of naturalized plants and to then write this becoming into *Wild Grass on the Riverbank*, where the link between immigration and botanical empathy is far more pronounced.

Seeking Asylum

It is Ito's follow-up to *La Niña*, titled *Three Lil' Japanese* (*Surii riro jyapaniizu*, 2001), that tackles the issue of immigration in the most straightforward manner of any of Ito's poems, novellas, or prose pieces. *Three Lil' Japanese* diverges from Ito's early novellas written in California. It is set in Japan and is not as directly autobiographical in nature as *House Plant* or *La Niña*. Nevertheless, it speaks to Ito's experience as an immigrant in the United States and belies an anxiety over the biopolitical control of immigration. The story is narrated by a woman named Rika, whose husband, Taku, runs an English-language school somewhere in Kyushu. The two have a young child named Tamara. Driven by a vague but fervent frustration with Japanese society, Taku and Rika express a strong desire to immigrate to the United States (where Taku had previously lived as an exchange student). They enter their names into the "Diversity Immigrant Visa Program," a lottery-based system that promotes the emigration of people from countries with historically low rates of immigration into the United States.

The novella portrays the extremely unlikely odds of being chosen for this program and the arbitrariness of legal immigration into the United States. Rika lays out the statistics in direct narration to the reader: "Anyone with more than a high school education can apply, and if chosen in the lottery, you can get a permanent resident visa. If you get chosen, your spouse automatically gets a permanent resident visa as well. Every year, 55,000 people are chosen from all over the world. In 1997, 448 Japanese people were chosen. 367 were chosen in 1998. I don't know the numbers after that. There's no information."[87]

Rika and Taku are not chosen in the lottery, which prompts Rika to suggest that they go on a tourist visa instead. Taking a page from Ito's own life (and replaying a scenario from *House Plant*), Taku confesses to Rika that he cannot return to the United States on a tourist visa, as he overstayed his last tourist visa and was refused entry when he attempted to reenter the country. Feeling as if they have no other options, Taku and Rika decide to drive to the Yokota Air Base in Western Tokyo—a military base operated jointly by the United States Air Force and the Japanese Air Self-Defense Force. Upon arriving at the base, they declare that they are seeking asylum in the United States. The novella ends with Taku, Rika, and Tamara being handled roughly by "large, fat" American soldiers, as Tamara wails in Rika's arms.

The botanical realm enters the story as Taku and Rika drive from southern Japan up north to Western Tokyo.[88] In line with both *House Plant* and *La Niña* (and unlike its role in Ito's later work), plant life does not offer Rika an alternative model to rethink her subjective experience as a migrant. Instead, the rootedness of plant life keeps Rika and Taku tethered to Japan, rooted in a country they desperately wish to leave behind. As they make their way to Yokota, Rika comments several times on the many cherry trees they pass. Cherry trees are an overwrought and overdetermined image in Japan, one that Emiko Ohnuki-Tierney has called "the master troupe of Japan's imperial nationalism" in her examination of the militarization of Japanese aesthetics.[89] The cherry tree follows Rika and Taku as they attempt to escape their native home. Rika mentions the almost horrifically overabundant trees alongside violent headlines taken from the newspapers that she buys at each stop along the way. The headlines include things like: "Taxi driver is killed and robbed," "A girl is killed in a car in the parking lot in front of the train station," and "8 dogs are found dead in town."[90] It seems these "incidents," as Rika refers to them, are meant to illustrate a violent instability in Japanese society that she and her husband are desperate to escape.

The unending sight of blooming cherry trees takes on an ominous character as Rika becomes increasingly panicked about the state of Japan. She puts it simply: "The cherry trees blossomed, and the incidents continued on."[91] Ito links the trees directly to military control, echoing Ohnuki-Tierney's claim. The Yokota Air Base itself is covered in cherry trees, and they appear to physically prevent Rika and Taku from entering:

On the other side of the "Do Not Enter" sign were cherry trees in full bloom. Over the fence and grounds of the base, cherry blossoms hung down like a low hanging haze or cloud.

I read it out loud: "'Do Not Enter.'"

My husband read it too: "'Do Not Enter.' It sounds like a curse."

We had been cursed, and so we couldn't get inside. We had been cursed, and so the flowers bloomed. They bloomed in full.[92]

Three Lil' Japanese is, like much of Ito's work, a story about family. Yet unlike her other work, and unlike the work of Osaki Midori explored in chapter 1 of this book, the plant life of *Three Lil' Japanese* does not become kin. The "cursed" trees that line the roads and block the entrance to the Yokota base function symbolically, on an abstract level far removed from the personal, close attention paid to the eucalyptus and acacia trees in *House Plant* and *La Niña*, respectively. The cherry trees are of a different sort than the naturalized plants such as *Sorghum halepense*, *Conyza sumatrensis*, and *Solidago altissima* that populate later texts like *Wild Grass on the Riverbank* and *Tree Spirits Grass Spirits*. In their abstraction and ties to nationalism, the cherry trees in *Three Lil' Japanese* lack the possibility of self-identification with the botanical realm that leads to botanical empathy.

Ito has written how, with *Three Lil' Japanese*, she wanted to create a narrating "I" that was not self-identified.[93] She based the story on a real-life event, in which a husband and wife (along with their two-year-old daughter) drove illegally into Yokota Air Base in May of 2000 and boarded a military plane bound for the United States. Like Taku and Riku, the couple requested asylum.[94] All the same, elements of Ito's experience in Southern California are legible in the narrative. Although the name of the city in which Taku had once studied in the United States is not given, it is clearly within the San Diego area of Southern California.[95] Taku describes the city as having a military base nearby (likely the Marine Corps base Camp Pendleton, which is in San Diego County) and road signs warning of "illegal immigrants" crossing the border from Mexico:

> It was a natural place with an army training base, wide with nothing else around. It was eerie because there really wasn't anything else around. Of course, places operated by the authorities have a different feel to them. A highway ran right through the middle of the grounds. There was a checkpoint, and as you got close to the checkpoint, there was a sign asking you to watch out for people. You see them a lot, right, on highways and whatnot, the ones that have pictures of deer or raccoons on them? If I remember correctly, it was a picture of a woman running and holding a child, and she's holding the child's hand and their hair is dishev-

eled. There were many illegal immigrants that would do that: cross the street and get hit by cars. Because there was a checkpoint there, and they would strictly control illegal immigration.[96]

Here and throughout *Three Lil' Japanese*, Ito writes of the potential perils of immigration in a matter-of-fact way, drawing from the visible evidence of state control she encountered in Southern California (both the immigration checkpoints and road signs warning drivers to be careful not to hit immigrants crossing into California on foot), rather than recasting these perils through a creative engagement with plant life.

Curiously, *Three Lil' Japanese* reaches, *without* becoming botanical, a realization that Ito finds through botanical empathy in her later works. Taku explains to Rika that he initially thought, having moved to the United States, that "illegal immigrants" all had "Mexican-like faces," as these were the people he saw get stopped at the immigration checkpoint.[97] After being deported due to overstaying his tourist visa, however, Taku comes to realize that he was similar to the other immigrants in California: "It was an area with many Mexicans. Every day, I would see illegal immigrants get caught and be deported on a worn-down bus. I watched this, thinking: 'those people and I, we're different.' But we're not different. It's not like we were different at all."[98] Taken together with the dinner party scene in *House Plant*, in which non-US citizens from Europe argue with the narrator about whether or not overstaying one's visa causes problems, this moment in *Three Lil' Japanese* offers an understated critique of racial profiling in the United States. Taku thinks, based on what he witnesses at an immigration checkpoint in Southern California, that US Immigration Officers are only concerned with undocumented immigrants that he believes look to be from Mexico. He recounts how the officers would check drivers' faces but only stop those that had "faces that looked like illegal immigrants."[99] Taku is thus surprised to learn that he, too, is subject to the same immigration laws when he attempts to reenter the United States after overstaying his visa.

"Dying Is Not Dying, and Not Dying Is Living, Right?"

Taku learns the hard way what Natsukusa learns by becoming botanical in *Wild Grass on the Riverbank*, that the act of migration is a shared experience that can lead to new alliances across species. For Natsukusa, this realization leads to an empowering botanical empathy. In *Three Lil' Japanese*, it leads to a notion of shared punishment: deportation, arrest, and potentially even death. It is unclear what becomes of Taku and Rika, just as it is unclear what became of the real-life figures on which these characters are based. However, the escalation of panic and violence palpable at the end of *Three Lil' Japanese* could easily lead to death if the narrative were to continue on. The novella's ending suggests that all immigrants, including asylum seekers, share in the potential for a violent response at the hands of the state. It is a dark realization devoid of hope.

Like all of Ito's early novellas written in California, *Three Lil' Japanese* presents immigration into the United States as something of a dead end. It would take Ito opening up the experience of migration to the botanical realm in order for this dead end to be washed away in the "never-ending stream" that Deleuze and Guattari recognize as the middle. The figurative waters of this stream were necessary to help the seeds that Ito planted in her early California novellas bloom, seeds that would grow into the radical (and botanical) hope written into works like *Wild Grass on the Riverbank*, where immigrants may wither and die but continue on in their path toward naturalization. As Natsukusa becomes botanical at the poem's end, producing bud after bud with the promise of secular migration, she gives birth to a form of hope that, phytomorphically, can overcome death.

Throughout *Wild Grass on the Riverbank*, bodies both human and more-than-human come back to life after dying. The poem links the ability to overcome death to plant life:

> Living is
> More commonplace
> Than dying for plants
> They come later
> They do not end
> They do not die
> They live from death
> They come back to life
> They grow again no matter what end they meet
> They give birth to any number of children[100]

That plants never truly die is a sentiment Ito returns to time and again throughout her work.[101] In *Aunt Green-Thumb*, she explains simply that: "for plants, 'dying' is 'not dying.' Their 'death,' 'birth,' 'living,' and 'flourishing' are fundamentally different from how we understand these concepts."[102] This is a philosophical take on life that Ito learned from tending to plants in her home and garden, where plants would die only to bloom again when the season was right. In *Tree Spirits Grass Spirits*, she writes of caring for an *agave attenuata* and learning of their ability to continue living beyond death through secular migration:

> The bulbs of these *attenuata*—which hang down their curious flowers here and there around town—will all, before long, die. If they were

> human, they'd be elderly people close to 100 years old. They will, before long, die—but it's not sad. Up until this point, they've made new bulbs to their hearts' content. Each new bulb is the spitting image of its parent bulb. Their death is neither sad nor painful. It's not even the end.
>
> I think as I gaze at them: Dogs and humans "grow old and die," but for plants, "dying" is "not dying," and "not dying" is "living," right? This is the karma unique to them and them alone.[103]

Ito claims here that plants alone have the karmic ability to overcome death, but she extends this ability to humans (and dogs, as well) within the poetic realm of *Wild Grass on the Riverbank*. Natsukusa's fathers (there is one in the wasteland and one in the riverbank) are "corpses" that can talk, existing somewhere in the middle of life and death. Her dog in the riverbank, who runs and plays with the children, is also a "corpse." As Natsukusa returns to the wasteland of Southern California at the end of the poem, she is reunited with her father and notes that "the law of the plants had extended to this man who had been our father, living had become more commonplace than dying for him, it had become possible for him to return, the end had vanished, and it didn't matter how often he died, he could come back to life again."[104] From here, Natsukusa becomes botanical and produces endless buds, just like the *agave attenuata* written into *Tree Spirits Grass Spirits*. Likely, the buds she produces are the "spitting image of its parent bulb."

In its closing moments, *Wild Grass on the Riverbank* stands in the middle of the botanical realm and offers hope for the future. It is a hope that looks beyond the immediate experience and hardships of the individual immigrant and focuses instead on the long durée of secular migration. It is a hope extended to all migratory bodies, alive and dead—a dichotomy that has been rethought through the model of plant life. It is a hope, however naive, that Ito extended in a gesture of botanical empathy during her poetry reading at Waseda University in 2019, to Óscar Alberto Martínez Ramírez and Valeria—that father and daughter who died along the riverbank while seeking asylum in the United States.

Wither Hope? Or, Hope Withered

The hope written into *Wild Grass on the Riverbank* was hard earned, and in recent years, Ito's writing on immigration has taken on a far more pessimistic hue. Having left the United States and returned to Japan following her partner's death, Ito's reflections on her experience as an immigrant in the United States have come to express a deep-seated fear and unease. In the afterword to the 2016 republication *Three Lil' Japanese*, Ito writes about how the United States fundamentally changed in the years following the initial publication of the story:

> I came to America in November 1997. I got my Permanent Resident Visa in June of the following year. The small incident (on which *Three Lil' Japanese* is based) occurred in May 2000. In January 2001, George W. Bush became president. On September 11th of that year, there were multiple, simultaneous terrorist attacks. And then from there, everything broke down and got weird.
>
> There was now a before and an after, and America truly changed. The change was irreversible, and I understood clearly that the sense of calm and the dreams I'd had before were now gone (those things probably hadn't actually existed, but anyway), and that all I could do was go on living. As an immigrant living there, as someone raising kids there, that's how it felt. And then afterwards a bleak period of not wanting to go to America continued on for a long time, even for our household. Actually, I wonder if it isn't still continuing on even now.[105]

Although she is vague about the specifics, Ito hints at the increased surveillance and violence that immigrants faced in the wake of September 11, 2001. She expresses a deep dissatisfaction and anxiety as an immigrant in the United States. Published three years and one month after the events of 9/11, *Wild Grass on the Riverbank* somehow found a way to resist this dissatisfaction and anxiety by becoming botanical.

Ito's anxiety only increased with the election of Donald Trump as president in 2016. In a short essay titled *Trump* (*Toranpu*) from her 2018 collection *Twilight Child*, Ito expresses disbelief at Trump's election, stating that she does not know a single person in California who supported his candidacy. Written around the time Ito was debating whether or not to return to Japan after her partner's death, the essay is uncharacteristically bleak. Upon learning of Trump's victory, Ito expresses a strange, pessimistic curiosity about the fate of the country that had been her home for decades: "It'll be interesting if America falls into chaos, if abortion and same-sex marriage are prohibited, if health care is repealed, if there is a recession, if its land gets polluted, if it comes to feel like all international relations deteriorate, if all ties are cut with Mexico, and if things get touch-and-go with China. I want to see how the American people recover from that."[106]

Ito follows this (sarcastically?) dire prediction with a statement of empathy for fellow immigrants having to deal with the consequences of Trump's election: "As I say these somewhat careless things, restrictions have already begun on the immigration of people from predominantly Islamic countries. There are stories of people with permanent resident visas also being stopped at airports."[107] She then once again recounts her experience overstaying her visa, and explains that the increased surveillance after George W. Bush took office felt draconian:

> I illegally overstayed my visa a long time ago. After that, whenever I entered the United States, I was always brought to a special room and cross-examined. I would be let through in the end, but I was prepared to be deported. Before I got permanent residency, I paid a fine to erase the record of my illegal stay. But despite this, I started getting harassed at the airport again the moment the Bush administration took power.
>
> It felt really terrible. An illogical door closed right before my eyes and I was treated like a criminal. But I had made a mistake, and all I could do in response was give in and agree. I couldn't talk back.[108]

Ito's "terrible" experience navigating immigration during the Bush presidency clearly continues to haunt her. A considerable amount of Ito's *Travels* (*Michiyukiya*, 2020) discusses her efforts to help other women struggling to make sense of the US immigration policy. In one particularly poignant section, she writes of a friend named Yoko and her difficult decision of whether to divorce her American husband and relocate her children to Japan. Yoko expresses concern that relocating her children would violate the Hague Abduction Convention.[109] Ito speaks with an immigration officer on the phone to get clarification for her friend but ends up thoroughly frustrated. She arrives at a bitter conclusion:

> As someone who has been through it, as a woman who has gone through it before, whenever I see a young woman who is in love with someone not Japanese, I want to give them advice: Don't get divorced. If you do, you'll have to leave your child and return to Japan alone. Wait, no, let's back up.
>
> Don't have children. Actually, let's back even up more. If I don't share my opinion, then it'll be too late. Ladies: don't fall in love with men from other countries. Don't fall in love and leave Japan for a foreign country.[110]

Ito's hope for secular migration seems to have all but withered. The water of the supposedly "never-ending" stream that runs through the zone of the middle has evaporated. Even plants seem to no longer offer potential for change. As the chapter concludes, Ito's disillusionment with state control of migration and reproduction extends into the fields of naturalized plants that populate the riverbank near Ito's Kumamoto home (a place Natsukusa also called home for a short while):

> The leaves of the kudzu squirm along the riverbank in Kumamoto in Japan. In the gaps between them bloom bright yellow *Coreopsis lanceo-*

late (*ōkinkeigiku*). There were more of them a few years back. It seems that someone familiar with the Invasive Alien Species Act, someone who is passionate about environmental protection and truly detested those species designated as invasive, walks through and pulls them out. The following was written on the website for the Kyushu Ministry of the Environment: "In order to help prevent the flourishing of *Coreopsis lanceolate*, it is important to exterminate them before they drop their seeds on the ground, or before they go to seed." That's what *Coreopsis lanceolate*'s problem was.[111]

Like children under the Hague Convention, naturalized plants have been subjected to biopolitical control under the Invasive Alien Species Act, which took effect in Japan in 2004 (see figure 5.4). The "that" that Ito claims is the problem

FIGURE 5.4. Flier created by the Kyushu Environmental Agency warning that "*Coreopsis lanceolate* is an invasive species!" Source: Japanese Ministry of Environment (https://kyushu.env.go.jp/wildlife/mat/m_2_3.html).

with *Coreopsis lanceolate* is its reproducing, its going to seed—the very thing Natsukusa accomplishes at the end of her narrative journey through secular migration. Naturalized plants no longer serve as role models for Ito but rather as cautionary tales meant to warn humans not to migrate or give birth.

Ito claims that her own dreams died in the wake of 9/11 and that her hopes for immigrants (and the United States at large) died with the election of Donald Trump. As Ito's writing teaches us, however, "For plants, 'dying' is 'not dying.'" Like the plants she has so carefully thought about and described throughout her writing career—those persistent plants always struggling for naturalization in the face of all obstacles—her dreams and hopes may indeed spring back to life in the right season, either within Ito herself or within a botanical subjectivity shared with her children, who live, as the result of secular migration, in the United States. As *Wild Grass on the Riverbank* states: "Living is/ More commonplace/ Than dying for plants."[112] The same is true, one can hope, for dreams of becoming botanical.

Epilogue

BOTANICAL MODELS

In the introduction of this book, I introduced Gregory Bateson's "syllogism in grass":

> Grass dies.
> Men die.
> Men are grass.[1]

Such phytomophoric logic has been at the heart of this book. It served as a starting point meant to shake up the way we conventionally think about both humans and plants and to help us consider the ways in which we share more in common with botanical life than we usually admit. Now, in this epilogue, I would like to take Bateson's syllogism one step further, drawing from the insights of the preceding chapters:

> Men are grass.
> Grass does not die.
> Men do not die.

We might call this the phytomorphic extreme, a "syllogism in undying grass" that pushes us to consider how humans live on beyond death, much like plants themselves. This idea—that in becoming more plantlike humans can rethink death—was envisioned by all of the figures discussed in the book. In one way or another, each chapter here has ended with the idea that plant life challenges clear notions of life and death, and as such, each chapter has ended by challenging the very notion of an ending. Chapter 1 closed with the image of Osaki Midori springing back to life like dried moss given water. Chapter 2 ended with the dark legacy of scientific naming, a kind of afterlife of the dendrocacalia plant that keeps it frozen in colonial time. The end of chapter 3 found dead spirits continuing to speak through writers who themselves searched for a way to communicate with the dead via botanical media. Chapter 4 focused on the ongoing cycles of death and rebirth found in disturbance ecology. Chapter 5 hoped that Hiromi Ito's own hope for becoming botanical through secular migration would come back to life like the plants and plantlike humans found in her poetry and prose. In the spirit of these artists and the plants with which they were engaged, I want to end this book by tying it back to the beginning, thereby embodying a rhizomatic structure that defies the notion of an ending.

It is fitting that a book about rethinking plants (and rethinking the human through plant life) should resist closure. The relatively long span of time covered in this book—beginning in the early Shōwa era and ending in the contemporary moment—is only a blip of time for some of the plants discussed in these pages. Take, for example, the Jakushinsan camphor discussed in chapter 5. The stretch of turbulent history discussed in this book, with all its various crises, is but a fraction of the lifespan of this over eight-hundred-year-old tree. It lived long before Osaki Midori began writing, and it will live long after the writer of this book (i.e., me) has passed on. To think in a more plantlike way is to acknowledge that the botanical realm ultimately exceeds the boundaries of our human knowledge production, including our periodization of history and our paradigms for understanding plant life, be they scientific, aesthetic, spiritual, or some combination of these three. By letting plants guide our way of thinking, we can think anew about the ways in which historical crises borne of Japanese imperialism and capitalist exploitation are themselves not yet finished. Like plants, the systems that have perpetuated violence have adapted and taken on new forms. The extractive system of Japanese colonial botany discussed in chapters 1 and 2 lives on in the exploitative timber extraction from Southeast Asia discussed in chapter 4. The scientific categorization of plant life likewise discussed in the first two chapters of this book sprouts anew as a means of controlling both human and plant migration in chapter 5. Remember the aspen discussed in the introduction, that grove of seemingly separate trees that, deep down, was one organism? The crises brought together in this book are entangled in a similar way. Deep down, they share roots and continue to grow and change. If we think of them like plants, might we not be better able to tend to them and trace their entanglements across decades, and perhaps even further?

With this in mind, I want to conclude with one last look at how plant life defies human-centered ideas of temporality. Nearly a century after Osaki Midori wrote about mosses falling in love in *Wandering in the Realm of the Seventh Sense*, the popular novelist and essayist Miura Shion published a botanical novel titled

A World Without Love (*Ai naki sekai*, 2018) that reads like a contemporary reimagining (or what we might consider a rebirth) of Osaki's novella. There is an uncanny overlap between the two stories, as if Miura's tale is a vegetal offspring of Osaki's, one that had been buried in the soil waiting to sprout. As outlined in chapter 1 of this book, the protagonist of *Wandering in the Realm of the Seventh Sense*, Machiko, watches from the sidelines as her brothers engage in scientific research. She cleans, cooks, fails at writing poetry, and dreams of becoming botanical to escape the confines of the small house that she shares with her male family members. In *A World Without Love*, it is a young female graduate student named Motomura Sae who studies plant biology. At T University (which is almost certainly meant to be Tokyo University, a site for botanical knowledge that has appeared many times throughout this book), Motomura researches the leaves of *Arabidopsis thaliana*, commonly known in English as thale cress and in Japanese as *shiroinunazuna*.

Motomura becomes acquainted with Fujimaru Yōta, a twenty-something-year-old delivery man who works at a restaurant (and lives in a small apartment above it) near her research lab. In an inversion of Machiko learning of plants from her scientist brother Ichisuke, in *A World Without Love*, it is Motomura who opens Fujimaru's eyes to the wonders of plant life. She invites him to view a leaf under her microscope, and Fujimaru sees the secret life of the botanical realm: "A galaxy spread out before his eyes. Within the darkness was scattered countless silver specks. . . . A beautiful, lonely galaxy existing inside of a tiny leaf."[2] Fujimaru sees the infinitesimally small world of the leaf become the expanse of a star-filled galaxy. Osaki saw something similar when she wrote of there existing "within a thin reed/a spirit as wide as the cosmos."[3] In the microscope, Fujimaru glimpses the potential of becoming botanical, just as Machiko did looking over the mosses on her brother's desk. The world of plants once again becomes a potential site of change, as it offers Fujimaru a sense of wonder that has been absent in his constricted life centered around the restaurant.

Motomura grounds Fujimaru's poetic vision of becoming botanical in scientific fact. She explains that the nucleus of each cell shines during the process of DNA duplication. She tells Fujimaru that humans are, to a certain extent, not so different from the plant he just looked at, as "Even within our own bodies, cells are moving around in the same way."[4] Motomura diminishes the ontological distance between humans and plants but quickly stresses that the vegetal world is fundamentally different from the human world: "Plants do not have brains or nervous systems. In other words, they have no thoughts and no feelings. They have no concept of what humans call 'love.' In spite of this, they reproduce vigorously, take on all varieties of forms, acclimatize to their environment, and live all over the Earth. Don't you think that's miraculous?"[5]

The novel's title, *A World Without Love*, thus refers to the world of plants, a world that Motomura believes is devoid of thinking and feeling. In addition to Miura's novel presenting the inverse of the gender dynamics found in Osaki's *Wandering in the Realm of the Seventh Sense*, it also comes to the inverse conclusion of Osaki's moss-love, namely, that plants categorically cannot experience emotions such as love. Although she finds in plants a reproductive power that Hiromi Ito has written about envying (as discussed in chapter 5), Motomura's interest in and envy of the botanical realm stems from her belief that plants have no emotions whatsoever and thus no emotional attachments. This may seem like a far cry from the other works I have discussed in these pages. Throughout, I have been discussing writers and filmmakers who saw in the botanical realm a means to inhabit the world differently. Whether through evolutionary thinking, botanical science, spirituality, or ecology, these novelists, poets, and filmmakers all thought plants were more like humans than conventionally believed. Indeed, this is the starting point for critical plant studies (CPS). The works brought together in these pages have imagined what it could mean for humans to become more plantlike. In the process, they have experimented with plant vision, plant perception of time, plant movement, plant communication, and, yes, plant emotions. *A World Without Love* denies plant life these capacities. One gets the sense that Motomura and her colleagues would scoff at the extraordinary claims put forth in Tompkins and Bird's *The Secret Life of Plants*, as discussed in chapter 3 of this book. The tarnished legacy of that work permeates Miura's novel and gives us a glimpse into the uphill battle thinkers in CPS have had to grapple with by taking plants and their capacities seriously.

All the same, *A World Without Love* is a tale of becoming botanical. Like *Wandering the Realm of the Seventh Sense* before it, Miura's novel portrays a woman yearning to move beyond the gendered expectations of a patriarchal society and finding the capacity to do so in the botanical realm. To be sure, *A World Without Love* grants Motomura a certain degree of agency as a woman in STEM research (a field heavily dominated by men in Japan), but the novel also sets up a narrative that seems destined to end with Motomura leaving plants behind and falling in love with Fujimaru. As Motomura teaches Fujimaru about plant science, he develops romantic feelings for her, and the dramatic tension of the story revolves around the conventional will-they-or-won't-they trope of romance novels. Surprisingly, Motomura refuses Fujimaru's advances to the very end. In this subversion of genre, we find the novel's plantlike form. Miura takes the conventions of the romance novel and rethinks them to be more plantlike. It is as if she is experimenting on the form of the genre in a way analogous to her character's experiments on thale cress. If we accept the novel's premise that the world of plants is a world without love, then it makes a certain sense to have a botanical romance novel without any romance.

Once again, however, if we follow the plant in the story (thale cress) and give it its history, we can see how *A World Without Love* may be a novel without romance, but it is not a novel devoid of desire. This is because thale cress (*Arabidopsis thaliana*) is one of the most common plant species currently experimented with/on in botanical research. It is often called "the model plant" for its unique *shokubutsusei*, which a listing on the US National Science Foundation website describes as follows:

> Arabidopsis is not an economically important plant. Despite this, it has been the focus of intense genetic, biochemical and physiological study for over 40 years because of several traits that make it very desirable for laboratory study. As a photosynthetic organism, *Arabidopsis* requires only light, air, water and a few minerals to complete its life cycle. It has a fast life cycle, produces numerous self progeny, has very limited space requirements, and is easily grown in a greenhouse or indoor growth chamber. It possesses a relatively small, genetically tractable genome that can be manipulated through genetic engineering more easily and rapidly than any other plant genome.[6]

The desire to control and modify thale cress has been strong in botanical science for decades. It was the first plant to have its entire genome sequenced, which was completed in the year 2000. It is often considered a weed, but it has accomplished extraordinary and fantastical things in its history. This is another reason why *The Secret Life of Plants* permeates *A World Without Love*. Motomura may indeed scoff at Tompkins and Bird, but scientifically credible experiments with thale cress in the 2020s sound much like the incredible claims of their pseudoscience. For example, thale cress was the first plant successfully grown in lunar soil, albeit in a laboratory on Earth using moon dust retrieved from a lunar mission.[7] Thale cress has likewise been grown aboard the International Space Station (ISS) to study the effect of microgravity on plant life.[8] These experiments were conducted at the ISS's KIBO laboratory, named after the Japanese word for *hope* (see figure 6.1).

In 2023, researchers in Japan published a paper on an experiment conducted on thale cress by which they used a fluorescence microscope and a green fluorescent biosensor to help make visible how the plant uses volatile organic compounds (VOC) to warn neighboring plants of threats such as insects.[9] Aesthetically, the videos these researchers have produced of thale cress communicating via VOC are strikingly beautiful. Green fluorescent light spreads across leaves against a black background in what could easily pass for an experimental art film.[10]

FIGURE 6.1. Thale cress being grown aboard the International Space Station KIBO Laboratory. Source: NASA Johnson Space Center / Wikimedia Commons / Public Domain.

A botanical poetics that lies in between science and poetry can be glimpsed in these videos. It is easy to imagine that Fujimaru saw something similar in the plant when "A galaxy spread out before his eyes. Within the darkness was scattered countless silver specks.... A beautiful, lonely galaxy existing inside of a tiny leaf."[11] What Fujimaru likely did not know was that the tiny leaves of thale cress were simultaneously spreading out into the galaxy aboard the ISS.

Thale cress is a model plant for the study of plasticity, that *shokubutsusei* discussed throughout this book. Experiments with thale cress aim to better help humans understand epigenetics, or how environmental factors influence the expression of genes without change to DNA sequence. It may not be "an economically important plant," but it is poised to serve a major role in how agriculture (and the industry thereof) adapts to climate change.[12] In 2022, for example, a research team at the University of Hiroshima conducted experiments on thale cress and rice to help identify genes that could be manipulated to engineer crop plants that would better withstand flooding and drought.[13] Epigenetic research on and manipulation of thale cress are concerned with rethinking the biological model of the plant, of engineering it to better serve human needs amid anthropogenic climate change.

If we allow thale cress to guide our reading of *A World Without Love*, we can find the desire to manipulate and rethink the model plant in ways that echo colonial botany, insofar as the research on thale cress in space serves the desire to eventually colonize other planets. More down to earth, however, is an undercurrent of crisis that runs quietly under the text's surface. Miura is also rethinking models in her novel, both literary and broadly cultural. She does so by critiquing and manipulating a cultural phenomenon that has grown out of a botanical imagination in contemporary Japan, the emergence of the so-called herbivore man who lacks sexual desire. This is to say, in *A World Without Love*, thale cress shows both its material and semiotic face. It draws our attention to material concerns about future food scarcity and semiotic concerns about the metaphorical male preference for plants over sex. These two concerns may seem far afield, but they share roots in the botanical realm of *A World Without Love*.

Herbivore Men

Motomura, the female scientist at the center of *A World Without Love*, has no interest in romance. Instead, she tells her family that she is "married to the plants." With this new form of becoming botanical, *A World Without Love* entangles the writing of plant life in the social phenomenon of the herbivore man (*sōshoku danshi* or *sōshoku-kei danshi*). The concept of the herbivore man emerged in Japan around the end of the first decade of the 2000s. Promotional copy for Miura's novel alerts potential buyers that *A World Without Love* is an "Herbivore Love Novel" (*Sōshiku-kei ren'ai shōsetsu*). The cultural buzzword in question was first used by writer Fukasawa Maki in 2006 to refer to the purported rise of feminized young men in Japan who were not assertive in seeking out sexual relationships with women. The word *herbivore* (literally "grass-eater" in Japanese) marks this lack of assertion by implying that sexually assertive, masculine men are "carnivores."[14] In other words, a metaphorical preference for plants has come to name a societal change that the philosopher and critic Morioka Masahiro (another early adopter of the term) has called an "epochal event in the history of the male gender in Japan."[15] Morioka links the emergence of herbivore men to a decrease in violence in postwar Japan. In a 2013 essay, he calls the phenomenon "a byproduct of Japan's sixty-six years of peace following World War II" and includes data to argue that the number of homicides committed by men has steadily decreased in Japan since 1955.[16]

Of course, Morioka's definition of violence is extremely narrow and overlooks much of the unspectacular violence-as-backdrop that informed the botanical becomings I have discussed throughout this book. Nevertheless, there is a strange resonance between the books and films I have focused on here and Morioka's claim that a decrease in violence has resulted in a more plantlike form of subjectivity. Is this not, to a certain degree, what the writers and filmmakers that I have brought together in these pages imagined as they attempted to rethink what it means to be human in alliance with plant life? If so, is the herbivore man an embodiment of a botanical subjectivity, a product of becoming botanical?

Not exactly. Morioka may see the herbivore man as a kind of evolutionary movement in a utopian direction for Japanese society, but the more he develops a link between herbivore men and a notion of "peace," the more problematic his claims become:

> [If] the emergence of herbivore men is a byproduct of Japan's post-war peace, I think it is something that must be welcomed. There is nothing more valuable than the absence of war. Very few of the young people in today's Japan have been trained to kill, and none have experienced combat on the battlefield. If they were told to kill a person standing in front of them they would presumably not have any idea how to do so. Of course, there are many brutal crimes such as rape and murder committed in Japan, but in comparison to other countries their number is considered low. I think that one of the reasons for this is that for sixty-six years Japan has not directly taken part in a war and Japanese territory has not been the site of combat. We must not forget that the achievement of Japan's post-war peace has been made possible by American military power through the treaty of mutual security between the United States and Japan.[17]

Morioka positions herbivore men as the embodiment of a postwar peace that is ultimately structured by systemic violence. One need look no further than to the still-occupied colonial space of the Ryūkyū Islands (or Okinawa) to see how "American military power" perpetrates its own forms violence, be they sexual (in the case of numerous high-profile instances of rape) or environmental (in the case of a purposed base relocation that threatens coral reefs and the critically endangered dugong). One could also look to Hiromi Ito's *Three Lil' Japanese* (as discussed in chapter 5), a novella that ends on a violent note at the American-run Yokota Air Base in Western Tokyo. This novella and the other texts examined in this book are responses to precisely the kind of violence and catastrophe Morioka neglects in his praise of peace, the kind of violence that serves as "both a backdrop to and condition for the intimate terrain of . . . everyday lives," to return to Dole et al.'s words one last time. In its botanical becoming, the so-called Herbivore Love novel *A World Without Love* responds to a backdrop of normative gender roles that, while not explicitly presented as catastrophic or violent, nevertheless threaten to coerce its female protagonist into a life of heterosexual domesticity for which she has no desire.

A World Without Love takes the notion of the "herbivore man" (as defined by Morioka) and turns it on its head. It uses the model plant of thale cress to shatter Morioka's model of the peaceful herbivore male. It literalizes the metaphorical preference for plant life it names by having Motomura eschew heterosexual love in favor of a botanical subjectivity that survives and thrives without romantic attachments. It is a botanical subjectivity that rethinks the human by rethinking gender roles and resisting literary conventions associated with them. This is the novel's radical intervention, one that would likely have appealed to both Machiko, the protagonist of *Wandering in the Realm of the Seventh Sense*, and Osaki, the writer thereof.

Digging for Connectivity

A World Without Love takes the highly gendered concept of the "herbivore man" and reimagines it through the lens of the botanical realm, and what emerges is the figure of Motomura, a female protagonist of a romance novel that actively resists and subverts the conventions of the genre into which she is written. It is a romance novel in which there is no romance, only a desire for plants. Near the novel's end, Fujimaru comes to accept the fact that Motomura is devoted to plants and that her lack of interest in romance is not a personal slight. He reaches an epiphany about Motomura's devotion and experiences his own moment of becoming botanical that leads him to see humans and plants as "the same." He tells Motomura: "That passion you have, that feeling of wanting to know—can't we call that 'love?' You're the same: you, Motomura—you who desire to know all about plants—are the same as the plants here in this laboratory, which are the objects of the human desire to be known. You both live in a world in which love exists."[18] Fujimaru reimagines "love" as the desire to better understand the world of plants. For him, every text examined in this book could be considered a work of romance in this way, insofar as they all desire to better understand the botanical realm.

In her review of *A World Without Love*, Fukasawa Maki, the writer who first coined the term *herbivore man*, picks up on Fujimaru's reconfiguration of love and its supposed connection to the desire to know. She laments how the term she created, which initially was intended to refer to young people who placed value on things over romantic love and sex, has taken on a negative connotation and is now viewed as something "pathetic" (*nasakenai*).[19] *A World Without Love*, Fukasawa believes, restores the concept of the "herbivore man" to its intended meaning: "That 'productivity' is something that comes only from a man and a woman getting married and having children, or that 'rationality' is to be found in a phony, inadequate value system that says 'important research is that which has immediate use'—such things are not to be found in this story."[20] Following Fujimaru, Fukasawa finds in Miura's novel a kind of love not bound to notions of gender or even species: "The feeling of 'wanting to know,' whether that want is directed toward people or directed toward plants, is something that overflows with love."[21]

In Fukasawa's figuration of knowing plants we witness the ambivalence of becoming botanical. On the one hand, Fukasawa's botanical imagination is one that seemingly pushes back against capitalist instrumentalization, as it rejects what it calls a "phony, inadequate value system" that privileges rationality and productivity. At the same time, however, it renders the botanical abstract, denying plants their history. *A World Without Love*, for all of its attempts to break out of a model of gendered heteronormativity and reproductive futurity, is nevertheless entangled in the still-very-much-unfolding history of thale cress and its ethically questionable mass instrumentalization in botanical research. Was the desire to know this particular plant's genome sequence something that overflowed with love? Is the desire to modify thale cress to better withstand the extremes of drought and flooding something that overflows with love? Or is it rather, to quote the previously mentioned listing on the website for the National Science Foundation, a desire to "(exploit) the scientific and practical advantages of the model organism"?[22]

The plant scientist Nicholas Harberd, in his 2007 book devoted to thale cress titled *Seed to Seed: The Secret Life of Plants*, is inspired by the plant to question the very nature of scientific research and the desire to know the botanical realm:

> Yesterday, I reread some of what I've written here. I thought I'd see if I could identify threads, continuing themes. I think that some are clear: the advance of the seasons in garden, fen, and wood; the growth of the thale-cress plant as part of that advance; a record of events in the lab; an account of our research, of its deepening understanding of the hidden mysteries of growth.
>
> Yet I find myself stumbling as I write. The word *research* an impediment. Discomfort with the idea that I 'study' something, that that something is 'biology'. Why do I feel like this? Why do these words make me pause?
>
> Is it that they are isolating terms? That I 'study' the growth of the hazel leaf, or the activity of a gene, by isolating it from the rest of the world? That by doing so I cut it off, reduce the connectivity of one thing with another?[23]

Harberd's *Seed to Seed* (which was translated into Japanese in 2009) is full of such ruminations. Formally, the text resembles Itō Seikō's *Botanical Life* (discussed in chapter 3) in its use of daily entries to theorize plant life and record observations over the course of a year. It poetically captures his affinity-bordering-on-love for thale cress while also foregrounding his discomfort with the objectification of the model inherent in conventional science. Harberd's anxiety over reducing the "connectivity of one thing with another" gives way in the end to a botanical imagination that looks for connectivity and context: "This notebook has served its purpose. I have direction. Have shifted our science away from a focus on the hidden secrets of plant growth to a broader vision that considers simultaneously the plant in the world and the world in the plant."[24] Thale cress may point some scientists toward outer space, but it brought Harberd back down to Earth.

As I have tried to illustrate by following the plants in my readings of modern Japanese literary and filmic texts in this book, not all attempts at knowing plant life stem from love, and sometimes finding "the plant in the world" means digging in the soil of forgotten and unpleasant histories. Naming, categorizing, and experimenting with plants can certainly grow out of an affinity for the botanical realm, but these acts can also serve state violence. To reiterate a claim I made in the introduction, becoming botanical is a potential that can be mobilized to different ends, at different points in time. Context matters, or, to paraphrase Harberd, connectivity matters.

Given the 2023 experiments conducted in Japan with VOC use among thale cress, it seems safe to say that even if the botanical realm is a world without love, it is still a world with connectivity and concern and care for others (granted, of course, we remember the difficulty in determining the line between self and other among plant life). If we take seriously the fact that thale cress releases VOC to warn other plants about potential harm, then shouldn't we also take seriously the call to rethink the ethical obligation humans have to plant life? Such ethics should in turn inform our work with plants, including academic work. In this book, I have tried to demonstrate that part of this ethical obligation can be found in recognizing that plants have their history, to invoke Kliment Timiryazev one last time. An ethically informed approach to plants in both CPS and Japanese studies would locate plants in their time and place and follow the sometimes-uncomfortable entanglements they have in national, cultural, and intellectual histories. There is much potential for our fields to become botanical. Let us dig in and get started.

Notes

FOREWORD

1. De-nin D. Lee, ed., *Eco-Art History in East and Southeast Asia* (Newcastle upon Tyne: Cambridge Scholars Publishing, 2019), xix.
2. Michael Dylan Foster, "Walking in the City with Natsume Sōseki: The Metaphorical Landscape in 'Koto no sorane,'" *Proceedings of the Association for Japanese Literary Studies* 6 (Summer 2005): 138–139. I am indebted to the work of Haruo Shirane, Sonya Arntzen, Yuki Masami, and Mina Kaneko.

INTRODUCTION

1. I use the term "botanical imagination" in reference to the work of John Charles Ryan, whose notion of a "dialectical interchange of the imaginative potentialities of plants and non-plants" was an inspiration for this book. See John Charles Ryan, *Plants in Contemporary Poetry: Ecocriticism and the Botanical Imagination* (New York: Routledge, 2018), 11.
2. In theorizing botanical poetics, I am indebted to the work of Joela Jacobs, whose notion of *phytopoetics* names "both a poetic engagement with plants in literature and moments in which plants take on literary or cultural agency themselves." The botanical poetics I map out in this book resemble the phytopoetics of which Jacobs writes in her work; in particular, the poetics of Hiromi Ito, whom I discuss in chapter 5. The phytopoetic qualities of vegetal eroticism and violence are clearly legible in Ito's poetry. See Joela Jacobs, "Phytopoetics: Upending the Passive Paradigm with Vegetal Violence and Eroticism," *Catalyst: Feminism, Theory, Technoscience* 5, no. 2 (2019): 1–18.
3. See https://www.doaks.org/research/mellon-initiatives/plant-humanities-initiative and https://plants.arizona.edu/bibliography/.
4. Jeffrey T. Nealon, *Plant Theory: Biopower and Vegetable Life* (Stanford, CA: Stanford University Press, 2016), 1. Italics in the original.
5. Nealon, *Plant Theory*, x.
6. Not all theorists working within CPS discuss Foucauldian biopower in the manner Nealon does, but they are all, to some extent, concerned with the abjection of plant life within dominant regimes of knowledge. Michael Marder—arguably the leading voice in CPS and editor of Brill's CPS book series—has painstakingly worked to reintroduce the centrality of plant life in the classical canon of Western philosophy. Robin Wall Kimmerer—another leading voice of CPS and a MacArthur Genius Grant recipient who has inspired theorists and general readers alike to think deeply and differently about plants—has argued for the necessity of integrating forms of Indigenous sciences that do not denigrate plant life into the dominant sciences that have heretofore objectified plants as mere specimens. Stefano Mancuso and Monica Gagliano have in turn used unconventional methods within dominant scientific protocols to advocate for plant life's ability to communicate and experience the world in ways most humans have not anticipated. Both have written about their groundbreaking experiments in public-facing books that engage the humanities as much as they do the physical sciences, providing good examples of how CPS theorists strive for interdisciplinary engagement. The list of CPS thinkers goes on, from philosopher Emanuele Coccia and his focus on the metamorphic capabilities of plant life to usher in a new botanical metaphysics, to Beronda Montgomery, whose 2021 book

Lessons from Plants posits we have much to learn from plants about care work and creating supportive communities in academia and beyond.

7. BBC Earth's *The Green Planet* (2022) and Netflix's *Fantastic Fungi* (2019) are two such examples.

8. Gabriel Popkin, "'Wood Wide Web'—The Underground Network of Microbes That Connects Trees—Mapped for First Time," *Science*, May 15, 2019, https://www.science.org/content/article/wood-wide-web-underground-network-microbes-connects-trees-mapped-first-time.

9. This term was proposed by Kathryn M. Parsley as a corrective to the more common term *plant blindness*, which Parsley argues is problematic due to its ableist use of a disability metaphor to signify a negative trait. See Kathryn M. Parsley, "Plant Awareness Disparity: A Case for Renaming Plant Blindness," *Plants People Planet*, October 3, 2020, https://doi.org/10.1002/ppp3.10153.

10. Andrea Thompson, "Plants Are the World's Dominant Life-Form," *Scientific American*, August 1, 2018, https://www.scientificamerican.com/article/plants-are-the-worlds-dominant-life-form/.

11. Fujihara Tatsushi, *Shokubutsukō* (Tokyo: Ikinobiru Books, 2022), 15.

12. Kliment Timiryazev, *The Life of the Plant*, trans. A. Sheremetyeva (Moscow: Foreign Languages, 1958), 347.

13. Japanese environmental history is another story, however. Books such as David Fedman's *Seeds of Control* and Tom Haven's *Lands of Plants in Motion* demonstrate the willingness of historians to move plants to the foreground of historical narratives.

14. Emiko Ohnuki-Tierney has, for example, tied the cherry blossom to Japanese imperialism in her examination of the militarization of Japanese aesthetics. Emiko Ohnuki-Tierney, *Kamikaze, Cherry Blossoms, and Nationalisms: The Militarization of Aesthetics in Japanese History* (Chicago: University of Chicago Press, 2002), 3. Historians like Fujihara Tatsushi and Jung Lee have examined the role agriculture and botany have played in Japan's interwar colonial project, while David Fedman and Tessa Morris-Suzuki have demonstrated the impact of forestry on modes of control (both environmental and social) in Japan's colonial acquisitions. Tessa Morris-Suzuki, "The Nature of Empire: Forest Ecology, Colonialism and Survival Politics in Japan's Imperial Order," *Japan Studies* 33, no. 3 (2013): 225–242. See also David Fedman, *Seeds of Control: Japan's Empire of Forestry in Colonial Korea* (Seattle: University of Washington Press, 2020).

15. Fujihara, *Shokubutsukō*, 21.

16. Michael Marder, *Plant Thinking: A Philosophy of Vegetal Life* (New York: Columbia University Press, 2013), 10.

17. Robert Stolz's *Bad Water* (2014) and Brett Walker's *Toxic Archipelago* (2010) are good examples of this paradigm in the field of environmental history, while Karen Thornber's *Ecoambiguity* (2012) and Christine Marran's *Ecology Without Culture* (2017) are good examples from within the field of literary and film studies.

18. Kimura Saeko's 2013 book *A Theory of Post-3.11 Literature: Toward a New Japanese Literature* (*Shinsaigo bungakuron: Atarashii Nihon bungaku no tame ni*) and its 2018 follow-up *A Theory of Post-3.11 Literature after That* (*Sono go no shinsaigo bungakuron*) are key texts in a growing corpus of post-3.11 scholarship that also includes Rachel DiNitto's *Fukushima Fiction: The Literary Landscape of Japan's Triple Disaster* and Koichi Haga's *The Earth Writes: The Great Earthquake and the Novel in Post-3/11 Japan*, both published in 2019.

19. Yuki Masami, "On Harmony with Nature: Toward Japanese Ecocriticism," in *Ecocriticism in Japan*, ed. Hisaaki Wake, Yuki Masami, and Keijiro Suga (Lanham, MD: Lexington Books, 2018), 4.

20. Yuki, "On Harmony with Nature," 4.

21. Haruo Shirane, *Japan and the Culture of the Four Seasons: Nature, Literature, and the Arts* (New York: Columbia University Press, 2012), 8.

22. Shirane, *Japan and the Culture of the Four Seasons*, 1–4.

23. Yuki offers the following critique of Shirane's *Japan and the Culture of the Four Seasons*: "Ideological criticism rarely surfaces in Shirane's literary and historical examination of the cultural representation of the environment." Yuki, "Ecocriticism in Japan," 4. It is my contention that CPS is particularly good at fleshing out ideological critique/criticism in relation to conceptions of "nature."

24. Shirane, *Japan and the Culture of the Four Seasons*, 4.

25. Gregory Bateson, *Sacred Unity: Further Steps to an Ecology of Mind* (New York: Cornelia and Michael Bessie Books, 1991), 240.

26. Bateson, *Sacred Unity*, 241.

27. I recognize that Bateson's gendered use of *men* here to mean "human" in general is problematic. It is likely that Bateson uses *men* to keep symmetry with the classical syllogism he is amending. I, in turn, keep Bateson's phrasing throughout, with an implied "[sic]" attached to each usage of *men*.

28. Hara Shōji, *Hito wa kusa de aru: "ruji" to "zure" o meguru kōsatsu* (Tokyo: Sairyūsha, 2013), 236.

29. Elizabeth Grosz, *Becoming Undone: Darwinian Reflections on Life, Politics, and Art* (Durham, NC: Duke University Press, 2011), 13–14.

30. Bateson, *Sacred Unity*, 241.

31. Here I break the convention the rest of the book follows—which is to list names in Japanese order, with the family name first and given name second—and refer to Itō Hiromi as Hiromi Ito, with the given name first and without the elongated ō in her family name. This is the writer's preference when being discussed in English, and it helps me differentiate between her and writer Itō Seikō, whom I discuss in chapter 3.

32. Itō Hiromi and Machida Kō. *Futatsu no hamon* (Tokyo: Bungei Seishun, 2022), 79–80.

33. Itō and Machida, *Futatsu no hamon*, 80.

34. Laurel Rasplica Rodd and Mary Catherine Henkenius, trans., *Kokinshū: A Collection of Poems Ancient and Modern* (Boston: Cheng & Tsui, 1996), 35.

35. Matsuo Bashō, *Bashō's Journey: The Literary Prose of Matsuo Bashō*, trans. David Landis Barnhill (Albany: State University of New York Press, 2005), 62.

36. Hiromi Ito, *Tree Spirits Grass Spirits*, trans. Jon L. Pitt (New York: Nightboat Books, 2023), 57.

37. Gilles Deleuze and Félix Guattari, *A Thousand Plateaus: Capitalism and Schizophrenia*, trans. Brian Massumi (New York: Bloomsbury, 2016), 342.

38. Sumana Roy, *How I Became a Tree* (New Haven, CT: Yale University Press, 2021), 54.

39. Deleuze and Guattari, *A Thousand Plateaus*, 3.

40. In their as-yet-unpublished history of *The Secret Life of Plants* (a portion of which was presented at the 2024 Plant Animacies Workshop at Harvey Mudd College), Vivien Hamilton and Delia Garvus demonstrate the extent to which Tompkins and Bird were taken seriously upon their book's release and thus argue that the line between so-called legitimate science and pseudoscience is not as clear cut as we might wish to believe. I use the term *pseudoscience* throughout this book in reference to both *The Secret Life of Plants* and the work of Hashimoto Ken, but I simultaneously recognize the ideological bias this word implies. Insofar as this book is about varying ways of knowing plants, and how those ways become entangled within one another, I acknowledge that *The Secret Life of Plants* and the work of Hashimoto Ken were each taken as serious science by some and rejected as pseudoscience by others. This places these texts in the generative in-between space that this present book looks to identify.

41. I am indebted to Gregory Golley's 2008 monograph *When Our Eyes No Longer See: Realism, Science, and Ecology in Japanese Literary Modernism*, which was foundational in my thinking about the connections between Japanese literature and science.

42. Catherine Malabou, *Ontology of the Accident: An Essay on Destructive Plasticity*, trans. Carolyn Shread (Malden: Polity, 2012), 3.

43. Beronda Montgomery, *Lessons from Plants* (Cambridge, MA: Harvard University Press, 2021), 5.

44. "What Is Plant Plasticity?" VILLUM Research Center for Plant Plasticity, accessed January 23, 2024, https://plantplasticity.ku.dk/what_is_sb/#:~:text=Plant%20plasticity%20refers%20to%20a,with%20changes%20in%20its%20environment.

45. Malabou writes of the subject undergoing the radical changes of destructive plasticity: "We return nowhere. Between life and death we become other to ourselves." Malabou, *Ontology of the Accident*, 34.

46. David W. Bates, "Unity, Plasticity, Catastrophe: Order and Pathology in the Cybernetic Era," in *Catastrophes: A History and Theory of an Operative Concept*, ed. Nitzan Lebovic and Andreas Killen (Boston: de Gruyter, 2014), 54.

47. Christopher Dole, Robert Hayashi, Andrew Poe, Austin Sarat, and Boris Wolfson, "When Is Catastrophe? An Introduction," in *The Time of Catastrophe: Multidisciplinary Approaches to the Age of Catastrophe*, ed. Christopher Dole, Robert Hayashi, Andrew Poe, Austin Sarat, and Boris Wolfson (Burlington, VT: Ashgate, 2015), 1.

48. Michael Pollan, "The Intelligent Plant," *New Yorker*, December 15, 2013.

49. Pollan, "The Intelligent Plant."

50. Dawn Keetley, "Introduction: Six Theses on Plant Horror; or, Why Are Plants Horrifying?" in *Plant Horror: Approaches to the Monstrous Vegetal in Fiction and Film*, ed. Dawn Keetley and Angela Tenga (London: Palgrave Macmillan, 2016), 1.

51. Catherine Malabou distinguishes between the "ungovernable" and the "nongovernable," claiming the latter names something that is "not resisting the logic of government, but perfectly alien to it." See https://youtu.be/RoxM_7QVMnc. In a lecture given on May 12, 2023, at the University of California, Irvine, Malabou suggested plants may indeed fall under this category.

1. BOTANICAL FAMILIES

1. I follow the custom of referring to Osaki by this name rather than "Ozaki" (which is the more common reading of the characters that make up her family name), as this is the pronunciation used in her native Tottori Prefecture. Max Fleischer, who created the film *Evolution*, is the animator famous for adapting comic strips such as *Superman*, *Betty Boop*, and *Popeye* for the screen. He was not the famous bryologist of the same name who specialized in categorizing the mosses of Java. It is fitting, however, that the two share a name, as moss ties them together in a kind of doppelganger scenario that would certainly have appealed to Osaki. For an outline of screening dates at the Musashinokan theater that correlate with the films discussed in Osaki's *Jottings on Film*, see: Hideyama Yōko, *Osaki Midori e no tabi: hon to zasshi no meiro no naka de* (Tokyo: Shogakukan, 2009), 62–63.

2. Osaki Midori, *Osaki Midori Zenshū* (Tokyo: Sōjusha, 1979), 345–346.

3. Michael Weiner, "The Invention of Identity: Race and Nation in Pre-War Japan," in *The Construction of Racial Identities in China and Japan: Historical and Contemporary Perspectives*, ed. Frank Dikotter (London: Hurst, 1997), 102–110.

4. Sherrie Cross, "Prestige and Comfort: The Development of Social Darwinism in Early Meiji Japan, and the Role of Edward Sylvester Morse," *Annals of Science* 53, no. 4 (1996): 323–344. See also Mizuguchi Hajime, "Nihon ni okeru Darwin no juyō to eikyō," *Gakushutsu no dōkō* 3 (2010): 48–57.

5. Cross, "Prestige and Comfort," 336.

6. Robin Wall Kimmerer, *Gathering Moss: A Natural and Cultural History of Mosses* (Corvallis: Oregon State University Press, 2003), 14–15.

7. Kimmerer, *Gathering Moss*, 15.

8. The Machiko Cycle includes the following stories, all of which feature an intricate web of characters centered around Ono Machiko and seem to inhabit the same narrative universe: *Wandering in the Realm of the Seventh Sense*; "Walking" ("*Hokō*," 1931); "Miss Cricket" ("*Kōrogijō*," 1932); and "A Night in Anton's Basement" ("*Chikashitsu anton no hitoya*," 1932).

9. Seiji Lippit, *Topographies of Japanese Modernism* (New York: Columbia University Press, 2022), 208.

10. Lippit, *Topographies of Japanese Modernism*, 208.

11. See, for example, Nathan Clerici, "Performance and Nonsense: Osaki Midori's 'Strange Love,'" *Japanese Language and Literature* 51, no. 2 (2017) and Tomoko Aoyama, "Sweet Bean Paste and Excrement: Food, Humor, and Gender in Osaki Midori's Writings," *Gastro-Modernism: Food, Literature, Culture*, ed. Derek Gladwin (Clemson, SC: Clemson University Press, 2019).

12. Mure Yōko, *Osaki Midori* (Tokyo: Bungei Shunjū, 1998), 95.

13. Kawasaki Kenko, *Osaki Midori: Sakyū no anata e* (Tokyo: Iwanami Shoten, 2010), 85.

14. Hideyama, *Osaki Midori e no tabi*, 75.

15. Kimmerer, *Gathering Moss*, 38.

16. J. W. Bates, "Is 'Life-Form' a Useful Concept in Bryophyte Ecology?" *Oikos* 82 (1998): 224.

17. Kimmerer, *Gathering Moss*, 11.

18. Karen L. F. Houle, "Animal, Vegetable, Mineral: Ethics as Extension or Becoming? The Case of Becoming-Plant," *Journal for Critical Animal Studies* 9, nos. 1/2 (2011): 96.

19. Osaki, *Osaki Midori Zenshū*, 115.

20. Osaki, *Osaki Midori Zenshū*, 372.

21. Blaise Pascal, *Pascal's Pensées* (New York: E. P. Dutton, 1958), Project Gutenberg EBook, 97. https://www.gutenberg.org/files/18269/18269-h/18269-h.htm.

22. Osaki, *Osaki Midori Zenshū*, 371. For "doppelgänger," Osaki uses the word *bunshin*, with the characters for "divide" and "heart/mind," respectively, glossed with phonetic katakana characters reading *dopperugengeru*. The phrase I have rendered "split poet" is *bunretsu shijin*.

23. Osaki, *Osaki Midori Zenshū*, 367. It is somewhat difficult to capture the reversal in English. The parallelism is clearer in the Japanese.

24. As explained in chapter 3, Haniya Yutaka also writes of becoming botanical as both an expansion and a contraction in his novel *Dead Spirits*.

25. Gilles Deleuze and Félix Guattari, *A Thousand Plateaus: Capitalism and Schizophrenia*, trans. Brian Massumi (New York: Bloomsbury, 2016), 278.

26. Kimmerer, *Gathering Moss*, 10–11.

27. Osaki, *Osaki Midori Zenshū*, 386.

28. Osaki, *Osaki Midori Zenshū*, 14. To capture the repetition of this paragraph, I have attempted in my translation to use the words *mandarin orange* for every time Osaki uses them. While it sounds repetitious in English, the effect is even more noticeable in the Japanese.

29. Catherine Malabou, "Post-Trauma: Towards a New Definition?" in *Telemorphosis: Theory in the Era of Climate Change, Vol. 1*, ed. Tom Cohen (Ann Arbor: University of Michigan Open Humanities Press, 2012), 235.

30. Luce Irigaray and Michael Marder, *Through Vegetal Being: Two Philosophical Perspectives* (New York: Columbia University Press, 2016), 158. Italics in the original.

31. Osaki, *Osaki Midori Zenshū*, 17.

32. Osaki, *Osaki Midori Zenshū*, 34. In his essay on moss in *Wandering in the Realm of the Seventh Sense*, Arakawa Tomotsugu attempts to determine just what kind of moss Osaki is writing about in the novella. Based on Machiko's quote here, he determines they are likely *tamagoke* (*Bartramia pomiformis*). Arakawa Tomotsugu, "Kokegakusha ga yomitoku 'Dainana kankai hōkō,'" in *Osaki Midori o yomu: Kōenhen II* (Tottori: Osaki Midori fōramu jikkōiinkai, 2016), 80.

33. Osaki, *Osaki Midori Zenshū*, 33.

34. Osaki, *Osaki Midori Zenshū*, 25.

35. Osaki Midori and Nozoe Nobuhisa, *Dainana kankai hōkō* (Tokyo: Ohta Shuppan, 2018), 130–131.

36. Osaki, *Osaki Midori Zenshū*, 43–44.

37. Osaki, *Osaki Midori Zenshū*, 44.

38. Elizabeth Grosz, "Darwin and Feminism: Preliminary Investigations for a Possible Alliance," *Australian Feminist Studies*, 14, no. 29 (1999): 41. DOI: 10.1080/08164649993317.

39. Osaki, *Osaki Midori Zenshū*, 49.

40. Osaki, *Osaki Midori Zenshū*, 53.

41. Akiyama Hiroyuki, *Koke no hanashi* (Tokyo: Chukokoron: Shinsha, 2004), 32.

42. Stella Sandford, *Vegetal Sex: Philosophy of Plants* (London: Bloomsbury, 2023), 103.

43. Sandford, *Vegetal Sex*, 37.

44. Sandford, *Vegetal Sex*, 38.

45. Sandford, *Vegetal Sex*, 105.

46. Sandford, *Vegetal Sex*, 117.

47. Osaki, *Osaki Midori Zenshū*, 49.

48. Osaki, *Osaki Midori Zenshū*, 74.

49. Kimmerer, *Gathering Moss*, 20.

50. Osaki, *Osaki Midori Zenshū*, 74.

51. Tessa Morris-Suzuki, "Debating Racial Science in Wartime Japan," *Osiris* 13 (1998): 354–375.

52. Miriam Silverberg, *Erotic Grotesque Nonsense: The Mass Culture of Japanese Modern Times* (Berkeley: University of California Press, 2006).

53. See Livia Monnet, "Montage, Cinematic Subjectivity and Feminism in Ozaki Midori's Drifting in the World of the Seventh Sense," *Japan Forum* 11, no. 1 (1999): 57–82.

54. Silverberg, *Erotic Grotesque Nonsense*, 116.

55. Kawasaki, *Osaki Midori*, 88.

56. Kawasaki, *Osaki Midori*, 85–89.

57. Tessa Morris-Suzuki, "The Nature of Empire: Forest Ecology, Colonialism and Survival Politics in Japan's Imperial Order," *Japan Studies* 33, no. 3 (2013): 235.

58. Morris-Suzuki, "The Nature of Empire," 234.

59. Fujihara Tatsushi, *Sensō to nogyō* (Tokyo: Shūeisha International e-shinsho, 2017), Kindle edition.

60. See Vanessa Catherine Baker's 2022 dissertation "Entangled Ecologies of the Everyday: Gender, Labor, and Nature in Rural Proletarian Literature of Korea and Japan," University of California, Irvine.

61. Osaki, *Osaki Midori Zenshū*, 31.

62. Kawasaki, *Osaki Midori*, 90.

63. Kawasaki, *Osaki Midori*, 90.

64. Arakawa, "Kokegakusha ga yomitoku 'Dainana kankai hōkō.'" 85.

65. Oka Asajirō, *Seibutsugaku kōwa* (Tokyo: Kaiseikan, 1916), 443.

66. Oka Asajirō, *Seibutsugaku kōwa*, 447.

67. Gregory Sullivan, *Regenerating Japan: Organicism, Modernism and National Destiny in Oka Asajirō's "Evolution and Human Life"* (Budapest: CEU Press, 2018), 12.
68. Sullivan, *Regenerating Japan*, 5.
69. Arakawa, "*Kokegakusha ga yomitoku 'Dainana kankai hōkō*,'" 86.
70. Osaki, *Osaki Midori Zenshū*, 107.
71. Osaki, *Osaki Midori Zenshū*, 198.
72. Osaki, *Osaki Midori Zenshū*, 199.
73. Osaki, *Osaki Midori Zenshū*, 199.
74. Osaki, *Osaki Midori Zenshū*, 37.
75. Alan Richardson, "Erasmus Darwin and the Fungus School," *Wordsworth Circle* 33, no. 3 (2001): 113.
76. Erasmus Darwin, *The Botanic Garden Part II* (Dublin: J. Moore, 1796), 1.
77. Osaki, *Osaki Midori Zenshū*, 75.
78. Irigaray and Marder, *Through Vegetal Being*, 50.
79. Throughout *Jottings on Film*, Osaki expresses a deep nostalgia for silent film.
80. For example, author Mure Yōko writes of Osaki, "I was astonished such a writer as this had lived in Japan." Mure, *Osaki Midori*, 7.
81. Osaki, *Osaki Midori Zenshū*, 530.
82. Osaki, *Osaki Midori Zenshū*, 159.
83. Arakawa, "*Kokegakusha ga yomitoku 'Dainana kankai hōkō*.'" 12.
84. Kimmerer, *Gathering Moss*, 37.

2. BOTANICAL ALLEGORY

1. Margaret S. Key, *Truth from a Lie: Documentary, Detection, and Reflexivity in Abe Kōbō's Realist Project* (Plymouth, UK: Lexington Books, 2001), 10.
2. Abe Kōbō, *Abe Kōbō zenshū* (Tokyo: Shinchōsha, 2009), 30:13.
3. Hanada Kiyoteru, "*Dōbutsu—shokubutsu—kōbutsu*," in *Gendai Nihon bungaku taikei 77: Dazai Osamu—Sakaguchi Ango shū* (Tokyo: Chikuma shobō, 1969), 425.
4. Osaki Midori, *Osaki Midori Zenshū* (Tokyo: Sōjusha, 1979), 524–525.
5. Donna Haraway, *Staying with the Trouble: Making Kin in the Chthulucene* (Durham, NC: Duke University Press, 2016).
6. Sebastian Conrad, "Entangled Memories: Versions of the Past in Germany and Japan, 1945–2001," *Journal of Contemporary History* 38, no. 1 (2003): 85–99.
7. In his discussion of plants within the Foucauldian concept of biopower, Jeffrey T. Nealon outlines a systemic shift in the nineteenth century that Foucault recognized as a change from the study of natural science to that of biology. This shift entailed "a mutation of the dominant epistemic procedures—from a representational discourse that maps external similitude and resemblance, to the emergence of a speculative discourse that takes as its object hidden internal processes." Jeffrey T. Nealon, *Plant Theory: Biopower and Vegetable Life* (Stanford, CA: Stanford University Press, 2016), 7.
8. Mutsuko Motoyama, "The Literature and Politics of Abe Kōbō: Farewell to Communism in *Suna no Onna*," *Monumenta Nipponica* 50, no. 3 (1995): 309.
9. Mutsuko Motoyama recounts that Abe had been living in a boardinghouse next to factory workers' quarters at the time he was awarded the Akutagawa Prize in 1951. See Motoyama, "The Literature and Politics of Abe Kōbō," 314.
10. Tsuyama Takashi, "Plantæ Boninenses Novæ vel Criticæ. V," *Shokubutsugaku zasshi* 1, no. 591 (1936): 129–133.
11. See "Ogasawara World Heritage Centre," http://ogasawara-info.jp/. See also Kazuto Kawakami and Isamu Okochi, eds., *Restoring the Oceanic Island Ecosystem Impact and Management of Invasive Alien Species in the Bonin Islands* (New York: Springer, 2010).

12. Itō Motomi, "*Wadannoki—Taiyōtō de ki ni natta kiku*," *Gekkan hyakka* 401 (1996), 24.

13. David Chapman, *The Bonin Islanders, 1830 to the Present: Narrating Japanese Nationality* (Lanham, MD: Lexington Books, 2016), 37.

14. Chapman, *The Bonin Islanders*, 92.

15. Chapman, *The Bonin Islanders*, 105.

16. Chapman, *The Bonin Islanders*, 104.

17. Chapman, *The Bonin Islanders*, 140.

18. Chapman, *The Bonin Islanders*, 159.

19. Christy Wampole, *Rootedness: The Ramifications of a Metaphor* (Chicago: University of Chicago Press, 2016), 5.

20. My discussion of "Dendrocacalia" is drawn primarily from the 1952 version of the short story. Although the general outline of the plot remains the same between the 1949 and 1952 versions, the 1949 version is longer and features an opening section of direct address to the reader that is excised in the revised version of 1952. The identity of the narrating voice is less stable in the earlier version, and there is a greater sense of ambiguity over the roles certain characters play in the narrative. For a thorough explanation of the differences between the two versions, see Toba Kōji, *Undōtai—Abe Kōbō* (Tokyo: Ichiyōsha, 2007).

21. Abe Kōbō, *Abe Kōbō zenshū* (Tokyo: Shinchōsha, 1997), 3:350.

22. Abe, *Abe Kōbō zenshū*, 3:351.

23. My reading of the motif of interior/exterior in "Dendrocacalia" is informed by Toba Kōji's chapter "'Henbō' to riarizumu ronsō—'Dendorokakariya' 1949," in Toba, *Undōtai—Abe Kōbō*.

24. Abe, *Abe Kōbō zenshū*, 3:356.

25. Emanuele Coccia, *The Life of Plants: A Metaphysics of Mixture*, trans. Dylan J. Montanari (Medford, OR: Polity, 2019), 5.

26. Toba, *Undōtai*, 84.

27. Motoyama, "The Literature and Politics of Abe Kōbō," 320.

28. Sho Konishi, *Anarchist Modernity: Cooperatism and Japanese-Russian Intellectual Relations in Modern Japan* (Cambridge, MA: Harvard University Asia Center, 2013), 297–298.

29. Peter Kropotkin, *Anarchism: Its Philosophy and Ideal* (London: J. Turner, 1897), Nineteenth Century Collections Online, 4.

30. Kropotkin, *Anarchism*, 4.

31. Konishi, *Anarchist Modernity*, 238. Anarchist Ōsugi Sakae (who founded Japan's first Esperanto school) translated *Mutual Aid* into Japanese in 1917, having previously translated Darwin's *Origin of the Species* three years before in 1914. Ōsugi would go on to translate Jean-Henri Fabre's *Souvenirs entomologiques* in 1922. See Konishi, *Anarchist Modernity*, 318.

32. Peter Kropotkin, *Mutual Aid: A Factor of Evolution* (London: William Heinemann, 1915), 62. Quotation marks and italics in the original.

33. Meguro Jiro, "Soveto seibutsugaku no tenbō," *Kagaku to gijutsu* 11 (1948): 13–14.

34. The essays that compose *Mutual Aid* were originally published during the 1890s in the British literary magazine *The Nineteenth Century*.

35. Peter Kropotkin, *Modern Science and Anarchism* (London: Freedom, 1912), 46. Italics in the original.

36. Kliment Timiryazev, *The Life of the Plant*, trans. A. Sheremetyeva (Moscow: Foreign Languages, 1958), 347.

37. Abe, *Abe Kōbō zenshū*, 3:192.

38. Kropotkin, *Anarchism*, 4.

39. Abe, *Abe Kōbō zenshū*, 3:352.

40. Abe, *Abe Kōbō zenshū*, 3:352.

41. Stefano Mancuso, *The Revolutionary Genius of Plants: A New Understanding of Plant Intelligence and Behavior* (New York: Atria Books, 2017), 49.
42. "Kokudo ryokka suishin undo," *Sanrin—Journal of Forestry* 791 (1950): 1.
43. In Japanese, "*Areta kokudo o heiwa na midori de*." See "*Kokudo ryokka kanren no kitte ni shōkai*," *Kokudo ryokka suishin kikō*, http://www.green.or.jp/news/news-other/o_fukyu_entry_273/.
44. "*Kokushi rokka suishin undo*," 1.
45. Kropotkin, *Mutual Aid*, 11.
46. Abe, *Abe Kōbō zenshū*, 3:354.
47. Mancuso, *Revolutionary Genius of Plants*, 73.
48. Abe Kōbō, *Abe Kōbō zenshū* (Tokyo: Shinchōsha, 1997), 2:234.
49. Stefano Mancuso and Alessandra Viola, *Brilliant Green: The Surprising History and Science of Plant Intelligence*, trans. Joan Benham (Washington, DC: Island, 2015), 67.
50. Mancuso and Viola, *Brilliant Green*, 77.
51. Abe, *Abe Kōbō zenshū*, 3:352.
52. Abe, *Abe Kōbō zenshū*, 3:353.
53. Mancuso, *The Revolutionary Genius of Plants*, 21.
54. Kropotkin, *Anarchism*, 4.
55. Abe, *Abe Kōbō zenshū*, 3:355.
56. Abe, *Abe Kōbō zenshū*, 3:356.
57. Abe, *Abe Kōbō zenshū*, 3:356.
58. Luce Irigaray and Michael Marder, *Through Vegetal Being: Two Philosophical Perspectives* (New York: Columbia University Press, 2016), 158.
59. Abe, *Abe Kōbō zenshū*, 3:356.
60. Abe Kōbō, *Abe Kōbō zenshū* (Tokyo: Shinchōsha, 1999), 21:437.
61. Abe, *Abe Kōbō zenshū*, 3:356.
62. Abe, *Abe Kōbō zenshū*, 3:356.
63. Irigaray and Marder, *Through Vegetal Being*, 120.
64. Abe, *Abe Kōbō zenshū*, 3:357.
65. Abe, *Abe Kōbō zenshū*, 3: 362.
66. Timiryazev, *The Life of the Plant*, 70.
67. Abe, *Abe Kōbō zenshū*, 3:359.
68. Abe, *Abe Kōbō zenshū*, 3:362.
69. Nakajima Seinosuke, "*Shokubutsu no seikatsu*," *Yuibutsuron kenkyū* 20 (1934): 121.
70. Nakajima, "*Shokubutsu no seikatsu*," 124.
71. Kliment Timiryazev, *Shokubutsu no sekatsu*, trans. Ishii Tomoyuki (Tokyo: Iwasaki shoten, 1947), 1.
72. Timiryazev, *The Life of the Plant*, 340.
73. Timiryazev, *The Life of the Plant*, 337.
74. Timiryazev, *The Life of the Plant*, 347.
75. With Honda's help, the Shōwa emperor published a series of studies on the plants of Nasu and the Izu Peninsula between 1962 and 1985. See Kageyama Noboru, "*Shōwa Tenno no jiko jitsugen to seibutsugaku kenkyū—sasaeta chiteki tankyūshin to ōsei na kiryoku*," *Shizen kagaku no tobira* 5, no. 4 (1999): 26–27.
76. Terao Shin and Honda Masaji, *Shin Nihon shōnen shōjo bunko dai 7 hen: Dōbutsu to shokubutsu no seikatsu* (Tokyo: Shinchōsha, 1940), 2.
77. Terao and Honda, *Shin Nihon shōnen shōjo bunko dai 7 hen*, 2.
78. Abe, *Abe Kōbō zenshū*, 3:363.
79. Terao and Honda, *Shin Nihon shōnen shōjo bunko dai 7 hen*, 186.
80. Tessa Morris-Suzuki, "The Nature of Empire: Forest Ecology, Colonialism and Survival Politics in Japan's Imperial Order," *Japan Studies* 33, no. 3 (2013): 230.

81. *Forestry of Japan* (Tokyo: Bureau of Forestry, Department of Agriculture and Commerce, 1910), 1.
82. Terao and Honda, *Shin Nihon shōnen shōjo bunko dai 7 hen*, 182.
83. Tsuyama, "Plantæ Boninenses Novæ vel Criticæ. V," 129.
84. Jung Lee, "Between Universalism and Regionalism: Universal Systematics from Imperial Japan," *British Society for the History of Science* 48, no. 4 (2015): 663.
85. Lee, "Between Universalism and Regionalism," 676. Thomas Havens claims Nakai made eighteen trips to Korea between 1908 and 1940. See Thomas R. H. Havens, *Land of Plants in Motion: Japanese Botany and the World* (Honolulu: University of Hawai'i Press, 2020), 117.
86. Havens, *Land of Plants in Motion*, 118.
87. Lee, "Between Universalism and Regionalism," 665.
88. Lee, "Between Universalism and Regionalism," 667.

3. BOTANICAL MEDIA

1. Haniya Yutaka and Tachibana Takashi, *Mugen no sō no moto ni* (Tokyo: Heibonsha, 1997), 111–112.
2. Thomas R. H. Havens, *Parkscapes: Green Spaces in Modern Japan* (Honolulu: University of Hawai'i Press, 2011), 95.
3. "Panel Documents: November 24, 1944, Musashino Air Raids and Nakajima Aircraft Co." Committee for the Promotion of Peace under the Declaration of Musashino as a Nuclear-Free City, accessed March 3, 2023, https://www.city.musashimurayama.lg.jp/.
4. Hattori Kenshō, *"Kichijōji de no kūshū taiken," Musashino no kūshū to sono kioku*, accessed March 3, 2023, https://www.city.musashimurayama.lg.jp/.
5. Shirakawa Masayoshi, ed., *Haniya Yutaka dokuji "Shirei" no sekai* (Tokyo: NHK Shuppan, 1997), 12.
6. Haniya Yutaka, *Shirei I* (Tokyo: Kōdansha, 1981), 28.
7. Haniya and Tachibana, *Mugen no sō no moto ni*, 26. The term Haniya uses, *bunretsukei*, contains the same word (*bunretsu*) that Osaki Midori uses throughout *Wandering in the Realm of the Seventh Sense* to discuss "split psychology."
8. Haniya and Tachibana, *Mugen no sō no moto ni*, 26.
9. *Haniya Yutaka dokuji "Shirei" no sekai*, 61.
10. For a 1946 account of the different factions associated with the agrarian movement, see Seiyei Wakukawa, "Japanese Tenant Movements," *Far Eastern Survey* 15, no. 3 (1946): 40–44.
11. *Nihon anakizumu undō jinmei jiten* (Tokyo: Parushuppan, 2004), 516.
12. Yoshiki Taijiri, "Beckett and Haniya Yutaka: Two Versions of the Ontological Enquiry," *Journal of Irish Studies* 17 (2002): 109.
13. Haniya and Tachibana, *Mugen no sō no moto ni*, 195.
14. Almost twenty years passed between the publications of the initial run of four volumes and the fifth volume, which was published in 1975 in the magazine *Gunzō*. The remaining volumes, all published in *Gunzō*, saw several years between publications: volume 6 in 1981, volume 7 in 1984, volume 8 in 1986, and volume 7 in 1995.
15. *Haniya Yutaka dokuji "Shirei" no sekai*, 13.
16. *Haniya Yutaka dokuji "Shirei" no sekai*, 13. Ellipses in the original.
17. Shinsuke Tsurumi, *An Intellectual History of Wartime Japan 1931–1945* (London: KPI, 1986), 65.
18. *Haniya Yutaka dokuji "Shirei" no sekai*, 64.
19. Haniya, *Shirei I*, 11.

20. James Dorsey, "The Art of War: Sakaguchi Ango's 'Pearls' and the Nature of Literary Resistance," in *Literary Mischief: Sakaguchi Ango, Culture, and War*, ed. James Dorsey and Doug Slaymaker (Lanham, MD: Lexington Books, 2010), 98.

21. Luce Irigaray and Michael Marder, *Through Vegetal Being: Two Philosophical Perspectives* (New York: Columbia University Press, 2016), 174.

22. Jane Bennett, *Vibrant Matter: A Political Ecology of Things* (Durham, NC: Duke University Press, 2010), 24.

23. Haniya, *Shirei I*, 30.

24. Haniya, *Shirei I*, 108–109.

25. Haniya, *Shirei I*, 24.

26. Haniya, *Shirei I*, 15.

27. Haniya, *Shirei I*, 16.

28. Haniya, *Shirei I*, 16.

29. Takizawa Kenji, *Ki to ke to ki: hirogari to gyōshuku no bigaku* (Tokyo: Hozansha, 1993), 97.

30. Takizawa, *Ki to ke to ki*, 101.

31. See Fabio Rambelli's chapter "The Cultural Imagination of Trees and the Environment" in *Buddhist Materiality: A Cultural History of Objects in Japanese Buddhism* (Stanford, CA: Stanford University Press, 2007) for a discussion of the entangled histories of *somoku jōbutsu*, Shinto ideology, and land preservation.

32. John Durhman Peters, *The Marvelous Clouds: Toward a Philosophy of Elemental Media* (Chicago: University of Chicago Press, 2015), 47.

33. Peters, *The Marvelous Clouds*, 3.

34. Takemura Shinichi, *Uchūju* (Tokyo: Chuo Seihan, 2018), 44.

35. Takemura, *Uchūju*, 44.

36. Haniya, Shirei I, 110.

37. Haniya, *Shirei I*, 110.

38. Catherine Malabou, *Ontology of the Accident: An Essay on Destructive Plasticity*, trans. Carolyn Shread (Malden, MA: Polity, 2012), 6.

39. Malabou, *Ontology of the Accident*, 34.

40. Fujii Takashi, "'Jinshinsei' no Haniya Yutaka: "Shirei" to posuto 'ningenchūshinshūgi,'" *Shōwa Bungaku Kenkyū* 84 (2022).

41. Haniya, *Shirei I*, 107.

42. Haniya, *Shirei I*, 107–108.

43. Emanuele Coccia, *The Life of Plants: A Metaphysics of Mixture*, trans. Dylan J. Montanari (Medford, OR: Polity, 2019), 37.

44. Quoted in Coccia, *The Life of Plants*, 87.

45. Haniya, *Shirei I*, 108.

46. Haniya, *Shirei I*, 108.

47. Haniya, *Shirei I*, 110.

48. Haniya, *Shirei I*, 48

49. Haniya, *Shirei I*, 48. Ellipses in the original.

50. Haniya, *Shirei I*, 48.

51. Coccia, *The Life of Plants*, 8.

52. Haniya and Tachibana, *Mugen no sō no moto ni*, 114–115.

53. Haniya and Tachibana, *Mugen no sō no moto ni*, 116.

54. Haniya and Tachibana, *Mugen no sō no moto ni*, 116.

55. For a summary of the impact and controversy of *The Secret Life of Plants*, see Michael Pollan, "The Intelligent Plant," *New Yorker*, December 15, 2013. https://michaelpollan.com/articles-archive/the-intelligent-plant/.

56. Peter Tompkins and Christopher Bird, *The Secret Life of Plants* (New York: Harper, 2002), 152.
57. Cleve Backster, *Primary Perception: Biocommunication with Plants, Living Foods, and Human Cells* (Anza, CA: White Rose Millennium, 2003).
58. At various points, *Dead Spirits* directly references literary and philosophical works such as Lao Tzu's *Dao de jing* and Algernon Charles Swinburne's poem "A Ballad of François Villion, Prince of All Ballad-Makers."
59. Hashimoto Ken, "Aruhuakoiru wo hatsumei suru made," *Nihon Chōkagakkai*, accessed January 28, 2024, http://www.alphacoil.com/kisekiap.htm.
60. Hashimoto, "*Aruhuakoiru wo hatsumei suru made.*"
61. Hashimoto, "*Aruhuakoiru wo hatsumei suru made.*"
62. Hashimoto Ken, *Kagaku ka? Shūkyō ka?* (Tokyo: Weagle Books, 1988).
63. Tompkins and Bird, *The Secret Life of Plants*, 44.
64. Hashimoto Ken, *Shokubutsu ni wa kokoro ga aru* (Tokyo: Goma Shobō, 1997), 147.
65. Hashimoto Ken, "Utau saboten," *Seishin kagaku* 291 (1971): 42.
66. Tompkins and Bird, *The Secret Life of Plants*, 43.
67. Haniya, *Shirei I*, 108.
68. Hashimoto, "*Utau saboten,*" 42.
69. Hashimoto, "*Utau saboten,*" 42.
70. Haniya Yutaka, *Shirei II* (Tokyo: Kōdansha, 1981), 38.
71. *Haniya Yutaka dokuji "Shirei" no sekai*, 128.
72. Hashimoto, "*Utau saboten,*" 42.
73. Hashimoto, "*Utau saboten,*" 42.
74. Hashimoto, *Kagaku ka? Shūkyō ka?*, 18.
75. Hashimoto Ken, *Yojigensekai no shinpi* (Tokyo: Ikeda, 1966).
76. Hashimoto, *Kagaku ka? Shūkyō ka?*, 17.
77. Hashimoto Ken, *Shokubutsu to ohanashi suru hō* (Tokyo: Goma Shobō, 1995), 133.
78. Hashimoto, *Shokubutsu to ohanashi suru hō*, 133.
79. Hashimoto, *Shokubutsu to ohanashi suru hō*, 134.
80. Hashimoto, *Shokubutsu to ohanashi suru hō*, 134.
81. Takemura. *Uchūju*, 47. Emphasis in original.
82. Directors' Statement from Press Packet for *Conversation with a Cactus* (received via personal correspondence).
83. Ryūtanji Yū, *Shaboten gensō* (Tokyo: Chikuma Shobō, 2016), 187–207.
84. Itō Seikō, *Botanikaru raifu—shokubutsu seikatsu* (Tokyo: Shinchōsha, 1999), 98.
85. Itō, *Botanikaru raifu*, 100.
86. Itō, *Botanikaru raifu*, 100.
87. Itō Seikō, *Sōzō rajio* (Tokyo: Kawade Shobō Shinsha, 2013), 101–102. The majority of the ellipses are in the original.
88. Itō, *Sōzō rajio*, 33.
89. Catherine Malabou, "Post-Trauma: Towards a New Definition?," in *Telemorphosis: Theory in the Era of Climate Change, Vol. 1*, ed. Tom Cohen (Ann Arbor: University of Michigan Open Humanities Press, 2012). Italics in the original.
90. Itō, *Sōzō rajio*, 132.
91. Itō, *Sōzō rajio*, 132.
92. Satoru Miura, "The Effects of Radioactive Contamination on the Forestry Industry and Commercial Mushroom-Log Production in Fukushima, Japan," in *Agricultural Implications of the Fukushima Nuclear Accident*, ed. Tomoko Nakanishi and Keitaro Tanoi (Tokyo: Springer, 2016), 145–160.
93. Miura, "The Effects of Radioactive Contamination," 147.
94. Haniya Yutaka, *Shirei III* (Tokyo: Kōdansha, 1996), 232.

95. Haniya, *Shirei III*, 232.
96. Haniya, *Shirei III*, 232.
97. Haniya Yutaka, "*Kodama*," *Haniya Yutaka Zenshū* (Tokyo: Kōdansha, 1999), 11:55.
98. Haniya, "*Kodama*," *Haniya Yutaka Zenshū*, 11:56.
99. Peters, *The Marvelous Clouds*, 3. Peters claims "we can regard media as enabling environments that provide habitats for diverse forms of life, including other media."
100. Itō, *Sōzō rajio*, 71.
101. Haniya, *Shirei III*, 234.

4. BOTANICAL REGENERATION

1. maffchannel, "'*Ki de tsukurō*' hen," YouTube video, 1:02, November 27, 2023, https://youtu.be/4I-L1R_54z4?si=yQBoVf_JpHVEFxxr.
2. "*Ki de mirai tsukurō*," *Yomiuri Shinbun*, October 23, 2013.
3. Japanese Forestry Agency, "Annual Report on Forest and Forestry in Japan Fiscal Year 2014 (Summary)," (Tokyo: Japanese Forestry Agency, 2014), 3, http://www.rinya.maff.go.jp/j/kikaku/hakusyo/26hakusyo/pdf/h26summary.pdf.
4. "*Chikyū ondanka bōshi no tame no kokusaiteki na torikumi*," Kizukai.com, accessed January 28, 2024, https://www.kidukai.com/learn/undou_non.php.
5. Conrad Totman, *The Green Archipelago: Forestry in Preindustrial Japan* (Berkeley: University of California Press, 1989), 1.
6. Peter Dauvergne, *Shadows in the Forest: Japan and the Politics of Timber in Southeast Asia* (Cambridge, MA: MIT Press, 1997), 5–6.
7. Dauvergne, *Shadows in the Forest*, 2.
8. John Knight, *Waiting for Wolves in Japan: An Anthropological Study of People-Wildlife Relations* (Honolulu: University of Hawai'i Press, 2006), 35.
9. Christopher Dole et al., "When Is Catastrophe? An Introduction," in *The Time of Catastrophe: Multidisciplinary Approaches to the Age of Catastrophe*, Christopher Dole et al. (Burlington, VT: Ashgate, 2015), 1.
10. The authoritative Japanese dictionary *Nihonkokugo daijiten* lists the first occurrence of the term (in its variant form of *somaudo*) in the *Tonyōshū*, a text dating to the late fourteenth century/early fifteenth century.
11. Anna Lowenhaupt Tsing, "A Threat to Holocene Resurgence Is a Threat to Livability," in *The Anthropology of Sustainability*, ed. Marc Brightman and Jerome Lewis (New York: Palgrave Macmillan, 2017), 52. Italics in the original.
12. Catherine Malabou, *Ontology of the Accident: An Essay on Destructive Plasticity*, trans. Carolyn Shread (Malden, MA: Polity, 2012), 4.
13. Jasper Sharp, "*Fire Festival*," *Midnight Eye*, accessed January 28, 2024, http://www.midnighteye.com/reviews/fire-festival. See also Elliot Stein, Stephan Harvey, and Harlan Jacobson. "The 23rd New York Film Festival," *Film Comment* 21, no. 6 (1985): 68.
14. Anne McKnight, *Nakagami, Japan: Buraku and the Writing of Ethnicity* (Minneapolis: University of Minnesota Press, 2011).
15. In addition to criticism of Kawase's decision to minimize anti-Olympic protestors and blur out their faces in her official film, Kawase has also received criticism for suggesting that those opposing the Olympics were paid protestors in an NHK program about the making of the documentary. See Masato Nishida, "NHK Apologizes for False Label of 'Paid Protester' Against Olympics," *The Asahi Shimbun*, January 10, 2022, https://www.asahi.com/ajw/articles/14518868.
16. Nina Cornyetz, "Peninsular Cartography: Topology in Nakagami Kenji's Kishū," in *Perversion and Modern Japan: Psychoanalysis, Literature, Culture*, ed. Nina Cornyetz and J. Keith Vincent. (London: Routledge, 2010), 133. Emphasis in original.

17. D. Max Moerman, *Localizing Paradise: Kumano Pilgrimage and the Religious Landscape of Premodern Japan* (Cambridge, MA: Harvard University Asia Center, 2005), 44.

18. Moerman, *Localizing Paradise*, 1.

19. Yamaguchi Masao/, *Himatsuri* (Tokyo: Riburopōto, 1985), 60.

20. Moerman, *Localizing Paradise*, 43.

21. Gotō Shin, *Asu naki mori: kamemushi sensei ga kumano de kataru* (Tokyo: Shinhyōron, 2008), 217.

22. Totman, *The Green Archipelago*, 139.

23. "*Kaso taisaku*," Ministry of Internal Affairs and Communications, accessed January 28, 2024, https://www.soumu.go.jp/main_sosiki/jichi_gyousei/c-gyousei/2001/kaso/kasomain0.htm.

24. "*Kaso taisaku*."

25. Yamaguchi, *Himatsuri*, 30.

26. Arthur Nolletti Jr., "Mitsuo Yanagimachi's 'Himatsuri': An Analysis," *Film Criticism* 10, no. 3 (1986): 53.

27. *Himatsuri*, Promotional Pamphlet (Tōhō Films, 1985).

28. *Himatsuri*, Promotional Pamphlet.

29. *Himatsuri*, Promotional Pamphlet.

30. Inamoto Tadashi, *Ki no koe* (Tokyo: Shogakukan, 1997), 94.

31. John Knight, "Rural Revitalization in Japan: Spirit of the Village and Taste of the Country," *Asian Survey* 34, no. 7 (1994): 636.

32. For information on the incident and its influence on Nakagami's screenplay and novelization of *Himatsuri*, see Moriyasu Toshihisa, "Nakagami Kenji 'Himatsuri'—eiga kara shōsetsu e," *Utsunomiya Daigaku kenkyū gakubu kiyō* 61, no. 1 (2011): 17–28.

33. Yamaguchi, Himatsuri, 70.

34. Nakagami Kenji, *Nakagami Kenji Zenshū* (Tokyo: Shueisha, 1996), 8:583.

35. Yamaguchi, *Himatsuri*, 52. The summary of the film included in its promotional pamphlet describes Tatsuo's actions as "*aibu*," a kind of loving caress that has romantic, if not sexual, overtones. Nakagami's screenplay is less overt: "Tatsuo raises both hands and clings to the tree as the rain falls on his face." Nakagami, *Nakagami Kenji Zenshū*, 8:584.

36. In an interview with Ueno Chizuko, Nakagami Kenji posits that the high-angle shot used in the film's climax represents "the point of view of the goddess [*kami no shiten*]." See Yamaguchi, *Himatsuri*, 27.

37. The *Kumano nendaiki* (*Chronicles of Kumano*, ~sixteenth century) locates the origin of the ritual to the reign of Emperor Bidatsu (572–585). See Miyake Hitoshi, ed., *Yama no matsuri to geinō* (Tokyo: Hirakawa shuppansha, 1984), 181.

38. *Yama no matsuri to geinō*, 181.

39. Sara E. Jensen and Guy R. McPherson, *Living with Fire: Fire Ecology and Policy for the Twenty-First Century* (Berkeley: University of California Press, 2008), 2.

40. Nathaniel Brodie, Charles Goodrich, and Frederick J. Swanson, eds., *Forest Under Story: Creative Inquiry in an Old-Growth Forest* (Seattle: University of Washington Press, 2016), 122.

41. Yamaguchi, *Himatsuri*, 34.

42. "*Kaso taisaku*."

43. Hiroki Koizumi, "More Than Half of All Municipalities in Japan Defined as 'Depopulated,'" *The Asahi Shimbun*, February 7, 2022, https://www.asahi.com/ajw/articles/14532405.

44. *Vision*, Promotional Pamphlet (LDH Pictures, 2018).

45. "The Weald (1997)," *Kawase Naomi*, accessed January 28, 2024, http://www.kawasenaomi.com/kumie/en/works/2015/03/post_23.html.

46. "The Weald (1997)."

47. See Totman's *The Green Archipelago* for a thorough analysis of just how much lumber was used during the Nara period to build both religious and imperial buildings. According to Totman, Tōdaiji alone used enough wood in its construction to build "three thousand ordinary 1950s-style (18-by-24-foot) Japanese dwellings." Totman, *The Green Archipelago*, 17.

48. Katherine Connell, "Kawase Naomi's 'Vision': Poetic Worlds and Vegetal Camerawork," *Another Gaze*, October 2, 2018, https://www.anothergaze.com/naomi-kawases-vision-poetic-worlds-vegetal-camerawork/.

49. According to the films' promotional materials, this tree is named the *moronjo no ki* and is known for its medicinal properties. The entry for the *nezumisashi* tree on Uekipedia (an online field guide of Japanese trees) states that the medicine made from *moronjo no ki* is used for urinary problems, rheumatism, nerve pain, and the common cold.

50. *Vision*, Promotional Pamphlet.
51. *Vision*, Promotional Pamphlet.
52. *Vision*, Promotional Pamphlet.
53. *Forest Under Story*, 121.
54. *Vision*, Promotional Pamphlet.
55. Elizabeth Grosz, *The Nick of Time: Politics, Evolution, and the Untimely* (Durham, NC: Duke University Press, 2004), 49.
56. *Vision*, Promotion Pamphlet. There is a particular irony at work in *Vision*'s hope to destroy the ego. Kawase has been criticized throughout her career for an egoistic focus in her films, particularly in her early documentary work. See Abé Markus Nornes, "The Postwar Documentary Trace: Groping in the Dark," *Positions: East Asia Culture Critique* 10 (2002): 39–78.
57. *Vision*, Promotion Pamphlet.

5. BOTANICAL MIGRATION

1. As mentioned earlier in this book, "Hiromi Ito" is what the writer prefers to be called in English, and this helps me differentiate between her and writer Itō Seikō.

2. Itō Hiromi, *Kodama kusadama* (Tokyo: Iwanami Shoten, 2014), 136.

3. Itō, *Kodama kusadama*, 135.

4. Dawn Keetley, "Introduction: Six Theses on Plant Horror; or, Why Are Plants Horrifying?" in *Plant Horror: Approaches to the Monstrous Vegetal in Fiction and Film*, ed. Dawn Keetley and Angela Tenga (London: Palgrave Macmillan, 2016), 1.

5. The unruly qualities of Ito's poetry fit within the parameters of "phytopoetics," as theorized by Joela Jacobs. Jacobs's phytopoetics identify a vegetal agency in literature about plant life that stems from unruly qualities of sexuality and violence, both of which are easily found in Ito's *Wild Grass on the River Bank*. See Joela Jacobs, "Phytopoetics: Upending the Passive Paradigm with Vegetal Violence and Eroticism," *Catalyst: Feminism, Theory, Technoscience* 5, no. 2 (2019): 1–18.

6. Hiromi Ito, *Wild Grass on the Riverbank*, trans. Jeffrey Angles (Notre Dame, IN: Action Books, 2015), 35. Ito has written about how she feels that Angles's English translation of *Wild Grass on the Riverbank* (from which I quote throughout) has become the "original" version, and that her actual original Japanese version is somehow a translation of Angels's version (despite having been written earlier). See Itō, *Kodama kusadama*, 138–139.

7. Ito, *Wild Grass on the Riverbank*, 57. In the English translation, Angles decided to use Latinized names for the plants. He explains his decision, in the introduction to his translation, as a combination of wanting to add to the feeling of becoming botanical in the poem and as a means of defamiliarization.

8. Hiromi Ito, *Tree Spirits Grass Spirits*, trans. Jon L. Pitt (New York: Nightboat Books, 2023), 4.

9. "Shocking Photo of Drowned Father and Daughter Highlights Migrants' Border Peril," *Guardian*, June 26, 2019, https://www.theguardian.com/us-news/2019/jun/25/photo-drowned-migrant-daughter-rio-grande-us-mexico-border.

10. Jeannie N. Shinozuka, *Biotic Borders: Transpacific Plant and Insect Migration and the Rise of Anti-Asian Racism in America, 1890–1950* (Chicago: University of Chicago Press, 2022), 3.

11. Christy Wampole, *Rootedness: The Ramifications of a Metaphor* (Chicago: University of Chicago Press, 2016), 2.

12. The word *naturalization* in Japanese is *kika*, which uses the Chinese characters for *return* and *change*.

13. Ito, *Wild Grass on the Riverbank*, 55.

14. Shinozuka, *Biotic Borders*, 218.

15. Catriona Sandilands, "Vegetate," in *Veer Ecology: A Companion for Environmental Thinking*, ed. Jeffrey Jerome Cohen and Lowell Duckert (Minneapolis: University of Minnesota Press, 2017), 22. Italics in the original.

16. Sandilands, "Vegetate," 22.

17. Sandilands attempts, in this essay, to reclaim the term *vegetate* and rethink it not as a term referring to a lack of action but rather as an active verb. Hence her use of the gerund form: "Grow*ing*. Populat*ing*. Spread*ing*. Invad*ing*" (emphasis added). Ito's work likewise understands plants in this way, as full of motion and activity.

18. Karen L. F. Houle, "Animal, Vegetable, Mineral: Ethics as Extension or Becoming? The Case of Becoming-Plant," *Journal for Critical Animal Studies* 9, nos. 1/2 (2011), 112.

19. The poem is included in Ito's 1985 collection *Teritorii-ron 2* (*On Territory 2*). A translation of the poem by Jeffrey Angles is included in a collection bearing the poem's name. See Hiromi Ito, *Killing Kanoko: Selected Poems of Hiromi Ito*, trans. Jeffrey Angles (Notre Dame: Action Books, 2009).

20. Ito, *Killing Kanoko*, vii. The quote belongs to poet Kido Shuri.

21. For a more detailed accounting of Ito's biography, see Jeffrey Angles's introduction to *Wild Grass on the Riverbank*, as well as his introductory article to the 2007 *U.S.-Japan Women's Journal* issue dedicated to Ito.

22. Ito recounts in *Midori no obasan* (*Aunt Green-Thumb*), her 2005 prose collection that is equal parts gardening advice and personal memoir, that growing plants in the Araceae family (*satoimoka*, in Japanese) gave her a feeling of "the scent of dusk in the Japanese countryside in spring, here within my home in California." See Itō Hiromi, *Midori no obasan* (Tokyo: Chikuma Shobō, 2005), 66.

23. According to the US Department of Justice, between 1994 and 1997 (the year Ito obtained legal immigration status in the United States), California admitted 203,305 legal immigrants. This number constituted 25.5 percent of all immigrants into the United States over this period of time. See "Legal Immigration, Fiscal Year 1997," US Department of Justice, January 1999, https://www.dhs.gov/sites/default/files/publications/INS_AnnualReport_LegalImmigration_1997_1.pdf. According to the American Immigration Council, by the year 2018, the number of immigrants living in California numbered 10.6 million, half of which had been naturalized. In 2016, undocumented immigrants made up 20 percent of the immigrant population in California. See "Immigrants in California," American Immigration Council, August 6, 2020, https://www.americanimmigrationcouncil.org/research/immigrants-in-california.

24. Herbert L. Mason, "Migration and Evolution in Plants," *Madroño* 6, no. 4 (2013): 162.

25. Sandilands, "Vegetate," 22.

26. Ito, *Wild Grass on the Riverbank*, 91.

27. Ito, *Wild Grass on the Riverbank*, 96.
28. Mason, "Migration and Evolution in Plants," 162.
29. Ito, *Wild Grass on the Riverbank*, 23.
30. Gilles Deleuze and Félix Guattari. *A Thousand Plateaus: Capitalism and Schizophrenia*, trans. Brian Massumi (New York: Bloomsbury, 2016), 27. Italics in the original.
31. Ito, *Tree Spirits Grass Spirits*, 44.
32. Ito, *Tree Spirits Grass Spirits*, 152. The APG (Angiosperm Phylogeny Group) system is the current scientific method of classifying plants. It was introduced in 1998, right around the time Ito began writing about the plants of Southern California.
33. Ito, *Tree Spirits Grass Spirits*, 49.
34. Ito, *Wild Grass on the Riverbank*, 43.
35. Sandilands, "Vegetate," 19.
36. Ito, *Tree Spirits Grass Spirits*, 39–40.
37. Ito, *Tree Spirits Grass Spirits*, 40.
38. Ito, *Tree Spirits Grass Spirits*, 41.
39. Deleuze and Guattari, *A Thousand Plateaus*, 27.
40. Deleuze and Guattari, *A Thousand Plateaus*, 27.
41. Michael Marder, *Grafts: Writings on Plants* (Minneapolis: University of Minnesota Press, 2016), 94.
42. Itō, *Midori no obasan*, 80–81. Ellipses in the original. The image of vines having "violated" (*oakasareteita*) Ito is repeated several times in *Wild Grass on the Riverbank*, as vines are repeatedly described as entering Natsukusa's mother's vagina. A troubling scene occurs late in the poem in which Natsukusa herself is violated by vines, seemingly against her will.
43. In a particularly graphic scene, Natsukusa's mother uses pruning shears to remove her dead husband's penis while cutting back dead leaves off plants. See Ito, *Wild Grass on the Riverbank*, 41.
44. Ito, *Wild Grass on the Riverbank*, 81.
45. Ito, *Tree Spirits Grass Spirits*, 142.
46. Ito, *Wild Grass on the Riverbank*, 52.
47. Ito, *Tree Spirits Grass Spirits*, 143.
48. Ito, *Tree Spirits Grass Spirits*, 3.
49. Ito, *Tree Spirits Grass Spirits*, 9. In her diagnosis of how plant life comes to be horrific, Dawn Keetley lists, as her third thesis, "Plants Menace with Their Wild, Purposeless Growth" (Keetley, "Six Theses on Plant Horror," 13). The excessive growth of vines and other active plants in *Wild Grass on the Riverbank* borders, at times, on being, if not exactly horrific, certainly grotesque. But it is this grotesque penchant for excessive reproduction that Ito laments not being able to achieve in *Tree Spirits Grass Spirits*.
50. Ito, *Wild Grass on the Riverbank*, 93.
51. Ito, *Tree Spirits Grass Spirits*, 63.
52. Banu Subramaniam, *Ghost Stories for Darwin: The Science of Variation and the Politics of Diversity* (Urbana: University of Illinois Press, 2014), 121.
53. Subramaniam, *Ghost Stories for Darwin*, 122.
54. Michael Marder, "The Life of Plants and the Limits of Empathy," *Dialogue* 51 (2012): 263.
55. Ito, *Tree Spirits Grass Spirits*, 64.
56. Michael Marder, *Plant-Thinking: A Philosophy of Vegetal Life* (New York: Columbia University Press, 2013), 162.
57. Marder, "The Life of Plants and the Limits of Empathy," 265.
58. Marder, "The Life of Plants and the Limits of Empathy," 264.
59. Ito, *Tree Spirits Grass Spirits*, 28.
60. Ito, *Wild Grass on the Riverbank*, 27.

61. Ito, *Wild Grass on the Riverbank*, 90.
62. Ito, *Wild Grass on the Riverbank*, 92–93.
63. Ito, *Wild Grass on the Riverbank*, 89–90. Italics in original.
64. Ito, *Wild Grass on the Riverbank*, 87.

65. They were also attempts at writing in a new genre for Ito. In an afterword to the 2016 republication of *La Niña* (which also includes *House Plant* and *Three Lil' Japanese*), Ito writes of the difficulty she experienced in switching from poetry to literary prose (*shōsetsu*). In 1999, however, Ito characterized her experiments with prose as an expression of freedom. See Kyōko Ōmori, "'Finding Our Own English': Migrancy, Identity, and Language(s) in Itō Hiromi's Recent Prose," *U.S.-Japan Women's Journal* 32 (2007): 93.

66. Ito writes in the 2016 afterword to *La Niña* that the narrating "I" of *House Plant* and *La Niña* is Ito herself. See Itō Hiromi, *Ra nīnya* (Tokyo: Iwanami Shoten, 2016), p. 281. Both novellas were nominated for the prestigious Akutagawa Prize for Literature, although neither won. Ito expresses some relief in the 2016 afterword at not having won in either case. *La Niña* did, however, win the Noma Literary Award for New Writers.

67. See Ōmori's "'Finding Our Own English'" for a discussion of the generative potential of the multilingual qualities of *House Plant*.

68. Itō Hiromi, "House Plant," trans. Itō Hiromi and Harold Cohen, *U.S.-Japan Women's Journal* 32 (2007): 115. Throughout, I quote from this English translation, which was rendered by Itō herself and her then-partner Harold Cohen.

69. Itō, "House Plant," 115.
70. Itō, *Ra nīnya*, 111.
71. Itō, "House Plant," 134.
72. Itō, "House Plant," 133.
73. Wampole, *Rootedness*, 7.
74. Itō, "House Plant," 127.

75. In 2003, the INS functions were transferred to three new departments within the newly formed Department of Homeland Security: US Citizenship and Immigration Services (USCIS), US Immigration and Customs Enforcement (ICE), and US Customs and Border Protection (CBP).

76. Itō, "House Plant," 129.
77. Itō, *Ra nīnya*, 199–200.
78. Itō, "House Plant," 132.
79. Itō, "House Plant," 121.
80. Itō, "House Plant," 120.
81. Ito, *Tree Spirits Grass Spirits*, 64.
82. Itō, "House Plant," 119.
83. Itō, "House Plant," 119.
84. Ito, *Wild Grass on the Riverbank*, 92–93.
85. Itō, *Ra nīnya*, 55.

86. Itō, *Ra nīnya*, 190–191. Ito quotes here from a poem by Yamamura Bochō (1884–1924) titled "Landscape" (*Fūkei*), in which the line "A full field of rape blossoms" is repeated for twenty-four of the twenty-seven lines that make up the poem. Ito references this poem many times throughout her oeuvre, often as a means to describe the overwhelming vitality of plant life.

87. Itō, *Ra nīnya*, 238.

88. Ito has described this section of the narrative as a *michiyuki*: a narrative device used in premodern Japanese theater and storytelling in which the main characters (often a pair of doomed lovers) travel together before reaching their tragic end. See Itō, *Ra nīnya*, 284.

89. Emiko Ohnuki-Tierney, *Kamikaze, Cherry Blossoms, and Nationalisms: The Militarization of Aesthetics in Japanese History* (Chicago: University of Chicago Press, 2002), 3.

90. Itō, *Ra nīnya*, 268.
91. Itō, *Ra nīnya*, 268.
92. Itō, *Ra nīnya*, 272.
93. Itō, *Ra nīnya*, 283.
94. Itō, *Ra nīnya*, 284.
95. Rika makes a point of saying that she can never remember the name, as it "doesn't seem like English." The implication is that it has a Spanish name, much like Ito's home of Encinitas or La Jolla (where the University of California, San Diego is located).
96. Itō, *Ra nīnya*, 234–235.
97. Itō, *Ra nīnya*, 235.
98. Itō, *Ra nīnya*, 245.
99. Itō, *Ra nīnya*, 235.
100. Ito, *Wild Grass on the Riverbank*, 94.
101. It is a sentiment Ito shares with Arakawa Tomotsugu, as discussed in chapter 1 in reference to the writing of Osaki Midori and moss.
102. Itō, *Midori no obasan*, 182.
103. Ito, *Tree Spirits Grass Spirits*, 25.
104. Ito, *Wild Grass on the Riverbank*, 94.
105. Itō, *Ra nīnya*, 285.
106. Itō Hiromi, *Tasogareteyuku kosan* (Tokyo: Chūō Kōron, 2018), 120.
107. Itō, *Tasogareteyuku kosan*, 120.
108. Itō, *Tasogareteyuku kosan*, 120–121.
109. The Hague Abduction Convention is an international treaty meant to regulate the movement of children across national borders. Japan became a party to the Hague Convention in 2014.
110. Itō Hiromi, *Michiyukiya* (Tokyo: Shinchōsha, 2020), 157.
111. Itō, *Michiyukiya*, 157. The Alien Species Act was enacted to designate a species as invasive if it has "adverse effects on ecosystems." See "Invasive Alien Species Act," Ministry of Environment, June 2, 2004, https://www.env.go.jp/en/nature/as/040427.pdf.
112. Ito, *Wild Grass on the Riverbank*, 94.

EPILOGUE

1. Gregory Bateson, *Sacred Unity: Further Steps to an Ecology of Mind* (New York: Cornelia and Michael Bessie Books, 1991), 240.
2. Miura Shion, *Ai naki sekai* (Tokyo: Chūō Kōron Shinsha, 2018), 88.
3. Osaki Midori, *Osaki Midori Zenshū* (Tokyo: Sōjusha, 1979), 372.
4. Miura, *Ai naki sekai*, 92.
5. Miura, *Ai naki sekai*, 92.
6. "*Arabidopsis*: The Model Plant," US National Science Foundation, accessed January 28, 2024, https://www.nsf.gov/pubs/2002/bio0202/model.htm.
7. Ian Sample, "Cress Seeds Grown in Moon Dust Raise Hopes for Lunar Crops," *Guardian*, May 12, 2022, https://www.theguardian.com/science/2022/may/12/cress-seeds-grown-in-moon-dust-raise-hopes-for-lunar-crops.
8. Masataka Nakano et al., "Entanglement of Arabidopsis Seedings to a Mesh Substrate under Microgravity Conditions in KIBO on the ISS," *Plants* 11, no. 7 (2022): 956, https://doi.org/10.3390/plants11070956.
9. Yuri Aratani et al., "Green Leaf Volatile Sensory Calcium Transduction in *Arabidopsis*," *Nature Communications* 14 (2023).
10. The videos can be seen here: https://phys.org/news/2023-10-real-time-visualization-plant-plant-communications-airborne.html.

11. Miura, *Ai naki sekai*, 88.

12. Noland Lendved, "Deep in the Weeds," *GROW Magazine* (Fall 2019), https://grow.cals.wisc.edu/departments/features/deep-in-the-weeds.

13. Keita Tamura and Hidemasa Bono, "Meta-Analysis of RNA Sequencing Data of Arabidopsis and Rice under Hypoxia," *Life* 12, no. 7 (2022).

14. Masahiro Morioka, "A Phenomenological Study of 'Herbivore Men,'" *Review of Life Studies* 4 (September 2013), 1.

15. Morioka, "A Phenomenological Study of 'Herbivore Men,'" 1.

16. Morioka, "A Phenomenological Study of 'Herbivore Men,'" 13–15.

17. Morioka, "A Phenomenological Study of 'Herbivore Men,'" 15.

18. Miura, *Ai naki sekai*, 444.

19. Fukasawa Maki, "*Shokubutsu no kenkyū ni bottō suru joshi to, yōshokuya minari danshi no yukue*," *Shūkan bunshun*, November 15, 2018, https://bunshun.jp/articles/-/9613.

20. Fukasawa, "*Shokubutsu no kenkyū*."

21. Fukasawa, "*Shokubutsu no kenkyū*."

22. "*Arabidopsis*: The Model Plant."

23. Nicholas Harberd, *Seed to Seed: The Secret Life of Plants* (London: Bloomsbury, 2006), 96.

24. Harberd, *Seed to Seed*, 300.

Bibliography

Abe Kōbō. *Abe Kōbō zenshū*. Vol. 2. Tokyo: Shinchōsha, 1997.
Abe Kōbō. *Abe Kōbō zenshū*. Vol. 3. Tokyo: Shinchōsha, 1997.
Abe Kōbō. *Abe Kōbō zenshū*. Vol. 21. Tokyo: Shinchōsha, 1999.
Abe Kōbō. *Abe Kōbō zenshū*. Vol. 30. Tokyo: Shinchōsha, 2009.
Abé Markus Nornes. "The Postwar Documentary Trace: Groping in the Dark." *Positions: East Asia Culture Critique* 10 (2002): 39–78.
Akiyama Hiroyuki. *Koke no hanashi*. Tokyo: Chukokoron: Shinsha, 2004.
Aoyama, Tomoko. "Sweet Bean Paste and Excrement: Food, Humor, and Gender in Osaki Midori's Writings." In *Gastro-Modernism: Food, Literature, Culture*, edited by Derek Gladwin, 21–34. Clemson, SC: Clemson University Press, 2019.
Arakawa Tomotsugu. "Kokegakusha ga yomitoku 'Dainana kankai hōkō.'" In *Osaki Midori o yomu: Kōenhen II*, 71–89. Tottori: Osaki Midori fōramu jikkōiinkai, 2016.
Aratani, Yuri, Takuya Uemura, Takuma Hagihara, Kenji Matsui, and Masatsugu Toyota. "Green Leaf Volatile Sensory Calcium Transduction in *Arabidopsis*." *Nature Communications* 14 (2023).
Backster, Cleve. *Primary Perception: Biocommunication with Plants, Living Foods, and Human Cells*. Anza, CA: White Rose Millennium, 2003.
Baker, Vanessa Catherine. "Entangled Ecologies of the Everyday: Gender, Labor, and Nature in Rural Proletarian Literature of Korea and Japan." PhD diss., University of California, Irvine, 2022.
Bates, David W. "Unity, Plasticity, Catastrophe: Order and Pathology in the Cybernetic Era." In *Catastrophes: A History and Theory of an Operative Concept*, edited by Nitzan Lebovic and Andreas Killen, 32–53. Boston: de Gruyter, 2014.
Bates, J. W. "Is 'Life-Form' a Useful Concept in Bryophyte Ecology?" *Oikos* 82 (1998): 223–227.
Bateson, Gregory. *Sacred Unity: Further Steps to an Ecology of Mind*. New York: Cornelia and Michael Bessie Books, 1991.
Bennett, Jane. *Vibrant Matter: A Political Ecology of Things*. Durham, NC: Duke University Press, 2010.
Brodie, Nathaniel, Charles Goodrich, and Frederick J. Swanson, eds. *Forest Under Story: Creative Inquiry in an Old-Growth Forest*. Seattle: University of Washington Press, 2016.
Chapman, David. *The Bonin Islanders, 1830 to the Present: Narrating Japanese Nationality*. Lanham, MD: Lexington Books, 2016.
Clerici, Nathan. "Performance and Nonsense: Osaki Midori's 'Strange Love.'" *Japanese Language and Literature* 51, no. 2 (2017): 271–304.
Coccia, Emanuele. *The Life of Plants: A Metaphysics of Mixture*. Translated by Dylan J. Montanari. Medford, OR: Polity, 2019.
Committee for the Promotion of Peace under the Declaration of Musashino as a Nuclear-Free City. "Panel Documents: November 24, 1944, Musashino Air Raids and Nakajima Aircraft Co." Accessed March 3, 2023. https://www.city.musashimurayama.lg.jp/

Connell, Katherine. "Kawase Naomi's 'Vision': Poetic Worlds and Vegetal Camerawork." *Another Gaze.* October 2, 2018. https://www.anothergaze.com/naomi-kawases-vision-poetic-worlds-vegetal-camerawork/.

Conrad, Sebastian. "Entangled Memories: Versions of the Past in Germany and Japan, 1945–2001." *Journal of Contemporary History* 38, no. 1 (2003): 85–99.

Cornyetz, Nina. "Peninsular Cartography: Topology in Nakagami Kenji's Kishū." In *Perversion and Modern Japan: Psychoanalysis, Literature, Culture*, edited by Nina Cornyetz and J. Keith Vincent, 125–146. London: Routledge, 2010.

Cross, Sherrie. "Prestige and Comfort: The Development of Social Darwinism in Early Meiji Japan, and the Role of Edward Sylvester Morse." *Annals of Science* 53, no. 4 (1996): 323–344.

Darwin, Erasmus. *The Botanic Garden Part II.* Dublin: J. Moore, 1796.

Dauvergne, Peter. *Shadows in the Forest: Japan and the Politics of Timber in Southeast Asia.* Cambridge, MA: MIT Press, 1997.

Deleuze, Gilles, and Félix Guattari. *A Thousand Plateaus: Capitalism and Schizophrenia.* Translated by Brian Massumi. New York: Bloomsbury, 2016.

Dole, Christopher, Robert Hayashi, Andrew Poe, Austin Sarat, and Boris Wolfson. "When Is Catastrophe? An Introduction." In *The Time of Catastrophe: Multidisciplinary Approaches to the Age of Catastrophe*, edited by Christopher Dole, Robert Hayashi, Andrew Poe, Austin Sarat, and Boris Wolfson, 1–18. Burlington, VT: Ashgate, 2015.

Dorsey, James. "The Art of War: Sakaguchi Ango's 'Pearls' and the Nature of Literary Resistance." In *Literary Mischief: Sakaguchi Ango, Culture, and War*, edited by James Dorsey and Doug Slaymaker, 97–136. Lanham, MD: Lexington Books, 2010.

Fedman, David. *Seeds of Control: Japan's Empire of Forestry in Colonial Korea.* Seattle: University of Washington Press, 2020.

Forestry of Japan. Tokyo: Bureau of Forestry, Department of Agriculture and Commerce, 1910.

Fujihara Tatsushi. *Sensō to nogyō.* Tokyo: Shūeisha International e-shinsho, 2017. Kindle edition.

Fujihara Tatsushi. *Shokubutsukō.* Tokyo: Ikinobiru Books, 2022.

Fujii Takashi. "'Jinshinsei' no Haniya Yutaka: "Shirei" to posuto 'ningenchūshinshūgi.'" *Shōwa Bungaku Kenkyū* 84 (2022): 120–133.

Fukasawa Maki. "Shokubutsu no kenkyū ni bottō suru joshi to, yōshokuya minari danshi no yukue." *Shūkan bunshun*, November 15, 2018. https://bunshun.jp/articles/-/9613.

Golley, Gregory. *When Our Eyes No Longer See: Realism, Science, and Ecology in Japanese Literary Modernism.* Cambridge, MA: Harvard University Press, 2008.

Gotō Shin. *Asu naki mori: kamemushi sensei ga kumano de kataru.* Tokyo: Shinhyōron, 2008.

Grosz, Elizabeth. *Becoming Undone: Darwinian Reflections on Life, Politics, and Art.* Durham, NC: Duke University Press, 2011.

Grosz, Elizabeth. "Darwin and Feminism: Preliminary Investigations for a Possible Alliance." *Australian Feminist Studies*, 14, no. 29 (1999): 31–45.

Grosz, Elizabeth. *The Nick of Time: Politics, Evolution, and the Untimely.* Durham, NC: Duke University Press, 2004.

Hanada Kiyoteru. "Dōbutsu—shokubutsu—kōbutsu." In *Gendai Nihon bungaku taikei 77: Dazai Osamu—Sakaguchi Ango shū*, 411–425. Tokyo: Chikuma shobō, 1969.

Haniya Yutaka. *Shirei I.* Tokyo: Kōdansha, 1981.

Haniya Yutaka. *Shirei II.* Tokyo: Kōdansha, 1981.

Haniya Yutaka. *Shirei III.* Tokyo: Kōdansha, 1996.

Haniya Yutaka and Tachibana Takashi. *Mugen no sō no moto ni.* Tokyo: Heibonsha, 1997.

Hara Shōji. *Hito wa kusa de aru: "ruji" to "zure" o meguru kōsatsu*. Tokyo: Sairyūsha, 2013.
Haraway, Donna. *Staying with the Trouble: Making Kin in the Chthulucene*. Durham, NC: Duke University Press, 2016.
Harberd, Nicholas. *Seed to Seed: The Secret Life of Plants*. London: Bloomsbury, 2006.
Hashimoto Ken. "*Aruhuakoiru wo hatsumei suru made*." *Nihon Chōkagakkai*. Accessed January 28, 2024. http://www.alphacoil.com/kisekiap.htm.
Hashimoto Ken. *Kagaku ka? Shūkyō ka?* Tokyo: Weagle Books, 1988.
Hashimoto Ken. *Shokubutsu ni wa kokoro ga aru*. Tokyo: Goma Shobō, 1997.
Hashimoto Ken. *Shokubutsu to ohanashi suru hō*. Tokyo: Goma Shobō, 1995.
Hashimoto Ken. "*Utau saboten*." *Seishin kagaku* 291 (1971): 42–45.
Hashimoto Ken. *Yojigensekai no shinpi*. Tokyo: Ikeda, 1966.
Hattori Kenshō. "*Kichijōji de no kūshū taiken*." *Musashino no kūshū to sono kioku*. Accessed March 3, 2023. https://www.city.musashimurayama.lg.jp/.
Havens, Thomas R. H. *Land of Plants in Motion: Japanese Botany and the World*. Honolulu: University of Hawai'i Press, 2020.
Havens, Thomas R. H. *Parkscapes: Green Spaces in Modern Japan*. Honolulu: University of Hawai'i Press, 2011.
Hideyama Yōko. *Osaki Midori e no tabi: hon to zasshi no meiro no naka de*. Tokyo: Shogakukan, 2009.
Himatsuri. Promotional Pamphlet. Tōhō Films, 1985.
Houle, Karen L. F. "Animal, Vegetable, Mineral: Ethics as Extension or Becoming? The Case of Becoming-Plant." *Journal for Critical Animal Studies* 9, nos. 1/2 (2011): 89–116.
"Immigrants in California." American Immigration Council. August 6, 2020. https://www.americanimmigrationcouncil.org/research/immigrants-in-california.
Inamoto Tadashi. *Ki no koe*. Tokyo: Shogakukan, 1997.
"Invasive Alien Species Act." Ministry of Environment. June 2, 2004. https://www.env.go.jp/en/nature/as/040427.pdf.
Irigaray, Luce, and Michael Marder. *Through Vegetal Being: Two Philosophical Perspectives*. New York: Columbia University Press, 2016.
Itō Hiromi. "House Plant." Translated by Itō Hiromi and Harold Cohen. *U.S.-Japan Women's Journal* 32 (2007): 115–163.
Itō Hiromi. *Killing Kanoko: Selected Poems of Hiromi Ito*. Translated by Jeffrey Angles. Notre Dame, IN: Action Books, 2009.
Itō Hiromi. *Kodama kusadama*. Tokyo: Iwanami Shoten, 2014.
Itō Hiromi. *Michiyukiya*. Tokyo: Shinchōsha, 2020.
Itō Hiromi. *Midori no obasan*. Tokyo: Chikuma Shobō, 2005.
Itō Hiromi. *Ra nīnya*. Tokyo: Iwanami Shoten, 2016.
Itō Hiromi. *Tasogareteyuku kosan*. Tokyo: Chūō Kōron, 2018.
Itō Hiromi. *Tree Spirits Grass Spirits*. Translated by Jon L. Pitt. New York: Nightboat Books, 2023.
Itō Hiromi. *Wild Grass on the Riverbank*. Translated by Jeffrey Angles. Notre Dame, IN: Action Books, 2015.
Itō Hiromi and Machida Kō. *Futatasu no hamon*. Tokyo: Bungei Seishun, 2022.
Itō Motomi. "*Wadannoki—Taiyōtō de ki ni natta kiku*." *Gekkan hyakka* 401 (1996): 23–26.
Itō Seikō. *Botanikaru raifu—shokubutsu seikatsu*. Tokyo: Shinchōsha, 1999.
Itō Seikō. *Sōzō rajio*. Tokyo: Kawade Shobō Shinsha, 2013.
Jacobs, Joela. "Phytopoetics: Upending the Passive Paradigm with Vegetal Violence and Eroticism." *Catalyst: Feminism, Theory, Technoscience* 5, no. 2 (2019): 1–18.
Japanese Forestry Agency. "Annual Report on Forest and Forestry in Japan Fiscal Year 2014 (Summary)." Tokyo: Japanese Forestry Agency, 2014.

Jensen Sara E., and Guy R. McPherson. *Living with Fire: Fire Ecology and Policy for the Twenty-First Century*. Berkeley: University of California Press, 2008.

Kageyama Noboru. "Shōwa Tenno no jiko jitsugen to seibutsugaku kenkyū—sasaeta chiteki tankyūshin to ōsei na kiryoku." *Shizen kagaku no tobira* 5, no. 4 (1999): 26–27.

Kawakami, Kazuto, and Isamu Okochi, eds. *Restoring the Oceanic Island Ecosystem Impact and Management of Invasive Alien Species in the Bonin Islands*. New York: Springer, 2010.

Kawasaki Kenko. *Osaki Midori: Sakyū no anata e*. Tokyo: Iwanami Shoten, 2010.

Kawase Naomi. "The Weald (1997)." Accessed January 28, 2024. http://www.kawasenaomi.com/kumie/en/works/2015/03/post_23.html.

Keetley, Dawn. "Introduction: Six Theses on Plant Horror; or, Why Are Plants Horrifying?" In *Plant Horror: Approaches to the Monstrous Vegetal in Fiction and Film*, edited by Dawn Keetley and Angela Tenga, 1–30. London: Palgrave Macmillan, 2016.

Key, Margaret S. *Truth from a Lie: Documentary, Detection, and Reflexivity in Abe Kōbō's Realist Project*. Plymouth, UK: Lexington Books, 2001.

"Ki de mirai tsukurō." *Yomiuri Shinbun*. October 23, 2013.

Kimmerer, Robin Wall. *Gathering Moss: A Natural and Cultural History of Mosses*. Corvallis: Oregon State University Press, 2003.

Kizukai.com. "Chikyū ondanka bōshi no tame no kokusaiteki na torikumi." Accessed January 28, 2024. https://www.kidukai.com/learn/undou_non.php.

Knight, John. "Rural Revitalization in Japan: Spirit of the Village and Taste of the Country." *Asian Survey* 34, no. 7 (1994): 634–646.

Knight, John. *Waiting for Wolves in Japan: An Anthropological Study of People-Wildlife Relations*. Honolulu: University of Hawai'i Press, 2006.

"Kokudo ryokka suishin undo." *Sanrin—Journal of Forestry* 791 (1950): 1–2.

Koizumi, Hiroki. "More Than Half of All Municipalities in Japan Defined as 'Depopulated.'" *The Asahi Shimbun*. February 7, 2022.

Konishi, Sho. *Anarchist Modernity: Cooperatism and Japanese-Russian Intellectual Relations in Modern Japan*. Cambridge, MA: Harvard University Asia Center, 2013.

Kropotkin, Peter. *Anarchism: Its Philosophy and Ideal*. London: J. Turner, 1897.

Kropotkin, Peter. *Modern Science and Anarchism*. London: Freedom, 1912.

Kropotkin, Peter. *Mutual Aid: A Factor of Evolution*. London: William Heinemann, 1915.

Lee, Jung. "Between Universalism and Regionalism: Universal Systematics from Imperial Japan." *British Society for the History of Science* 48, no. 4 (2015): 661–684.

"Legal Immigration, Fiscal Year 1997." US Department of Justice. January 1999. https://www.dhs.gov/sites/default/files/publications/INS_AnnualReport_LegalImmigration_1997_1.pdf.

Lendved, Noland. "Deep in the Weeds." *GROW Magazine*, Fall 2019. https://grow.cals.wisc.edu/departments/features/deep-in-the-weeds.

Lippit, Seiji. *Topographies of Japanese Modernism*. New York: Columbia University Press, 2022.

maffchannel. "'Ki de tsukurō' hen." YouTube video, 1:02, November 27, 2024. https://youtu.be/4I-L1R_54z4?si=yQBoVf_JpHVEFxxr.

Malabou, Catherine. *Ontology of the Accident: An Essay on Destructive Plasticity*. Translated by Carolyn Shread. Malden, MA: Polity, 2012.

Malabou, Catherine. "Post-Trauma: Towards a New Definition?" In *Telemorphosis: Theory in the Era of Climate Change, Vol. 1*, edited by Tom Cohen, 226–238. Ann Arbor: University of Michigan Open Humanities Press, 2012.

Mancuso, Stefano. *The Revolutionary Genius of Plants: A New Understanding of Plant Intelligence and Behavior*. New York: Atria Books, 2017.

Mancuso, Stefano, and Alessandra Viola. *Brilliant Green: The Surprising History and Science of Plant Intelligence*. Translated by Joan Benham. Washington, DC: Island, 2015.
Marder, Michael. *Grafts: Writings on Plants*. Minneapolis: University of Minnesota Press, 2016.
Marder, Michael. "The Life of Plants and the Limits of Empathy." *Dialogue* 51 (2012): 259–273.
Marder, Michael. *Plant-Thinking: A Philosophy of Vegetal Life*. New York: Columbia University Press, 2013.
Mason, Herbert L. "Migration and Evolution in Plants." *Madroño* 6, no. 4 (2013): 161–169.
Matsuo Bashō. *Bashō's Journey: The Literary Prose of Matsuo Bashō*. Translated by David Landis Barnhill. Albany: State University of New York Press, 2005.
McKnight, Anne. *Nakagami, Japan: Buraku and the Writing of Ethnicity*. Minneapolis: University of Minnesota Press, 2011.
Meguro Jiro. "*Soveto seibutsugaku no tenbō*." *Kagaku to gijutsu* 11 (1948): 13–14.
Ministry of Internal Affairs and Communications. "*Kaso taisaku*." Accessed January 28, 2024. https://www.soumu.go.jp/main_sosiki/jichi_gyousei/c-gyousei/2001/kaso/kasomain0.htm.
Miura, Satoru. "The Effects of Radioactive Contamination on the Forestry Industry and Commercial Mushroom-Log Production in Fukushima, Japan." In *Agricultural Implications of the Fukushima Nuclear Accident*, edited by Tomoko Nakanishi and Keitaro Tanoi, 145–160. Tokyo: Springer, 2016.
Miura Shion. *Ai naki sekai*. Tokyo: Chūō Kōron Shinsha, 2018.
Miyake Hitoshi, ed. *Yama no matsuri to geinō*. Tokyo: Hirakawa shuppansha, 1984.
Mizuguchi Hajime. "*Nihon ni okeru Darwin no juyō to eikyō*." *Gakushutsu no dōkō* 3 (2010): 48–57.
Moerman, D. Max. *Localizing Paradise: Kumano Pilgrimage and the Religious Landscape of Premodern Japan*. Cambridge, MA: Harvard University Asia Center, 2005.
Monnet, Livia. "Montage, Cinematic Subjectivity and Feminism in Ozaki Midori's Drifting in the World of the Seventh Sense." *Japan Forum* 11, no. 1 (1999): 57–82.
Montgomery, Beronda. *Lessons from Plants*. Cambridge: Harvard University Press, 2021.
Morioka, Masahiro. "A Phenomenological Study of 'Herbivore Men.'" *Review of Life Studies* 4 (September 2013): 1–20.
Moriyasu Toshihisa. "*Nakagami Kenji 'Himatsuri'—eiga kara shōsetsu e*." *Utsunomiya Daigaku kenkyū gakubu kiyō* 61, no. 1 (2011): 17–28.
Morris-Suzuki, Tessa. "Debating Racial Science in Wartime Japan." *Osiris* 13 (1998): 354–375.
Morris-Suzuki, Tessa. "The Nature of Empire: Forest Ecology, Colonialism and Survival Politics in Japan's Imperial Order." *Japan Studies* 33, no. 3 (2013): 225–242.
Motoyama, Mutsuko. "The Literature and Politics of Abe Kōbō: Farewell to Communism in *Suna no Onna*." *Monumenta Nipponica* 50, no. 3 (1995): 305–323.
Mure Yōko. *Osaki Midori*. Tokyo: Bungei Shunjū, 1998.
Nakagami Kenji. *Nakagami Kenji Zenshū* Vol. 8. Tokyo: Shueisha, 1996.
Nakajima Seinosuke. "'*Shokubutsu no seikatsu*.'" *Yuibutsuron kenkyū* 20 (1934): 121–124.
Nakano, Masataka, Takuya Furuichi, Masahiro Sokabe, Hidetoshi Iida, Sachiko Yano, and Hitoshi Tatsumi. "Entanglement of Arabidopsis Seedings to a Mesh Substrate under Microgravity Conditions in KIBO on the ISS." *Plants* 11, no. 7 (2022): 956.
Nealon, Jeffrey T. *Plant Theory: Biopower and Vegetable Life*. Stanford, CA: Stanford University Press, 2016.
Nihon anakizumu undō jinmei jiten. Tokyo: Parushuppan, 2004.

Nishida, Masato. "NHK Apologizes for False Label of 'Paid Protester' against Olympics." *The Asahi Shimbun*. January 10, 2022. https://www.asahi.com/ajw/articles/14518868.
Nolletti Jr., Arthur. "Mitsuo Yanagimachi's 'Himatsuri': An Analysis." *Film Criticism* 10, no. 3 (1986): 49–59.
Ohnuki-Tierney, Emiko. *Kamikaze, Cherry Blossoms, and Nationalisms: The Militarization of Aesthetics in Japanese History*. Chicago: University of Chicago Press, 2002.
Oka Asajirō. *Seibutsugaku kōwa*. Tokyo: Kaiseikan, 1916.
Ōmori, Kyōko. "'Finding Our Own English': Migrancy, Identity, and Language(s) in Itō Hiromi's Recent Prose." *U.S.-Japan Women's Journal* 32 (2007): 92–114.
Osaki Midori. *Osaki Midori Zenshū*. Tokyo: Sōjusha, 1979.
Osaki Midori and Nozoe Nobuhisa. *Dainana kankai hōkō*. Tokyo: Ohta Shuppan, 2018.
Parsley, Kathryn M. "Plant Awareness Disparity: A Case for Renaming Plant Blindness." *Plants People Planet*, October 3, 2020. https://doi.org/10.1002/ppp3.10153.
Pascal, Blaise. *Pascal's Pensées*. New York: E. P. Dutton, 1958.
Peters, John Durham. *The Marvelous Clouds: Toward a Philosophy of Elemental Media*. Chicago: University of Chicago Press, 2015.
Pollan, Michael. "The Intelligent Plant." *New Yorker*, December 15, 2013.
Popkin, Gabriel. "'Wood Wide Web'—The Underground Network of Microbes That Connects Trees—Mapped for First Time." *Science*, May 15, 2019. https://www.science.org/content/article/wood-wide-web-underground-network-microbes-connects-trees-mapped-first-time.
Rambelli, Fabio. *Buddhist Materiality: A Cultural History of Objects in Japanese Buddhism*. Stanford, CA: Stanford University Press, 2007.
Richardson, Alan. "Erasmus Darwin and the Fungus School." *Wordsworth Circle* 33, no. 3 (2001): 113–116.
Rodd, Laurel Rasplica, and Mary Catherine Henkenius, trans. *Kokinshū: A Collection of Poems Ancient and Modern*. Boston: Cheng & Tsui, 1996.
Roy, Sumana. *How I Became a Tree*. New Haven, CT: Yale University Press, 2021.
Ryan, John Charles. *Plants in Contemporary Poetry: Ecocriticism and the Botanical Imagination*. New York, NY: Routledge, 2018.
Ryūtanji Yū. *Shaboten gensō*. Tokyo: Chikuma Shobō, 2016.
Sample, Ian. "Cress Seeds Grown in Moon Dust Raise Hopes for Lunar Crops." *Guardian*. May 12, 2022.
Sandilands, Catriona. "Vegetate." In *Veer Ecology: A Companion for Environmental Thinking*, edited by Jeffrey Jerome Cohen and Lowell Duckert, 16–29. Minneapolis: University of Minnesota Press, 2017.
Sanford, Stella. *Vegetal Sex: Philosophy of Plants*. London: Bloomsbury, 2023.
Sharp, Jasper. "Fire Festival." *Midnight Eye*. Accessed January 28, 2024. http://www.midnighteye.com/reviews/fire-festival.
Shinozuka, Jeannie N. *Biotic Borders: Transpacific Plant and Insect Migration and the Rise of Anti-Asian Racism in America, 1890–1950*. Chicago: University of Chicago Press, 2022.
Shirakawa Masayoshi, ed. *Haniya Yutaka dokuji "Shirei" no sekai*. Tokyo: NHK Shuppan, 1997.
Shirane, Haruo. *Japan and the Culture of the Four Seasons: Nature, Literature, and the Arts*. New York: Columbia University Press, 2012.
"Shocking Photo of Drowned Father and Daughter Highlights Migrants' Border Peril." *Guardian*. June 26, 2019.
Silverberg, Miriam. *Erotic Grotesque Nonsense: The Mass Culture of Japanese Modern Times*. Berkeley: University of California Press, 2006.

Stein, Elliot, Stephan Harvey, and Harlan Jacobson. "The 23rd New York Film Festival." *Film Comment* 21, no. 6 (1985): 60–71.
Subramaniam, Banu. *Ghost Stories for Darwin: The Science of Variation and the Politics of Diversity*. Urbana: University of Illinois Press, 2014.
Sullivan, Gregory. *Regenerating Japan: Organicism, Modernism and National Destiny in Oka Asajirō's "Evolution and Human Life."* Budapest: CEU Press, 2018.
Taijiri, Yoshiki. "Beckett and Haniya Yutaka: Two Versions of the Ontological Enquiry." *Journal of Irish Studies* 17 (2002): 109–115.
Takemura Shinichi. *Uchūju*. Tokyo: Chuo Seihan, 2018.
Takizawa Kenji. *Ki to ke to ki: hirogari to gyōshuku no bigaku*. Tokyo: Hozansha, 1993.
Tamura, Keita, and Hidemasa Bono. "Meta-Analysis of RNA Sequencing Data of Arabidopsis and Rice under Hypoxia." *Life* 12, no. 7 (2022).
Terao Shin and Honda Masaji. *Shin Nihon shōnen shōjo bunko dai 7 hen: Dōbutsu to shokubutsu no seikatsu*. Tokyo: Shinchōsha, 1940.
Thompson, Andrea. "Plants Are the World's Dominant Life-Form." *Scientific American*, August 1, 2018. https://www.scientificamerican.com/article/plants-are-the-worlds-dominant-life-form/.
Timiryazev, Kliment. *The Life of the Plant*. Translated by A. Sheremetyeva. Moscow: Foreign Languages, 1958.
Timiryazev, Kliment. *Shokubutsu no sekatsu*. Translated by Ishii Tomoyuki. Tokyo: Iwasaki shoten, 1947.
Toba Kōji. *Undōtai—Abe Kōbō*. Tokyo: Ichiyōsha, 2007.
Tompkins, Peter, and Christopher Bird. *The Secret Life of Plants*. New York: Harper, 2002.
Totman, Conrad. *The Green Archipelago: Forestry in Preindustrial Japan*. Berkeley: University of California Press, 1989.
Tsing, Anna Lowenhaupt. "A Threat to Holocene Resurgence Is a Threat to Livability." In *The Anthropology of Sustainability*, edited by Marc Brightman and Jerome Lewis, 51–65. New York: Palgrave Macmillan, 2017.
Tsurumi, Shinsuke. *An Intellectual History of Wartime Japan 1931–1945*. London: KPI, 1986.
Tsuyama Takashi. "Plantæ Boninenses Novæ vel Criticæ. V." *Shokubutsugaku zasshi* 1, no. 591 (1936): 129–133.
US National Science Foundation. "*Arabidopsis*: The Model Plant." Accessed January 28, 2024. https://www.nsf.gov/pubs/2002/bio0202/model.htm.
VILLUM Research Center for Plant Plasticity. "What Is Plant Plasticity?" Accessed January 23, 2024. https://plantplasticity.ku.dk/what_is_sb/#:~:text=Plant%20plasticity%20refers%20to%20a,with%20changes%20in%20its%20environment.
Vision. Promotional Pamphlet. LDH Pictures, 2018.
Wakukawa, Seiyei. "Japanese Tenant Movements." *Far Eastern Survey* 15, no. 3 (1946): 40–44.
Wampole, Christy. *Rootedness: The Ramifications of a Metaphor*. Chicago: University of Chicago Press, 2016.
Weiner, Michael. "The Invention of Identity: Race and Nation in Pre-War Japan." In *The Construction of Racial Identities in China and Japan: Historical and Contemporary Perspectives*, edited by Frank Dikotter, 102–110. London: Hurst, 1997.
Yamaguchi Masao, ed. *Himatsuri*. Tokyo: Riburopōto, 1985.
Yuki Masami. "On Harmony with Nature: Toward Japanese Ecocriticism." In *Ecocriticism in Japan*, edited by Hisaaki Wake, Yuki Masami, and Keijiro Suga, 1–20. Lanham, MD: Lexington Books, 2018.

Index

Page numbers in *italics* refer to illustrations.

Abe Kōbō, ix, 13–14, 28, 33, 55–79; "Dendrocacalia," 21–23, 55–79, *63*, 82, 102, 109, 210n20, 210n23; *Green Stockings*, 65; *Inter Ice Age 4*, 101; *Kangaroo Notebook*, 65; "Lead Egg," 65; *For the Night with No Name*, 71; *Woman of the Dunes*, 65
Abe Machiko, 55, *63*
acacia trees, 180–81, 183
acclimatization, 125, 153, 155, 157, 173–81, 193
adaptation, 6, 14, 19–20, 23, 30, 109–11, 145, 153, 163, 174–75, 179
Airin shisō (Forest-Love Ideology), 77, 90, 117
Akiyama Hiroyuki, 44
alterity, 53, 147, 154, 155, 165
Anarcho-Marxists, 21, 56, 63–64, 67, 70, 71, 76, 84
animal studies, 3
Anthropocene, 94
anthropocentrism, 2–3, 7, 12, 93–94, 96, 134, 168–69
anthropomorphism, 12–13, 36, 47, 50, 99–100, 164
anti-immigration policies, 150, 152–53, 155, 166–68, 183–90
Arakawa Tomotsugu, 50, 54, 208n32, 221n101
Arishima Takeo, 64
aspens, 3–4, 14, 19, 141, 192
assemblages, 88, 102. *See also* forests
asylum seekers, 152, 155, 182–86

Backster, Cleve, 97, 99–100
Bates, J. W., 34
Bateson, Gregory, 12–16, 51, 191
becoming, as process, 19–20
becoming botanical, trope of, 1–28. *See also* botanical form/poetics; botanical subjectivity
Bennett, Jane, 88
biopower, 3, 203n6, 209n7

Bird, Christopher. See *The Secret Life of Plants*
Bonin (Ogasawara) Islands, 55, 57–60, 73, 77
botanical empathy, 154, 163, 166–70, 174, 176–77, 179–81, 183–84, 186
botanical form/poetics, 1–2, 6–7, 16–20, 39–42, 71, 85, 106, 120, 150, 174
Botanical Society of Japan, 58
botanical subjectivity, 6, 13–16, 19; botanical-anarchist subjectivity, 55–56, 63–68; cinematic-botanical subjectivity, 120, 127–31, *138*; disturbance and destruction, 119, 123; dystopian, 21, 32, 56, 67–70, 133; forests and, 56, 80–95, 127; as humanlike, 100; interior/exterior divide, 61–62, 66, 68, 70, 72–73, 75, 77; liberatory, 71–72 (*see also* resistance); migration and, 172; moss-like, 41–47; multiple, 14, 19, 31, 34–38, 44–45, *45*, 91–92, 105, 110, 120, 127, 143, 163, 175; resilience and, 32, 109–10, 113–14; silence and, 53; utopian, 21, 30, 46–47, 55, 56, 64–68, 70, 72, 127, 147, 198; violence and, 127, 131–33, 197–98
Brodie, Nathaniel, 132, 144
Buddhism, 90, 93, 108, 120, 122–23, 137, 151, 217n47

cacti, 100–103, 106
cedar trees (*sugi*), 80–81, *81*, 83, 108–10, 123, 128–30, 159–60
Chapman, David, 59–60
cherry blossoms, 1, 8, 12, 16, 80, 161, 182–83, 204n14
Chisso factory, 48–49
cinematic-botanical subjectivity, 120, 127–31, *138*
classical Japanese aesthetics, x, 1, 8, 10–11, 16–17
climate change, 2, 59, 116–17, 196
Coccia, Emanuele, 8, 62, 94, 95, 203n6

231

INDEX

colonialism, Japanese, 6, 8, 20–23, 204n14; internal *naichi* and external *gaichi*, 59–62, 65, 72–73, 77, 78–79; in Korea, 48–49, 59, 78; patriotism and, 90; in postwar era memory, 55–79; propagandistic literature on, 75–78; resistance to, 30, 32–33, 46–49; resource extraction, 60, 117; scientific naming and, 78–79, 151; scientific research and, 32, 47–49, 60, 77; in Taiwan, 59, 84; violence of, 48–49, 56–57, 65, 75
connectivity, 91, 200–201
Connell, Katherine, 137
consciousness, 31, 44, 68, 74–75, 94, 101, 104
Conversation with a Cactus (2017), 106
crises, 10, 22–23, 109, 192. *See also* climate change; colonialism, Japanese; migration; 3.11; World War II
critical plant studies (CPS), ix–x, 2–12, 15–20, 23–26, 34, 168, 194, 201, 203n6, 204n9, 205n23; Japanese studies and, 7–12, 28; plant awareness disparity, 4–10, 204n9
cyclical time, 39, 135, 137–42, 145, 147

Darwin, Charles, 30, 43, 45, 59, 61–62, 64. *See also* social Darwinism
Darwin, Erasmus, 52
Darwin, Francis, 66–67
Dauvergne, Peter, 117
death, 25–26, 80–83, 90–91, 192; communication with spirits, 83, 96, 99, 101–3, 108–11, 113; futurity and, 119; rethinking, 191–92; trauma of, 81–82, 86. *See also* rebirth; suicide
Deborin, Abram Moiseevich, 64
deforestation, 10–11, 117, 137, 217n47
dehumanization, 56, 153
Deleuze, Gilles, 6, 19–21, 38, 157, 160, 162–63, 177, 185
destructive plasticity, 93, 119–21, 123, 131–34, 148, 206n45
disturbance ecology, 118–23, 127, 130–31, 136, 139, 144–45, 147, 192
Dodo Arata, 137, *138*, 147
Dole, Christopher, 23, 83, 118, 198
doppelgangers, 34, 37, 41, 42, 207n22
Dorsey, James, 87

earthquakes, 10, 24, 33, 83, 109
Edison, Thomas, 99
emotions, 42, 50, 56, 87, 165, 168, 194
endemic species, 55, 57, 59–60, 62

environmental degradation, 10–11, 48, 117, 187
environmental history, 10, 204n17; Japanese, 204n13
environmental humanities, ix–x, 2–3
environmental texts, 11, 23, 93–94
ero-guro-nansensu (erotic-grotesque-nonsensical), 47, 50
eucalyptus trees, 178–79, 183
evolution, 13, 15, 20; destruction of human ego and, 144–48; disturbance events and, 145; in early twentieth-century Japan, 49–50; hierarchical, 102; love and, 49–50; mutual aid and, 64–65; in Osaki's work, 29–30, 32, 37–38, 42–47, 49–50, 52–54, 65, 102, 144–45, 169. *See also* social Darwinism
Evolution (1925), 29–31, 37, 48, 206n1
experimental narratives, 18, 21, 39, 63, 106

Fabre, Jean-Henri, 64, 210n31
Fedman, David, 204n13, 204n14
fertilizer, 32, 39, 47–49
Fire Festival (1985), 24, 118–27, *124*, *131*, 136, 137, 139, 144, 145, 216nn35–36
Fleischer, Max, *Evolution* (1925), 29–31, 37, 48, 206n1
Florenty, Elise, 106
forest love ideology, 77, 90, 117
forestry industry, 115–23, 126, 134. *See also somabito* (foresters)
forests, 23–24, 28; assemblage, 88, 91–92, 108, 119–20, 128, 130, 137–39, 141–42; botanical subjectivity and, 56, 80–95, 127; conservation and reforestation, 67–68, 70, 73, 80, 82, 116–17, 134; destruction and renewal through fire, 119–23, 131–34, 136, 140–48 (*see also* disturbance ecology); destructive plasticity, 93; domestic lumber consumption, 115–18; multiplicity of, 91–92; spiritual relationship to, 118–23, 125–31; 3.11 disaster and, 83, 111. *See also* deforestation; trees
forest time, 86, 139–41
Foucault, Michel, 3, 203n6, 209n7
fractured subjectivity, 31, 34–38, 84–87, 95
Freud, Sigmund, 31
Fujihara Tatsushi, 8–9, 18, 32, 48, 204n14
Fujii Takashi, 94
Fukasawa Maki, 197, 199–200
Fukushima Daiichi Nuclear Power Plant, 3.11 disaster, 10, 12, 24, 83, 102, 106–11
fungal networks, 4

futurity, 19; abstract, *146*, 146–47; cyclical time and, 135 (*see also* cyclical time); death and, 119; destruction of present and, 132–33, 144; evolutionary thought and, 43; reproductive, 200; revitalization and, 118; unified subjectivity and, 112

Gagliano, Monica, 26, 203n6
Galapagos Islands, 59
Garvus, Delia, 205n40
gender norms, 28, 44–45, 194, 197–200
Giacometti, Alberto, 65–66
Gotō Shin, 123
grass, 16; "men are grass" syllogism, 12–17, 51, 191
Green, Walon, 97
Greening Week, *67*, 67–68, 70, 73
Grosz, Elizabeth, 14–15, 43, 145
Guattari, Félix, 6, 19–21, 38, 157, 160, 162–63, 177, 185

Haberlandt, Gottlieb, 66
Hamano Sachi, 42, *43*, 54
Hamilton, Vivien, 205n40
Hanada Kiyoteru, 33, 53–56, 66, 71, 76
Hana no Iwa Shrine, 122
Haniya Yutaka, 17, 28, 55–56, 63, 115–16; *Dead Spirits*, 23–24, 26, 56, 81–105, 107, 112–14, 120, 127, 207n24, 214n58; "Echo," 113
Hara Shōji, 14
Haraway, Donna, 57, 110
Harberd, Nicholas, 200–201
Hashimoto Ken, 25–26, 83–84, 96–106, *101*, 108, 205n40
haunting, 17, 26, 80–83, 86, 88, 91, 93, 99, 105, 107, 111, 114
Haven, Tom, 204n13
Hayashi Fumiko, 33
herbivore men, 197–99
Hiroshima, 34, 110, 113
Hiroshima, University of, 196
Hofmeister, William, 45
Honda Masaji, 76–78, 211n75
Hongū Shrine, 123
Houle, Karen L. F., 35, 154
humanities, 2–3. *See also* environmental humanities
human subjectivity, 1, 13–15, 19, 27; becoming botanical, 19–20 (*see also* botanical subjectivity); destruction and evolution of, 136, 142–48; fluid, 29–30; fractured, 31, 34–38, 84–87, 95; plasticity of, 22, 53, 105; postwar, 62, 70; revolutionary, 56, 64; singular/unified, 35–36, 41, 94–95, 112

ice plant, 166–69, *167*
Imperial Japan: celebration of, 124–25; ideology of, 93–94, 104. *See also* colonialism; World War II
Inamoto Tadashi, 126
Inokashira Park, 80–82, *81*, 96, 105, 111
Inukai Tsuyoshi, 33
Invasive Alien Species Act, 189, 221n111
invasive plant species, 14, 149, 152–53, 166–74, *167*, 179–81, 189, *189*, 221n111
involution, 38, 45
Irigaray, Luce, 53
Ishii Tomoyuki, 74
Ishikawa Chiyomatsu, 30
Ito, Hiromi, ix, 15–16, 27, 58, 86, 107, 154–55, 192, 203n2, 205n31, 218n17, 218n22; *Aunt Green-Thumb*, 163, 185; *Coyote Song*, 170; *A Father's Life*, 157; *Good Breasts, Bad Breasts*, 154; *House Plant*, 174–84, 220nn65–66; "Killing Kanoko," 154, 218n19; *La Niña*, 174–83, 220nn65–66; *Sky of Plants*, 154; *The Thorn-Puller*, 157; *Three Lil' Japanese*, 181–85, 187, 198; *Travels*, 157, 188; *Tree Spirits Grass Spirits*, 16–17, 151, 157–65, 167, 170, 174, 179, 181, 183, 185–86, 219n49; *Trump*, 187; *Twilight Child*, 157; *Wild Grass on the Riverbank*, 149–57, 160, 163–67, 170–74, 179, 181, 183–88, 190, 217nn5–7, 219nn42–43, 219n49
Itō Motomi, 59
Itō Seikō, 8, 99, 106–16; *Botanical Life*, 107–8; *Radio Imagination*, 12, 24, 26, 83, 102, 106–14
Izanagi and Izanami, 29, 122
Izu Peninsula, 211n75

Jacobs, Joela, 203n2, 217n5
Jakushinsan camphor tree, 161–62, 192
Japanese Communist Party (JCP), 28, 63, 70, 84, 85, 87
Japanese Forestry Agency, 111, 115–16, 131
Japanese studies, 6–9, 201; critical plant studies and, 7–12, 28; environmental scholarship, 10–11
Jensen, Sara E., 132
Jimmu (emperor), 124–25
Jōmon era, 125–26

INDEX

kami (spirits or local gods), 90, 120, 122, 216n36
Kawabata Yasunari, 31
Kawasaki Kenko, 33, 49
Kawase Naomi, ix, 17, 24, 107, 121, 134–36, 149, 215n15; *Vision* (2018), 24, 28, 118–20, 135–48, *138*, *143*, 151, 217n56
Keetley, Dawn, 26–27, 150, 219n49
kehai (presence or trace), 83, 89–90, 92, 96, 97, 100, 102, 107, 112, 113, 120
Kenji, Miyazawa, 8
Ketsumiko no Ōkami, 123
Kii Peninsula, 120, 121–22, 124
Kimmerer, Robin Wall, 5–8, 24, 26, 31, 34, 38, 46, 54, 203n6
Ki no Tsurayuki, 16
Kizukai Movement, 115–18, 120, 134
Knight, John, 118, 126
Koishikawa Botanical Gardens, *58*, 79
Kokinwakashū (poetry anthology), 16
Korea, 73; Japanese colonialism in, 48–49, 59, 78
Kropotkin, Peter, 64–68, 71, 75
Kumamoto, 149, 154–58, 161–62, 164–65, 172, 188
Kumano region, 122–23, 125, 127
kyotai (empty body), 93–96, 100

language: loss of, 53, 86–89, 93; scientific naming, 57–59, 61, 62, 72–73, 78–79, 151, 192; status of, in postwar era, 86–87; words as plants, 15–18, 58, 86, 150; writing as voice of dead spirits, 113
Lee, Jung, 78, 204n14
Lippit, Seiji, 31
Literary Signpost (journal), 86–87
The Lives of Animals and Plants, 75–78
love, 193–201; evolution and, 49–50

Machida Kō, 15
Malabou, Catherine, 21–22, 40, 41, 93, 109, 112, 119, 206n45, 206n51
Mancuso, Stefano, 8, 26, 68, 203n6
Marder, Michael, 10, 40–41, 53, 71–72, 87, 163, 168–69, 203n6
Marxism, 63–64. *See also* Anarcho-Marxists; Japanese Communist Party
Mason, Herbert, 155–56
Matsumura Jinzō, 79
Matsuo Bashō, 16
McLuhan, Marshall, 93
McPherson, Guy R., 132
Mechnikov, Ilya, 64

Meeker, Natania, 7
Meiji era, 30, 59
mental illness, 31–36, 54, 61, 86–87, 89, 95
metaphysics, 82, 88, 94, 98
michiyuki (narrative device), 220n88
migration, 27, 149–90, 218n23. *See also* anti-immigration policies; asylum seekers; naturalization
Miura, Satoru, 111
Miura Shion, *A World Without Love*, 28, 192–200
Modern Literature (literary magazine), 85, 86
Moerman, D. Max, 122–23
Montgomery, Beronda, 22, 203n6
Morioka Masahiro, 197–99
Morris-Suzuki, Tessa, 46, 77, 204n14
Morse, Edward, 30
mosses, 5, 6–7, 23, 29–32, 34–35, 38–51, 54, 86, 191–92, 208n32; moss-like botanical subjectivity, 41–47; multiplicity of, 34–35, *35*, 50; rebirth of, 54
Murasaki Shikibu, 11
Mure Yōko, 209n80
Mutsuko Motoyama, 58
mutual aid, 64
mythological figures, 122, 125–26, 139–42

Nakagami Kenji, 121–22, 125, 133, 144, 216nn35–36
Nakai Takenoshin, 57, 78
Nakajima Plant, 81
Nakajima Seinosuke, 74
Nara Prefecture, 135–36. *See also* Yoshino region
nationalism, 28, 76–77, 98, 103, 121, 168, 182–83
Native Americans, 169–70
naturalization, 153, 158–59, 164, 166, 169–74, 177–81, 185, 188–90, 218n12
nature: harmony with, 11; material face of (primary nature), 7, 16, 197; nonobjectification of, 40–42, 165; right relation between humans and, x; semiotic face of (second nature), 11, 16, 197. *See also* plant life
Nealon, Jeffrey T., 3, 209n7
neoliberalism, 116, 118, 134, 153
Night Group, 55, 57, 63, 70, 76, 82
Nihon shoki (mytho-history), 122
9/11 terrorist attacks, 155, 187, 190
Nixon, Rob, 23
Nozoe Nobuhisa, 42

nuclear crises, 10, 109; at Fukushima (3.11), 10, 12, 24, 83, 102, 106–11

Ogi Masahiro, 125–26, 140
Ohnuki-Tierney, Emiko, 182, 204n14
Oka Asajirō, 49–50, 52
Okamoto Tarō, 55, 66
Ōka Shōhei, 33
Okinawa, 73, 198
Osaki Midori, ix, 5, 6–7, 13, 20–23, 27, 29–56, 65, 71, 102, 127, 140, 144–45, 151, 161, 169, 183, 221n101; *Jottings on Film*, 29, 31, 41, 209n79; "Machiko Cycle," 31, 51–53, 207n8; "Miss Cricket," 36; "A Night in Anton's Basement," 51; "Osmanthus," 54; *Poems Dedicated to the Gods*, 36; "Walking," 51; *Wandering in the Realm of the Seventh Sense*, 23, 31, 33–34, 38–54, 43, 56, 57, 61, 68–69, 72, 85–87, 145, 150, 165, 191–94, 199, 208n32, 212n7
Ōsugi Sakae, 210n31
Ōta Yōko, 33

parascience, 96–105, 108
Parsley, Kathryn M., 204n9
Pascal, Blaise, 36–37
patriarchy, 32, 46, 47, 136, 194
Perry, Matthew, 59
Peters, John Durham, 91–92, 113, 215n99
Pfeffer, Wilhelm Friedrich Philipp, 69
phenotypic plasticity, 22, 169
photosynthesis, 85, 94, 195
phytomorphism, 13–14, 23, 27, 36, 42, 92, 113, 163, 164, 169, 191
phytophenomenology, 66–70
phytopoetics, 203n2, 217n5
plant awareness disparity, 4–10, 204n9
plant humanities, 3–5, 26, 28
plant life, 2–9, 203n6; alterity of, 53, 147, 154, 155, 165; communication with, 96–106, 101, 195; compared to animal life, 74–78; death and rebirth (*see* disturbance ecology; rebirth and regeneration); decentralization in, 68; dibionic life cycle, 45; green life force of, 107–8; historicity of, 5–6, 9; as horrific, 27, 61, 62, 68, 150, 182, 219n49; interior life, 61–62; metamorphosis, 42, 55–57, 60–79; nonviolence of, 85; senses, 66–68; sexual differentiation, 44–45; temporality of, 68–69, 192–93 (*see also* forest time); as untamable, 26–28. *See also* botanical empathy; botanical subjectivity; critical plant studies (CPS); forests; grass; invasive plant species; mosses; scientific research; *shokubutsusei*; trees
"plant-thinking," 10
plasticity, 21–24, 27, 196, 205n45; botanical media and, 109; destructive, 93, 119–21, 123, 131–34, 148, 206n45; human ego and, 141, 145; migration and, 153, 174–81; phenotypic, 22, 169; plant metamorphosis, 42, 55–57, 60–79; repetition and, 40–41; of subjectivity, 22, 53, 105. *See also* transformation
poetry: classical Japanese, x, 16–17; Osaki, 51–53; science as, 51–53; *shokubutsusei* of Ito's poetry, 150
Pollan, Michael, 25
polygraph machines, 97, 99–102, 104, 106
post-humanism, 56, 106
post-traumatized subjects, 109
postwar era: colonial memory in, 55–79; economic imperialism and resource extraction, 117–18, 126; economic miracle, 117–18, 124; greening efforts, 67–68, 70, 73, 80, 82, 116–17, 134; Japanese literature in, 23–24 (*see also* Haniya Yutaka); *yakeato* ruins, 70. *See also* colonialism, Japanese; World War II
Powers, Richard, 4
pseudoscience, 20, 25–26, 83–84, 96–97, 195, 205n40
psychoanalysis, 31–32, 105

racial ideologies, 30, 46
radioactivity, 111
rebirth and regeneration, 25, 53–54, 95, 107, 118, 132, 164–65, 185–86, 190. *See also* disturbance ecology
religion, 90, 103–4. *See also* Buddhism; Shinto cosmology
repetition, 39–42, 140, 150
reproduction, 4, 50, 156, 163–66, 193–94, 219n49
resistance, 6, 27–28, 99; to anthropocentrism, 93; to biopolitical control over migration, 153–54, 169–74, 181–90; to capitalism, 120; to colonialism, 30, 32–33, 46–49; to gender norms, 28, 44–45, 197–200; against patriarchy, 32, 47, 194
resource extraction, 60, 115–18, 126
revolutionary subjectivity, 56, 64
rhizomatic logic, 19–20, 163, 192
Rilke, Rainer Maria, 71–72

INDEX

rootlessness, 152–54, 163. *See also* uprootedness
Roy, Sumana, 19–20
rural communities: depopulation (*kasoka*), 12, 118, 123–27, 134–35, 137, 147; economic crisis and revitalization, 118, 120, 123–36, 147. See also *somabito* (foresters)
Ryan, John Charles, 203n1
Ryūkyū Islands, 73, 198
Ryūtanji Yū, 32, 106

Sandford, Stella, 44–45
Sandilands, Catriona, 153, 155, 160, 171, 218n17
Sartre, Jean-Paul, 65–66
Satō Haruo, 32
science, 7, 20; literature and, 30–54; objectivity and, 76; as poetry, 51–53; popular, 74; spirituality and, 23–26, 151
scientific epistemology, 75
scientific naming, 57–59, 61, 62, 72–73, 78–79, 151, 192
scientific research, 201, 211n75; colonialism and, 47–49, 60, 76–77; on thale cress, 195–97, *196*, 199, 200–201
Sconce, Jeffrey, 99
The Secret Life of Plants (Tompkins and Bird), 20, 25–26, 83–84, 97, 99–101, 105, 109, 194–95, 205n40
secular migration, 155–56, 160, 162, 166, 169, 172, 174, 178, 185–90
settler colonialism, 8, 21, 169. *See also* colonialism, Japanese
Sharp, William/Fiona Macleod, 36–38
shinboku (sacred trees), 90–91, *91*, 103–6, 108
Shinchōsha, 75
Shinozuka, Jeannie N., 152–53, 168
Shinto cosmology: divine wind (kamikaze), 98, 103; trees and forests, 90–91, *91*, 103–5, 120
Shirane, Haruo, 11, 16, 205n23
shokubutsusei, 26–28, 65; concept of, 8–13, 16, 18–19; dibiontic life cycle, 45; disturbance ecology, 118–21; environmental texts and, 11; of forests, 83, 121, 139; of Ito's poetry, 150; migration, 149; moss, 35; in Osaki, 32, 35, 37; rebirth, 25, 164; repetition and, 150; of trees, 110
shokumin ("people planting"), 60
Shōwa era, 20, 22, 30, 32, 33, 37, 46, 53, 80, 192, 211n75
Shūgendō, 122
Shyamalan, M. Night, 27

silence, 53, 176, 209n79; loss of language, 53, 86–89, 93
slow violence, 23
Smith, F. Percy, 69
social Darwinism, 30, 46, 50, 64–65, 169
somabito (foresters), 118–19, 121, 123, 125–29, 134–42, 144–45, 147, 215n10
spirit radio, 99–103, 106–11
spirituality: forests and, 118–23, 125–31; nationalism and, 76–77; plants and, 83, 119–20; science and, 23–26, 151; trees and, 108–9
state power and control, 201; colonial memory and, 62, 72–73; over migration, 150, 152–55, 166–71, 183–90; resistance to (*see* resistance); service to, 98–99. *See also* colonialism; Imperial Japan; nationalism
subjectivity. *See* botanical subjectivity; human subjectivity
Subramanian, Banu, 168
suicide, 74, 95, 121, 127, 131–33, 136, 144
Sullivan, Gregory, 50
Susanoo, 125
Suzaku (1997), 135–36
syllogisms, 13–14, 191, 205n27
Szabri, Antonia, 7

Tachibana Takashi, 96–97
Taiwan, 59, 84
Takemitsu Tōru, 121, 129–30, 133
Takemura Shinichi, 91–93, 105, 109–10
Takizawa Kenji, 89–90
The Tale of Genji (Murasaki), 11
Tamura Masaki, 128, 135
Tamura Taijirō, 94
Taniguchi Masaharu, 98
Tatsushi, Fujihara, 4
thale cress, 195–97, *196*, 199, 200–201
3.11 (earthquake, tsunami, and nuclear meltdown at Fukushima), 10, 12, 24, 83, 102, 106–11
Timiryazev, Kliment, 6, 64–66, 73, 80, 94, 104, 201; *The Life of the Plant*, 57, 61–62, 74–75, 78
Toba Kōji, 210n23
Tōdaiji, 137, 217n47
Toda Toyoko, 33
Tokyo Imperial University, 30, 48, 57, 59, 78–79, 98, 193
Tokyo Olympics (2020), 28, 121, 215n15
Tompkins, Peter. See *The Secret Life of Plants*
Totman, Conrad, 10–11, 117, 123, 137, 217n47

transformation, 21–23, 42, 53–54; evolution and, 53; forests as site of, 90–93; violent, 119. *See also* plasticity
trees: classification of, 159–60; multiplicity of, 105, 110; plasticity of, 105; in Shinto cosmology, 90–91, *91*, 103–5, 120; *shokubutsusei* of, 110. *See also* cedar trees; cherry blossoms; eucalyptus trees; forests; Jakushinsan camphor tree
Trump, Donald, 155, 187, 190
Tsing, Anna, 119, 120, 127, 134, 137, 139
tsunamis, 10, 24, 83, 109
Tsuyama Takashi, 78
Türkowsky, Marcel, 106

Ueno Chizuko, 125, 133, 216n36
United States, 26–27, 62, 98, 150, 152–90, 198
uprootedness, 60, 149, 153, 165, 167, 174–76, 178; of colonial modernity, 32–34, 36, 38–39, 44, 48, 57, 62. *See also* rootlessness

violence, 6, 89, 182; botanical subjectivity and, 127, 131–33, 197–98; colonial, 48–49, 56–57, 65, 75; decrease in, 197–98; gendered, 49, 53; of humanity, 147; political, 33; postwar, 72–73, 82–85, 118; spiritual relationship to forest and, 118–19, 127–31; of twenty-first century, 150; of war, 98
Vision (2018), 24, 28, 118–20, 135–48, *138*, *143*, 151, 217n56
vitalism, 33, 74

Wager, Harold, 67
Wampole, Christy, 60, 152, 176
Watanabe Masao, 30
The Weald (1997), 136
weeds, 16–17, 27, 71, 166, 195
Wohlleben, Peter, 4
World War II, 23, 56, 70, 80–82, 86, 93–94, 97–98, 103–5, 117. *See also* postwar era

xenophobia, 168, 170

Yamamoto Reiji, 144
Yamamura Bochō, 220n86
Yama no Kami (mountain goddess), 122, 128–31, *131*, 139
Yanagimachi Mitsuo, 17, 24, 107, 121–22; *Fire Festival* (1985), 24, 118–27, *124*, *131*, 136, 137, 139, 144, 145, 216nn35–36
Yokomitsu Riichi, 31–32
Yoshino region, 120, 135, 136–37, 139–42, 145
Yuki Masami, 11, 205n23

www.ingramcontent.com/pod-product-compliance
Lightning Source LLC
Chambersburg PA
CBHW021854230426
43671CB00006B/386